Cooking for all Occasions

Ellen Sinclair

HAMLYN

LONDON · NEW YORK · SYDNEY · TORONTO

First published as *The Australian Women's Weekly*
New Cookbook in 1978 by
Golden Press Pty. Ltd.
2–12 Tennyson Road
Gladesville, NSW 2111
This edition published 1978 by
The Hamlyn Publishing Group Limited
London · New York · Sydney · Toronto
Astronaut House, Feltham, Middlesex, England

© Copyright 1978 Australian Consolidated Press Ltd.
ISBN 0 600 32070 7

Printed in Italy

Contents

Soups & First Courses

The entree — or entry to the meal — should be light, full of flavour, stimulating appetite for the good things to come. Apart from the selection of recipes given here, look also at the Fish and Dinner Party sections for further ideas. We also give recipes for some good hearty soups — meals in themselves — and for light soups as meal-starters.

Vegetable Platter

3 sticks celery	6 shallots or spring onions
125 g (4 oz.) green beans	2 tomatoes
2 carrots	4 hard-boiled eggs
125 g (4 oz.) broccoli	125 g (4 oz.) black olives
250 g (8 oz.) cauliflower	
125 g (4 oz.) small mushrooms	

Curry Mayonnaise

1½ cups mayonnaise	few drops tabasco sauce
1 tablespoon curry powder	1 tablespoon chopped parsley
1 clove garlic	
1 teaspoon lemon juice	salt, pepper

Cut celery into 6 cm (2½ in.) strips; slice one end to make into curls. Put into iced water while preparing other vegetables. Top, tail and string beans; leave whole. Scrape carrots; cut into thin straws. Remove leaves from broccoli and cauliflower; cut into small flowerets; trim stalks. Trim stalks from mushrooms. Individually cook the beans, broccoli and cauliflower in large saucepan of boiling, salted water for 1 minute. Remove from saucepan immediately; rinse under cold water; this helps keep their bright colour.

Put bowl of Curry Mayonnaise in centre of large platter. Arrange prepared vegetables, tomatoes cut into wedges, shelled and halved eggs, trimmed shallots and black olives decoratively around mayonnaise. Guests pick up a vegetable with hand or fork and dip it into the mayonnaise.

Curry Mayonnaise: Combine crushed garlic and all remaining ingredients in small bowl. Refrigerate before serving.

Serves 6.

Vegetable Platter — crisp, colourful vegetables are dipped into a creamy Curry Mayonnaise; a delightfully light first course.

Asparagus and Artichokes

2 x 315 g (10 oz.) cans asparagus spears	470 g (15 oz.) can artichoke hearts
lettuce	

Vinaigrette Dressing

1 onion	1 teaspoon capers
¼ cup chopped parsley	1 hard-boiled egg
⅓ cup oil	salt, pepper
⅓ cup white vinegar	

Drain asparagus spears; drain and halve artichoke hearts. Arrange lettuce on platter; place asparagus and artichoke hearts on lettuce, spoon dressing over.

Dressing: Peel and finely chop onion; put in bowl; add parsley, oil, vinegar, finely-chopped capers, salt and pepper. Remove yolk from egg (use for another purpose); finely chop egg white; add to dressing; mix well.

Serves 4.

Hot Asparagus with Curry Butter

2 x 440 g (14 oz.) cans asparagus spears	½ cup plain flour
flour	2 teaspoons baking powder
salt, pepper	1 teaspoon salt
⅔ cup cornflour	1 cup milk
	oil for deep-frying

Curry Butter

4 egg yolks	2 teaspoons curry powder
1 tablespoon white vinegar	2 tablespoons chopped parsley
2 tablespoons lemon juice	salt, pepper
250 g (8 oz.) softened butter	

Drain asparagus; place on absorbent paper to absorb liquid. Allow to stand on paper 30 minutes. Gently coat asparagus with flour seasoned with salt and pepper. Sift plain flour, cornflour, baking powder and salt into bowl; make a well in centre of dry ingredients; gradually add milk; stir until combined. Spoon asparagus into batter; drain off excess batter, then spoon into deep hot oil; cook until golden. Remove from oil; drain on absorbent paper. Serve immediately with prepared Curry Butter.

Curry Butter: Place egg yolks in top of double saucepan; add vinegar, lemon juice, butter and curry powder; mix well. Place over simmering water; stir until butter melts and sauce thickens. Remove from heat immediately. Add salt, pepper and parsley; stir until combined.
NOTE: The 440 g cans of asparagus labelled 'giant' or 'large' are ideal for this.

Serves 6.

Asparagus with Smoked Salmon

500 g (1 lb.) fresh asparagus or 2 x 470 g (15 oz.) cans asparagus spears	2 tablespoons lemon juice
	2 teaspoons sugar
	2 tablespoons chopped parsley
125 g (4 oz.) butter	6 slices smoked salmon
30 g (1 oz.) flaked almonds	lettuce

If using fresh asparagus, cut off tough ends; scrape spears several centimetres up from end; tie in a bunch. Stand in a deep saucepan and add boiling water to come halfway up spears. Cover tightly; bring to boil; reduce heat and simmer until asparagus is tender (approx. 20 minutes); drain well.

Melt butter; add almonds; saute over low heat until almonds are golden. Add lemon juice and sugar; combine well. Bring to boil; add parsley; remove from heat.

Arrange a lettuce leaf on each plate; place drained asparagus on lettuce (allow approx. 6 spears per serve). Spoon the almond butter over. Top with a rolled slice of salmon.
NOTE: Smoked salmon can be bought in slices from food counters of most large stores or in 90 g (3 oz.) cans. You will need two of these cans.

Serves 6.

Crab and Salmon Pate

60 g (2 oz.) butter	250 g (8 oz.) can red salmon
2 tablespoons flour	
½ cup milk	220 g (7 oz.) can crab
½ cup cream	3 teaspoons gelatine
⅓ cup dry white wine	¼ cup water
salt, pepper	
1 teaspoon french mustard	

Heat butter in pan; add flour; stir until combined; remove pan from heat. Add milk and cream; stir until combined. Return pan to heat; stir until sauce boils and thickens. Reduce heat; simmer 2 minutes; remove pan from heat. Gradually stir in wine. Season with salt and pepper. Add mustard; mix well. Sprinkle gelatine over water; when softened add to white sauce mixture. Return pan to heat; stir for 4 minutes; do not boil.

Put sauce into electric blender; add undrained salmon which has had bones and any dark skin removed. Blend on medium speed for 2 minutes or until very smooth. Add undrained, coarsely flaked crab; mix well (do not blend). Pour into four individual bowls. Cover bowls, refrigerate several hours or overnight.

Serves 4.

Haddock Pate

500 g (1 lb.) smoked haddock	½ cup mayonnaise
½ cup short-grain rice	⅓ cup cream
1 small onion	salt, pepper
2 shallots or spring onions	½ teaspoon dry mustard
2 tablespoons chopped parsley	1 teaspoon lemon juice
	30 g (1 oz.) butter

Cook rice in boiling salted water 12 minutes or until tender; drain. Cover fish with water; bring to boil. Reduce heat; simmer until tender, approx. 5 to 10 minutes; drain and flake, removing any bones and skin. Combine fish with rice, finely-chopped onion, chopped shallots and parsley. Fold in mayonnaise and whipped cream. Stir in pepper, lemon juice and mustard. (Taste; add a little salt if necessary.) Stir in softened butter; mix well. Refrigerate before serving. Serve with Melba Toast. Serves 4.

Melba Toast: Take a square loaf of unsliced bread; remove all crusts. Cut bread in half, giving two half-loaves (this way, it is easier to handle the cutting of individual slices). Now cut each loaf diagonally in half, giving four thick triangle-shaped bread pieces. Place flat side down on board. Cut into wafer-thin slices. Place on ungreased baking trays; bake in moderate oven 15 to 20 minutes, turning frequently.

Caviar Pate

250 g (8 oz.) pkt cream cheese	2 teaspoons worcester-shire sauce
500 g (1 lb.) liverwurst	salt, pepper
4 tablespoons tomato sauce	¼ cup sour cream
4 tablespoons dry sherry	105 g (3½ oz.) jar red caviar

Place cream cheese in small bowl of electric mixer. Beat until soft and creamy. Add remaining ingredients, except sour cream and caviar; beat until mixture is combined and creamy. Spoon pate into serving bowl or individual serving bowls. Cover and refrigerate until ready to serve.

To serve, place a spoonful of sour cream in centre of pate; spoon caviar around sour cream. Serve with triangles of toast.

Serves 4.

Tahitian Fish Soup

2 sticks celery	1½ litres (6 cups) chicken stock
125 g (4 oz.) mushrooms	250 g (8 oz.) fresh prawns
1 green pepper	2.5 cm (1 in.) piece green ginger
1 clove garlic	¼ teaspoon saffron
1 onion	
30 g (1 oz.) butter	
3 medium tomatoes	6 shallots or spring onions
salt, pepper	

Crab Meat Balls

155 g can crab	½ cup dry breadcrumbs
250 g (8 oz.) fresh prawns	1 egg
2 shallots or spring onions	1 tablespoon water
1 teaspoon dry sherry	salt

Chop celery finely; chop mushrooms finely; cut pepper in half, remove seeds and chop finely; peel onion, chop finely. Melt butter in large saucepan; add celery, mushrooms, pepper, crushed garlic and onion; saute 2 minutes. Add peeled and chopped tomatoes and chicken stock; bring to boil; reduce heat; simmer covered 25 minutes. Add shelled and chopped prawns, crab balls, grated ginger, saffron, salt and pepper. Bring to boil; reduce heat; simmer 5 minutes. Just before serving, add chopped shallots.

Crab Meat Balls: Combine crab, peeled and chopped prawns, chopped shallots and bread-crumbs. Beat egg lightly with water and sherry; add to crab mixture with salt. Take heaped teaspoonfuls of crab mixture and form into balls.

Serves 6.

Cream of Avocado Soup

1½ litres (6 cups) chicken stock	1 ripe avocado
2 chicken stock cubes	1 cup cream
3 large onions	30 g (1 oz.) red caviar
250 g (8 oz.) potatoes	30 g (1 oz.) butter
salt, pepper	2 tablespoons plain flour
	5 cm (2 in.) strip lemon rind

Place chicken stock, stock cubes, peeled and sliced onions, peeled and sliced potatoes, salt, pepper and lemon rind in pan. Bring to boil; reduce heat; simmer covered 45 minutes. Remove lemon rind. Place quarter of the soup in electric blender; blend on medium speed until smooth. Repeat with remaining soup.

Remove skin and stone from avocado; place avocado in electric blender with 1 cup of the soup; blend on medium speed 1 minute. Return soup and avocado mixture to pan with cream; stir until combined. Place softened butter on plate; gradually work in flour until mixture is combined and very smooth. Gradually add flour mixture to soup; stir until melted and combined, then stir until boiling; reduce heat; simmer 5 minutes. Spoon soup into serving bowls; top with a spoonful of caviar.

This soup is best made a few hours before serving and then gently reheated.

Serves 6.

Cauliflower Rice Soup

½ medium size cauliflower	2 tablespoons flour
2 onions	3 cups milk
2 carrots	¾ cup long-grain rice
60 g (2 oz.) butter	1 cup yoghurt
2 teaspoons turmeric	3 tablespoons chopped
¼ teaspoon chilli powder	parsley
3 chicken stock cubes	salt, pepper
3 cups water	

Cook rice in boiling salted water until tender; drain. Trim cauliflower; cut into small flowerets. Heat butter in pan; add cauliflower, peeled and chopped onions and carrots, turmeric, chilli powder, stock cubes and water. Stir until combined; bring to boil. Reduce heat; simmer covered 30 minutes.

Push vegetables and liquid through fine sieve or puree in electric blender. Return vegetable puree to pan; stir in flour which has been mixed to a paste with a little of the milk; gradually add remaining milk; stir until boiling. Reduce heat; simmer 2 minutes. Stir in rice, yoghurt and parsley. Season with salt and pepper; heat gently; do not boil.

Serves 4 to 6.

Cream of Chicken Soup

1.25 kg (2½ lb.) chicken	90 g (3 oz.) butter
(or chicken pieces)	⅓ cup plain flour
2 litres (8 cups) water	salt, pepper
2 large onions	2 chicken stock cubes
4 sticks celery	½ cup cream
1 medium parsnip	chopped parsley

Wash and clean chicken; place into large pan; add water, 1 peeled and chopped onion and 2 chopped sticks celery. Bring to boil; reduce heat; simmer covered 2 hours. Remove chicken from stock; reserve 7 cups of strained stock.

In separate pan, melt butter; add remaining peeled and finely-chopped onion, remaining finely-chopped celery and peeled and finely-chopped parsnip; saute gently until onion is tender. Add flour; stir until combined; remove pan from heat. Add reserved stock to pan all at once; stir until combined. Return pan to heat; stir until sauce boils and thickens. Reduce heat; simmer gently 2 minutes. Season with salt and pepper; add crumbled stock cubes. Cover pan; simmer gently 60 minutes.

Remove skin from chicken; remove meat from bones. Cut meat into very small pieces. Just before serving, add chicken and cream to pan; heat through gently. Stir in parsley.

Serves 6.

Crab and Asparagus Soup

500 g (1 lb.) chicken thighs	1 egg
2¼ litres (9 cups) water	2 tablespoons soy sauce
2.5 cm (1 in.) piece green	1 tablespoon dry sherry
ginger	1 teaspoon sugar
salt, pepper	6 shallots or spring onions
250 g (8 oz.) can crab	2 tablespoons water, extra
470 g (15 oz.) can green	1 tablespoon cornflour
asparagus tips	

Put chicken thighs, water and peeled and grated green ginger into large pan; bring to boil. Reduce heat; simmer covered 2 hours. Strain; reserve 6 cups of the chicken stock. Put reserved chicken stock, soy sauce, sherry and sugar into pan; stir until boiling. Add beaten egg gradually to soup mixture, whisking constantly. Add undrained flaked crab, drained asparagus and finely chopped shallots. Simmer gently 3 minutes. Mix cornflour to smooth paste with extra water; add to soup; stir until boiling. Reduce heat; simmer 2 minutes. Season with salt and pepper. (Chicken thighs can be used for another meal.)

Serves 6.

Minestrone

½ cup haricot beans	2 potatoes
30 g (1 oz.) butter	125 g (4 oz.) green beans
2 onions	3 courgettes
60 g (2 oz.) bacon pieces	4 tomatoes
2 cloves garlic	⅓ cup small macaroni
2½ litres (10 cups) water	2 tablespoons chopped
6 beef stock cubes	parsley
3 carrots	salt, pepper
2 sticks celery	grated parmesan cheese

Soak haricot beans overnight in plenty of cold water to cover. Heat butter in large pan; add peeled and chopped onions, chopped bacon pieces and crushed garlic. Saute gently until onions are transparent. Add water, crumbled stock cubes and drained haricot beans; bring to boil. Reduce heat; simmer covered 2¼ hours.

Peel and dice carrots; slice celery; peel and dice potatoes; top, tail and slice beans; slice courgettes; remove skins from tomatoes and chop tomatoes finely. Add vegetables to simmering stock; bring to boil. Reduce heat; simmer covered 1 hour. Remove lid from pan; add macaroni. Simmer, stirring occasionally, until pasta is cooked, 10 to 15 minutes. Stir in parsley; season with salt and pepper. Serve grated parmesan cheese separately to sprinkle on top of soup.

Serves 6.

Minestrone — hot, hearty, a meal in itself. Serve with crusty bread.

Goulash Soup

30 g (1 oz.) butter	2 litres (8 cups) water
2 large onions	2 beef stock cubes
2 large carrots	2 chicken stock cubes
3 sticks celery	¼ teaspoon caraway
500 g (1 lb.) pork (see Note)	seeds
125 g (4 oz.) bacon pieces	salt, pepper
1½ tablespoons paprika	⅓ cup tomato paste
60 g (2 oz.) butter, extra	3 tablespoons chopped
2 tablespoons oil	parsley.
½ cup flour	cream

Cut meat and bacon pieces into 1 cm (½ in.) pieces. Heat butter in large pan; add peeled and chopped onions and carrots and chopped celery. Saute gently until golden brown; remove from pan. Add extra butter and oil to pan; add pork and bacon pieces; cook gently until meat is golden brown; remove from pan.

Add flour to pan; stir until dark golden brown; add paprika; stir 1 minute more. Remove pan from heat; add water; stir until combined. Return pan to heat; stir until soup comes to boil; reduce heat.

Add pork, bacon and vegetables; stir until combined. Add caraway seeds, crumbled stock cubes and tomato paste. Stir until combined; season with salt and pepper. Cover; simmer gently 1½ hours. Add parsley; heat until boiling. Spoon into serving dishes; swirl a little cream on top of each.

Serves 6 to 8.

NOTE: Two large thick pork chops can be used for this soup: or ask your butcher for any economical cut of lean pork.

Seafood Soup

Seafood Soup

1½ litres (6 cups) water	2 medium potatoes
500 g (1 lb.) fish fillets	2 small carrots
250 g (8 oz.) fresh prawns	1 stick celery
250 g (8 oz.) scallops	1 cup dry white wine
2 teaspoons salt	pepper
90 g (3 oz.) butter	½ cup cream
1 teaspoon curry powder	2 tablespoons chopped
⅓ cup flour	parsley
⅓ cup tomato paste	

Cheese Croutons

1 small stick french bread	2 tablespoons grated
45 g (1½ oz.) butter	parmesan cheese
60 g (2 oz.) cheese	

Shell prawns; reserve prawn shells. Put water, fish fillets, prawn shells and salt into large pan; bring to boil. Reduce heat; simmer covered 30 minutes. Strain; reserve stock and fish fillets.

Heat butter in large pan; add curry powder and flour; stir until combined. Remove pan from heat; add reserved stock and wine; stir until combined. Return pan to heat; add tomato paste, peeled and diced potatoes, peeled and diced carrots and celery; stir until mixture boils. Reduce heat; simmer gently, covered, 30 minutes. Season with pepper.

Clean prawns; cut into pieces; clean scallops; cut in half. Remove skin and bones from fish; flake into large pieces. Add all these to soup; simmer 5 minutes uncovered. Add cream and parsley; stir until combined.

Serve with Cheese Croutons.

Croutons: Cut bread diagonally into 1 cm (½ in.) slices. Melt butter; brush one side of each slice of bread with butter; bake in moderate oven 10 minutes or until crisp and golden brown. Sprinkle combined grated cheeses over unbuttered side of bread; bake in moderate oven a further 10 minutes or until cheese has melted and browned slightly.

Serves 6.

Veal and Broccoli Consomme

1 veal knuckle	125 g (4 oz.) mushrooms
1¾ litres (7 cups) water	6 shallots or spring onions
2 tablespoons rice	½ teaspoon cinnamon
500 g (1 lb.) broccoli	salt, pepper
(or 375 g (12 oz.) pkt	
frozen broccoli)	

Put veal, water and cinnamon in saucepan; bring to boil. Reduce heat; simmer covered 1½ hours. Remove knuckle; discard veal; strain stock twice through fine sieve.

Remove stems and leaves from broccoli. Cut broccoli into flowerets. (If using frozen broccoli, defrost and cut into small flowerets.) Drop broccoli into boiling salted water; cook 1 minute; drain and rinse under cold running water. Put veal stock in saucepan; bring to boil. Add rice; boil until tender, approx. 10 minutes. Add sliced mushrooms, sliced shallots, broccoli, salt and pepper; reduce heat; simmer 2 minutes.

Serves 4.

Spinach and Bacon Soup

1½ litres (6 cups) water	salt, pepper
3 chicken stock cubes	125 g (4 oz.) lean bacon
250 g (8 oz.) old potatoes	pieces
2 large onions	½ cup cream
1 small bunch spinach	

Place water, crumbled stock cubes, peeled and sliced potatoes, peeled and chopped onions in pan; bring to boil. Reduce heat; simmer covered 45 minutes. Add roughly chopped spinach which has had white stalks removed; simmer a further 5 minutes. Season with salt and pepper.

Place mixture in electric blender; blend on medium speed until pureed. (You will need to do this in two lots.) If you do not have a blender, push mixture through fine sieve. Return soup to pan; add finely-chopped bacon; simmer further 15 minutes. Just before serving, add cream; stir until heated through.

Serves 4.

Country Potato Soup

500 g (1 lb.) potatoes	2 tablespoons flour
1 litre (4 cups) water	2 beef stock cubes
30 g (1 oz.) butter	½ teaspoon caraway seeds
1 onion	2 tablespoons chopped
125 g (4 oz.) bacon pieces	parsley

Peel potatoes; cut into 2.5 cm (1 in.) cubes. Put potatoes into the water; cook until tender. Heat butter in pan; add peeled, chopped onion and chopped bacon; saute until onion is well browned. Add flour, stir until golden brown. Add onion and bacon mixture to potatoes; stir until soup boils and thickens. Add crumbled stock cubes, caraway seeds and chopped parsley.

Serves 4.

Chinese Hot Sour Soup

125 g (4 oz.) sliced ham	½ teaspoon salt
125 g (4 oz.) small mushrooms	2 tablespoons cornflour
	¼ cup water
250 g (8 oz.) lean pork	2 teaspoons white vinegar
30 g (1 oz.) sweet chinese pickles	1 teaspoon sesame oil
	1 egg
125 g (4 oz.) bamboo shoots	6 shallots or spring onions
	250 g (8 oz.) fresh or canned bean curd
1¾ litres (7 cups) chicken stock	soy sauce
¼ cup dry white wine	

Cut ham into very fine shreds; slice mushrooms thinly; cut pork, pickles and bamboo shoots into very fine shreds. Place chicken stock in very large pan; add wine and salt; bring to boil. Boil uncovered 5 minutes; remove pan from heat.

Place cornflour and water in bowl; stir until combined. Gradually add cornflour mixture to chicken stock, stirring until combined. Return pan to heat; stir until soup comes to boil. Reduce heat; add ham, mushrooms, pork, pickles and bamboo shoots. Simmer uncovered 5 minutes. Add vinegar and oil; stir until combined.

Beat egg until combined. Gradually add to chicken stock, stirring constantly. Add chopped shallots and bean curd cut into 1 cm (½ in.) cubes. Simmer 3 minutes. Spoon into individual bowls; top each with a teaspoon of soy sauce.

Serves 6.

NOTE: Chinese pickles are available in cans, or are sold in bulk from all Chinese food stores.

Cream of Mushroom Soup

1½ litres (6 cups) chicken stock	1 large onion
	4 shallots or spring onions
250 g (8 oz.) mushrooms	½ cup cream
1 large potato	salt, pepper

Shallot Cream

6 shallots or spring onions	¼ cup sour cream
¼ cup parsley sprigs	1 tablespoon milk

Slice 185 g (6 oz.) of the mushrooms; peel and roughly chop potato; peel and roughly chop onion. Put chicken stock in saucepan; add mushrooms, potato and onion. Bring to boil; reduce heat; simmer covered 20 minutes or until vegetables are tender. Remove from heat; put vegetables and liquid in blender; blend until smooth. Return soup to saucepan; add remaining thinly-sliced mushrooms and chopped shallots; simmer 5 minutes. Add cream; reheat without boiling. Season with salt and pepper. Pour soup into individual dishes; swirl Shallot Cream through soup.

Shallot Cream: Put roughly-chopped shallots and parsley sprigs into blender; blend well. Add the sour cream and milk; blend until smooth.

Serves 4.

Italian Stracciatella

1½ litres (6 cups) chicken stock	1 tablespoon chopped parsley
2 eggs	pinch nutmeg
1 tablespoon grated parmesan cheese	salt, pepper

Beat together eggs and cheese; add parsley and nutmeg. Bring chicken stock to boil; reduce heat; gradually whisk in the egg mixture; simmer 2 minutes. Season with salt and pepper.

Serves 4 to 6.

Fish & Shellfish

Fish and shellfish are high in food value, low in calories. Preparation and cooking times are short. Recipes given provide interesting ideas for entrees or main courses.

Seafood Cocktail

A seafood cocktail can be any combination of seafood — prawns, crab, lobster, oysters — or you could use just prawns alone. Allow about 125 g (4 oz.) seafood per serving. (If using prawns alone, this would be 125 g (4 oz.) shelled prawns, or 250 g (8 oz.) unshelled prawns; about half the weight is lost when prawn shells are removed.)

Shred some washed, crisp lettuce finely; arrange in the base of cocktail glasses. A little very finely-chopped celery and parsley can be mixed in with the lettuce. Arrange seafood over; top with the sauce, or serve sauce separately. Quantities given here for sauce will serve 4.

Seafood Cocktail Sauce

¼ cup tomato sauce	2 tablespoons brandy
1 teaspoon worcester-shire sauce	¼ cup cream
	few drops tabasco sauce
½ cup mayonnaise	salt, pepper

Combine tomato sauce, worcestershire sauce, mayonnaise, brandy, tabasco sauce, salt and pepper. Whip cream lightly; fold into sauce.

Prawns Creole

500 g (1 lb.) prawns	470 g (15 oz.) can whole peeled tomatoes
3 cups water	
45 g (1½ oz.) butter	¼ cup dry white wine
1 onion	1 teaspoon sugar
1 clove garlic	1½ tablespoons tomato paste
2 rashers bacon	
1 green pepper	salt, pepper
1 stick celery	2 tablespoons chopped parsley
1 tablespoon flour	

Shell prawns; remove back vein; reserve shells. Put reserved prawn shells in saucepan with water; bring to boil. Reduce heat; simmer covered 15 minutes. Drain; reserve 1 cup stock.

Heat butter in pan; add peeled and chopped onion, crushed garlic and chopped bacon; saute

Recipe continued overleaf:

Seafood Cocktail — a seafood combination is topped with a superb brandied cocktail sauce. It makes a perfect first course.

until bacon is crisp. Add seeded and finely-chopped pepper and sliced celery; saute until pepper is tender. Add flour; cook until golden brown. Add undrained mashed tomatoes, reserved prawn stock and white wine; stir until sauce boils and thickens. Add sugar, tomato paste, salt and pepper; stir until combined. Reduce heat; simmer covered 10 minutes. Add prawns and parsley; cook further 5 minutes. Serve with hot rice.

Serves 4.

Prawn Cutlets with Crab

1 kg (2 lb.) large fresh **prawns**	¾ cup plain flour
2 eggs	1½ cups packaged dry breadcrumbs
¼ cup milk	oil for deep-frying

Filling

2 x 170 g cans crab	1 tablespoon flour
1 tablespoon finely-chopped celery	⅓ cup milk
1 tablespoon finely-chopped green pepper	½ cup fresh breadcrumbs
	½ teaspoon worcester-shire sauce
1 clove garlic	½ teaspoon lemon juice
30 g (1 oz.) butter	1 teaspoon salt

Shell prawns, leaving tail intact; remove back vein. Wash prawns; drain; dry well. Using sharp, pointed knife, cut deep slit down back of each prawn, taking care not to cut through flesh completely. Put approx. 1 tablespoon of filling into each slit and reshape prawn. Refrigerate 1 hour.

Roll prawns in flour; shake off excess flour. Dip in combined beaten eggs and milk; roll in breadcrumbs. Dip in egg mixture again; roll in breadcrumbs again. (Prawns can be returned to refrigerator at this stage until required.) Deep-fry prawns in hot oil a few at a time for 3 minutes or until golden brown and crisp; drain. Serve prawns with Creamy Tartare Sauce and lemon wedges.

Filling: Melt butter in saucepan; add celery, pepper and crushed garlic; saute 2 minutes until vegetables are tender. Add flour; stir until smooth; cook 1 minute. Remove from heat; add milk; stir until smooth. Return to heat; stir until sauce boils and thickens. Reduce heat; simmer 1 minute; remove from heat. Add drained, flaked crab, breadcrumbs, worcestershire sauce, lemon juice and salt; mix well.

Creamy Tartare Sauce

¾ cup mayonnaise	1 teaspoon lemon juice
2 gherkins	salt, pepper
6 shallots or spring onions	½ teaspoon dry mustard
1 tablespoon chopped parsley	½ cup cream

Combine mayonnaise, finely-chopped gherkins, finely-chopped shallots, parsley, lemon juice, salt, pepper and dry mustard. Whip cream; fold into mayonnaise mixture. Refrigerate until ready to use.

Serves 6 as an entree.

Fish Pate

125 g (4 oz.) butter	1 chicken stock cube
500 g (1 lb.) fish fillets	½ cup mayonnaise
½ cup dry white wine	1 teaspoon grated lemon rind
salt, pepper	
½ cup cream	

Remove skin and all bones from fish; cut fish into large pieces. Melt butter in pan; add fish, wine, salt, pepper and crumbled stock cube. Cover, bring to boil. Reduce heat; simmer 5 minutes or until fish is just cooked.

Remove fish from liquid. Bring liquid to boil; boil uncovered until about ¼ cup liquid remains. Add cream; stir until combined.

Put fish in blender; add cream mixture. Blend on medium speed until smooth. Spoon into serving dish or individual dishes; refrigerate until firm. Combine mayonnaise and lemon rind; spoon this mixture over pate. Refrigerate.

Serves 4.

Curried Cream Scallops

60 g (2 oz.) butter	500 g (1 lb.) scallops
1 onion	2 egg yolks
2 tablespoons flour	2 tablespoons chopped parsley
3 teaspoons curry powder	
1 cup milk	½ cup rice
½ cup mayonnaise	45 g (1½ oz.) butter, extra
2 tablespoons sour cream	1½ cups fresh breadcrumbs
1 tablespoon lemon juice	
salt, pepper	

Wash scallops; remove dark vein; slice in half. Melt butter; add peeled and finely-chopped onion; saute until onion is transparent. Add flour and curry powder; stir until smooth; cook 1 minute. Remove from heat; add milk; stir until smooth. Return to heat; stir over medium heat until sauce boils and thickens. Add mayonnaise, sour cream, lemon juice, salt, pepper and scallops; simmer covered 5 minutes. Add lightly beaten egg yolks and parsley; mix well; reheat without boiling.

Cook rice in boiling salted water 12 minutes or until tender; drain. Spoon rice evenly over base of 4 individual dishes; spoon scallop mixture evenly over rice.

Combine extra melted butter and breadcrumbs; sprinkle evenly over top of each casserole. Bake in moderate oven 15 to 20 minutes or until golden brown.

Serves 4.

Braised Scallops with Ham

3 tablespoons oil	1 cup water
2.5 cm (1 in.) piece green ginger	2 chicken stock cubes
	3 teaspoons cornflour
500 g (1 lb.) scallops	1 teaspoon soy sauce
125 g (4 oz.) sliced leg ham	1 tablespoon oyster sauce
315 g (10 oz.) can champignons	1 tablespoon sate sauce
	salt
6 shallots or spring onions	1 tablespoon dry sherry

Wash and dry scallops; cut ham into 2.5 cm x 1 cm (1 in. x ½ in.) strips; peel and grate green ginger; drain champignons; cut shallots into 2.5 cm (1 in.) pieces. Heat oil in frying pan or wok; add ginger, scallops, ham, champignons; toss quickly 2 minutes over very high heat. Add combined water, crumbled stock cubes, cornflour, soy sauce, oyster sauce, sate sauce, salt and dry sherry; toss quickly until sauce is boiling; boil uncovered 1 minute, tossing constantly. Add shallots; boil a further 20 seconds.

Serves 4.

NOTE: Oyster sauce and sate sauce can be bought in small bottles from large supermarkets or Chinese food stores.

Souffle Oysters

12 oysters in the shell	1 teaspoon prepared mustard
3 rashers bacon	
60 g (2 oz.) butter	salt, pepper
1½ tablespoons flour	60 g (2 oz.) cheddar cheese
½ cup milk	2 eggs, separated

Put oysters on to oven tray. Remove rind from bacon; chop into small pieces. Put in frying pan; cook until bacon is crisp; sprinkle evenly over oysters.

Heat butter in pan; add flour; stir until combined; remove from heat. Gradually add milk; stir until combined. Add mustard, salt and pepper. Return pan to heat; stir until sauce boils and thickens; remove from heat. Add grated cheese and egg yolks; stir until combined. Allow mixture to cool until warm.

Beat egg whites until soft peaks form; gently fold into cheese mixture. Spoon heaped teaspoonfuls of mixture on to each oyster. Bake in hot oven 5 minutes or until puffed and golden brown. Serve immediately.

Serves 2.

Scallops en Brochette

500 g (1 lb.) scallops	butter
lemon juice	lemon wedges
salt, pepper	parsley

Saffron Rice

1 cup long grain rice	¼ teaspoon saffron
½ teaspoon salt	30 g (1 oz.) butter

Wash and trim scallops; thread on to thin bamboo skewers. Allow 4 to 6 scallops for each skewer. Brush with melted butter; sprinkle with lemon juice, salt and pepper.

Put under hot griller 3 to 4 minutes or until scallops are just golden brown; turn and cook other side, basting with melted butter. Serve on bed of hot saffron rice; garnish with lemon and parsley.

Saffron Rice: Put a large saucepan of water on to boil; add salt and saffron. When boiling, gradually add rice; cook 12 minutes or until tender. Drain rice well; stir in butter; mix butter through rice until melted.

Serves 4 as an entree.

Fish Puffs

750 g (1½ lb.) fish fillets	salt, pepper
3 slices bread	1 egg, extra
½ cup milk	2 tablespoons milk, extra
1 teaspoon curry powder	flour, extra
1 tablespoon flour	packaged dry breadcrumbs
1 egg	oil for deep-frying

Curry Sauce

30 g (1 oz.) butter	¼ cup sour cream
1 tablespoon flour	1 tablespoon parsley
2 teaspoons curry powder	salt, pepper
1 cup milk	

Remove skin and all bones from fish; chop fish finely. Remove crusts from bread; break up bread roughly; cover with the milk and let stand 20 minutes. Combine chopped fish, soaked bread and milk, curry powder, flour, egg, salt and pepper; mix well. Refrigerate 1 hour. Form mixture into balls; coat with extra flour, then combined beaten extra egg and extra milk; coat well with breadcrumbs. Refrigerate 30 minutes to firm. Deep-fry in hot oil until golden brown. Serve hot with curry sauce.

Curry Sauce: Melt butter in small pan; add flour and curry powder; stir until smooth. Cook 1 minute; remove from heat. Add milk gradually; stir until smooth. Return to heat; stir until sauce boils and thickens. Add sour cream, chopped parsley, salt and pepper.

Makes approx. 30.

Italian Fish

4 large fish fillets
30 g (1 oz.) butter
1 onion
470 g (15 oz.) can whole tomatoes
salt, pepper
½ teaspoon basil
1 teaspoon sugar
1 tablespoon chopped parsley
1 tablespoon capers
30 g (1 oz.) stuffed olives
2 sticks celery
1 tablespoon chopped parsley, extra

Skin fish fillets; remove bones. Put fish in base of greased shallow ovenproof dish. Melt butter in pan; saute peeled and finely-chopped onion until onion is transparent. Add tomatoes with liquid from can, salt, pepper, basil and sugar. Bring to boil; reduce heat; simmer uncovered 15 minutes, or until nearly all liquid has evaporated. Remove from heat; stir in parsley, finely-chopped capers, sliced olives and chopped celery. Pour tomato mixture over fish; cover; bake in moderate oven 20 minutes or until cooked. Sprinkle with extra parsley.
  Serves 4.

Golden Oat Trout

6 trout
¾ cup fine oatmeal
1 cup rolled oats
1½ cups fresh breadcrumbs
salt, pepper
2 eggs
¼ cup milk
flour
60 g (2 oz.) butter
3 tablespoons oil

Parsley Lemon Butter

125 g (4 oz.) butter
1 tablespoon chopped parsley
salt, pepper
2 teaspoons lemon juice
1 teaspoon grated lemon rind

Clean and scale fish. Combine oatmeal, rolled oats, breadcrumbs, salt and pepper. Coat fish with flour; dip in combined beaten eggs and milk; coat well with crumb mixture. Heat butter and oil in large frying pan (or several pans); fry fish on both sides until golden brown. Put on serving plate; garnish with lemon slices or wedges and slices of Parsley Lemon Butter.

Parsley Lemon Butter: Beat butter until light and creamy; fold in parsley, lemon rind, lemon juice, salt and pepper. Spoon mixture into rough log shape about a quarter of the way down a sheet of greaseproof paper. Fold paper over roll, then, with ruler, push against the butter so that mixture forms a smooth roll. Roll butter in the greaseproof paper; refrigerate until firm; cut into slices.
  Serves 6.

NOTE: Fine oatmeal is available in 500 g (1 lb.) packs at health food stores.

Chinese Bream

500 g to 750 g (1 lb. to 1½ lb.) whole bream
water
salt
2.5 cm (1 in.) piece green ginger
2 tablespoons soy sauce
4 shallots or spring onions
2.5 cm (1 in.) piece green ginger, extra
3 tablespoons oil

Clean and scale fish. Put on to boil a shallow pan with water (enough to cover fish), salt and crushed ginger; boil 5 minutes. Reduce heat; put in fish; cover. Cook over low heat 10 to 15 minutes, or until fish is cooked.
  Remove fish from water; drain well; place on heated serving dish. Pour soy sauce over; sprinkle with finely-sliced shallots and sliced extra ginger. Heat oil until nearly boiling; pour over fish.
  Serves 2.

Steamed Ginger Fish

4 x 500 g (1 lb.) whole bream or snapper
1 red pepper
1 green pepper
2 sticks celery
10 shallots or spring onions

Ginger Sauce

2.5 cm (1 in.) piece green ginger
2 cups water
1½ tablespoons cornflour
1 tablespoon soy sauce
2 tablespoons dry sherry
salt
3 chicken stock cubes
1 thick slice lemon
1 teaspoon sugar

Wash and clean fish. Place fish in two large baking dishes; cover completely with water. Place baking dishes on top of stove over medium heat; bring to simmering point. Reduce heat; simmer uncovered very slowly until fish is tender, approx. 15 to 20 minutes.
  Seed red and green peppers; cut peppers into very thin slices. Cut celery into 5 cm (2 in.) lengths, then cut into very thin slices. Cut shallots into very thin diagonal slices. Drop peppers and celery into saucepan of boiling salted water; boil 1 minute; drain.
  Place fish on serving plates; spoon peppers and celery down centre of each fish. Spoon over prepared Ginger Sauce; top with shallots.

Ginger Sauce: Peel ginger; cut into very thin slices, then cut slices into very thin strips. Place ginger and remaining ingredients in pan; stir until combined. Place pan over heat; stir until sauce boils and thickens. Reduce heat; simmer uncovered 5 minutes. Remove lemon before serving.
  Serves 4.

Steamed Ginger Fish — Chinese-style, with colourful vegetables.

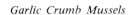
Garlic Crumb Mussels

Garlic Crumb Mussels

1 kg (2 lb.) mussels	2 tablespoons chopped
125 g (4 oz.) butter	parsley
2 cloves garlic	60 g (2 oz.) butter, extra
salt, pepper	1½ cups fresh
4 shallots or spring onions	breadcrumbs
1 tablespoon lemon juice	

Scrub mussels and remove beards. Place mussels in large pan of simmering water; cover and boil gently 2 minutes or until mussel shells open; remove immediately from water. Discard any shells which do not open. Open shells; leave mussel on one side of shell; discard empty shells.

Beat butter until soft and creamy. Add crushed garlic, salt, pepper, finely-chopped shallots, parsley and lemon juice; mix well. Take teaspoonfuls of mixture and spoon over each mussel. Heat extra butter in pan; add breadcrumbs; mix well. Spoon breadcrumbs over mussels, pressing lightly into butter mixture.

Arrange mussels on oven slide. Put under hot griller until golden brown and heated through, approx. 2 minutes.

Serves 4 (approx. 6 mussels per serving).

Crisp Fried Fish

6 fish fillets	salt, pepper
cornflour	1¼ cups water, approx.
2 cups self-raising flour	oil for deep-frying

Tartare Sauce

¾ cup mayonnaise	1 teaspoon chopped chives
2 tablespoons capers	1 tablespoon chopped
2 tablespoons chopped	parsley
gherkins	salt, pepper

Skin fish; remove as many bones as possible. Lightly coat fish fillets in cornflour; shake off the excess. Sift flour, salt and pepper into small bowl. Add water gradually, beating well until smooth and of a good pouring consistency. Using tongs, coat fish well with batter; allow excess batter to drain from fish. Lower fish into deep hot oil, cooking only one or two pieces at a time. Deep-fry 1 minute or until pale golden colour. Remove from oil; allow oil to reheat; re-fry fish until golden brown and cooked through. Drain on absorbent paper. Serve with chips and Tartare Sauce.

Tartare Sauce: In a small bowl combine mayonnaise, finely-chopped capers, gherkins, chives, parsley; season with salt and pepper; mix well.

Serves 3 or 6.

Salmon Quiche

Pastry

1 cup plain flour	1 egg yolk
pinch salt	1 tablespoon lemon juice
90 g (3 oz.) butter	

Filling

250 g (8 oz.) can red	½ teaspoon paprika
salmon	2 tablespoons chopped
4 rashers bacon	parsley
1 cup cream	1 tablespoon grated
3 eggs	parmesan cheese
salt, pepper	

Pastry: Sift flour and salt into bowl. Rub in butter until mixture resembles fine breadcrumbs. Mix to a firm dough with lightly beaten egg yolk and lemon juice; add one to two teaspoons of water, if necessary. Turn pastry on to lightly floured surface; knead lightly. Roll out to line base and sides of 23 cm (9 in.) flan tin. Cut a circle of greaseproof paper to fit base and sides of flan tin; press lightly on to pastry. Spoon approx. 250 g (8 oz.) dried beans or rice evenly on to greaseproof paper. Bake in hot oven 8 minutes. Remove beans and greaseproof paper; bake further 3 minutes. Remove from oven; allow to become cold. (The beans or rice can, of course, be used again for ordinary cooking purposes.)

Filling: Drain salmon, reserving liquid; flake salmon lightly; remove bones. Dice bacon; fry until crisp; remove from pan; drain well. Beat together cream, eggs, salt and pepper, paprika, parsley, parmesan cheese and reserved salmon liquid. Place flan tin on oven tray. Place salmon evenly in base of pastry shell; sprinkle bacon over; carefully pour egg mixture over. Bake in moderately slow oven 30 to 35 minutes or until set.

Fish Fillets with Artichokes

8 bream (or other) fillets	3 cups fresh breadcrumbs
flour	60 g (2 oz.) butter
2 eggs	2 tablespoons oil
2 tablespoons milk	

Sauce

30 g (1 oz.) butter	½ cup cream
1 onion	470 g (15 oz.) can artichoke
3 teaspoons french	hearts
mustard	1 tablespoon chopped
2 tablespoons flour	parsley
1 cup milk	salt, pepper
½ cup dry white wine	

Skin fish; remove bones. Coat fish with flour; dip in combined beaten eggs and milk; coat well with breadcrumbs. Heat butter with oil in large pan; add fish; cook until well browned on both sides. Serve hot with sauce.

Sauce: Melt butter; add peeled and finely-chopped onion; saute until onion is transparent. Add flour and mustard; stir until smooth. Remove from heat; add milk and wine. Return to heat; stir over medium heat until sauce boils and thickens. Add drained, sliced artichokes; simmer 2 minutes. Add cream, parsley, salt and pepper; reheat without boiling.

Serves 4.

Calamari

1 kg (2 lb.) fresh squid	salt, pepper
2 eggs	oil for deep-frying
flour	

Hold squid firmly with one hand; with other hand, hold head and pull gently. Head and inside of body of squid will come away in one compact piece. Remove bone which will be found at open end of squid; it looks like a long, thin piece of plastic. Clean squid under cold running water, then rub off the brown outer skin.

Cut squid into 5 mm (¼ in.) rings. Dip rings into beaten eggs. Toss well in flour seasoned with salt and pepper. Repeat egg-and-flouring. Cook in deep hot oil until golden brown; drain on absorbent paper. (Oil should be hot, but not too hot, or calamari will brown before they are properly cooked and tender. Cooking time is approx. 3 minutes.) Serve with lemon wedges and Tartare Sauce (see recipe for Crisp Fried Fish).

Serves 4.

NOTE: Some large food stores or supermarkets sell squid already cleaned, ready for cooking as above.

Curried Salmon Mornay Slice

1 cup long grain rice	1½ cups milk
220 g can salmon	½ cup mayonnaise
30 g (1 oz.) butter	2 teaspoons lemon juice
1 egg	2 tablespoons chopped
salt, pepper	parsley
45 g (1½ oz.) butter, extra	1 egg, extra
2 tablespoons flour	60 g (2 oz.) cheese
1½ tablespoons curry powder	

Cook rice in boiling salted water 12 minutes or until tender; drain. Combine with butter, egg, salt and pepper. Line 18 cm x 28 cm (7 in. x 11 in.) lamington tin with aluminium foil, bringing it above sides of tin on each side; this makes it easy to lift out slice when cooked. Press rice mixture over base and sides of tin to make a pie case. Arrange drained flaked salmon over rice base.

Melt extra butter; add flour and curry powder; stir until smooth; cook 1 minute. Remove from heat; add milk gradually; stir until smooth; add mayonnaise. Return to heat; stir until sauce boils and thickens. Add lemon juice and parsley. Reduce heat; simmer 1 minute. Remove from heat; add extra beaten egg; cool slightly. Spoon mixture evenly into rice shell; sprinkle with grated cheese. Bake in moderate oven 25 to 35 minutes or until golden brown on top.

Serves 4 to 6.

Tuna and Vegetable Patties

425 g can tuna	2 potatoes
45 g (1½ oz.) butter	flour, extra
1 onion	1½ cups packaged dry
2 sticks celery	breadcrumbs
1 carrot	1 tablespoon chopped
1 tablespoon flour	parsley
3 teaspoons prepared mustard	1 egg
	1 tablespoon milk, extra
salt, pepper	30 g (1 oz.) butter, extra
½ cup milk	2 tablespoons oil

Sauce

45 g (1½ oz.) butter	2 tablespoons chopped
1½ tablespoons flour	parsley
3 teaspoons prepared mustard	30 g (1 oz.) grated cheese
	salt, pepper
1½ cups milk	

Peel and finely chop onion; chop celery and carrot finely. Melt butter in pan; add onion, celery and carrot; saute gently 5 minutes. Add flour, mustard, salt and pepper; stir until smooth. Add milk; stir until smooth, then stir over medium heat until mixture boils and thickens. Reduce heat; simmer 2 minutes. Add drained, flaked tuna.

Peel and roughly chop potatoes; cook in boiling salted water until tender. Drain; mash until smooth; add to tuna mixture; mix well. Allow mixture to become cold.

Shape mixture into 12 patties; coat lightly with extra flour. Dip in combined beaten egg and extra milk; coat well with combined breadcrumbs and parsley. Heat extra butter and oil in large pan; cook patties until golden brown on both sides. Serve hot with sauce.

Sauce: Melt butter; add flour and mustard; cook 1 minute. Remove from heat; add milk; stir until smooth. Return to heat; stir until sauce boils and thickens. Add cheese and chopped parsley; stir over low heat until cheese melts. Season with salt and pepper.

Serves 4.

Bream with Asparagus

4 large bream (or other) fillets	¼ cup water
	1 tablespoon lemon juice
470 g (15 oz.) can asparagus spears	¼ cup mayonnaise
	¼ cup cream
60 g (2 oz.) butter	½ teaspoon thyme
6 shallots or spring onions	salt, pepper
2 tablespoons flour	2 tablespoons chopped
½ cup dry white wine	parsley

Remove any skin or bones from fish. Put fish in shallow ovenproof dish. Arrange drained asparagus over fish, reserving 2 tablespoons of the asparagus liquid.

Melt butter over low heat; add shallots; cook until shallots are tender. Remove pan from heat; stir in flour; stir until smooth. Return to heat; cook a few minutes. Remove from heat; gradually add wine and water, then lemon juice, mayonnaise, cream, thyme, salt, pepper, chopped parsley and reserved asparagus liquid. Return to heat, stir until sauce boils and thickens. Pour sauce over fish. Bake covered in moderate oven 30 minutes.

Serves 4.

Meat Dishes

Beef

Beef is a great family favourite — as simple steaks, succulent roasts, substantial casseroles. You'll want to try so many of these delicious recipes, and you'll enjoy every one.

Tournedos with Mustard Bearnaise

4 fillet steaks, each about 2.5 cm (1 in.) thick
60 g (2 oz.) butter
4 slices bread, about 2.5 cm (1 in.) thick

90 g (3 oz.) butter, extra
345 g (11 oz.) can artichoke bottoms
375 g (12 oz.) can asparagus tips

Mustard Bearnaise

½ cup white vinegar
8 peppercorns
1 bayleaf
¼ teaspoon tarragon
4 egg yolks

2 teaspoons prepared mustard
250 g (8 oz.) butter
salt, pepper
6 shallots or spring onions

Trim steaks to neat shape; cut bread into rounds same shape as steaks. Melt 90 g (3 oz.) butter; brush liberally over both sides of bread. Put bread slices on oven tray; bake in moderate oven 10 to 15 minutes or until crisp and golden, turning once. Pan-fry steaks in 60 g (2 oz.) butter until cooked as desired — rare, medium or well-done. Put a steak on top of each slice of bread. Drain asparagus and artichoke bottoms. Fill four artichoke bottoms with asparagus tips; put on top of steaks; pour Mustard Bearnaise over.

Mustard Bearnaise: Put vinegar, peppercorns, bayleaf and tarragon in saucepan. Bring to boil; reduce heat; simmer uncovered until mixture is reduced by half. Strain; reserve 2 tablespoons of the liquid. Put egg yolks, mustard and cooled, reserved liquid in top of double saucepan over barely simmering water; stir in gradually the melted and cooled butter; stir until mixture is thick; remove from heat immediately. Add salt, pepper and finely-chopped shallots.
    Serves 4.

Tournedos with Mustard Bearnaise — an easily made, elegant way with steak, combining artichokes, asparagus and a superb sauce.

Rich Beef Casserole

1 kg (2 lb.) round steak	½ cup dry red wine
60 g (2 oz.) butter	425 g (14 oz.) can whole
8 small onions	tomatoes
30 g (1 oz.) butter, extra	2 beef stock cubes
250 g (8 oz.) carrots	salt, pepper
125 g (4 oz.) bacon pieces	½ teaspoon basil
3 tablespoons flour	½ teaspoon oregano
2 cups water	

Trim excess fat from meat; cut meat into 2.5 cm (1 in.) cubes. Melt butter in pan; brown meat well; remove from pan. (Do this in batches so meat browns well.) Melt extra butter in pan. Peel onions; leave whole; slice carrots; add to pan with chopped bacon pieces; saute until onions are lightly browned; remove from pan. Add flour to pan; stir until flour is golden brown; remove pan from heat. Add water, wine, undrained mashed tomatoes, crumbled stock cubes, salt, pepper, basil and oregano; stir until combined. Return pan to heat; stir until sauce boils and thickens. Return meat and vegetables to pan; bring to boil; reduce heat; simmer covered 1½ hours or until meat is tender.

Serves 4 to 6.

All-in-one Casserole

1 kg (2 lb.) round steak	2 large potatoes
60 g (2 oz.) butter	3 tablespoons flour
2 tablespoons oil	3 cups water
2 large onions	salt, pepper
2 medium parsnips	½ teaspoon thyme
2 medium carrots	2 tablespoons tomato
2 sticks celery	sauce
45 g (1½ oz.) butter, extra	3 beef stock cubes

Remove all fat from meat; cut meat into 2.5 cm (1 in.) cubes. Heat butter and oil in large frying pan; add quarter of the meat; fry on all sides until golden brown; remove meat from pan. Repeat with remaining meat in batches; remove from pan. To fat in pan, add peeled and chopped onions, peeled and sliced carrots, peeled and sliced parsnips and sliced celery. Saute gently until golden brown; remove from pan. Add extra butter to pan; when melted, add flour; stir until combined. Remove pan from heat; add water; stir until combined. Return pan to heat; stir until sauce boils and thickens. Add meat, vegetables, salt, pepper, thyme, tomato sauce and crumbled stock cubes; stir until combined. Reduce heat; simmer, covered, 1 hour; add peeled and cubed potatoes; simmer a further 30 minutes or until potatoes are tender.

Serves 6.

Shepherd's Pie

750 g (1½ lb.) minced	½ teaspoon thyme
steak	salt, pepper
30 g (1 oz.) butter	3 cups water
1 large onion	2 tablespoons flour
1 large carrot	¼ cup water, extra

Topping

750 g (1½ lb.) old potatoes	salt
60 g (2 oz.) butter	1 egg
⅓ cup milk	

Place steak, butter, peeled and finely-chopped onion and peeled and finely-chopped carrot in frying pan; stir over high heat until golden brown, mashing meat well. Add thyme, salt, pepper and water; stir until combined. Bring to boil; reduce heat; simmer covered 45 minutes or until meat is tender. Remove pan from heat; add combined flour and extra water; stir until combined. Return pan to heat; stir until sauce boils and thickens; reduce heat; simmer 5 minutes. Spoon meat mixture into medium-sized ovenproof dish, or 4 individual ovenproof dishes. Spoon potato mixture evenly over meat, spreading out evenly. With knife, mark a diamond pattern on potato. Brush lightly with beaten egg. Bake in moderate oven 45 minutes or until potato is golden brown.

Topping: Place peeled, washed and quartered potatoes in boiling salted water; boil, covered, 20 minutes or until potatoes are tender; drain. Add butter and milk; mash well. Use while still hot.

Serves 4.

Beef Curry

1 kg (2 lb.) round steak	1 large onion
60 g (2 oz.) butter	1 tablespoon curry powder
2 tablespoons oil	¼ teaspoon chilli powder
1 ripe banana	1 teaspoon cumin
1 green apple	salt, pepper
5 cm (2 in.) piece green	2 cups water
ginger	2 beef stock cubes

Remove all fat from meat; cut meat into 2.5 cm (1 in.) pieces. Heat butter and oil in frying pan; add quarter of the meat; brown on all sides; remove from pan. Repeat with remaining meat in batches; remove from pan. Add to pan peeled and finely-chopped banana, peeled and finely-chopped apple, peeled and grated ginger, peeled and finely-chopped onion, curry powder, chilli powder, cumin, salt and pepper; saute gently 4 minutes, stirring occasionally. Add water and crumbled stock cubes; stir until combined. Bring to boil; reduce heat; simmer covered 1½ hours or until meat is tender. Remove lid from pan; simmer uncovered 10 minutes or until curry has thickened slightly.

Serves 4.

Cabbage Rolls

16 large cabbage leaves	250 g (8 oz.) sausage
30 g (1 oz.) butter	mince
1 onion	salt, pepper
2 sticks celery	2 teaspoons basil
½ green pepper	2 tablespoons tomato
1 medium carrot	sauce
500 g (1 lb.) minced steak	½ cup rice

Lemon Sauce

½ cup lemon juice	¼ cup water
1 tablespoon oil	salt, pepper
1 tablespoon tomato paste	1 chicken stock cube

Drop cabbage leaves gradually into large saucepan of boiling water; boil uncovered 15 minutes; drain. When cool, remove any hard central core in the leaves. Melt butter in pan; add peeled and finely-chopped onion, diced celery, seeded and finely-chopped pepper and grated carrot; cook 2 minutes. Add minced steak, sausage mince, salt, pepper, basil and tomato sauce. Cook, stirring, until meat is well browned. Remove from heat; drain off excess fat; cool.

Cook rice in boiling salted water for 12 minutes or until tender; drain; add to meat mixture; mix well. Place equal portions of meat in centre of each cabbage leaf; carefully fold into neat parcels. Arrange rolls in ovenproof dish.

Make sauce by combining lemon juice, oil, tomato paste, water, salt, pepper and crumbled stock cube; mix well. Pour lemon sauce over cabbage rolls; cover; bake in moderate oven 40 to 45 minutes or until the rolls are tender.

Serves 4.

Crumbed Steak with Avocado

4 scotch fillet (or other) steaks	2 tablespoons chopped parsley
salt, pepper	60 g (2 oz.) butter
2 eggs	2 tablespoons oil
3 cups fresh white bread-crumbs (approx. ½ loaf)	1 avocado

Mustard Sauce

3 egg yolks	2 teaspoons french
1 tablespoon lemon juice	mustard
salt, pepper	125 g (4 oz.) butter

Remove any fat from each steak. Pound the steaks out to 1 cm (½ in.) thickness. Coat steaks lightly with flour seasoned with salt and pepper. Dip steaks into lightly-beaten eggs, then coat with combined breadcrumbs and parsley, pressing on firmly. Heat butter and oil in large frying pan; fry steaks until golden brown on both sides, approx. 3 minutes each side. Remove from pan; keep warm. Place steaks on serving plate. Peel and slice avocado; place two slices of avocado on each steak; spoon prepared Mustard Sauce over. avocado; place two slices of avocado on each steak; spoon prepared Mustard Sauce over.

Mustard Sauce: Place egg yolks, lemon juice, salt, pepper and mustard in top of double saucepan; stir until combined. Add chopped, softened butter; mix well. Place saucepan over simmering water; stir until sauce is thick and creamy. Remove from heat immediately.

Serves 4.

Grand Marnier Steaks

4 pieces fillet steak	60 g (2 oz.) butter, extra
60 g (2 oz.) butter	3 tablespoons Grand
250 g (8 oz.) mushrooms	Marnier
1 clove garlic	3 tablespoons cream
¼ teaspoon rosemary	2 tablespoons chopped
freshly ground black	chives
pepper	2 tablespoons chopped
salt	parsley

Heat butter in large frying pan; add fillet steaks and whole mushrooms; cook over high heat until steaks are cooked to required doneness. Turn mushrooms frequently. Remove steaks and mushrooms from pan; keep warm. Add crushed garlic, rosemary, black pepper, salt and extra butter; stir until butter has melted. Remove pan from heat; add Grand Marnier; return pan to heat; set aflame. When flames die down, add cream, chives and parsley; boil uncovered, stirring constantly, 2 minutes or until mixture has thickened slightly. Place steaks on serving plates; spoon mushrooms beside steaks; spoon sauce over.

Serves 4.

Chinese Ginger Beef

500 g (1 lb.) fillet steak, in one piece	2 tablespoons white vinegar
2 teaspoons cornflour	2 teaspoons sugar
2 teaspoons oil	1 teaspoon salt
1 teaspoon soy sauce	2 tablespoons oil, extra
125 g (4 oz.) piece green ginger	1 green pepper
	6 shallots or spring onions

Recipe continued overleaf:

Trim all fat and sinew from meat; slice meat into 5 mm (¼ in.) slices. Put meat in bowl; combine with cornflour, oil and soy sauce; mix well; marinate 20 minutes. Peel and thinly slice green ginger; combine with vinegar, sugar and salt in separate bowl; marinate 20 minutes or longer.

Heat extra oil in pan; add meat slices gradually, spreading out in pan. When brown on one side, turn to brown other side; don't overlap slices or meat will not brown well. Cook quickly and only until meat is tender; remove from pan.

Add ginger with liquid to pan with chopped pepper and shallots; cook quickly, stirring, 2 to 3 minutes. Return meat to pan; continue cooking a further 1 minute, stirring constantly.

Serves 4.

Tournedos Provencale

4 fillet steaks, each about 2.5 cm (1 in.) thick	30 g (1 oz.) butter, extra
	1 tomato
4 (or 8) slices bread, about 2.5 cm (1 in.) thick	1 red pepper
	4 shallots or spring onions
oil for shallow-frying	125 g (4 oz.) small mushrooms
60 g (2 oz.) butter	

Tomato Basil Sauce

2 tablespoons oil	1 beef stock cube
1 large onion	2 tablespoons chopped fresh basil or 1 teaspoon dried
1 clove garlic	
2 tablespoons flour	
2 cups water	2 tablespoons chopped parsley
¼ cup dry red wine	
⅓ cup tomato paste	salt, pepper

Press steaks to a neat shape; cut bread into rounds. Heat oil in pan; add bread; fry until golden brown on both sides; drain on absorbent paper. Heat butter in pan; fry steaks until cooked as desired — rare, medium or well-done. While steaks are cooking, heat extra butter in separate pan; add peeled, quartered tomatoes and whole mushrooms; saute until mushrooms are tender. Add seeded, finely-chopped pepper and chopped shallots; cook a further 1 minute. Put steak on top of each slice of bread; spoon sauce over steak; top with vegetables.

Tomato Basil Sauce: Heat oil in pan; add peeled and chopped onion and crushed garlic; saute until onion is golden brown. Add flour; cook until light golden brown. Add water and red wine; stir until sauce boils and thickens. Add tomato paste, crumbled stock cube, basil, parsley, salt and pepper; reduce heat; simmer covered 15 minutes.

Serves 4.

Lamb

There's nothing nicer than a golden, crisp-skinned leg of lamb for a family meal, with the traditional accompaniment of mint sauce. But there are many other ways of cooking lamb, using the various cuts; here we give a wide variety of recipes.

Lamb with Savoury Beans

2 kg (4 lb.) forequarter of lamb	3 large carrots
	470 g (15 oz.) can whole tomatoes
375 g (12 oz.) pkt haricot beans	pinch mixed herbs
30 g (1 oz.) butter	salt, pepper
3 tablespoons oil	1 cup water
2 large onions	2 tablespoons chopped parsley
1 clove garlic	
125 g (4 oz.) bacon pieces	

Place beans in large heatproof bowl; cover with hot water. Cover bowl; stand overnight. Next day drain; place beans in large pan; cover well with water. Bring to boil; cover pan; reduce heat; simmer 1½ hours or until beans are tender; add more water, if necessary. Drain.

Place meat in baking dish; add butter and oil. Bake in moderate oven 1½ hours. Remove meat from baking dish; pour off excess fat from dish, leaving approx. 4 tablespoons of fat. Place baking dish on top of stove over medium heat. Add peeled and chopped onions, crushed garlic and chopped bacon; saute until onions are light golden brown. Add peeled and sliced carrots, undrained mashed tomatoes, mixed herbs, water, salt, pepper and beans. Stir until boiling. Return meat to baking dish with beans. Return dish to oven; bake a further 30 minutes or until cooked, stirring bean mixture occasionally. Sprinkle parsley over bean mixture; mix through lightly.

Serves 6.

Crumbed Noisettes of Lamb

8 lamb short-loin chops	flour
⅓ cup chutney	dry breadcrumbs
2 teaspoons french mustard	4 eggs
	60 g (2 oz.) butter
salt, pepper	3 tablespoons oil
¼ teaspoon thyme	

Mint and Chive Butter

125 g (4 oz.) butter	1 tablespoon chopped parsley
3 tablespoons chopped mint	2 tablespoons chopped chives
salt, pepper	

Lamb with Savoury Beans — an economical forequarter, cooked with vegetables and beans, makes a substantial family meal.

Ask butcher to cut each chop 3 cm (approx. 1¼ in.) thick. Remove bones, or ask butcher to do this for you. Combine sieved chutney, mustard, salt, pepper and thyme in bowl. Spread chutney mixture evenly over both sides of chops, then roll up each firmly into neat round; secure with small wooden stick. Coat chops with flour seasoned with salt and pepper. Dip into beaten eggs, then coat firmly with breadcrumbs. Repeat egg-and-breadcrumb process. Put chops on to tray; refrigerate until ready to cook. Heat butter and oil in large frying pan. Put chops into pan; cook over very low heat until golden brown and cooked through, approx. 8 minutes on each side. Drain on absorbent paper. Put on to serving plate; top each with a thick slice of Mint and Chive Butter.

Mint and Chive Butter: Put softened butter and remaining ingredients into bowl; mix well. With wet hands, form into roll approx. 2.5 cm (1 in.) in diameter. Roll up in greaseproof paper; refrigerate until set and ready to serve.

Serves 4.

Lamb Curry

1.5 kg (3 lb.) leg of lamb	2 teaspoons poppy seeds
flour	2 teaspoons cinnamon
30 g (1 oz.) butter	1 teaspoon ground ginger
2 tablespoons oil	2 teaspoons ground cloves
1 large onion	salt, pepper
2 teaspoons coriander	1 cup water
2 teaspoons ground cardamom	½ cup natural yoghurt

Ask butcher to bone meat; cut meat into 2.5 cm (1 in.) cubes. Toss meat in flour seasoned with salt and pepper. Heat butter and oil in large frying pan; fry meat until golden brown; remove meat from pan. Add peeled and chopped onion to pan; saute until onion is transparent. Add to pan coriander, cardamom, poppy seeds, cinnamon, ginger, cloves, salt, pepper, water and yoghurt. Stir until sauce is smooth and comes to the boil. Reduce heat; add meat; cover; simmer 1 hour or until meat is tender.
Serves 4.

Lamb Casserole

750 g (1½ lb.) best end lamb neck chops	3 tablespoons tomato paste
flour	470 g (15 oz.) can beef consomme
30 g (1 oz.) butter	½ cup water
2 tablespoons oil	2 tablespoons dry sherry
1 onion	1 tablespoon worcester-
1 clove garlic	shire sauce
1 tablespoon flour, extra	salt, pepper
2 teaspoons french mustard	

Toss chops lightly in flour seasoned with salt and pepper. Melt butter and oil in large frying pan; add chops; brown well. Remove chops from pan; put in casserole dish. Add peeled and finely-chopped onion and crushed garlic to pan; saute until onion is transparent. Add extra flour; stir until well browned; add mustard, tomato paste, consomme, water, sherry, worcestershire sauce, salt and pepper. Stir until smooth; stir until sauce boils and thickens; reduce heat; simmer 1 minute. Pour sauce over chops; cover; bake in moderate oven 1½ hours or until chops are tender.
Serves 4.

Glazed Minted Racks of Lamb

4 racks lamb (approx. 4 chops in each)	2 tablespoons brown vinegar
½ cup tomato sauce	2 tablespoons bottled mint jelly
2 tablespoons brown sugar	½ cup water

Trim excess fat from lamb. Put lamb in baking dish; bake in hot oven 15 minutes. Combine tomato sauce, brown sugar, vinegar, mint jelly and water in saucepan; bring to boil; remove from heat. Pour sauce over lamb; reduce heat to moderate; bake a further 40 to 45 minutes or until meat is tender, basting frequently with sauce. Serve sauce separately.
Serves 4.

Garlic Chops

8 lamb chump chops	¼ cup dry sherry
1 onion	30 g (1 oz.) butter
2 cloves garlic	2 tablespoons oil
1 tablespoon soy sauce	1 tablespoon flour
2 teaspoons worcester- shire sauce	1 cup water
1 tablespoon tomato sauce	salt, pepper

Combine peeled and finely-chopped onion, crushed garlic, soy sauce, worcestershire sauce, tomato sauce and sherry. Pour over chops; marinate 2 hours. Melt butter and oil in large frying pan; add drained chops (reserve marinade); saute until chops are golden brown and tender. Remove from pan; keep warm. Add flour to pan drippings; stir until smooth and brown. Add water and reserved marinade; stir until sauce boils; reduce heat; add chops; season with salt and pepper; cover; simmer 30 minutes.
Serves 4.

Curried Lamb Ribs

1 kg (2 lb.) lamb rashers	1 teaspoon cumin
2 large onions	1 teaspoon coriander
2 tablespoons oil	1 teaspoon salt
¼ teaspoon chilli powder	pepper
1 teaspoon turmeric	1 cup water

Peel and chop onions; put in electric blender with oil, chilli powder, turmeric, cumin, coriander, salt and pepper. Blend on medium speed 3 minutes or until very finely ground. Place lamb rashers in large bowl; pour onion mixture over; mix well; cover; allow to stand 2 hours. Place lamb and marinade in baking dish; bake in moderate oven 1 to 1½ hours or until tender. Skim off excess fat; put baking dish on top of stove over medium heat; add water to pan; mix well; bring to boil; reduce heat; simmer 1 minute. Serve meat with sauce spooned over.
Serves 4.
NOTE: Lamb rashers are breast of lamb cut into approx. 3.5 cm (1½ in.) x 10 cm (4 in.) strips.

Tomato Lamb Casserole

750 g (1½ lb.) lamb leg chops
flour
1 onion
1 clove garlic
30 g (1 oz.) butter
1 tablespoon oil
1 tablespoon flour, extra

470 g (15 oz.) can tomato soup
2 teaspoons dry mustard
1 tablespoon worcester- shire sauce
¼ cup dry red wine
salt, pepper

Remove any excess fat from chops. Coat chops lightly in flour. Heat butter and oil in large frying pan; add chops; brown well on both sides; remove chops from pan. Add peeled and finely-chopped onion and crushed garlic to pan; saute until onion is transparent. Add extra flour to pan; stir until smooth; cook 1 minute or until well browned. Add undiluted tomato soup, mustard, worcester- shire sauce, red wine, salt, pepper. Stir until sauce boils and thickens; reduce heat; add chops; simmer covered 35 to 40 minutes or until chops are cooked.

Serves 4.

Lamb and Bacon Casserole

750 g (1½ lb.) lamb neck chops
flour
30 g (1 oz.) butter
2 tablespoons oil
125 g (4 oz.) bacon pieces
1 large onion

1½ tablespoons flour, extra
salt, pepper
1 teaspoon worcester- shire sauce
1 tablespoon tomato sauce
1½ cups water
1 chicken stock cube

Dust chops lightly with flour seasoned with salt and pepper. Heat butter and oil in large frying pan; add chops; brown well. Remove chops from pan; put in casserole dish. Add peeled and chopped onion and chopped bacon pieces to pan; saute until onion is transparent. Put onion and bacon mixture over chops in casserole dish. Add extra flour to pan; cook until brown; add water, worcestershire sauce, tomato sauce, crumbled stock cube, salt and pepper. Stir until sauce boils and thickens; reduce heat; simmer 1 minute. Pour sauce over chops; cover; bake in moderate oven 1½ hours or until chops are tender.

Serves 4.

Crunchy Cutlets with Curry Sauce

8 lamb cutlets
3 cups fresh white or wholemeal bread- crumbs
2 tablespoons chopped parsley
6 shallots or spring onions
1 teaspoon mixed herbs

salt, pepper
½ teaspoon turmeric
½ cup bottled fruit chutney
flour
1 egg
2 tablespoons milk
60 g (2 oz.) butter
2 tablespoons oil

Sauce

1½ tablespoons flour
1 tablespoon curry powder
1½ cups water
1 beef stock cube

2 tablespoons mayonnaise
2 tablespoons chopped parsley
salt, pepper

Combine breadcrumbs, parsley, chopped shallots, mixed herbs, salt, pepper and turmeric. Spread each side of each cutlet with chutney; coat cutlets with flour; dip in combined beaten egg and milk; coat well with prepared crumbs. Heat butter and oil in large frying pan; add cutlets; cook until golden brown on both sides and cooked through. Remove cutlets from pan; keep warm; reserve pan drippings.

Sauce: Add flour and curry powder to pan; stir until smooth. Add crumbled stock cube and water; stir until smooth; stir until sauce boils. Add mayonnaise; stir until smooth; reduce heat; simmer 2 minutes. Add parsley, salt and pepper. Spoon sauce over cutlets.

Serves 4.

Mongolian Garlic Lamb

1 kg (2 lb.) lamb chump chops, in one piece
½ cup water
1 tablespoon sesame oil
1 tablespoon oil
1 tablespoon soy sauce
1 teaspoon sugar
2 tablespoons oil, extra

1 onion
6 shallots or spring onions
2 cloves garlic
2 teaspoons cornflour
2 teaspoons oyster sauce
1 tablespoon hoi sin sauce
½ cup water, extra

Remove meat from bone; trim all fat from meat; remove sinews. Cut meat into wafer-thin slices. It may be easier to freeze meat first until firm, then slice. It is important slices be wafer-thin. Marinate meat in combined water, sesame oil, oil, soy sauce and sugar for 2 hours. Drain marinade from meat; reserve marinade. Heat extra oil in large pan; add peeled and chopped onion, chopped shallots and crushed garlic; saute 1 minute; remove from pan. Add meat slices to pan; don't overlap meat slices or they will not brown well. Brown meat on both sides; remove from pan. Add reserved marinade to pan. Dissolve cornflour in extra water; add oyster sauce and hoi sin sauce; add to marinade in pan; stir until sauce boils and thickens. Return onion mixture and meat to sauce; simmer 1 minute.

Serves 4.

NOTE: Oyster sauce and hoi sin sauce are available in small bottles from large supermarkets or Chinese food stores.

Veal

Tender veal lends itself well to colourful, rich tasting sauces and accompaniments.

Veal with Prosciutto

6 veal steaks	¼ cup dry white wine
2 eggs	¼ cup water
flour	1 chicken stock cube
salt, pepper	1 teaspoon cornflour
60 g (2 oz.) butter	1 tablespoon marsala
3 tablespoons oil	¼ teaspoon oregano
6 thin slices prosciutto	⅓ cup cream
185 g (6 oz.) small mushrooms	125 g (4 oz.) mozzarella cheese
1 clove garlic	2 tablespoons grated parmesan cheese
60 g (2 oz.) butter, extra	

Pound veal steaks out very thinly. Dip into flour which has been seasoned with salt and pepper; place in beaten eggs; drain well, then coat again with flour. Heat butter and oil in frying pan; add veal steaks; cook until golden brown on both sides and cooked through; place on ovenproof serving plate. Remove all fat from pan. Heat extra butter in pan; add sliced mushrooms and crushed garlic; saute 2 minutes. Add combined wine, water, crumbled stock cube, cornflour and marsala; stir until boiling; reduce heat; simmer uncovered 2 minutes. Add salt, pepper, oregano and cream; simmer 3 minutes. Place a slice of prosciutto over each veal steak; spoon the sauce over. Top with sliced mozzarella cheese; sprinkle with parmesan cheese. Bake uncovered in moderate oven 20 minutes or until heated through and golden brown.

Serves 6.

NOTE: Prosciutto is Italian raw ham, available at most large food stores. If unavailable, substitute ordinary ham.

Veal with Crab

6 veal steaks	packaged dry breadcrumbs
flour	90 g (3 oz.) butter
salt, pepper	155 g can crab
3 eggs	3 shallots or spring onions

Sauce

60 g (2 oz.) butter	¼ cup dry white wine
3 shallots or spring onions	2 egg yolks
60 g (2 oz.) mushrooms	⅔ cup cream
2 teaspoons cornflour	2 tablespoons mayonnaise
¾ cup water	1½ teaspoons french mustard
1 chicken stock cube	

Pound veal steaks out thinly. Coat veal in flour seasoned with salt and pepper. Dip into beaten eggs, then coat veal in breadcrumbs. Heat butter in pan; add veal; saute on both sides until golden brown and cooked through, approx. 8 to 10 minutes. Remove from pan; keep warm while making sauce. To serve, put veal on to serving dish; spoon sauce over; top with drained lightly-flaked crab and chopped shallots.

Sauce: Heat butter in pan; add chopped shallots and sliced mushrooms; saute until mushrooms are just tender. Blend cornflour with water; add to pan with crumbled stock cube and white wine; stir until sauce boils and thickens. Reduce heat; simmer uncovered 2 minutes. Combine lightly-beaten egg yolks, cream, mayonnaise, mustard, salt and pepper in bowl; mix well. Add cream mixture to pan, whisking well until sauce thickens; do not allow to boil.

Serves 6.

Tomato Veal

6 veal steaks	½ cup dry red wine
flour	¼ cup water
salt, pepper	3 tablespoons tomato paste
2 eggs	
2 tablespoons milk	2 tablespoons marsala
dry breadcrumbs	1 clove garlic
60 g (2 oz.) butter	½ teaspoon basil
3 tablespoons oil	1 teaspoon sugar
60 g (2 oz.) butter, extra	90 g (3 oz.) black olives
1 red pepper	6 shallots or spring onions
185 g (6 oz.) mushrooms	

Pound veal steaks out thinly. Coat veal lightly in flour seasoned with salt and pepper. Dip into combined beaten eggs and milk, then coat with dry breadcrumbs. Heat butter and oil in frying pan; add veal steaks; cook on both sides until golden brown and cooked through; place on heatproof serving plate; keep warm.

Remove all fat from pan; add extra butter, seeded and sliced pepper, sliced mushrooms and crushed garlic; saute gently 3 minutes. Add combined wine, water, tomato paste, basil, marsala, sugar, salt and pepper; bring to boil; reduce heat; simmer uncovered 3 minutes or until sauce is slightly thickened; add black olives and chopped shallots; simmer 1 minute. Spoon sauce over veal.

Serves 6.

Tomato Veal with a wine-flavoured sauce is a delicious-tasting recipe from Italy.

Veal Goulash

1 kg (2 lb.) stewing veal	¼ teaspoon thyme
60 g (2 oz.) butter	salt, pepper
3 tablespoons oil	⅓ cup tomato paste
1 clove garlic	2 cups water
2 medium onions	2 chicken stock cubes
250 g (8 oz.) mushrooms	300 ml (½ pint) sour cream
1 tablespoon paprika	

Remove all fat and gristle from meat; cut meat into 2.5 cm (1 in.) cubes. Heat butter and oil in large frying pan; add one quarter of the meat; cook quickly until golden brown; remove from pan. Repeat with remaining meat in quarter quantities; remove from pan. Add peeled and chopped onions and crushed garlic; saute gently until onions are tender. Add sliced mushrooms, paprika and thyme; saute 2 minutes. Return meat to pan; add water, crumbled stock cubes, tomato paste, salt and pepper; stir until combined. Bring to boil; reduce heat; simmer covered 1 hour or until veal is tender. Just before serving, add sour cream; stir until combined; heat through gently.

Serves 4.

Veal Italian

500 g (1 lb.) veal steak	1 teaspoon worcestershire
flour	sauce
30 g (1 oz.) butter	½ teaspoon paprika
30 g (1 oz.) butter, extra	1 teaspoon sugar
2 onions	½ teaspoon basil
2 shallots or spring onions	salt, pepper
2 cloves garlic	1 tablespoon chopped
1½ tablespoons flour,	parsley
extra	125 g (4 oz.) mozzarella
470 g (15 oz.) can whole	cheese
tomatoes	2 tablespoons grated
2 chicken stock cubes	parmesan cheese

Pound veal steak out thinly. Toss in flour seasoned with salt and pepper. Heat butter in pan; cook veal on both sides until golden brown. Remove from pan; drain well. In the same pan heat extra butter; add peeled and chopped onions, chopped shallots and crushed garlic; saute until onions are tender. Add extra flour; stir until golden brown. Remove from heat. Add undrained roughly-chopped tomatoes, crumbled stock cubes, worcestershire sauce, paprika, sugar, basil, salt and pepper. Return to heat; stir until mixture boils and thickens. Reduce heat; cover; simmer 10 minutes. Stir in parsley. Place veal in ovenproof dish. Pour sauce over. Place sliced mozzarella cheese on top; sprinkle with parmesan cheese. Bake uncovered in moderate oven 30 minutes.

Serves 4.

Veal and Ham Pie

Pastry

1 cup plain flour	375 g (12 oz.) packaged
90 g (3 oz.) butter	puff pastry
1 egg yolk	1 egg yolk, extra
2 tablespoons water	1 tablespoon water, extra
1 teaspoon lemon juice	

Filling

500 g (1 lb.) stewing veal	2 teaspoons worcester-
30 g (1 oz.) butter	shire sauce
2 onions	½ teaspoon oregano
4 shallots or spring onions	salt, pepper
1 tablespoon flour	125 g (4 oz.) ham or ham
2 cups water	pieces
2 chicken stock cubes	2 tablespoons chopped
2 teaspoons prepared	parsley
mustard	2 hard-boiled eggs
1 tablespoon tomato paste	

Pastry: Sift flour into basin; rub in butter until mixture resembles dry breadcrumbs. Mix to pliable dough with egg yolk, water and lemon juice. Turn out on to lightly-floured board; knead lightly; roll out to fit 20 cm (8 in.) pie plate; glaze edge of pie with combined extra egg yolk and extra water. Spread cold filling in evenly. Roll out puff pastry on lightly-floured surface; arrange over pie. Press edges together; trim and decorate. Brush top of pie with egg yolk mixture. Make slit in top of pie. Bake in very hot oven 10 minutes; reduce heat to moderate; bake a further 15 to 20 minutes or until golden brown.

Filling: Cut veal into 2.5 cm (1 in.) cubes. Heat butter in pan; add veal; cook until veal is well browned. Add peeled and chopped onions and chopped shallots; saute until onions are tender. Add flour; stir until flour is golden brown. Remove pan from heat; add water, crumbled stock cubes, mustard, tomato paste, worcester-shire sauce, oregano, salt and pepper. Return to heat; stir until sauce boils and thickens; reduce heat; cover; simmer gently 50 to 55 minutes or until veal is tender; stir frequently. Remove from heat. Cut ham into 2.5 cm (1 in.) cubes; add to pan with parsley and sliced hard-boiled eggs; allow to become cold.

Steaks with Ham

6 veal steaks	6 slices prosciutto (Italian
flour	raw ham) or ham
salt, pepper	150 g (5 oz.) pkt mozzarella
2 eggs	cheese slices
90 g (3 oz.) butter	2 tomatoes

Flatten veal steaks out thinly with rolling pin or mallet. Coat veal with flour, then dip in beaten eggs. Heat butter in large frying pan; fry two veal steaks until golden brown on both sides and cooked through; remove from pan; repeat with remaining steaks. Top each steak with a slice of prosciutto, a slice of mozzarella cheese and a slice of tomato. Sprinkle with salt and pepper. Place on oven tray. Bake in moderate oven 5 minutes or until cheese has melted.

Serves 6.

Gnocchi

| 500 g (1 lb.) old potatoes | 1 egg |
| 1½ cups self-raising flour | ½ teaspoon salt |

Veal and Tomato Sauce

60 g (2 oz.) butter	2 cups dry white wine
1 large onion	1 cup water
2 cloves garlic	2 chicken stock cubes
500 g (1 lb.) minced veal	1 teaspoon sugar
470 g (15 oz.) can whole tomatoes	1 teaspoon basil
2 tablespoons tomato paste	salt, pepper

Peel and quarter potatoes; place in boiling, salted water; cover pan; reduce heat; simmer 20 minutes or until potatoes are very tender; drain well; push through fine sieve into bowl. Add sifted flour and salt, and lightly-beaten egg; mix well. Turn mixture out on to a lightly-floured surface and knead for about 2 minutes. Take a quarter of the mixture; roll into sausage shape on floured surface. Roll should be 2.5 cm (1 in.) in diameter. Repeat with remaining dough. Cut rolls into 2.5 cm (1 in.) lengths. With two fingers, press each of the gnocchi against cheese grater to roughen the surface on one side and to make a dent in the other where the fingers press. Repeat with remaining gnocchi. Place quarter of the gnocchi in large pan of boiling, salted water; they will go straight to the bottom of the pan. When gnocchi rise to top of water, boil 1 minute, then remove from pan. Repeat with remaining gnocchi in batches. Add gnocchi to prepared Veal and Tomato Sauce; simmer uncovered 5 minutes. Put gnocchi into serving bowl; spoon over half the sauce. Serve remaining sauce and grated parmesan cheese separately.

Veal and Tomato Sauce: Heat butter in frying pan; add peeled and chopped onion, crushed garlic and veal; mash well. Fry meat until light golden brown. Add undrained mashed tomatoes, tomato paste, wine, water, chicken stock cubes, sugar, basil, salt and pepper; mix well. Bring to boil; reduce heat; simmer very slowly uncovered 1½ hours until sauce is reduced and thickened.

Serves 6.

Crunchy Crumbed Veal Chops

8 veal chops	125 g (4 oz.) cheddar cheese
flour	60 g (2 oz.) butter
salt, pepper	3 tablespoons oil
2 eggs	grated parmesan cheese
¼ cup milk	
packaged dry breadcrumbs	

Tomato Sauce

30 g (1 oz.) butter	½ teaspoon basil
1 large onion	salt, pepper
1 clove garlic	1 teaspoon sugar
470 g (15 oz.) can whole tomatoes	

Carefully cut meat from around bone of each veal chop. Wrap tail of veal chop around thick part of meat. Secure with small wooden stick. Coat chops with flour seasoned with salt and pepper. Dip chops into combined beaten eggs and milk, then coat with breadcrumbs. Repeat egg-and-bread-crumbing to give chops firm coating. Heat butter and oil in large pan; add chops; cook slowly 5 to 8 minutes on each side (depending on thickness of chops) until golden brown and cooked through. Place chops on oven tray in single layer. Spoon tomato mixture down centre of each chop. Top each chop with a slice of cheese. Sprinkle with grated parmesan cheese. Place under hot griller until cheese has melted and turns light golden brown, or cook in moderately hot oven 8 minutes.

Tomato Sauce: Heat butter in pan; add peeled and chopped onion and crushed garlic; saute gently until onion is light golden brown. Add undrained mashed tomatoes, basil, salt, pepper and sugar; stir until boiling. Reduce heat; simmer uncovered 10 minutes or until mixture is of a good thick consistency.

Serves 4.

Veal Chops with Curry Sauce

750 g (1½ lb.) veal chops	1 clove garlic
flour	2 rashers bacon
60 g (2 oz.) butter	1 tablespoon curry powder
2 tablespoons oil	1 teaspoon salt
2 large onions	1 cup milk

Roll chops in flour. Heat butter and oil in pan; add chops; cook until golden brown and cooked through; remove from pan; keep warm. Remove rind from bacon; chop bacon finely; add to pan with peeled and finely-chopped onions and crushed garlic; cook until onions are tender. Stir in curry powder and salt; cook 1 minute; add milk; simmer 3 minutes. Serve chops with sauce spooned over.

Serves 4.

Pork

Here are new and interesting ways of serving this popular meat, for both family and special occasion meals.

Golden Pork with Lychees

1 kg (2 lb.) lean short loin pork chops	565 g can lychees
flour	½ small cabbage
salt, pepper	2 tablespoons white vinegar
2 eggs	1 teaspoon soy sauce
¼ cup milk	2 chicken stock cubes
3 cups fresh breadcrumbs (approx. ½ loaf)	2 tablespoons dry sherry
oil for deep-frying	1 tablespoon honey
5 cm (2 in.) piece green ginger	1 cup water
1 red pepper	1 tablespoon cornflour
	8 shallots or spring onions

Remove rind and excess fat from pork. Cut meat into 2.5 cm (1 in.) cubes. Coat meat lightly with flour seasoned with salt and pepper. Dip into combined beaten eggs and milk, then coat with breadcrumbs. Fry a quarter of the pork in deep hot oil 3 minutes or until cooked through and golden brown; remove from oil; drain on absorbent paper. Repeat with remaining pork in batches. Do not have oil too hot or bread-crumbs will brown too quickly and pork will not cook through.

Place 2 tablespoons of the oil in frying pan or wok; add peeled and very thinly-sliced ginger; toss gently over medium heat 1 minute. Add pork, drained lychees, seeded and cubed pepper; toss a further 2 minutes. Add combined vinegar, soy sauce, crumbled stock cubes, sherry, honey, water, salt and cornflour. Increase heat; toss ingredients in sauce until sauce boils and thickens. Add coarsely-shredded cabbage. Continue cooking 1 minute. Add shallots cut into 2.5 cm (1 in.) pieces; toss until just combined.

Serves 4.

NOTE: If available, Chinese cabbage gives the best texture to the finished dish.

Pork Spareribs

1 kg (2 lb.) pork spareribs	2 cloves garlic
¼ cup honey	1 onion
¼ cup soy sauce	½ teaspoon ground ginger
½ cup canned pineapple juice	2 tablespoons lemon juice
	salt, pepper

Combine honey, soy sauce, pineapple juice, crushed garlic, peeled and chopped onion, ginger, lemon juice, salt and pepper; mix well. Pour over spareribs; marinate 2 to 3 hours, turning occasionally. Bake ribs, with marinade, in moderately hot oven 50 to 60 minutes or until tender. Turn ribs and brush with marinade occasionally during cooking.

Serves 4.

Pork Sate

500 g (1 lb.) pork fillets	2 teaspoons ground cumin
1 teaspoon turmeric	2 tablespoons sugar
2 teaspoons ground coriander	1 teaspoon salt
	¼ cup oil

Sate Sauce

2 cloves garlic	1 teaspoon salt
1 cm (½ in.) piece green ginger	¼ cup raisins
½ cup brown vinegar	¼ cup sultanas
½ cup sugar	¼ cup peanut butter
	¾ cup water

Cut pork into pieces about 2.5 cm (1 in.) long by 1 cm (½ in.) wide. Combine remaining ingredients; add pork; stir well; cover; refrigerate 1 hour or overnight.

Thread meat on to thin bamboo skewers. Grill, turning skewers occasionally. Keep meat moist by brushing with remaining marinade during grilling. Serve with Sate Sauce.

Sate Sauce: Chop garlic, ginger, raisins and sultanas very finely or blend in blender. Combine all ingredients in pan; heat slowly, stirring to dissolve sugar. When sugar is dissolved, bring to boil; reduce heat; simmer uncovered 30 minutes.

Serves 4.

Pork with Mustard Glaze

500 g (1 lb.) pork fillet (in one piece)	½ cup orange juice
1 clove garlic	2 tablespoons french mustard
½ teaspoon rosemary	2 tablespoons marmalade
2 tablespoons oil	1 tablespoon brown sugar

Place pork in baking dish; brush with oil; sprinkle with rosemary. Bake in moderate oven 45 minutes. Remove meat from oven; combine crushed garlic and remaining ingredients; pour over meat; return to oven. Bake a further 15 to 20 minutes, basting frequently.

Serves 2.

Golden Pork with Lychees — there's a delightful contrast of colours, flavours, textures in this Oriental-inspired dish.

Roast Pork with Minted Apple Stuffing

2.5 kg (5 lb.) loin of pork	1½ cups water, extra
2 teaspoons salt	2 chicken stock cubes
¼ cup oil	½ cup dry white wine
60 g (2 oz.) butter	2 tablespoons port
1 cup water	pepper
3 tablespoons flour	

Minted Apple Stuffing

2 rashers bacon	salt, pepper
1 large onion	¼ teaspoon mixed herbs
60 g (2 oz.) butter	pinch rosemary
1 teaspoon grated lemon rind	1 green apple
2 cups fresh white breadcrumbs	2 tablespoons chopped mint
	1 egg

Ask butcher to bone loin of pork, then carefully remove the rind keeping it in one piece. Place pork, fat side down, on board. Spread prepared stuffing down centre of pork. Roll up pork; secure with string at 2.5 cm (1 in.) intervals. Rub rind of pork with 1 teaspoon of the salt. Place pork rind on baking tray. Bake in hot oven 45 minutes, draining off fat as it accumulates. Place rind under hot griller until rind bubbles and is very crisp. When cold, break into small pieces.

Rub loin with remaining salt and the oil. Place in baking dish; dot with butter. Add water. Bake in moderately hot oven 1½ hours or until meat is cooked. Remove from oven; keep warm.

Drain all liquid from baking dish into bowl; allow to stand for a few minutes, then skim off all fat from pan juices. You will need 1 cup of the juices. Return ¼ cup of the skimmed-off fat to baking dish; add flour; stir over low heat until flour is golden brown; remove pan from heat; add reserved pan juices, extra water, crumbled stock cubes, wine and port; stir until combined. Return pan to heat; stir until sauce boils and thickens; season with pepper. Simmer 5 minutes. Serve sauce separately. Serve with Red Pepper Pickle.

Stuffing: Place finely-chopped bacon, peeled and finely-chopped onion, butter and grated lemon rind in pan; saute gently until onion is light golden brown. Add peeled, cored and finely-chopped apple; saute 5 minutes; remove pan from heat; add remaining ingredients; mix well.

Serves 6.

Red Pepper Pickle

3 large red peppers	salt, pepper
3 large green peppers	1 teaspoon sugar
4 ripe tomatoes	4 tablespoons white vinegar
2 large onions	
3 tablespoons oil	

Remove seeds from peppers; cut peppers into 2.5 cm (1 in.) cubes. Place peppers, roughly-chopped tomatoes, peeled onions cut into thin wedges, oil, salt, pepper and sugar into pan. Cover; bring slowly to boil; reduce heat; simmer very gently 45 minutes, stirring occasionally. Add vinegar; mix well. Keep refrigerated.

This pickle is best if made several days before serving.

Pork Pasties

500 g (1 lb.) minced pork	salt, pepper
30 g (1 oz.) butter	1 tablespoon soy sauce
1 large onion	3 tablespoons chopped parsley
2 medium carrots	
3 tablespoons plain flour	375 g (12 oz.) puff pastry
2½ cups water	1 egg yolk
¼ teaspoon mixed herbs	1 tablespoon water, extra

Heat butter in pan; add peeled and chopped onion and pork; cook until pork is golden brown, mashing meat well. Add peeled and chopped carrots and flour; stir until combined; remove pan from heat. Add water; stir until combined. Return pan to heat; stir until sauce comes to boil; reduce heat; add mixed herbs, salt, pepper and soy sauce. Reduce heat; simmer covered 45 minutes; remove lid; increase heat slightly; simmer 15 minutes or until meat mixture is thick. Add parsley; stir until combined. Allow meat mixture to become cold.

Roll out puff pastry very thinly; cut six 15 cm (6 in.) circles of pastry; a saucer is a good guide. You may have to re-roll pastry for last one or two circles of pastry. Brush edge of each pastry circle with combined beaten egg yolk and extra water; divide meat mixture evenly into centre of each pastry circle. Pick up each pasty in hand and press edges together firmly. Place on greased baking tray; brush top of each with egg glaze; bake in very hot oven 5 minutes or until golden brown; reduce heat to moderate; cook a further 15 minutes or until golden brown and heated through.

Makes 6 pasties.

Pineapple Glazed Pork Rashers

1 kg (2 lb.) lean pork rashers	6 whole peppercorns
¼ teaspoon rosemary	1 teaspoon salt
	2 tablespoons vinegar

Pineapple Glaze

470 g (15 oz.) can crushed pineapple	1 tablespoon soy sauce
¼ cup honey	1 clove garlic
⅓ cup dry white wine	1 cm (½ in.) piece green ginger

Cut pork into slices. Put in saucepan; cover with water; add rosemary, peppercorns, salt and vinegar. Cover; bring to boil; reduce heat; simmer uncovered 20 minutes; drain well. Put pork pieces in single layer in baking dish; spoon pineapple glaze over. Bake in hot oven, uncovered, 25 minutes or until pineapple glaze has evaporated, and pork pieces are golden brown and tender.

Pineapple Glaze: Place ½ cup drained crushed pineapple (reserve syrup), honey, white wine, soy sauce, crushed garlic, finely-chopped green ginger and ½ cup of the reserved syrup in saucepan. Bring to boil; remove from heat.

Serves 4.

Pork Chops L'Orange

4 pork chops	1 chicken stock cube
1 large orange	3 teaspoons arrowroot
2 teaspoons white vinegar	2 teaspoons dry sherry
1 tablespoon sugar	1 tablespoon brandy
1½ cups water	1 tablespoon oil

Remove rind thinly from orange; make sure there is no white pith. Cut orange rind into very thin strips; you will need 2 tablespoons of orange rind. Drop these into a small saucepan of boiling water; boil 1 minute; drain. Squeeze juice from orange.

Heat oil in pan; add chops; cook until golden brown and cooked through. Remove chops from pan; add sugar and vinegar to pan; stir over low heat until sugar caramelises slightly. Add to pan the water, crumbled stock cube, juice and rind of orange; bring to boil; boil 1 minute. Blend arrowroot with sherry and brandy; stir gradually into sauce; stir until sauce boils and thickens. Spoon hot orange sauce over chops.

Serves 4.

Pork Chops with Apple Gravy

4 pork chops	¼ teaspoon ground cloves
30 g (1 oz.) butter	½ teaspoon grated lemon
2 tablespoons oil	rind
1 onion	1 large green cooking
1½ tablespoons flour	apple
1 beef stock cube	salt, pepper
1½ cups apple cider	

Heat butter and oil in pan; add peeled and sliced onion; cook until onion is transparent; remove from pan. Add chops; cook until brown on both sides; remove from pan. Add flour to pan; cook 1 minute, stirring; add crumbled stock cube, ground cloves, grated lemon rind and apple cider;

mix well; stir until sauce boils and thickens. Reduce heat; return chops and onion to pan. Peel apple; slice thinly; spread over top of chops; cover; cook over low heat 15 to 20 minutes or until chops are tender. Season with salt and pepper.

Serves 4.

Chinese Barbecued Pork

750 g (1½ lb.) lean pork fillets	2 teaspoons red food colouring
¼ cup soy sauce	1 clove garlic
2 tablespoons red wine	½ teaspoon cinnamon
1 tablespoon honey	1 shallot or spring onion
1 tablespoon brown sugar	

Combine soy sauce, red wine, honey, brown sugar, food colouring, crushed garlic and halved shallot in large bowl. Sprinkle cinnamon on top; add pork; marinate 1 hour, or cover and refrigerate overnight; turn occasionally. Drain from marinade; put on rack in baking dish. Bake in moderate oven 30 minutes, turning frequently with tongs and basting with marinade and drippings from pork. Cut into thin slices to serve.
NOTE: The red food colouring gives the traditional appearance to the pork, but can be omitted, if desired.

Crumbed Pork Schnitzels

4 short loin pork chops	salt, pepper
flour	packaged dry breadcrumbs
1 egg	oil for frying

Brandied Spiced Peaches

440 g (14 oz.) can peach halves	5 cm (2 in.) piece cinnamon stick
⅓ cup brandy	

Remove rind and any excess fat from chops; leave bone in; secure in round shape with small wooden sticks. Roll in flour seasoned with salt and pepper; dip in beaten egg; press breadcrumbs on firmly. Heat oil in frying pan; fry chops until golden and cooked through, approx. 20 minutes, turning occasionally. Cooking time will depend on thickness of chops. Serve with Brandied Spiced Peaches.

Brandied Spiced Peaches: Drain peaches; reserve syrup. Place peach syrup in saucepan with cinnamon stick; bring to boil; reduce heat; simmer gently 5 minutes. Remove cinnamon stick from syrup; stir in brandy. Add peach halves; heat through gently.

Serves 4.

Chicken & Duck

Here's a tempting variety of praise-winning ways with chicken. Some are for every day while others are more exotic. We've also added some superb, special occasion recipes for duck.

Indian Chicken Curry

1.5 kg (3 lb.) chicken (or chicken pieces)	2 teaspoons ground coriander
1 large onion	1 teaspoon ground cumin
2 sticks celery	½ teaspoon ground cloves
2 tablespoons oil	½ cup boiling water
2.5 cm (1 in.) piece green ginger	2 teaspoons tomato paste
2 cloves garlic	2.5 cm (1 in.) piece creamed coconut
1 teaspoon turmeric	salt
2 teaspoons chilli powder	1 cup boiling water, extra

Saffron Rice

1½ cups rice	60 g (2 oz.) slivered almonds
4½ cups boiling water	
¼ teaspoon saffron	1 tablespoon oil
1 small onion	4 chicken stock cubes
¾ cup sultanas	6 shallots or spring onions

Cut chicken into serving pieces. Peel onion; chop finely; chop celery finely. Heat oil in large pan; saute onion, celery, peeled and grated ginger and crushed garlic until golden brown. Combine turmeric, chilli powder, coriander, cumin and ground cloves; add to pan; cook 1 minute, stirring constantly. Add water, then chicken. Bring to boil; reduce heat; simmer covered 30 minutes.

Combine extra boiling water, tomato paste and cream of coconut; add to pan; bring to boil. Reduce heat; simmer uncovered a further 30 to 35 minutes or until chicken is cooked and sauce has thickened. Season with salt; remove from heat. Serve with Saffron Rice.

NOTE: Creamed coconut is available in 227 g cartons at most large food stores and super-markets.

Recipe continued overleaf:

Indian Chicken Curry — spicy, full of rich flavour. And there's an interesting Saffron Rice for accompaniment.

Saffron Rice: Wash rice; cover with water; soak 10 minutes; drain. Peel and finely chop onion; saute in oil until light golden brown; remove from pan. Add sultanas and almonds to pan; saute 1 minute; remove from pan. Add drained rice to pan; saute 1 minute. Add saffron, water and crumbled stock cubes; bring to boil; boil uncovered 10 to 15 minutes or until rice is tender, adding a little more boiling water, if necessary. When cooked, drain well. Add onion, sultanas and almonds; combine well. Top with finely-sliced shallots.

Serves 4.

Chicken and Champagne Mousse

1.25 kg (2½ lb.) chicken	1 cup thickened cream
60 g (2 oz.) butter	1 teaspoon grated lemon
4 tablespoons flour	rind
1½ cups dry champagne	¼ cup water
(or dry white wine)	1 tablespoon gelatine
salt, pepper	4 eggs, separated
1 teaspoon french	2 sticks celery
mustard	3 tablespoons chopped
½ teaspoon sugar	parsley

Steam or boil chicken until tender; allow to become cold. Remove skin and bones from chicken; chop chicken meat finely.

Heat butter in pan; add flour; stir until combined. Remove pan from heat; add champagne; stir until combined. Return pan to heat; add salt, pepper, mustard, sugar and lemon rind; stir until sauce boils and thickens. Reduce heat; simmer 3 minutes. Remove pan from heat; add egg yolks one at a time, beating well. Cool a little, until warm.

Place chicken meat, finely-chopped celery, parsley and sauce into bowl; mix well. Sprinkle gelatine over cold water; stand over simmering water until gelatine has dissolved; add to chicken mixture; mix well. Beat cream until soft peaks form; fold into chicken mixture with mayonnaise. Beat egg whites until firm peaks form; fold into chicken mixture. Pour into large serving dish or individual dishes. Refrigerate until firm.

Serves 6.

Wine Cream Chicken

1.5 kg (3 lb.) chicken	1 tablespoon flour, extra
(or chicken pieces)	1 cup milk
flour	½ cup water
60 g (2 oz.) butter	½ cup dry white wine
2 tablespoons oil	salt, pepper
1 onion	470 g (15 oz.) can artichoke
3 rashers bacon	hearts
2 teaspoons prepared	½ cup cream
mustard	

Topping

1 cup fresh breadcrumbs	2 tablespoons chopped
2 teaspoons dry mustard	parsley
salt, pepper	60 g (2 oz.) butter
1 teaspoon rosemary	

Cut chicken into serving pieces; coat lightly with flour. Heat butter and oil in large pan; add chicken pieces; saute until golden brown; remove from pan.

Add peeled and finely-chopped onion and chopped bacon to pan; saute until onion is transparent. Add extra flour and mustard to pan; stir until smooth; cook 1 minute. Remove pan from heat; add milk, water and wine; stir until smooth. Return pan to heat; stir until sauce boils and thickens; reduce heat. Add chicken to pan; simmer covered 40 to 45 minutes or until chicken is tender.

Add drained artichokes to pan 10 minutes before end of cooking time. Add cream; reheat without boiling; season with salt and pepper. Spoon chicken and sauce into casserole dish; sprinkle prepared topping over chicken; bake in moderate oven 15 minutes or until topping is golden brown.

Topping: Combine in bowl breadcrumbs, mustard, salt, pepper, parsley and rosemary. Add melted butter; stir until combined.

Serves 4.

Herbed Chicken

4 whole chicken breasts	1 teaspoon oregano
60 g (2 oz.) butter	½ cup dry white wine
1 tablespoon oil	1 cup milk
flour	1 cup water
125 g (4 oz.) mushrooms	2 chicken stock cubes
2 tablespoons flour, extra	½ cup cream
½ teaspoon mixed herbs	6 shallots or spring onions
½ teaspoon sage	salt, pepper
½ teaspoon thyme	

Remove chicken breasts from bones, giving eight individual pieces; flatten slightly; coat lightly with flour. Heat butter and oil in large pan; add chicken; saute until light golden brown and cooked through; remove from pan.

Add mushrooms to pan; saute until tender; remove from pan. Add extra flour, mixed herbs, sage, thyme and oregano to pan drippings; mix until smooth and golden brown. Add milk, wine and water to pan; stir until sauce boils and thickens. Add crumbled stock cubes; reduce heat; simmer 5 minutes. Return chicken and mushrooms to pan; simmer 2 minutes. Add cream, shallots, salt and pepper; reheat without boiling.

Serves 4.

Asparagus Chicken Casserole

1.5 kg (3 lb.) chicken (or chicken pieces)	470 g (15 oz.) can asparagus cuts
⅓ cup oil	2 chicken stock cubes
1 onion	1 tablespoon lemon juice
125 g (4 oz.) bacon	salt, pepper
¼ cup flour	90 g (3 oz.) cheddar cheese
1 cup milk	2 tablespoons chopped parsley
1 cup water	

Cut chicken into serving pieces. Heat oil in pan; add chicken pieces; cook, turning occasionally, until chicken is well browned on all sides. Remove chicken; reserve pan drippings. Place chicken in ovenproof dish.

Add peeled and sliced onion and chopped bacon to reserved pan drippings; saute until onion is transparent. Add flour; stir until flour is combined. Remove pan from heat. Add milk, water, undrained asparagus, crumbled stock cubes, lemon juice, salt and pepper; stir until mixture is combined. Return to heat; stir until sauce boils and thickens. Stir in grated cheese; stir until cheese melts.

Pour sauce over chicken. Bake, covered, in moderate oven 45 to 55 minutes or until chicken is tender. Stir in chopped parsley.

Serves 4.

Swiss Chicken

4 whole chicken breasts	1 teaspoon french mustard
flour	½ cup cream
salt, pepper	3 shallots or spring onions
90 g (3 oz.) butter	8 slices ham
1 clove garlic	8 slices swiss cheese
¾ cup dry white wine	

Carefully remove chicken meat from bones, giving eight individual pieces; flatten out slightly. Dust chicken breasts lightly with flour seasoned with salt and pepper. Heat butter in frying pan; add crushed garlic and chicken; saute gently until chicken is light golden brown. Add wine; bring to boil. Reduce heat; simmer covered 20 minutes or until chicken is tender; remove chicken from pan.

Trim ham and cheese to approximately same size as chicken. Put a slice of ham on each piece of chicken, then top with a slice of cheese. Put on heatproof serving dish. Cook in moderate oven, uncovered, for 10 minutes or until cheese has melted.

While chicken is in oven, bring liquid in pan to boil; boil uncovered until approx. a half-cup of liquid remains in pan. Reduce heat; add cream, chopped shallots and mustard; stir until combined. Season with salt and pepper. Pour sauce over chicken.

Serves 4.

Creamy Tarragon Chicken

2 x 1.25 kg (2½ lb.) chickens	½ cup dry white wine
60 g (2 oz.) butter	1 cup cream
1 cup water	2 chicken stock cubes
2 teaspoons tarragon	salt, pepper
3 tablespoons plain flour	1 teaspoon french mustard
1½ cups water, extra	½ cup cream, extra

Place chickens in baking dish; add butter, water and tarragon. Bake in moderately hot oven for 60 minutes, basting frequently with pan juices. Remove chickens from baking dish; cut each chicken in half, lengthwise.

Pour fat and pan drippings into bowl; allow to stand for 5 minutes; skim off all fat. Return 4 tablespoons of this fat to baking dish. Measure remaining pan drippings; you will need ½ cup. (Make up to ½ cup with water, if necessary.) Place baking dish over heat; add flour; stir until smooth; remove pan from heat. Add the ½ cup of pan drippings, extra water, wine, cream, crumbled stock cubes, salt, pepper and mustard; stir until combined. Return pan to heat; stir until sauce boils and thickens; remove pan from heat.

Return chickens to pan skin side up; spoon sauce over. Place dish in moderate oven for 30 minutes, spooning sauce over frequently. Remove chickens from baking dish on to serving plate. Add extra cream to pan; stir over low heat until combined. Do not boil. Spoon sauce over chickens.

Serves 4.

Creamy Chicken

1.5 kg (3 lb.) chicken (or chicken pieces)	2 chicken stock cubes
flour	4 shallots or spring onions
60 g (2 oz.) butter	salt, pepper
2 tablespoons oil	125 g (4 oz.) mushrooms
1 clove garlic	30 g (1 oz.) butter, extra
1 cup dry white wine	½ cup milk
1½ cups water	2 tablespoons flour, extra
	¼ cup cream

Cut chicken into serving pieces; roll in flour. Heat butter and oil in large pan; saute chicken pieces until golden brown. Add crushed garlic, wine, water and crumbled stock cubes; cover; simmer 30 minutes or until chicken is tender. Remove chicken from pan.

Melt extra butter in separate pan; saute sliced mushrooms and chopped shallots. Blend extra flour with milk; stir until smooth; add gradually to chicken liquid in pan; stir until sauce boils and thickens; season with salt and pepper.

Return chicken pieces to pan with sauteed mushrooms 'and shallots; reduce heat; reheat gently. Just before serving, stir in cream.

Serves 4.

Chicken Casserole

1.5 kg (3 lb.) chicken (or chicken pieces)	3 cups water
flour	salt, pepper
60 g (2 oz.) butter	2 chicken stock cubes
2 tablespoons oil	470 g (15 oz.) can whole peeled tomatoes
2 medium potatoes	2 tablespoons tomato paste
2 medium carrots	
2 sticks celery	1 cup dry white wine
2 parsnips	½ teaspoon basil
1 onion	½ teaspoon thyme
¼ cup flour, extra	

Cut chicken into serving pieces; coat lightly with flour. Heat butter and oil in large pan; saute chicken until golden brown; remove from pan; reserve fat in pan.

Peel potatoes; cut into quarters; peel carrots; cut into 5 cm (2 in.) diagonal slices; cut celery into 5 cm (2 in.) diagonal slices; peel parsnips; cut into 5 cm (2 in.) diagonal slices. Add vegetables to pan; saute 2 minutes; remove from pan.

Add peeled and finely-chopped onion to pan; saute until golden brown. Add extra flour; stir until smooth and well-browned. Add water, salt, pepper and crumbled stock cubes; stir until sauce boils and thickens. Reduce heat; simmer covered 10 minutes. Add mashed undrained tomatoes, tomato paste, wine, basil and thyme. Stir until boiling; reduce heat; simmer 2 minutes.

Put chicken into large casserole; pour sauce over; cook covered in moderate oven 1 hour. Add vegetables; bake covered a further 30 minutes or until vegetables are tender.
Serves 4 to 6.

Tarragon Chicken

1.5 kg (3 lb.) chicken (or chicken pieces)	1 chicken stock cube
flour	2 teaspoons french mustard
30 g (1 oz.) butter	salt, pepper
2 tablespoons oil	1 teaspoon tarragon
1 onion	2 teaspoons lemon juice
1 tablespoon flour, extra	2 tablespoons chopped parsley
1½ cups milk	
½ cup water	½ cup cream

Cut chicken into serving pieces; coat with flour seasoned with salt and pepper. Heat butter and oil in large pan; add chicken pieces. Cook until chicken is golden brown; remove from pan.

Add peeled and finely-chopped onion to pan; saute until onion is transparent; add flour; cook 1 minute. Add milk, water and crumbled stock cube; stir until smooth and sauce boils and thickens. Add mustard, salt, pepper and tarragon; mix well. Add chicken; reduce heat; simmer covered 30 to 40 minutes or until chicken is tender. Add lemon juice, parsley and cream. Reheat without boiling.
Serves 4.

Lemon-Crumbed Chicken

4 whole chicken breasts	2 tablespoons chopped parsley
¼ cup lemon juice	
½ cup dry white wine	1 teaspoon grated lemon rind
2 tablespoons oil	
salt, pepper	1 tablespoon grated parmesan cheese
flour	
2 eggs	90 g (3 oz.) butter
1½ cups packaged dry breadcrumbs	1 tablespoon oil, extra
	2 teaspoons flour, extra
60 g (2 oz.) ground almonds	½ cup cream
	1 tablespoon chopped parsley, extra
¼ teaspoon oregano	

Remove skin from chicken breasts. Carefully remove chicken meat from bones, giving 8 individual pieces. Gently pound out each chicken breast. Combine lemon juice, wine, oil, salt and pepper; pour over chicken breasts; allow to stand 2 hours.

Drain chicken breasts; reserve marinade. Coat chicken lightly in flour seasoned with salt and pepper; dip in beaten eggs, then coat chicken in combined breadcrumbs, ground almonds, oregano, parsley, lemon rind and parmesan cheese.

Heat butter and extra oil in a large frying pan; add chicken; cook on both sides until golden brown and cooked through. Remove from pan; keep warm. Add extra flour to pan; cook 1 minute; add reserved marinade; stir until smooth; bring to boil. Reduce heat; simmer 1 minute. Add cream and extra parsley; reheat without boiling. Put chicken on serving-plate; spoon sauce over.
Serves 4.

Honey Chicken

1.5 kg (3 lb.) chicken (or chicken pieces)	1 tablespoon lemon juice
	2 teaspoons grated green ginger
60 g (2 oz.) butter	
¼ cup honey	1 chicken stock cube
3 teaspoons soy sauce	1 cup water
2 teaspoons worcester-shire sauce	3 teaspoons cornflour
	salt, pepper

Cut chicken into serving pieces; put in baking dish. Melt butter; pour over chicken; bake uncovered in moderate oven 30 minutes, brushing occasionally with pan drippings. Remove from oven; pour off fat.

Combine in saucepan honey, soy sauce,

Chinese Lemon Chicken

worcestershire sauce, lemon juice, ginger, crumbled stock cube and combined cornflour and water. Stir over medium heat until sauce boils and thickens. Reduce heat; simmer 1 minute.

Pour sauce over chicken; return to oven; bake uncovered a further 30 to 35 minutes or until chicken is tender and golden brown, basting occasionally with sauce. Season with salt and pepper. Serve with any remaining sauce poured over.

Serves 4.

Chinese Lemon Chicken

4 whole chicken breasts	salt, pepper
½ cup cornflour	6 shallots or spring onions
3 tablespoons water	oil for deep-frying
4 egg yolks	

Lemon Sauce

2 tablespoons rice flour	2 teaspoons soy sauce
2 tablespoons sugar	1 teaspoon grated green
2 cups water	ginger
⅔ cup lemon juice	salt, pepper
2 chicken stock cubes	2 teaspoons dry sherry

Remove chicken breasts from bone; separate along centres to form 8 individual pieces; pound chicken breasts lightly. Put cornflour into bowl; gradually add water and beaten egg yolks; add salt and pepper; mix until combined. Dip chicken breasts into this batter; drain well. Place two pieces in deep hot oil; fry until golden brown and cooked through; drain on absorbent paper. Keep warm while cooking remainder of chicken. Slice each breast across into three or four pieces; re-assemble on serving plate. Spoon the hot Lemon Sauce over. Sprinkle with finely-chopped shallots.

Sauce: Put rice flour and sugar into pan; gradually add water, then crumbled stock cubes and lemon juice; stir until combined. Add soy sauce, ginger and sherry; stir until boiling. Reduce heat; simmer 2 minutes. Season with salt and pepper.

Serves 4.

Chicken in Wine

1.5 kg (3 lb.) chicken (or chicken pieces)	1 clove garlic
flour	1 onion
salt, pepper	2 x 470 kg (15 oz.) cans whole peeled tomatoes
60 g (2 oz.) butter	1 cup dry white wine
2 tablespoons oil	½ cup water

Topping

30 g (1 oz.) butter	2 tablespoons chopped parsley
2 rashers bacon	2 tablespoons grated parmesan cheese
1 cup fresh bread-crumbs	

Cut chicken into serving pieces; coat with flour seasoned with salt and pepper. Heat butter and oil in large pan; cook chicken until golden brown; remove from pan.

Add crushed garlic and peeled and chopped onion to pan; saute until onion is transparent. Add undrained mashed tomatoes, wine, water, salt and pepper.

Put chicken in ovenproof dish; pour sauce over. Bake covered in moderate oven 35 to 45 minutes or until chicken is cooked. Before serving, sprinkle prepared topping over.

Topping: Melt butter in pan; saute finely-chopped bacon and breadcrumbs until bacon is crisp and breadcrumbs golden. Add parsley and cheese.

Serves 4.

Chicken Loaf

½ x 375 g (12 oz.) pkt puff pastry	½ teaspoon thyme
1.5 kg (3 lb.) chicken	½ cup cream
30 g (1 oz.) butter	2 eggs
1 small onion	salt, pepper
1 clove garlic	1 egg yolk
	1 tablespoon water

Mushroom Sauce

60 g (2 oz.) butter	salt, pepper
1 tablespoon flour	1 tablespoon chopped parsley
½ cup cream	4 shallots or spring onions
½ cup milk	125 g (4 oz.) small mushrooms
1 teaspoon lemon juice	
1 teaspoon prepared mustard	

Boil chicken in usual way until tender; cool. Remove skin and bones from chicken; chop meat finely or put chicken meat through mincer. Combine minced chicken, beaten eggs, cream, thyme, salt and pepper.

Melt butter in pan; add peeled and chopped onion wind crushed garlic; saute until onion is transparent. Add onion mixture to chicken; mix well; cool.

Thaw pastry to room temperature; roll out on lightly floured board to 30 cm x 43 cm (12 in. x 17 in.) rectangle; trim to 28 cm x 40 cm (11 in. x 16 in.). Spoon chicken mixture down centre of pastry, leaving 2.5 cm (1 in.) free at each end; press chicken mixture into loaf shape. Combine egg-yolk and water; brush edges of pastry; fold over to enclose loaf; press edges neatly and firmly together at sides and top.

Put loaf on greased oven tray with folded edge down. Make three or four slits on top of loaf; brush with egg yolk mixture. Bake in hot oven 10 minutes; reduce heat to moderate; bake further 20 minutes. Serve hot, cut into slices, with Mushroom Sauce spooned over, or serve cold with salad.

Mushroom Sauce: Melt butter; add sliced mushrooms; saute until tender. Add flour; cook 1 minute. Remove from heat; add cream and milk; return to heat; stir until sauce boils and thickens. Add lemon juice, mustard, parsley, chopped shallots, salt and pepper. Bring to boil; reduce heat; simmer 1 minute.

Serves 4 to 6.

Chicken in Oyster Sauce

4 whole chicken breasts	¼ cup dry sherry
flour	salt, pepper
60 g (2 oz.) butter	1 tablespoon brandy
2 tablespoons flour, extra	1 teaspoon lemon juice
1 cup milk	about 10 canned fresh oysters
½ cup water	6 shallots or spring onions

Remove chicken breasts from bone, giving eight individual pieces; flatten out slightly. Coat lightly with flour. Heat butter in large pan; add chicken; saute until golden brown and cooked through; remove from pan.

Add extra flour to pan; stir until smooth; cook 1 minute. Remove pan from heat; add milk, water and dry sherry; stir until smooth. Return to heat; stir until sauce boils and thickens. Add salt, pepper, brandy and lemon juice; combine well. Add chicken and drained oysters; bring to boil. Reduce heat; simmer 2 minutes. Add cream and shallots; mix well; reheat without boiling.

Serves 4.

Camembert Chicken

2 x 1 kg (2 lb.) chickens	90 g (3 oz.) butter, extra
2 cloves garlic	3 cups fresh white breadcrumbs
30 g (1 oz.) butter	60 g (2 oz.) almonds
2 x 125 g (4 oz.) pkts camembert cheese	salt, pepper

Rub chicken skins with cut cloves of garlic. Gently lift skin covering breasts. Cut 30 g (1 oz.) butter into small pieces; put under skin of each chicken breast. Cut each camembert cheese into quarters; put four quarters in each chicken cavity. Put chickens into baking dish; brush over 30 g (1 oz.) of the melted extra butter. Bake in moderate oven for 30 minutes, basting frequently.

Melt remaining 60 g (2 oz.) butter in frying pan; add breadcrumbs; toss gently in butter until all butter has been absorbed. Season with salt and pepper.

Remove chickens from oven after 30 minutes cooking time. Carefully remove cheese from cavity and spread over chickens. Then pack breadcrumbs firmly on to each chicken. Cut almonds in half lengthways; sprinkle over breadcrumbs. Return chickens to oven for a further 1 hour or until golden brown and tender, basting frequently. Cut chickens in half lengthways; allow one half per serving.

Serves 4.

Chicken in Champagne

6 whole chicken breasts	1 cup dry champagne
flour	(or dry white wine)
salt, pepper	60 g (2 oz.) butter, extra
¼ cup oil	250 g (8 oz.) small
60 g (2 oz.) butter	mushrooms
2 tablespoons flour, extra	½ cup cream
2 cups water	6 shallots or spring onions
3 chicken stock cubes	

Cut chicken breasts in half. With sharp knife, carefully remove chicken meat from bones, keeping in one piece; this gives 12 pieces. Pound each chicken breast out thinly. Lightly coat chicken with combined flour, salt and pepper. Heat oil and butter in large frying pan; add a few of the chicken breasts; cook gently until golden brown on both sides; remove from pan. Repeat with remaining chicken; remove from pan.

Drain off excess fat from pan, leaving ¼ cup fat. Add extra flour; stir until light golden brown; remove pan from heat. Add water, crumbled stock cubes and champagne; stir until combined. Return pan to heat; stir until sauce boils and thickens. Season with salt and pepper.

Heat extra butter in separate pan; add sliced mushrooms; saute gently until mushrooms are just tender. Add to sauce mixture; stir until combined.

Return chicken breasts to pan; reduce heat; simmer covered 20 minutes. Add cream; stir until combined. Simmer a further 5 minutes. Just before serving, add chopped shallots.

Serves 6.

Chicken Drambuie

4 whole chicken breasts	1 cup cream
flour	6 shallots or spring onions,
salt, pepper	chopped finely
90 g (3 oz.) butter	2 tablespoons chopped
2 cloves garlic	parsley
2 cups water	2 tablespoons Drambuie
3 chicken stock cubes	

Remove chicken breasts from bones, giving 8 individual pieces; pound each piece lightly with mallet or rolling pin. Coat chicken breasts with flour seasoned with salt and pepper. Melt butter in pan; saute chicken breasts until golden brown on both sides; remove from pan. Drain excess fat from pan; add crushed garlic, water and crumbled stock cubes. Bring to boil; reduce heat; return chicken to pan; cover; simmer gently until chicken is tender, approx. 20 to 25 minutes. Remove chicken from pan; stir in cream; stir until sauce is thick. Stir in shallots, parsley and Drambuie. Return chicken to pan; stir to coat with sauce.

Serves 4.

Chicken with Crab

1.5 kg (3 lb.) chicken	1 teaspoon french mustard
60 g (2 oz.) butter	3 teaspoons lemon juice
1 cup milk	250 g (8 oz.) can crab
½ cup cream	60 g (2 oz.) butter, extra
½ cup mayonnaise	2 cups fresh white
3 tablespoons flour	breadcrumbs (approx.
salt, pepper	½ loaf)

Steam or boil chicken in usual way until tender; allow to become cold. Reserve ½ cup of the chicken stock. Remove skin and bones from chicken meat; cut meat into 2.5 cm (1 in.) cubes. Put chicken into greased, shallow ovenproof dish.

Heat butter in pan; add flour; stir until combined. Remove pan from heat; add milk, cream, mayonnaise, reserved chicken stock, salt, pepper, mustard and lemon juice; stir until combined. Return pan to heat; stir until sauce boils and thickens. Reduce heat; simmer 5 minutes. Add undrained flaked crab; simmer a further 3 minutes. Pour sauce over chicken.

Heat extra butter in pan; add breadcrumbs; stir until well coated with butter. Sprinkle breadcrumbs over sauce. Bake uncovered in moderate oven 30 minutes.

Serves 4.

Curried Glazed Chicken

1.5 kg (3 lb.) chicken	5 cm (2 in.) piece green
1 tablespoon curry powder	ginger
½ teaspoon chilli powder	2 cups water
2 tablespoons dry sherry	salt, pepper
1 tablespoon soy sauce	1 chicken stock cube
1 tablespoon honey	1 tablespoon cornflour

Pineapple Stuffing

⅓ cup rice	salt, pepper
60 g (2 oz.) butter	1 clove garlic
470 g (15 oz.) can crushed	2 tablespoons chopped
pineapple	mint
1 small green apple	1 tablespoon chopped
1 medium onion	parsley

Press prepared stuffing into chicken cavity. Secure cavity with skewer. Place in baking dish. Combine curry powder, chilli powder, sherry, soy sauce, honey, peeled and grated green ginger and ½ cup of the water; pour over chicken. Bake in moderate oven for 1 hour, basting chicken frequently.

Remove chicken from baking dish. Skim fat from pan drippings, leaving pan drippings in baking dish. Add combined remaining water, salt, pepper, crumbled stock cube and cornflour. Stir over medium heat until sauce boils and thickens.

Return chicken to baking dish; spoon sauce over. Return chicken to moderate oven for a further 30 minutes or until chicken is tender; spoon sauce over frequently.

Pineapple Stuffing: Gradually add rice to large quantity of boiling salted water; boil uncovered 12 minutes or until rice is tender; drain well. Heat butter in pan; add well-drained pineapple, peeled, cored and finely-chopped apple, peeled and finely-chopped onion, salt, pepper and crushed garlic; saute for 5 minutes, stirring occasionally. Remove pan from heat; add rice, mint and parsley; mix well.

Serves 4.

Egyptian Lemon Chicken

2 x 1 kg (2 lb.) chickens	1 teaspoon grated lemon
(or chicken pieces)	rind
4 tablespoons oil	½ teaspoon thyme
1 large clove garlic	salt, pepper
2 tablespoons lemon	60 g (2 oz.) butter
juice	chopped parsley

Cut chickens into serving pieces. Combine oil, crushed garlic, lemon juice and rind, thyme, salt and pepper. Add chicken pieces; cover; marinate at least 2 hours, turning occasionally.

Put chicken and marinade into ovenproof dish; dot with butter. Cook, uncovered, in moderate oven 50 minutes, or until tender. Sprinkle with parsley. Spoon some cooking liquid over each serving.

Serves 6.

Curried Glazed Chicken

How to Roast a Chicken

Roast chicken, golden brown and glistening, perhaps with a savoury stuffing added, is one of the most popular of all meals. Here's how to make sure it's golden, moist and succulent every time.

You will need:

1 chicken
prepared stuffing
60 g (2 oz.) butter
1 cup water
1 chicken stock cube
salt, pepper

Herb Stuffing: Combine 2 cups fresh breadcrumbs, 30 g (1 oz.) melted butter, 2 tablespoons chopped parsley, 1 teaspoon grated lemon rind, 1 teaspoon mixed herbs, 1 small chopped onion, salt, pepper, 1 beaten egg.

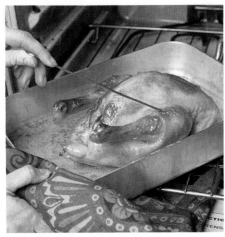

1. If using stuffing, fill this loosely into chicken (stuffing will swell during cooking); secure vent with small skewer. Put chicken in baking dish, rub well with softened butter — particularly over the breast and legs; add salt and pepper.

2. Add water and crumbled stock cube to pan. Roast in moderately hot oven 30 minutes, then brush chicken well with the pan juices. Move chicken around a little in the pan, so that the skin of the chicken does not stick to the pan during cooking. Add an extra ½ cup of water to pan if water evaporates too quickly.

3. Continue cooking in moderately hot oven until chicken is tender; allow approx. 1½ hours for a 1.5 kg (3 lb.) chicken. Brush with pan juices about every 15 minutes. Twice during cooking time (if cooking chicken without stuffing) tilt chicken so that any water inside cavity runs out (this water slows down the cooking time). To test if chicken is cooked, pierce with skewer at the thick second joint of leg; the juices will run clear, not pink. The leg will also move easily to and fro and the skin will start to shrink slightly from the bones.

Orange Chicken

1.5 kg (3 lb.) chicken
60 g (2 oz.) butter
½ cup water

1 chicken stock cube
8 small onions

Stuffing

2½ cups fresh
    breadcrumbs
60 g (2 oz.) butter
6 shallots or spring onions
1 tablespoon chopped
    parsley

1 teaspoon oregano
2 teaspoons grated orange
    rind
1 teaspoon grated lemon
    rind
1 egg

Sauce

½ cup orange juice
1 cup water
1 tablespoon sugar
1 chicken stock cube
2 teaspoons lemon juice

1 teaspoon grated green
    ginger
3 teaspoons cornflour
¼ cup Grand Marnier

Fill chicken with prepared stuffing; secure opening. Put in baking dish; brush with melted butter; pour over combined water and crumbled stock cube. Bake uncovered in moderate oven 1 hour or until chicken is golden brown, brushing frequently with pan drippings. While chicken is cooking, peel onions and leave whole. Cook in boiling salted water until just tender; drain.

Drain fat from pan; add onions to pan; pour prepared sauce over chicken and onions. Bake uncovered a further 30 minutes or until chicken and onions are cooked and well-glazed, brushing frequently with sauce.

Stuffing: Combine in bowl breadcrumbs, parsley, oregano, orange and lemon rind. Saute finely-chopped shallots in butter 1 minute. Add shallots and butter to breadcrumb mixture with beaten egg; mix well.

Sauce: Mix cornflour to smooth paste with water; add remaining ingredients. Stir over medium heat until sauce boils and thickens. Reduce heat; simmer 2 minutes.
    Serves 4.

Pineapple Chicken

1.5 kg (3 lb.) chicken
    (or chicken pieces)
flour
60 g (2 oz.) butter
2 tablespoons oil
1 tablespoon flour, extra
1 pkt french onion soup
    mix

2 teaspoons grated green
    ginger
470 g (15 oz.) can
    pineapple pieces
2 teaspoons soy sauce
2 tablespoons lemon juice
1½ cups water
salt, pepper

Cut chicken into serving pieces; coat with flour. Heat butter and oil in large frying pan; fry chicken

until golden brown; remove from pan. Pour off fat, reserving 2 tablespoons of fat in pan.

Add extra flour, dry soup mix and ginger; stir until golden brown. Drain pineapple; reserve pineapple pieces; add syrup to pan with soy sauce, lemon juice and water. Stir until sauce boils and thickens; add chicken pieces. Reduce heat; simmer covered 30 minutes. Add reserved pineapple pieces, salt and pepper; continue to simmer covered a further 15 minutes or until chicken is tender.
    Serves 4.

Pineapple-Curry Chicken

1.5 kg (3 lb.) chicken
    (or chicken pieces)
⅓ cup oil
2 onions
1 clove garlic
¼ cup flour
1 tablespoon curry powder
¼ teaspoon chilli powder
2 cups water

470 g (15 oz.) can
    unsweetened pineapple
    juice
2 chicken stock cubes
¼ cup tomato paste
salt, pepper
2 tablespoons chopped
    parsley
4 shallots or spring onions

Cut chicken into serving pieces. Heat oil in pan; add chicken pieces; cook, turning occasionally, until chicken is well browned on all sides. Remove chicken from pan; reserve pan drippings. Place chicken in ovenproof dish.

Add peeled and sliced onions and crushed garlic to reserved pan drippings; saute until onions are golden brown. Stir in flour, curry powder and chilli powder; stir until flour is golden brown. Remove from heat. Add water, pineapple juice, crumbled stock cubes, tomato paste, salt and pepper; mix until smooth. Return to heat; stir until sauce boils and thickens.

Pour sauce over chicken. Bake, covered, in moderate oven 45 to 55 minutes or until chicken is tender. Stir in chopped shallots and chopped parsley.
    Serves 4.

Crumbed Chicken

1 kg (2 lb.) chicken
1½ cups dry white wine
salt, pepper
2 cloves garlic
2 tablespoons chopped
    parsley
½ teaspoon thyme

½ teaspoon basil
60 g (2 oz.) butter
1 egg
1½ cups fresh
    breadcrumbs
60 g (2 oz.) butter, extra

Sauce

30 g (1 oz.) butter
1 onion
2 tablespoons flour
1 cup water
salt, pepper

1 teaspoon soy sauce
1 teaspoon worcester-
    shire sauce
1 tablespoon brandy

Cut chicken in half; put in baking dish, skin side up. Combine wine, salt, pepper, crushed garlic, finely-chopped parsley, thyme and basil; mix well. Pour over chicken; cover; stand a few hours or overnight, basting frequently with marinade. Drain off marinade; reserve. Brush chicken with melted butter; add ¼ cup reserved marinade to pan; bake in moderate oven 1 hour, brushing frequently with pan juices. Remove from oven; pour off pan drippings.

Combine breadcrumbs, salt, pepper and extra melted butter; mix well. Brush chicken halves with beaten egg; press crumb mixture on to chicken. Return to moderate oven and cook a further 20 to 30 minutes or until golden brown. Serve with prepared sauce.

Sauce: Melt butter; add peeled and finely-chopped onion; saute until golden brown. Add flour; stir until smooth and well browned. Add water, remaining reserved marinade, salt, pepper, soy sauce, worcestershire sauce and brandy. Stir until smooth; stir until sauce boils and thickens. Reduce heat; simmer 2 minutes.

Serves 2.

Apricot Duck

2 x 1.25 kg (2½ lb.) ducks	60 g (2 oz.) butter

Sauce

1 onion	½ cup water
30 g (1 oz.) butter	1 tablespoon lemon juice
2 teaspoons grated green ginger	2 teaspoons soy sauce
1 tablespoon flour	1 teaspoon worcester- shire sauce
¼ cup hoisin sauce	1 tablespoon dry sherry
470 g (15 oz.) can apricot nectar	salt, pepper

Put ducks into baking dish; brush with melted butter; bake in moderate oven 1 hour or until golden brown. Put ducks into large casserole dish; pour sauce over; bake covered in moderate oven 1 hour or until tender, basting frequently with sauce. To serve, cut ducks in half lengthwise; allow half a duck per serving.

Sauce: Peel and finely chop onion; saute onion and ginger in butter until onion is transparent. Add flour; stir until smooth; cook 1 minute. Remove from heat; add hoisin sauce, apricot nectar, water, lemon juice, soy sauce, worcestershire sauce and sherry; stir until smooth. Return to heat; stir over medium heat until sauce boils and thickens. Reduce heat; simmer 5 minutes. Season with salt and pepper.

Serves 4.

NOTE: Hoisin sauce is available at most large supermarkets and Chinese food stores.

Duck with Mangoes

2 x 1.5 kg (3 lb.) ducks	2 tablespoons brandy
60 g (2 oz.) butter	½ cup orange juice
½ cup flour	salt, pepper
2 cups water	500 g (1 lb.) can mango slices
1 cup dry white wine	
2 tablespoons port	1 bayleaf
½ cup Grand Marnier	pinch thyme

Wash and dry ducks; put in baking dish. Brush each duck with melted butter. Bake in moderately hot oven 60 minutes or until golden brown, brushing ducks frequently with melted butter. Remove ducks from pan; drain all fat from pan; reserve fat.

Put baking dish on top of stove; stand over high heat until pan drippings have turned dark golden brown; do not allow to burn. Add ½ cup reserved fat; remove pan from heat; add flour; stir until combined. Return pan to heat; stir until flour is dark golden brown. Add combined water, wine, port, Grand Marnier, brandy and orange juice all at once; stir until sauce boils and thickens. Season with salt and pepper. Add bayleaf and thyme; stir until combined.

Put ducks into individual casserole dishes or one large casserole dish. Pour sauce over; cover; bake in moderate oven 1½ hours or until ducks are tender. Remove ducks from pan; cut in half lengthwise; put on serving plates. Remove bayleaf. Pour sauce over. Meanwhile heat mangoes in their own liquid; drain; serve with ducks.

Serves 4.

Duck with Cherry Sauce

2 x 1.25 kg (2½ lb.) ducks	60 g (2 oz.) butter

Cherry Sauce

470 g (15 oz.) can black cherries	¼ cup port
1½ tablespoons arrowroot	¼ cup brandy
1 teaspoon lemon juice	1 tablespoon bottled red currant jelly

Put ducks in baking dish; brush with melted butter. Bake in moderate oven approx. 1¼ hours or until tender, brushing occasionally with pan juices. When cooked, skim off fat from pan; strain pan juices and reserve for sauce.

Cherry Sauce: Drain cherries; reserve syrup. Blend arrowroot with lemon juice, port wine and brandy; add cherry syrup, reserved pan juices and red currant jelly. Stir over medium heat until boiling. Reduce heat; cook 2 minutes. Remove from heat; add cherries.

Serves 4.

Rice & Pasta

Rice and pasta, combined with meat, fish or vegetables, make excellent main courses. Or, served as an accompaniment, they give extra servings to a meal, making the meal go further. We give interesting recipes in this section for rice and pasta as both main meals and accompaniments; they're easy, economical, delicious!

Curried Salmon and Rice Slice

440 g (14 oz.) can salmon	1½ cups milk
1 cup long grain rice	½ cup mayonnaise
30 g (1 oz.) butter	2 teaspoons lemon juice
1 egg	2 tablespoons chopped
salt, pepper	parsley
45 g (1 ½ oz.) butter, extra	1 egg, extra
2 tablespoons flour	60 g (2 oz.) cheese
1½ tablespoons curry powder	

Cook rice in boiling, salted water 12 minutes or until tender; drain. Combine rice with butter, egg, salt and pepper. Line 18 cm x 28 cm (7 in. x 11 in.) lamington tin with aluminium foil, bringing it above sides of tin on each side (this makes it easy to lift out slice when cooked); press rice mixture over base and sides of tin. Arrange drained, flaked salmon over rice base.

Melt extra butter; add flour and curry powder; stir until smooth; cook 1 minute. Remove from heat; add milk gradually, stirring until smooth. Add mayonnaise; return to heat; stir until sauce boils and thickens. Add lemon juice and parsley; reduce heat; simmer 1 minute; remove from heat; add extra beaten egg; cool slightly. Spoon mixture evenly into rice shell; sprinkle with grated cheese. Bake in moderate oven 25 to 35 minutes or until golden brown on top.

Serves 4 to 6.

Curried Salmon and Rice Slice — a soft shell of rice holds a creamy curried salmon filling.

Crab and Rice Balls

½ cup rice	60 g (2 oz.) cheddar cheese
170 g (5½ oz.) can crab	salt, pepper
30 g (1 oz.) butter	flour, extra
2 tablespoons flour	2 eggs
½ cup milk	packaged dry breadcrumbs
4 shallots or spring onions	oil for deep frying
2 tablespoons chopped parsley	

Put rice in large saucepan of boiling, salted water; cook approx. 12 minutes or until rice is tender; drain well. Heat butter in pan; add flour; cook 1 minute. Gradually add milk; stir until sauce boils and thickens. Add drained, flaked crab, chopped shallots, parsley, grated cheddar cheese, salt, pepper and cooked rice; mix well. Roll heaped teaspoonfuls of mixture into balls. Roll in flour; coat with lightly-beaten eggs; toss in breadcrumbs. Deep-fry in hot oil until golden brown.

Makes approx. 30.

Curried Steak and Rice

1 tablespoon oil	1 banana
500 g (1 lb.) minced steak	salt, pepper
1 tablespoon curry powder	1 cup water
2 onions	1 beef stock cube
1 carrot	1 cup rice
1 potato	2 tablespoons chopped parsley
1 apple	

Heat oil in pan; add minced steak, curry powder and peeled and chopped onions; cook until meat is well browned; pour off any surplus fat. Add peeled and thinly-sliced carrot, peeled and cubed potato, peeled and chopped apple and peeled, chopped banana. Add salt, pepper, water and crumbled stock cube; bring to boil. Reduce heat; simmer covered 15 to 20 minutes or until vegetables and meat are tender. Put rice in large saucepan of boiling, salted water; cook 12 minutes or until rice is tender; drain well. Add rice to meat; cook a further 5 minutes. Stir in parsley.

Serves 6.

Savoury Wine Rice

90 g (3 oz.) butter	½ cup dry white wine
1 clove garlic	salt, pepper
1 onion	6 shallots or spring onions
1 cup rice	2 tablespoons chopped parsley
2½ cups water	
2 chicken stock cubes	

Heat butter in pan; add crushed garlic and peeled and chopped onion; saute until onion is tender. Add rice; stir 2 minutes. Add 1 cup of the water and crumbled chicken stock cubes; stir uncovered until nearly all liquid has evaporated. Add remaining water, wine, salt and pepper; bring to boil; reduce heat; simmer uncovered approx. 10 minutes or until rice is tender and nearly all liquid has been absorbed. Add chopped shallots; cook a further 1 minute. Remove from heat; stir in parsley.

Serves 4.

Spinach and Steak Casserole

Base

1 cup small macaroni	2 tablespoons chopped parsley
30 g (1 oz.) butter	
2 tablespoons grated parmesan cheese	

Filling

1 tablespoon oil	¼ cup dry red wine
2 onions	2 tablespoons tomato paste
1 clove garlic	
500 g (1 lb.) minced steak	¼ teaspoon oregano
470 g (15 oz.) can whole peeled tomatoes	salt, pepper

Topping

315 g (10 oz.) pkt frozen spinach	salt, pepper
125 g (4 oz.) ricotta cheese	¼ teaspoon nutmeg
¼ cup sour cream	125 g (4 oz.) mozzarella cheese
4 shallots or spring onions	

Base: Put macaroni in boiling, salted water; cook 10 to 15 minutes or until tender; drain. Add butter, parmesan cheese and parsley; stir until butter has melted. Put into base of ovenproof dish.

Filling: Heat oil in pan; add peeled and chopped onion, crushed garlic and minced steak; saute until meat is well browned, mashing meat well; pour off any surplus fat. Add undrained mashed tomatoes, wine, tomato paste, oregano, salt and pepper; stir until combined. Bring to boil; reduce heat; simmer covered 30 minutes or until mixture is very thick. Spread meat mixture evenly over macaroni.

Topping: Cook spinach according to directions on packet; drain well. Put into bowl with ricotta cheese, sour cream, chopped shallots, salt, pepper and nutmeg; mix well. Spread evenly over meat mixture. Arrange sliced mozzarella cheese over spinach topping. Bake in moderate oven 15 to 20 minutes or until heated through.

Serves 4 to 6.

Vegetable Rice Pie

Base

1 cup rice	1 egg
½ teaspoon saffron	

Filling

60 g (2 oz.) butter	1 cup milk
1 clove garlic	½ teaspoon oregano
1 onion	salt, pepper
1 small aubergine	125 g (4 oz.) feta cheese
250 g (8 oz.) courgettes	3 eggs
125 g (4 oz.) mushrooms	150 g (5 oz.) pkt mozzarella
1 small red pepper	cheese slices
15 g (½ oz.) butter, extra	paprika
2 tablespoons flour	

Base: Put saffron in large saucepan of boiling, salted water; add rice; mix well; cook approx. 12 minutes or until rice is tender; drain well. Add lightly-beaten egg; mix well. Press mixture over base and sides of greased 23 cm (9 in.) pie plate.

Filling: Cut aubergine into 2.5 cm (1 in.) cubes; sprinkle with salt; leave to stand 30 minutes; rinse under cold water; drain well. Heat butter in pan; add crushed garlic and peeled and chopped onion; saute until onion is golden brown. Add sliced courgettes, aubergine, sliced mushrooms and seeded and chopped pepper; cook, stirring, until vegetables are tender. Remove vegetables from pan. Heat extra butter in pan; add flour; cook 1 minute. Gradually add milk; stir until sauce boils and thickens. Add oregano, salt, pepper and crumbled feta cheese; stir until cheese has melted. Add vegetables; mix well. Remove from heat; cool slightly. Add lightly-beaten eggs; mix well. Put mixture into prepared rice base. Arrange mozzarella slices over vegetables; sprinkle with paprika. Bake in moderate oven approx. 30 minutes or until pie is set and cheese is golden brown.

Serves 4 to 6.

Curried Nut Rice

1½ cups rice	125 g (4 oz.) salted
125 g (4 oz.) butter	cashews
6 shallots or spring onions	salt, pepper
1 tablespoon curry	2 tablespoons chopped
powder	parsley

Put rice in large saucepan of boiling, salted water; cook 12 minutes or until tender; drain well. Heat butter in pan; add chopped shallots and curry powder; cook 1 minute. Add rice; cook a further 5 minutes. Add chopped cashews, salt, pepper and parsley; mix well.

Serves 6 as a meal accompaniment.

Asparagus and Corn Casserole

1 cup rice	2 x 300 g (10 oz.) can
60 g (2 oz.) butter	asparagus cuts
1 onion	300 g (10 oz.) can corn
3 tablespoons flour	niblets
¾ cup milk	90 g (3 oz.) ham
¼ cup dry white wine	¼ teaspoon thyme
1 chicken stock cube	2 tablespoons chopped
3 tablespoons mayonnaise	parsley
1 teaspoon french	90 g (3 oz.) cheddar cheese
mustard	1 teaspoon paprika
salt, pepper	

Drain asparagus cuts; reserve ¼ cup liquid. Put rice into large saucepan of boiling, salted water; boil 12 minutes or until rice is tender; drain. Put rice evenly into base of ovenproof dish. Heat butter in pan; add peeled and chopped onion; saute until onion is tender. Add flour; stir until golden brown. Gradually add milk, wine, reserved asparagus liquid and crumbled stock cube; stir over medium heat until sauce boils and thickens. Add mayonnaise and mustard; mix well. Add salt, pepper, drained asparagus cuts, well-drained corn niblets, chopped ham and thyme; stir until all ingredients are well combined; stir until mixture boils; stir in parsley. Spread mixture evenly over rice; sprinkle with grated cheese; dust with paprika. Bake in moderate oven 20 to 25 minutes or until cheese has melted and casserole is heated through.

Serves 6.

Wholemeal Macaroni and Vegetables

375 g (12 oz.) pkt	1 tablespoon oil
wholemeal macaroni	1 onion
¼ cauliflower	1 clove garlic
250 g (8 oz.) broccoli	60 g (2 oz.) mushrooms
250 g (8 oz.) courgettes	1 red pepper
2 carrots	salt, pepper
125 g (4 oz.) butter	¼ cup chopped parsley

Put macaroni in boiling, salted water; cook approx. 20 minutes or until tender; drain. Break cauliflower into flowerets; put into boiling water with chopped broccoli, sliced courgettes and sliced carrots; cook 4 minutes; drain well. Heat butter and oil in pan; add peeled and chopped onion and crushed garlic; saute until onion is tender. Add cauliflower, broccoli, courgettes, carrots, sliced mushrooms and seeded and sliced pepper; mix well; cook 3 minutes. Add well-drained macaroni, salt and pepper; stir until heated through and vegetables are just tender. Stir in parsley.

Serves 8.

Chicken and Macaroni Casserole

1.5 kg (3 lb.) chicken	1 cup milk
250 g (8 oz.) small macaroni	½ cup dry white wine
60 g (2 oz.) butter	2 teaspoons french mustard
2 tablespoons chopped parsley	1 teaspoon worcester-shire sauce
90 g (3 oz.) butter, extra	¼ teaspoon thyme
1 onion	pepper
185 g (6 oz.) mushrooms	½ cup sour cream
1 stick celery	4 shallots or spring onions
2 tablespoons flour	
440 g (14 oz.) can cream of chicken soup	

Topping

2 cups fresh breadcrumbs	60 g (2 oz.) butter
60 g (2 oz.) cheddar cheese	

Boil or steam chicken in usual way; cool. Remove skin. Remove all meat from chicken bones; chop roughly. Drop macaroni into boiling, salted water; cook 10 minutes or until tender; drain. Put into bowl with butter and parsley; mix well. Put into base of ovenproof dish. Heat extra butter in pan; add peeled and chopped onion, sliced mushrooms and sliced celery; saute until onion is tender. Add flour; stir until golden brown. Add undiluted chicken soup; stir until combined. Gradually add milk and white wine; stir until sauce boils and thickens. Add mustard, worcester-shire sauce, thyme and pepper; mix well. Reduce heat; simmer uncovered 5 minutes. Add sour cream, chicken and chopped shallots; cook until sauce is heated through. Spoon mixture over macaroni; sprinkle breadcrumb topping over evenly. Bake in moderate oven 20 to 25 minutes or until golden brown.

Topping: Put breadcrumbs and grated cheese in bowl. Add melted butter; mix well.

Serves 6.

Macaroni Cheese

250 g (8 oz.) small macaroni	salt, pepper
3 rashers bacon	90 g (3 oz.) cheddar cheese
30 g (1 oz.) butter	30 g (1 oz.) butter, extra
⅓ cup flour	½ cup packaged dry breadcrumbs
2¼ cups milk	30 g (1 oz.) cheddar cheese, extra
¼ teaspoon dry mustard	

Put macaroni in boiling, salted water; cook approx. 10 minutes or until tender; drain. Put into ovenproof dish. Put chopped bacon in pan; saute until crisp; remove from pan. Heat butter in pan; add flour; cook 1 minute. Gradually add milk; cook, stirring, until sauce boils and thickens; reduce heat; simmer 3 minutes. Add dry mustard, salt and pepper; mix well. Gradually add grated cheese, stirring until all cheese has melted. Pour cheese sauce over macaroni. Melt extra butter in pan; add breadcrumbs; mix well. Sprinkle over cheese sauce, then sprinkle extra grated cheese over breadcrumbs. Bake in moderate oven 25 minutes or until heated through.

Serves 4.

Creamy Spinach Macaroni

250 g (8 oz.) shell macaroni	1 chicken stock cube
315 g (10 oz.) pkt frozen spinach	⅓ cup sour cream
30 g (1 oz.) butter	¼ cup cream
6 shallots or spring onions	⅓ cup grated parmesan cheese
½ cup water	¼ cup chopped chives
	salt, pepper

Cook macaroni in large quantity of boiling, salted water 10 minutes or until tender; drain. Cook spinach as directed on packet. Heat butter in pan; add chopped shallots, water and crumbled stock cube; bring to boil; reduce heat; simmer 3 minutes. Add sour cream and cream; stir until combined. Add well-drained macaroni and cooked, drained spinach; cook until heated through. Remove from heat; add grated parmesan cheese, chives, salt and pepper; mix well.

Serves 6.

Garlic Mushroom Macaroni

250 g (8 oz.) macaroni	2 eggs
60 g (2 oz.) butter	⅓ cup cream
1 onion	¼ cup grated parmesan cheese
1 clove garlic	
60 g (2 oz.) bacon	2 tablespoons chopped parsley
90 g (3 oz.) mushrooms	salt, pepper
½ cup dry white wine	
1 chicken stock cube	

Cook macaroni in large quantity of boiling, salted water 10 minutes or until tender; drain. Heat butter in pan; add peeled and chopped onion, crushed garlic and chopped bacon; saute until bacon is crisp. Add sliced mushrooms, white wine and crumbled stock cube; bring to boil; reduce heat; simmer 2 minutes. Add macaroni; stir until heated through. Stir in lightly-beaten eggs; cook a further 3 minutes. Add cream and parmesan cheese; stir until mixture just boils. Add parsley, salt and pepper; mix lightly.

Serves 6.

Creamy Spinach with Macaroni — serve as an entree, or as an unusual meal accompaniment.

58 *Rice & Pasta*

Curried Chicken with Sultana Rice

1.5 kg (3 lb.) chicken	2 tablespoons curry
60 g (2 oz.) butter	powder
2 onions	salt, pepper
1 green pepper	1 tablespoon sugar
3 tablespoons flour	

Sultana Rice

1 cup rice	½ cup sultanas
salt, pepper	¼ cup chopped parsley

Put chicken in saucepan; cover with water; bring to boil; reduce heat; simmer covered 1 hour or until chicken is tender. Remove from saucepan; reserve 3 cups of the chicken stock. Discard skin and bones from chicken; chop meat into medium-sized pieces. Heat butter in pan; add peeled and chopped onions and seeded and chopped pepper; saute until onions are tender. Add flour and curry powder; cook 1 minute. Remove from heat; add salt, pepper, sugar and reserved chicken stock; stir until combined. Return to heat; stir until sauce boils and thickens. Add chicken; reduce heat; simmer covered 10 minutes. Serve with Sultana Rice.

Sultana Rice: Put rice and sultanas in large saucepan of boiling, salted water; cook approx. 12 minutes or until tender. Drain well. Add parsley, salt and pepper; mix well.

Serves 4.

Rice and Seafood Slice

1 cup rice	¼ cup sour cream
60 g (2 oz.) butter	2 tablespoons mayonnaise
1 onion	salt, pepper
500 g (1 lb.) fish fillets	¼ cup chopped parsley
1 clove garlic	250 g (8 oz.) prawns
2 tablespoons flour	3 eggs
2 teaspoons curry powder	60 g (2 oz.) cheddar cheese
1 cup milk	

Gherkin Mayonnaise

⅓ cup sour cream	5 gherkins
⅓ cup mayonnaise	2 tablespoons chopped
salt, pepper	parsley

Remove skin and bones from fish. Put rice in large saucepan of boiling, salted water; cook 12 minutes or until rice is tender; drain well. Heat butter in pan; add peeled and finely-chopped onion, finely-sliced fish fillets and crushed garlic; saute until onion is tender. Add flour and curry powder; cook 1 minute. Gradually add milk; stir until sauce boils and thickens. Add sour cream, mayonnaise, salt and pepper; reduce heat; simmer 3 minutes. Add parsley, shelled prawns, drained rice and lightly-beaten eggs; mix well. Put mixture evenly into greased 28 cm x 18 cm (11 in. x 7 in.)

lamington tin. Sprinkle with grated cheese. Bake in moderate oven 25 to 30 minutes or until cheese is golden brown and mixture set. Serve with Gherkin Mayonnaise.

Gherkin Mayonnaise: Put sour cream, mayonnaise, salt and pepper in bowl; mix well. Add finely-chopped gherkins and parsley; stir until combined.

Serves 6.

Curried Seafood Casserole

½ cup rice	1¼ cups milk
500 g (1 lb.) scallops	½ cup cream
500 g (1 lb.) prawns	salt, pepper
60 g (2 oz.) butter	paprika
2 tablespoons flour	2 tablespoons chopped
2 teaspoons curry powder	parsley
½ cup dry white wine	8 shallots or spring onions

Cook rice in boiling, salted water 12 minutes or until tender; drain. Wash and clean scallops; shell and devein prawns. Melt butter in pan; saute scallops 2 minutes. Remove scallops from pan. Add flour and curry powder to butter in pan; stir until smooth; cook 1 minute. Remove from heat; add wine and milk; stir until smooth; return to heat; stir until sauce boils and thickens. Add scallops and prawns; reduce heat; simmer uncovered 5 minutes. Add cream; season with salt and pepper; reheat without boiling.

Spoon rice evenly into base of 4 individual ovenproof dishes; spoon a little of the sauce over the rice; spoon over remaining scallop and prawn mixture. Sprinkle top of each dish with a little paprika; bake in moderate oven 15 to 20 minutes or until lightly browned on top and heated through. Remove from oven; sprinkle with chopped shallots and parsley.

Serves 4.

Creamy Seafood Pasta

250 g (8 oz.) pkt ribbon noodles	salt, pepper
30 g (1 oz.) butter	1 teaspoon french mustard
2 tablespoons chopped parsley	1 teaspoon worcester-shire sauce
¼ cup grated parmesan cheese	1 teaspoon lemon juice
90 g (3 oz.) butter, extra	2 tablespoons mayonnaise
1 onion	⅔ cup cream
1 clove garlic	6 shallots or spring onions
500 g (1 lb.) fish fillets	250 g (8 oz.) prawns
3 tablespoons flour	2 tablespoons chopped parsley, extra
¾ cup dry white wine	60 g (2 oz.) cheddar cheese
1¼ cups water	1 tablespoon grated parmesan cheese, extra
1 chicken stock cube	

Remove skin and bones from fish. Drop noodles into boiling, salted water; cook 10 minutes or until tender; drain. Put noodles into bowl with butter, parsley and parmesan cheese; mix well. Heat extra butter in pan; add peeled and chopped onion, crushed garlic and sliced fish fillets; saute until onions are tender. Add flour; stir until golden brown. Add white wine, water, crumbled stock cube, salt and pepper; stir until sauce boils and thickens; reduce heat; simmer uncovered 3 minutes. Add mustard, worcestershire sauce, lemon juice and mayonnaise; mix well; cook a further 3 minutes. Add cream, chopped shallots, shelled prawns and parsley; stir until sauce is heated through. Arrange half of noodles over base of ovenproof dish; spoon over half the seafood mixture; repeat layers with remaining half of mixture. Sprinkle with grated cheddar cheese and extra parmesan cheese. Bake uncovered in moderate oven 20 minutes or until heated through.

Serves 6.

Cannelloni

1 pkt cannelloni (approx. 15 tubes)
45 g (1½ oz.) butter
2 onions
750 g (1½ lb.) minced steak
3 teaspoons flour
½ cup tomato sauce
1½ cups water
2 beef stock cubes

3 teaspoons soy sauce
3 teaspoons worcestershire sauce
1 teaspoon oregano
1 teaspoon basil
150 g (5 oz.) pkt sliced mozzarella cheese
2 tablespoons grated parmesan cheese

Sauce

30 g (1 oz.) butter
1 onion
2 cloves garlic
470 g (15 oz.) can whole peeled tomatoes
⅓ cup tomato sauce

salt, pepper
1 teaspoon basil
1½ cups water
3 tablespoons chopped parsley

Drop cannelloni gradually into large saucepan of boiling, salted water; cook 15 to 20 minutes or until tender; drain. Rinse under cold water to prevent sticking; drain again. Heat butter in pan; add peeled and chopped onions; saute until onions are tender. Add meat; cook until well browned, mashing meat well; drain off excess fat. Add flour; cook 1 minute. Add tomato sauce, water, crumbled stock cubes, soy sauce, worcestershire sauce, oregano and basil; stir until sauce boils and thickens. Reduce heat; simmer uncovered 20 to 25 minutes or until mixture is thick; remove from heat; allow to cool.

Spoon approx. 3 tablespoons of mixture into each cannelloni tube. Put filled cannelloni into ovenproof dish; spoon sauce over. Arrange mozzarella slices over sauce; sprinkle with parmesan cheese. Bake in moderate oven 25 to 30 minutes or until golden brown and heated through.

Sauce: Heat butter in pan; add peeled and chopped onion and crushed garlic; saute until onion is tender. Add undrained mashed tomatoes, tomato sauce, salt, pepper, basil and water; stir until sauce boils. Reduce heat; simmer uncovered 20 to 25 minutes. Stir in parsley.

Serves 4 to 6.

Tortellini with Cream

500 g (1 lb.) tortellini
90 g (3 oz.) parmesan cheese
185 g (6 oz.) ham
125 g (4 oz.) small mushrooms

salt, pepper
1 cup cream
30 g (1 oz.) grated parmesan cheese, extra

Drop tortellini into large saucepan of boiling, salted water; boil uncovered 10 minutes; drain. Combine tortellini with grated cheese, chopped ham, thinly-sliced mushrooms, salt, pepper and cream; mix well. Put into greased ovenproof dish. Sprinkle with extra grated parmesan cheese. Bake in moderate oven 15 minutes.

Serves 6 to 8.

NOTE: If tortellini are difficult to obtain, any other small pasta can be substituted.

Tomato Anchovy Sauce

2 tablespoons oil
1 onion
2 cloves garlic
45 g (1½ oz.) can anchovies
470 g (15 oz.) can whole peeled tomatoes

1 tablespoon tomato paste
½ teaspoon basil
pepper
30 g (1 oz.) stuffed olives
1 teaspoon capers
grated parmesan cheese

Heat oil in pan; add peeled and chopped onion and crushed garlic; saute until onion is golden brown. Add drained chopped anchovies, undrained mashed tomatoes and tomato paste; stir until sauce boils; reduce heat; simmer uncovered 5 minutes. Add basil, pepper, sliced stuffed olives and chopped capers; stir until combined; simmer covered a further 5 minutes. Serve with grated parmesan cheese. This sauce is sufficient for 250 g (8 oz.) spaghetti.

Serves 4.

Rich Meat Sauce

2 tablespoons oil	1½ cups water
30 g (1 oz.) butter	1 beef stock cube
500 g (1 lb.) minced steak	2 tablespoons tomato
1 large onion	· sauce
250 g (8 oz.) mushrooms	salt, pepper
1 tablespoon flour	½ teaspoon basil
1 cup dry red wine	

Heat oil and butter in large frying pan; add meat; mash well. Stir meat until dark golden brown; pour off any surplus fat; add peeled and chopped onion and sliced mushrooms; saute 5 minutes. Add flour; stir until combined; remove pan from heat. Add wine, water and crumbled stock cube; stir until combined. Return pan to heat; stir until sauce boils and thickens. Add tomato sauce, salt, pepper and basil; mix well. Reduce heat; simmer covered 1 hour or until meat sauce is thick. This sauce is sufficient for 250 g (8 oz.) spaghetti.

Serves 4.

Spinach Pesto Sauce

1 large bunch spinach	2 tablespoons chopped
1 clove garlic	parsley
30 g (1 oz.) pine nuts	30 g (1 oz.) butter
1 teaspoon basil	grated parmesan cheese
salt, pepper	500 g (1 lb.) ribbon noodles
4 tablespoons oil	

Wash spinach; remove white stems; place spinach leaves in saucepan with water that clings to them. Cover; bring to boil. Reduce heat; simmer gently 5 minutes or until spinach is soft. (There should be enough spinach to give about 1½ cups.) Put spinach in electric blender with crushed garlic, pine nuts, basil and parsley. Blend on medium speed until smooth; gradually add oil in a thin stream. Remove from blender; season with salt and pepper.

Cook noodles in large quantity of boiling, salted water 10 minutes or until tender; drain. Return noodles to saucepan; add butter; stir lightly until butter is melted; add sauce; mix well. Serve with grated parmesan cheese.

Serves 6.

Spaghetti Amatriciana

2 tablespoons oil	salt, pepper
125 g (4 oz.) ham	4 tablespoons chopped
2 small onions	parsley
3 ripe tomatoes	

Heat oil in pan; add diced ham and peeled and finely-chopped onions. Saute gently until onions are tender. Add peeled and finely-chopped tomatoes. Bring to boil; reduce heat; simmer uncovered 5 minutes or until sauce is thick. Season with salt and pepper. Add parsley; mix well. This sauce is sufficient for 250 g (8 oz.) spaghetti.

Serves 4.

Summer Spaghetti

2 x 470 g (15 oz.) cans	1 teaspoon basil
whole peeled tomatoes	⅓ cup oil
3 small cloves garlic	500 g (1 lb.) spaghetti
½ cup chopped parsley	grated parmesan cheese
salt, pepper	

Drain tomatoes (liquid can be used for soups or casseroles). Cut each tomato into three pieces. Into each of six bowls, put the sliced tomatoes. Combine oil, crushed garlic, salt, pepper, chopped basil and parsley; mix to combine.

Gradually add spaghetti to large saucepan of boiling, salted water; boil uncovered 15 minutes; drain well. Return spaghetti to pan; add oil mixture; toss well. Spoon spaghetti into bowls; toss with the tomatoes. Offer parmesan cheese separately.

Serves 6.

Seafood Spaghetti

1 tablespoon oil	1 teaspoon basil
1 onion	1 teaspoon sugar
1 clove garlic	250 g (8 oz.) scallops
2 x 470 g (15 oz.) cans	250 g (8 oz.) prawns
whole peeled tomatoes	about 10 canned fresh
¼ cup dry white wine	oysters
1 tablespoon tomato	salt, pepper
paste	¼ cup chopped parsley
	250 g (8 oz.) mussels

Scrub mussels well. Bring 2 cups of water to boil in saucepan; add mussels; cover; boil 5 minutes or until shells open. Remove from pan.

Heat oil in pan; add peeled and chopped onion and crushed garlic; saute until onion is tender. Add undrained mashed tomatoes, white wine and tomato paste; bring to boil; add basil and sugar. Reduce heat; simmer 3 minutes. Add scallops; simmer covered a further 3 minutes. Add shelled prawns, drained oysters, salt and pepper; simmer a further 3 minutes. Stir in parsley and mussels. This sauce is sufficient for 250 g (8 oz.) to 375 g (12 oz.) spaghetti.

Serves 4 to 6.

Aubergine Spaghetti – aubergine, anchovies, tomatoes and other good things make this superb tasting spaghetti sauce.

Aubergine Spaghetti

1 aubergine	½ cup water
¼ cup oil	2 tablespoons tomato paste
2 cloves garlic	½ teaspoon basil
1 onion	pepper
1 red pepper	60 g (2 oz.) black olives
45 g (1½ oz.) can anchovies	1 teaspoon capers
	2 tablespoons chopped parsley
470 g (15 oz.) can whole peeled tomatoes	grated parmesan cheese

Cut unpeeled aubergine into 1 cm (½ in.) cubes; sprinkle with salt; leave 30 minutes. Rinse well under cold running water; pat dry. Heat oil in pan; add crushed garlic, peeled and chopped onion, seeded and sliced pepper and aubergine; saute until onion is tender. Add drained chopped anchovies, undrained mashed tomatoes, water, tomato paste, basil, pepper and chopped capers. Stir until combined; bring to boil; reduce heat; simmer covered 10 minutes. Stir in parsley and olives. Serve with grated parmesan cheese. This sauce is sufficient for 250 g (8 oz.) to 375 g (12 oz.) spaghetti.

Serves 4 to 6.

Spaghetti Vongole

2 tablespoons oil	4 ripe tomatoes
1 small clove garlic	2 tablespoons chopped parsley
315 g (10 oz.) can baby clams	salt, pepper
¼ teaspoon oregano	
½ teaspoon basil	

Heat oil and crushed garlic in pan; add drained clams; saute 1 minute. Add oregano and chopped basil; stir until combined. Add peeled, chopped tomatoes; bring to boil; reduce heat; simmer uncovered 15 minutes or until sauce is thick. Add parsley; season with salt and pepper. This sauce is sufficient for 250 g (8 oz.) spaghetti.

Serves 4.

Fruits in Season

Eat fruits in season – they're tops in quality then, and reasonably priced. Here we give you information on each fruit, and on seasonal times.

Apples

Apples of some sort are available all year round; over twenty varieties of dessert apple appear in the shops and these are some of the most popular:

Granny Smith: Available March to August. The crisp, sharp-flavoured flesh and juicy texture make this bright green skinless apple very refreshing.

Cox's Orange Pippin: Available September to May. Cox's have a golden-yellow skin streaked with orange and red; the flesh is crunchy and juicy with a delicate smell.

Golden Delicious: Available September to April. They ripen from a green colour to a light yellow, but are crispest before they get too ripe.

Russets, Laxton's Superb, Crispins, Jonathan, Red Delicious, Dunn's Seedling, Lord Lambourne, Worcester Pearmain, and many others supply a large variety in the shops. Bramley's and Newton's are among the best for cooking due to their sharp taste and fluffy texture when cooked.

Apricots

Available May to August and December to February. A small stone fruit of plum size, quite like a peach with a downy skin. Delicious fresh or cooked, apricots are a good accompaniment to meat.

Avocados

Available all the year round, from Israel or South Africa. Pear-shaped with a rough green skin, avocados are ripe when the flesh is soft and oily and pale yellow green. The large stone should come away from the flesh easily. If preparing in advance, brush cut surfaces with lemon juice to prevent discolouring.

Bananas

Available all the year round, always imported. The best fruit has a firm yellow skin with brown streaks. Slightly under-ripe fruit are easier to cook with.

Bilberries

Available July to August, but are in short supply. These small dull blue berries are not generally eaten raw, but have a subtle and delicious taste when cooked or in jam.

Blackberries

Available July to October. Often found growing wild, but are also cultivated commercially. The soft black fruit deteriorates quickly so use them on the day of purchase. Often stewed with apples, blackberries are delicious in pies and jams.

Blackcurrants

Available July to August. The round black berries have toughish skins and a lot of pips. Being rich in pectine, they are excellent in jams, jellies and fruit syrups, and the sharp flavour makes them ideal for hot desserts and pies.

Cherries

Available June to August. White and red cherries start the season, early imported fruit is found in the shops from April. The small stone fruit varies in sweetness and size according to type. Bitter Morello cherries are suitable for jam, while the big black cherries with deep red flesh are eaten as a dessert fruit or cooked.

Crab apples

Available September to October, crab apples are too sour to eat raw, but the small apple-like fruit is used in jams and pickles. When used they are usually home-grown, they are not often seen in shops.

Cumquats

Available all the year round, but are in short supply. These Japanese fruit are small, round or oval in shape with a light or dark orange skin. The fruit is eaten whole with the skin and the sharp, slightly bitter taste makes it ideal for jams and jellies.

Figs

Available August to December. Fresh figs are small, pear-shaped fruits with a bloom on the dull purple skin. The pulp inside is very sweet, and of a rich red colour when ripe. The pulp is full of seeds which are eaten with the fruit.

Gooseberries

Cape gooseberries: Available imported all the year. The fruit of the Japanese Lantern (Physalis), Cape gooseberries are small, round and golden in colour, encased in a papery yellow husk. They can be eaten as a dessert fruit, or served stewed in syrup or made into jams or jellies.

Chinese gooseberries: Available July to February. Sometimes called Kiwi fruit, they have brownish, bristly skins and sweet, juicy green flesh, speckled with black seeds.

Gooseberries: Available end April to September. The berries are slightly hairy, green to yellow in colour with a sharp tasting pulp full of seeds. Dessert varieties, such as Levellers, are larger, juicier and sweeter than the culinary gooseberry, whose sharp taste and harder texture makes them suitable for stewing, pie fillings and jam making.

Grapefruit

Imported fruit is available all the year round. It is the largest citrus fruit sold in this country, and is round and squat in shape. A tough yellow skin and spongy pith contains juicy flesh of varying sweetness.

Grapes

Imported fruit is available all the year. Small, sharp-tasting seedless grapes are in season in summer, when all grapes are at their cheapest and British fruit is ripe. All varieties, blue-black, red, amber and green should have a bloom on the skin.

Lemons

Available all the year round. The waxy skinned, smooth fruit is usually juicier than the knobbly, thick-skinned types. Although not eaten as a fruit, lemon rind and juice are used for flavour in both sweet and savoury dishes.

Limes

Available all the year round, but in short supply. Smaller than lemons, but with a similar sharp taste, limes are not eaten on their own, but give a fresh tang to drinks, desserts and curry dishes.

Loganberries

Available July to late August. They are the same shape as blackberries, growing up to 3·5 cm (1½ in.) in length, and are a darker red than raspberries. The flavour is quite sharp, so as well as being eaten fresh, loganberries make excellent pie fillings and jams.

Loquats

Available all the year round, but are in short supply. Although they are known as Japanese medlars, they are usually imported from Israel. A stone fruit similar to plums in size and shape, with yellow to reddish-brown skins, creamy coloured flesh and a tart flavour.

Lychees

Available December to February. The scaly skin on the cherry sized fruit turns from pink to brown, and they are best eaten when red in colour. The white flesh has a sweet taste and a slippery texture.

Mandarins

Available October to March. Imported from Spain, Italy and Morocco, the small squat oranges have loose skin and a large number of pips. Popular as a Christmas dessert fruit.

Mangoes

Available January to September. Mangoes can be almost any size, from that of a large peach to 1·5 kg (3 lb.) in weight. The skin is tough and leathery and varies in colour from greeny yellow to reddish orange. When ripe the flesh is a rich orange with a sweet spicy taste. Generally served as dessert or made into chutney.

Melons

Watermelon: Available May to September. The largest of the melon family, they have a dark green skin, pinkish-red watery flesh with a lot of black seeds.
Honeydew: Available all the year round. In shape very like a rugby ball, they vary in colour from whitish yellow to green, with a ridged skin. When ripe the greenish flesh turns a pinkish orange around the central seed-filled cavity.
Ogen: Available all the year. Ogen melons are the size of large grapefruit, the yellowy orange skin has longitudinal green stripes. The pale, yellow-green flesh is sweet and juicy.
Charantais: Available all the year. Smaller in size than the Ogen, with a rough yellow-green skin with slight downward indentations. The flesh is a rich orange with a sweet taste and delicate scent.
Canteloup: Available all the year. A large and slightly flattened melon with a rough yellow-green skin and juicy, highly scented orange flesh.

Mulberries

Available in August, but not often sold in shops as they bruise so easily. The dark purplish fruit is very soft and juicy, and quite like loganberries in appearance. As they are so hard to keep and squash so easily, they are usually home grown and are delicious made into jams or wine.

Nectarines

Available July to February, either imported or home grown. A member of the peach family, nectarines have a shinier skin than peaches but a similar sweet juicy flesh.

They are usually expensive to buy, and are best eaten on the day of purchase.

Oranges

Available all the year. Sevilles, the small bitter oranges used for marmalade, are only in season in January and February. Many other varieties of dessert orange are in season during the rest of the year. Valencia, Jaffa, Navel, blood and Malta oranges are all suitable for eating as fresh fruit as well as for cooking with the rind and juice.

Passionfruit

Available most of the year, but are in short supply. They are about the size of a large plum, but have a dull purple, leathery skin containing the delicately scented pulp, which is sweet and orange in colour, pitted with small black seeds, which are eaten with the rest of the pulp. If fresh passionfruit are not available, the small cans of pulp are just as good.

Pawpaws

Imported fruit is available from June to December. Green when unripe, these large pear-shaped fruit ripen to orange or yellow. The flesh is sweet and juicy with a central cavity full of small dark seeds.

Peaches

Imported or home-grown fruit available March to December. The free-stone peaches (with loose stones) have a better flavour, but cling peaches are more common in the shops. The thin velvety skin is usually yellow turning to deep red when ripe.

Pears

Available all the year, either home grown or imported. Cooking pears are in season from October to December. The colour varies from yellow-green to pinky gold. Some of the most popular dessert pears are Commice, Conference and William's; all should be handled with care as they bruise easily.

Persimmons

Available October to January. Also known as date plums. Like a large tomato in appearance, with a tough reddish skin. The sweet, juicy flesh is orange in colour and is very astringent if not ripe.

Pineapples

Available all the year. The fruit, all imported, should be bought when the top leaves are fresh and stiff. The flesh is yellow and the central core is slightly woody. Pineapple is delicious as a dessert, often served with pork and bacon dishes.

Plums

Available from January to March. Home-grown plums are in season around August and September. The colour varies from the bright green of greengages, to the yellow of Pershores, the red of Victorias and the blue-black of damsons and Czars. The juicy flesh is sweet only when ripe.

Pomegranates

Available September to January. The skin of this orange-sized fruit is thin and tough and orangey yellow to reddish in colour. The seeds and the red pulp which surrounds each one are the edible parts, delicious scooped out into fruit salads.

Quinces

Available October to November, but in short supply. The skin is tough and yellow and the flesh is firm and sharp-tasting. Not eaten fresh, quinces are used to make jam or jelly and to add flavour to pies.

Raspberries

Available July to August. There are two crops, one in summer and one in autumn. Like a blackberry in appearance, they are red and juicy, delicious eaten fresh or cooked in summer pudding or tarts.

Strawberries

Available May to July, and again in early autumn. Several varieties are grown, differing in size, taste and texture, Royal Sovereign are the sweetest and most popular along with Talisman, which are also sweet.

Redcurrants

Available July to August. The berries are small and bright red with large seeds and a very tart flavour. As they are not always sweet enough to eat fresh, they are often combined with other soft fruits for cooking, and being high in pectin, they are excellent for jams and jellies.

Rhubarb

Available December to June. The first rhubarb of the season is forced and is milder in flavour and less woody than the maincrop which ends the season. Never eaten raw, rhubarb makes good pie fillings, its tart flavour combining well with other fruit in compotes. Eat only the stems as the leaves are poisonous.

Ugli fruit

Available October to February, but in short supply. Also called a tangelo, it is a cross between a tangerine and a grapefruit. The loose yellow skin is coarse and the almost pipless flesh is sweeter than the ordinary grapefruit.

Freezing Vegetables & Fruit

It is preferable for vegetables to be blanched before freezing. Blanching is a heat treatment. It inactivates enzymes, checks respiration and destroys many of the micro-organisms. It is done by the immersing of food in boiling water or steam.

In a report on Home Frozen Foods it is recommended that:

'During storage before freezing and in some preparative steps, significant losses can occur, particularly of the water-soluble vitamin B group and vitamin C. In addition to being water-soluble, vitamin C is readily destroyed by heat or under alkaline or neutral conditions. Therefore, while it is quite stable in citrus juices and concentrates, it is not stable during blanching of vegetables — and blanching instructions should be strictly followed, using the minimum of water to do the job. The volume of water used for blanching is a more important factor in determining vitamin loss than the time or the temperature of heating.'

Choose very fresh vegetables: remove any blemished sections. Prepare as for normal cooking — pod peas, slice beans, scrape carrots, etc. Wash under cold, running water, then blanch as directed in the chart. Count blanching time from the moment vegetables are added to the water.

Method for Blanching Vegetables

In Boiling Water

Use a large saucepan or similar container; just over half fill the pan; bring the water to a vigorous boil; place prepared vegetables loosely in a container such as a wire basket, colander or cheesecloth bag; immerse vegetables completely in boiling water; bring water to the boil again as quickly as possible, increasing heat if necessary.

Time: start to time blanching process from the moment vegetables are added; for blanching times, see table on pages 66 and 67.

When blanching time has been reached, remove vegetables from pan of boiling water; cool vegetables rapidly in iced water, or under running water.

In Steam

Use a large saucepan or similar container with approx. 5 cm (2 in.) water in bottom of pan; bring water to a vigorous boil; place prepared vegetables loosely in a container such as a wire basket, colander or cheesecloth bag; place container of vegetables in pan, so that it is in steam, but not in water; cover pan with lid. Bring water to the boil again as quickly as possible, increasing heat if necessary.

Time: start to time blanching process from the moment vegetables are added; for blanching times, see table on pages 66 and 67.

When blanching time has been reached, remove vegetables from steam; cool vegetables rapidly in iced water, or under running water.

Vegetable Packaging for Freezing

There are two types of vegetable packs, the solid or loose.

Solid Pack: After blanching and draining, pack vegetables in container, leaving some space at top; seal; freeze.

Loose Pack: Useful when only part of pack will be used at one time. After blanching and draining, spread vegetables on trays; freeze. Scrape off trays, pack into containers. When needed, a portion of pack can be removed.

Cooking Frozen Vegetables

Remember the blanching process has already partially cooked vegetables. They do not need to be thawed before cooking. The only exception is corn-on-the-cob: thaw before cooking, otherwise, although the young kernels may be tender, the thick inside core could still be cold.

Fruits

Fruit should be just ripe, firm, and perfectly fresh. Pick carefully and discard any blemished or bruised pieces. Wash fruit; drain well. Fruits such as apples, apricots, peaches can be cut in halves or sliced.

There are four ways to pack fruit for the freezer (see list opposite). Fruits that discolour easily and tend to turn brown (apples, peaches etc.) should have vitamin C added in the form of lemon juice or ascorbic acid before packaging. Use ¼ teaspoon powdered ascorbic acid or 3 tablespoons lemon juice combined with ½ cup cold water for every 1 litre (2 pints) fruit.

Information in this chapter reproduced from *Home Freezing of Foods* by N.S.W. Dept. of Agriculture.

Dry Pack: Wash fruit, prepare, pack in freezer container. Seal and freeze. Do not use this method for any fruit that discolours. Fruits packed in this way are good for pies, also for use in any recipe specifying fresh fruit or berries.

Dry Sugar Pack: Slice fruit directly into container, filling to quarter-full; sprinkle with sugar. Repeat until container is full. Alternatively, the fruit can be sliced into large bowl, sugar added and stirred gently with spoon. Quantity of sugar used will vary, depending on type of fruit and individual tastes. Do not use this method for any fruit that discolours.

Syrup Pack: A syrup pack helps preserve colour of fruit. According to type of fruit, use light, medium or heavy syrup (see below). Prepare fruit, put in containers, pour chilled syrup over. Allow 1 cm (½ in.) for expansion between top of fruit and lid; fruit must be completely covered by syrup.

Light Syrup: Dissolve 1 cup sugar in 3 cups water. Use for pears, melons.

Medium Syrup: Dissolve 1 cup sugar in 2 cups water. Use for apricots, berries, cherries, peaches, pineapple, mangoes, strawberries and rhubarb.

Heavy Syrup: Dissolve 1 cup sugar in 1 cup water. Use for apricots, pineapple, cherries, plums, rhubarb. Some of the fruits can be frozen in medium or heavy syrup. It is a matter of personal taste for sweetness. To make the syrup, stir sugar and water over low heat until sugar is dissolved; do not boil. Allow to cool, then refrigerate before using. Syrup can be made the day before and refrigerated.

Special Fruits

Citrus Fruits

Grapefruit: Peel, divide into segments without pith or skin. Toss in sugar, allowing 1 tablespoon sugar to 2 grapefruit. Pack in plastic containers or bags, allowing 2.5 cm (1 in.) headspace for expansion. Seal, label. Keeping time: 6 months.

Oranges: As for grapefruit, allowing 1 tablespoon sugar to 3 oranges. Keeping time: 6 months.

Citrus Juices

Refrigerate fruit for several hours before squeezing out the juice, so that oil from the skins does not come out into the juice when squeezed. Squeeze juice from halved fruit; press lightly — also to ensure oil does not get into juice and retard freezing. Remove any seeds. The juice can be strained or left with some of the pulp still in it. Pour into plastic containers, leaving about 2.5 cm (1 in.) space at top of container; freeze. Alternatively, the juice can be poured into

Fruits in season make a pretty decoration when frosted, as shown. Brush them with lightly-beaten egg white, roll in castor sugar, then let stand until dry. Violets, for decoration, can also be frosted in this way.

ice-cube trays and frozen, then the cubes removed from trays and stored in freezer in plastic bags.

Grated lemon or orange rind can be wrapped in plastic and stored in freezer for use in cooking.

Keeping time: 6 months.

Soft Fruits (strawberries, mulberries, etc.)

Toss in sugar; allow ½ cup castor sugar per 500 g (1 lb.) fruit. Pack in plastic containers or bags; allow 2.5 cm (1 in.) headspace for expansion. Strawberries can also be frozen in ice-cube trays; when frozen, they can be removed from the trays and put in plastic containers or bags, then placed again in the freezer. This way strawberries keep their shape, although generally they can still only be used in cooking.

Passionfruit Pulp

Remove pulp from passionfruit; put into ice-cube trays and freeze as for citrus juices.

Apples

Peel, slice, blanch 2 to 3 minutes in boiling, salted water. Drain, plunge into ice-cold water, drain, pack firmly in containers. If desired, use ½ cup sugar to each 500 g (1 lb.) fruit; sprinkle sugar between layers.

Or alternatively, freeze in puree form, using minimum quantity of water in cooking; sweeten as desired. Allow headspace for packing.

Vegetable Blanching

Vegetable	Preparation	Water-blanch time	Steam-blanch time
Asparagus	Use only the top 15 cm to 20 cm (6 in. to 8 in.) of stem, which must be tender. Cut to 5 cm (2 in.) lengths, or to length to suit the container. Wash in cold water. Blanching time depends on thickness of stalk.	3 to 4 min.	4 to 6 min.
Aubergine	Peel, and slice into 8 mm (⅓ in.) slices, or dice in 8 mm (⅓ in.) cubes. Place slices or dice in a salt solution — 1 tablespoon salt to 1 litre (4 cups) cold water — to prevent discoloration before blanching. After blanching, and before chilling, dip eggplant into citric acid solution. Use ½ cup lemon juice, or 1 tablespoon citric acid to 1425 ml (2½ pints) cold water.	4 min.	5 min.
Beans, runner	Select when young and tender; stringless varieties are best. Remove tips and ends and cut into 2.5 cm (1 in.) lengths or slices.	*Whole:* 2 to 3 min. *Cut:* 2 min. *Slices:* 1 min.	3 to 4 min. 3 min. 2 min.
Beans, broad	Shell and wash beans.	1 min.	1¾ min.
Beetroot	Cut off tops. Wash well and scrub in cold water. Remove skins after blanching.	*Small, 2.5 to 3.5 cm (1 to 1½ in.) diam.:* 2½ min. *Large:* 4 min.	*Small:* 3½ min. Cook till tender.
Broccoli	Wash thoroughly in cold, running water. Remove coarse leaves. Cut into pieces no longer than 15 cm (6 in.) and no thicker than 2.5 cm (1 in.). Sort into small, medium and large pieces.	*Small:* 3 min. *Medium:* 4 min. *Large:* 5 min.	4 min. 5 min. 6 min.
Brussel sprouts	Cut sprouts from main stem. Trim off coarse leaves and discard those with insect blemishes. Wash thoroughly in cold, running water. Sort into small and medium sizes. Split stems into four sections.	*Small:* 3 min. *Medium:* 4 min. *Large:* 5 min.	4 min. 5 min. 6 min.
Cabbage and chinese cabbage (use only in cooked dishes)	Remove coarse leaves and part of stalk; wash if necessary. Shred, or cut into wedges, or separate leaves.	*Shredded:* 1½ min. *Wedges:* 3½ min.	*Shredded:* 2 min. *Wedges:* 5 min.
Carrots	Choose young or medium sized carrots. Remove tips, wash in cold, running water, and scrape. Use small young carrots whole; cut larger ones into slices or sticks, dice, or quarter lengthwise.	*Whole:* 4½ min. *Diced:* 1 min. *Small:* 3 min.	 1½ min. 3½ min.
Cauliflower	Choose firm, compact, creamy heads; trim, break or cut into small pieces 2.5 cm to 5 cm (1 in. to 2 in.) across. Wash in cold water.	*Small pieces:* 3 min. *Medium pieces:* 4 min.	*Small:* 4 min. *Medium:* 5 min.
Celery (only suitable for use in cooked dishes)	Trim stalks as for table use; wash thoroughly in cold, running water. After blanching, cool by placing pan of celery in bowl of water.	Blanch until tender.	Blanch until tender.
Corn	Corn should be tender and fresh. Remove husk and sort into sizes. *Kernel corn:* remove corn from cob after blanching.	*Small:* 6 min. *Medium:* 8 min. *Large:* 10 min.	7 min. 9 min. 11 min.

Vegetable Blanching

Vegetable	Preparation	Water-blanch time	Steam-blanch time
Marrow — very small — large	Wash and cut into 1 cm (½ in.) slices. Peel, remove seeds; after cooking, mash-pack.	3 min. 3 min.	4 min. Cook till soft.
Mushrooms	Use fresh mushrooms, free from decay and bruising. Cut off base of stem and wash in cold, running water. Sort into sizes, small, medium and large. Steam-blanching is preferable.	*Small:* 1½ min. *Medium:* 3 min. *Large:* 4½ min.	3 min. 4 min. 5 min.
Onions	Sliced, chopped or rings.	1½ min.	3 min.
Parsnips	Cut off tips, wash thoroughly in cold, running water, peel, then dice into 1 cm (½ in.) cubes or cut slices about 1.5 cm (¾ in.) thick. Steam-blanching is preferable.	*Cubes:* 1 min. *Slices:* 2 min.	1½ min. 3 min.
Peas	Shell peas, and discard those withered, or starchy and yellowed. Wash and use only young peas.	1 min.	2 min.
Peppers	Wash peppers and remove stem and seeds. Cut into halves and/or slice or dice. Blanching is optional. Omit it if the frozen peppers are needed for raw use; if not, blanch halves.	*Sliced or diced:* 2 min. *Halves:* 3 min.	3 min. 4 min.
Potatoes	Cut up as chips. Add the juice of half a lemon for every 1 litre (4 cups) blanching water. This gives a firmer, crisper result to the cooked product.	2 min.	3½ min.
Pumpkin	Select well-coloured, fine-textured pumpkin. Peel and cook until soft; steam, boil or bake. Mash pumpkin and pack cool pulp in containers.	No blanching required.	3½ min.
Spinach	Wash thoroughly in cold, running water and remove thick stems.	2 min.	3½ min.
Sweet potatoes	Choose smooth, firm roots. Wash, cook until soft, cool, and peel; mash to a fine pulp. Add 2 tablespoons lemon or orange juice to each 1 litre (4 cups) of mashed pulp, and mix well.		
Tomato — Puree	Do not freeze whole. Choose full, ripe fruit. Remove stem ends, dip in boiling water, peel and quarter, and remove pithy section at blossom end. Place in pan and cook gently until tender. Place pan of tomatoes in cold water to cool, then pack.		1 min.
— Juice	Use firm, ripe, mature fruit; wash and trim. Cut into quarters and eights. Simmer till just tender, press through a sieve, or use a blender. Season, if preferred, with 1 tablespoon salt to each 1 litre (4 cups) of juice. Pack into containers.		
Turnips, white	Use small or medium tender turnips with mild flavour. Prepare in same way as carrots.	1 min.	1½ min.

Vegetables

There are new ways here to cook all the popular vegetables, including many vegetable casseroles — which are great do-ahead dishes for parties. Many of the recipes are suitable for vegetarian meals.

Italian Aubergine Casserole

3 tablespoons oil
30 g (1 oz.) butter
500 g (1 lb.) courgettes
2 onions
1 clove garlic
1 green pepper
1 red pepper
125 g (4 oz.) mushrooms
470 g (15 oz.) can whole
　peeled tomatoes
½ teaspoon oregano
½ teaspoon mixed herbs
⅔ cup water
2 tablespoons tomato
　paste
300 g (10 oz.) can borlotti
　beans
300 g (10 oz.) can red
　kidney beans
salt, pepper
2 tablespoons chopped
　parsley
oil for shallow-frying
1 aubergine
125 g (4 oz.) mozzarella
　cheese
1 teaspoon paprika

Cut aubergine into 1 cm (½ in.) rounds; sprinkle each side with salt; stand 30 minutes; rinse.

Heat oil and butter in pan; add sliced courgettes, peeled and chopped onions and crushed garlic; saute 7 minutes or until courgettes are just tender. Add seeded and sliced peppers and sliced mushrooms; cook stirring over low heat until peppers are tender. Add undrained mashed tomatoes, oregano, mixed herbs, water and tomato paste; stir until combined; bring to boil; simmer uncovered 3 minutes. Add rinsed and well-drained borlotti and red kidney beans, salt, pepper and parsley; cook, stirring, uncovered a further 3 minutes or until beans are heated through. Put into large ovenproof dish.

Heat oil in pan; shallow-fry rinsed and dried aubergine on each side for 1 minute or until golden brown; drain. Overlap aubergine slices on vegetables; cover aubergine with thin slices of mozzarella cheese; sprinkle with paprika. Bake in moderate oven 30 minutes or until golden brown.

Serves 6 to 8.

Italian Aubergine Casserole — colourful vegetables team with crunchy beans in a delicious, herb-flavoured sauce.

Asparagus with Lemon

340 g (11 oz.) can asparagus spears	4 shallots or spring onions
¼ cup oil	pinch thyme
1 tablespoon lemon juice	1 tablespoon chopped parsley
2 gherkins	salt, pepper
1 teaspoon chopped capers	

Drain asparagus; reserve 1 tablespoon of liquid. Put asparagus in ovenproof dish; cover; bake in moderate oven 15 minutes or until heated through. Put oil, lemon juice, reserved asparagus liquid, chopped gherkins, capers, chopped shallots, thyme, parsley, salt and pepper in saucepan; bring to boil. Reduce heat; simmer uncovered 3 minutes. Pour sauce over hot asparagus.

Serves 4.

Beans with Tomatoes

1 tablespoon oil	½ teaspoon worcester-shire sauce
1 clove garlic	
1 onion	¼ teaspoon basil
1 teaspoon curry powder	salt, pepper
470 g (15 oz.) can tomatoes	500 g (1 lb.) pkt frozen beans
¼ cup water	60 g (2 oz.) cheddar cheese
1 tablespoon tomato paste	

Heat oil in pan; add crushed garlic, peeled and chopped onion and curry powder; saute until onion is golden. Add undrained mashed tomatoes, water, tomato paste, worcestershire sauce, basil, salt and pepper; stir until combined; bring to boil. Reduce heat; simmer uncovered 5 minutes.

Put beans in boiling salted water; boil 2 minutes; drain well. Add beans to tomato mixture; mix well. Put in ovenproof dish; sprinkle with grated cheddar cheese. Bake uncovered in moderate oven 10 minutes or until cheese has melted.

Serves 6.

Green Beans Italian

500 g (1 lb.) beans	¼ cup oil
2 medium onions	2 cloves garlic

Topping

1 cup fresh breadcrumbs	2 tablespoons grated parmesan cheese
30 g (1 oz.) butter	

Top, tail and string beans. Peel and slice onions. Put beans and onions into saucepan. Add enough boiling water to cover beans. Bring to boil again; reduce heat; simmer uncovered 5 minutes; drain.

Heat oil in frying pan; add crushed garlic; saute 1 minute. Add beans and onions; saute 2 minutes.

Put on serving plate; sprinkle with topping.

Topping: Melt butter in pan; add breadcrumbs; stir until golden brown. Remove from pan; allow to cool, then add parmesan cheese; stir until combined.

Serves 4.

Broccoli with Lemon

375 g (12 oz.) pkt frozen broccoli	1 tablespoon lemon juice
	¼ teaspoon basil
30 g (1 oz.) butter	½ teaspoon sugar
1 clove garlic	½ teaspoon soy sauce
1 chicken stock cube	salt, pepper
1 teaspoon flour	4 shallots or spring onions
¼ cup water	

Cook broccoli according to directions on packet. While broccoli is cooking, prepare sauce. Heat butter in saucepan; add crushed garlic and crumbled stock cube; cook 1 minute. Add flour; stir until golden brown. Gradually add water and lemon juice; stir until sauce boils and thickens. Add basil, sugar, soy sauce, salt and pepper; cook 1 minute. Add chopped shallots; cook a further 1 minute. Drain broccoli; spoon sauce over.

Serves 4.

Hot Broccoli-Macaroni Salad

250 g (8 oz.) large shell macaroni	250 g (8 oz.) mushrooms
	¼ cup oil
1 kg (2 lb.) fresh broccoli	2 teaspoons cornflour
1 large onion	¾ cup water
2 cloves garlic	1 chicken stock cube
1 red pepper	2 teaspoons soy sauce

Cook macaroni in boiling, salted water until tender, about 10 minutes; drain. Cut stalks off broccoli. Fill large saucepan with water; add 1 teaspoon salt; bring to boil. Add broccoli; return to boil; boil 2 minutes. Drain; rinse under cold water; drain again.

Heat oil in pan; saute peeled and sliced onion until transparent. Add crushed garlic, sliced mushrooms, chopped pepper; saute 2 minutes. Add broccoli; saute a further 2 minutes.

Combine cornflour, water, crumbled stock cube and soy sauce. Pour over vegetables in pan; combine thoroughly; stir until sauce comes to the boil. Reduce heat; add macaroni; simmer 1 minute longer.

Serves 6.

NOTE: When fresh broccoli is out of season, quick-frozen broccoli can be substituted. Let it thaw before dropping it into the boiling water.

Sherried Brussel Sprouts

500 g (1 lb.) brussel sprouts	¼ cup sour cream
30 g (1 oz.) butter	¼ cup dry sherry
2 rashers bacon	¼ teaspoon cinnamon
2 tablespoons flour	1 chicken stock cube
1 cup water	salt, pepper
¼ cup milk	1 tablespoon chopped parsley

Put brussel sprouts in boiling salted water; cook 10 to 15 minutes or until tender; drain; cool. Slice brussel sprouts crossways.

Heat butter in pan; add chopped bacon; saute until crisp; remove from pan. Add flour; stir until golden brown. Gradually add water, milk and sherry; stir until sauce boils and thickens. Add sour cream, cinnamon, crumbled stock cube, salt and pepper; stir until sauce boils; reduce heat; simmer a further 1 minute. Add sliced brussel sprouts; stir until heated through. Put into serving dish; sprinkle with bacon and parsley.

Serves 4.

Bacon-Cabbage

60 g (2 oz.) butter	salt, pepper
2 rashers bacon	1 teaspoon brown sugar
¼ cup white vinegar	¼ cabbage
¼ cup water	2 tablespoons chopped parsley
2 chicken stock cubes	

Heat butter in large pan; add chopped bacon; saute gently until bacon is crisp; remove bacon from pan. To fat in pan, add vinegar, water, crumbled stock cubes, salt, pepper and brown sugar; bring to boil. Boil uncovered until liquid is reduced by half.

Add shredded cabbage and bacon; toss well. Cover pan; reduce heat; simmer 5 minutes or until cabbage is just crisp. Remove lid; increase heat; stir until nearly all liquid has evaporated. Stir in parsley.

Serves 4.

Fried Aubergine

2 small aubergines	4 shallots or spring onions
salt	¼ cup chopped chives
2 eggs	¼ cup chopped parsley
2 tablespoons milk	salt, pepper
2 cloves garlic	¼ teaspoon mixed herbs
2½ cups fresh bread- crumbs (approx. ½ loaf)	oil for frying

Cut unpeeled aubergines into 1 cm (½ in.) rounds; sprinkle both sides with salt; leave to stand 30 minutes. Rinse well under cold running water; drain; dry with absorbent paper.

Combine lightly beaten eggs, milk and crushed garlic. Put breadcrumbs, chopped shallots, chives, parsley, salt, pepper and mixed herbs in bowl; mix well. Dip aubergine slices into egg mixture, then coat with breadcrumbs. Press breadcrumbs on firmly. Refrigerate 1 hour.

Shallow-fry aubergine slices on both sides until golden brown; drain.

Serves 4 to 6.

Brandied Cream Mushrooms

15 g (½ oz.) butter	1 tablespoon port
125 g (4 oz.) bacon	2 tablespoons brandy
30 g (1 oz.) butter, extra	2 tablespoons cream
250 g (8 oz.) small mushrooms	1 tablespoon chopped parsley
salt, pepper	

Heat butter in pan; add chopped bacon; cook until crisp; remove from pan. Heat extra butter in pan; add mushrooms, salt and pepper; cook 2 minutes or until mushrooms are just tender. Add port and brandy; cook over low heat a further 1 minute. Add cream and bacon; stir until sauce is heated through; stir in chopped parsley.

Serves 4.

Cauliflower Casserole

½ medium cauliflower	½ teaspoon prepared mustard
30 g (1 oz.) butter	½ cup milk
1 onion	¼ cup dry white wine
1 clove garlic	salt, pepper
430 g (14 oz.) can cream of mushroom soup	4 shallots or spring onions
2 tablespoons mayonnaise	

Topping

30 g (1 oz.) butter	1 cup fresh breadcrumbs

Separate cauliflower into flowerets; cook in lightly salted water until tender but still firm; drain.

Melt butter in pan; add peeled and chopped onion and crushed garlic; saute until onion is tender. Add undiluted mushroom soup, mayonnaise and mustard; stir until combined. Add milk, white wine, salt and pepper; stir over medium heat until sauce boils. Add chopped shallots; reduce heat; simmer a further 2 minutes.

Pour sauce over cauliflower; sprinkle on topping. Bake uncovered in moderate oven 15 minutes or until golden brown.

Topping: Melt butter in pan; add breadcrumbs; mix well.

Serves 6.

Cauliflower Cheese Paprika — a simple and deliciously different way of preparing a favourite vegetable.

Cauliflower Cheese Paprika

1 small cauliflower (or quick-frozen cauliflower)	½ cup mayonnaise
60 g (2 oz.) butter	salt, pepper
4 shallots or spring onions	60 g (2 oz.) cheddar cheese
	paprika

Separate cauliflower into flowerets; cook in lightly salted water until tender but still firm; drain. Melt butter; saute the chopped shallots for a few moments. Spread shallots and butter over base of ovenproof dish. Cover with the cauliflower; sprinkle lightly with salt and pepper. Spread mayonnaise over cauliflower; sprinkle the coarsely grated cheese on top, then sprinkle with paprika. Bake in moderate oven approx. 15 minutes.

Serves 4

Cauliflower with Curry Mayonnaise

½ cauliflower	2 tablespoons mayonnaise
2 chicken stock cubes	salt, pepper
30 g (1 oz.) butter	60 g (2 oz.) cheddar cheese
2 teaspoons flour	1 egg
2 teaspoons curry powder	¼ cup cream
¾ cup milk	4 shallots or spring onions
1 teaspoon lemon juice	

Put cauliflower and crumbled stock cubes in boiling salted water; cook 15 minutes or until cauliflower is tender; drain. Make sauce while cauliflower is cooking.

Heat butter in pan; add flour and curry powder; stir 1 minute. Gradually add milk, lemon juice, mayonnaise; add salt and pepper; stir until sauce boils and thickens. Reduce heat; gradually add grated cheese; stir until combined.

Beat together egg and cream; add to curry sauce with chopped shallots; stir over low heat until sauce thickens. Spoon sauce over cauliflower.

Serves 4.

Carrot Casserole

500 g (1 lb.) carrots	⅔ cup milk
60 g (2 oz.) butter	¼ cup dry white wine
1 onion	¼ cup chopped chives
2 sticks celery	salt, pepper
430 g (14 oz.) can cream of chicken soup	

Topping

1 cup fresh breadcrumbs	30 g (1 oz.) butter

Scrape carrots; cut into thin strips. Put in boiling, salted water; cook 10 minutes or until just tender; drain. Heat butter in pan; add peeled and chopped

onion, sliced celery and drained carrots; saute until onion is tender.

Remove from pan; put into ovenproof dish. Add undiluted chicken soup, milk and white wine to pan; stir until combined and sauce boils; reduce heat; simmer 3 minutes. Stir in chives, salt and pepper. Pour sauce over vegetables; sprinkle topping over. Bake uncovered in moderate oven 15 minutes or until golden brown.

Topping: Melt butter; add breadcrumbs; mix well.

Serves 6.

Carrot and Celery Saute

500 g (1 lb.) carrots	salt, pepper
60 g (2 oz.) butter	4 shallots or spring onions
2 sticks celery	½ cup cream
1 onion	2 tablespoons chopped
½ teaspoon oregano	parsley

Put sliced carrots in boiling salted water; cook until just tender; drain well. Heat butter in pan; add carrots, sliced celery, and peeled and chopped onion; saute until onion is tender. Add oregano, salt, pepper, chopped shallots and cream; stir until sauce just boils; sprinkle with parsley.

Serves 6.

Crispy Potatoes — soft, savoury, cheese-flavoured potato is encased in firm golden crumbs; they're a delightful accompaniment to grills.

Crispy Potatoes

500 g (1 lb.) old potatoes	flour
salt, pepper	2 eggs, extra
30 g (1 oz.) butter	¼ cup milk
1 egg	3 cups fresh white bread-
1 tablespoon grated	crumbs (approx. ½ loaf)
parmesan cheese	oil for deep-frying

Peel, quarter and wash potatoes; place in boiling salted water; cover pan. Reduce heat; simmer 20 minutes or until potatoes are tender; drain well. Return potatoes to pan; shake over high heat to evaporate any excess liquid. Push potatoes through fine sieve into bowl. Add salt, pepper, butter, egg and parmesan cheese; mix well. Refrigerate mixture until firm.

Take small tablespoonfuls of mixture; roll into cylindrical shape. Roll in flour, then dip in combined beaten extra eggs and milk. Coat again with flour. Dip into egg mixture again, then coat well with breadcrumbs. Refrigerate 1 hour.

Place in deep hot oil; cook until golden brown; drain on absorbent paper.

Serves 4.

Potatoes Romanoff

6 large potatoes	185 g (6 oz.) cheese
600 ml (1 pint) sour cream	salt, pepper
8 shallots or spring onions	1 teaspoon paprika

Peel potatoes; cut in halves. Cook in boiling salted water approx. 20 minutes or until just tender; drain; cool slightly.

Grate potatoes coarsely into large bowl; add sour cream, chopped shallots, half of the grated cheese, salt and pepper. Put into greased casserole dish; top with remaining grated cheese; sprinkle with paprika.

Cover; refrigerate several hours or overnight. Bake uncovered in moderate oven 35 minutes.

Serves 6 to 8.

Indian Potato Chahkee

500 g (1 lb.) potatoes	1 tablespoon curry powder
¼ cup oil	salt
3 onions	1 cup hot water

Peel and quarter potatoes. Heat oil in pan; cook peeled, sliced onions until golden, then stir in curry powder and salt. Add potatoes; cook 10 minutes. Add hot water; simmer covered approx. 15 minutes or until potatoes are tender.

Serves 4.

Potato and Carrot Casserole

750 g (1½ lb.) old potatoes	1 onion
60 g (2 oz.) butter	3 chicken stock cubes
¼ cup sour cream	1 teaspoon french mustard
¼ cup milk	⅓ cup mayonnaise
salt, pepper	30 g (1 oz.) butter, extra
750 g (1½ lb.) carrots	1 tablespoon milk, extra

Peel potatoes; chop roughly. Cook in salted water until tender; drain. Add butter; mash until smooth. Add sour cream, milk, salt and pepper; beat until smooth.

Peel carrots; chop roughly; put in separate saucepan with crumbled stock cubes and peeled and chopped onion. Cover with water; bring to boil. Reduce heat; simmer 15 to 20 minutes or until tender. Drain; reserve 2 tablespoons of the carrot liquid. Put carrot mixture, reserved carrot liquid, salt, pepper, mustard and mayonnaise into electric blender; blend until pureed, or mash until smooth.

Put potato and carrot mixtures in layers in ovenproof dish. Brush top of casserole with extra milk; dot with extra butter. Bake in moderate oven 30 to 35 minutes or until top is golden.

Serves 6.

Chips

Peel potatoes; wash well; dry. Cut potatoes into 1 cm (½ in.) slices, then into strips 1 cm (½ in.) wide. Roll chips in a clean teatowel to dry them well.

Heat oil in deep pan. Drop one chip into oil; when it rises to the surface surrounded by bubbles, oil is at correct temperature for cooking chips. A frying basket makes it easier to lower and raise a quantity of chips in the hot oil. If not using a frying basket, drop chips gradually into hot oil. Cook 6 minutes; remove; drain well. At this point chips are only partly cooked, or blanched. They can now be set aside for several hours, ready for final cooking; they will not discolour. Or, when cold, they can be packed in freezer bags and frozen.

Before serving, reheat oil. As before, drop one chip into it to test that it is the right heat. Cook chips quickly for about 3 minutes, until golden brown and crisp. Drain well; sprinkle with salt.

Shoestring potatoes make an attractive accompaniment to grills.

Cut potatoes into 5 mm (¼ in.) slices, then into strips 5 mm (¼ in.) wide. For speed, several potato slices can be put on top of one another and cut together. Cook in hot oil approx. 3 to 5 minutes.

Tomato Casserole

6 firm tomatoes	60 g (2 oz.) cheese
2½ cups fresh bread-crumbs	salt, pepper
	chopped parsley
60 g (2 oz.) butter	

Peel and slice tomatoes. Arrange layers of sliced tomatoes, breadcrumbs, dots of butter and salt and pepper in lightly-greased ovenproof dish. Finish with layer of breadcrumbs; dot with butter. Bake in moderately hot oven 20 minutes.

Sprinkle with grated cheese; bake a further 10 minutes or until brown. Sprinkle with chopped parsley.

Serves 4 to 6.

Tomato Potatoes

500 g (1 lb.) large old potatoes	2 tablespoons tomato paste
4 small onions	1 chicken stock cube
60 g (2 oz.) butter	salt, pepper
2 tablespoons oil	2 tablespoons chopped parsley
½ cup water	

Peel potatoes; cut into large cubes; wash and dry well. Peel onions; cut into thick wedges. Heat butter and oil in large frying pan; add potatoes; cook very gently until golden brown and cooked through, approx. 20 minutes. Add onions; cook 5 minutes or until just soft.

Combine water, tomato paste, crumbled chicken stock cube, salt, pepper and parsley in bowl. Add to potatoes; stir until potatoes are well coated and heated through.

Serves 4.

Creamed Spinach

1 bunch spinach	salt, pepper
60 g (2 oz.) butter	pinch nutmeg
1 onion	¼ cup sour cream
1 clove garlic	4 shallots or spring onions

Wash spinach; remove white stems; chop leaves roughly. Put spinach in saucepan with ¼ cup boiling water. Cover tightly; cook until tender, approx. 5 minutes. Drain, pressing out all moisture.

Heat butter in pan; add peeled and chopped onion and crushed garlic; saute until onion is tender. Add spinach, salt, pepper and nutmeg; stir until spinach is heated through. Add sour cream and chopped shallots; cook a further 3 minutes.

Serves 4.

Sherried Minted Peas

500 g (1 lb.) fresh peas	1 teaspoon flour
2 small onions	¼ cup dry sherry
1½ cups boiling water	2 tablespoons finely-chopped mint
2 chicken stock cubes	
1 teaspoon sugar	salt, pepper
30 g (1 oz.) butter	

Put shelled peas, sugar and peeled, finely-chopped onions into saucepan. Add boiling water and crumbled stock cubes; bring to boil again. Reduce heat; cook until tender. Drain; reserve 1 cup liquid.

Melt butter in pan; add flour; stir until smooth. Add reserved cooking liquid and sherry; stir until smooth, then stir until boiling. Add peas and chopped mint; season with salt and pepper.

Serves 4.

Minted Peas and Mushrooms

500 g (1 lb.) pkt frozen peas	2 tablespoons chopped mint
a few mint leaves	125 g (4 oz.) mushrooms
½ cup bottled french dressing	4 shallots or spring onions
1 clove garlic	½ teaspoon thyme
	salt, pepper

Put peas in boiling salted water with mint leaves; cook according to directions on packet. While peas are cooking, make sauce.

Heat dressing in pan; add crushed garlic, mint, sliced mushrooms and chopped shallots; saute until mushrooms are tender. Add drained peas, thyme, salt and pepper; cook a further 3 minutes.

Serves 4 to 6.

Herbed Potato Balls

1 kg (2 lb.) potatoes	2 tablespoons chopped parsley
3 tablespoons mayonnaise	
1 teaspoon french mustard	salt, pepper
1 clove garlic	2 eggs
4 shallots or spring onions	3 tablespoons milk
¼ cup chopped chives	packaged dry breadcrumbs
½ teaspoon mixed herbs	oil for deep-frying

Put peeled and halved potatoes in boiling salted water; cook until tender. Drain; mash well; cool. Add mayonnaise and mustard; mix well. Add crushed garlic, chopped shallots, chives, mixed herbs, parsley, salt and pepper; mix well.

Roll mixture into 2.5 cm (1 in.) balls. Dip in combined lightly beaten eggs and milk; coat in breadcrumbs. Repeat egg-and-breadcrumb process. Deep-fry in hot oil until golden brown.

Makes approx. 30.

Herbed Courgettes

750 g (1½ lb.) courgettes	¼ cup dry white wine
90 g (3 oz.) butter	¼ cup water
1 onion	1 chicken stock cube
1 clove garlic	salt, pepper
½ teaspoon mixed herbs	60 g (2 oz.) cheddar cheese
30 g (1 oz.) butter, extra	2 tablespoons chopped parsley
1 tablespoon flour	
½ cup milk	

Heat butter in pan; add sliced courgettes, peeled and chopped onion, crushed garlic and mixed herbs; stir over medium heat 5 minutes or until courgettes are just tender. Remove from pan; put into serving dish; keep warm.

Heat extra butter in pan; add flour; stir until golden brown. Gradually add milk, wine and water; add crumbled stock cube, salt and pepper. Stir over medium heat until sauce boils and thickens. Gradually add grated cheese; stir until cheese melts. Add parsley; mix well. Pour sauce over courgettes; mix through lightly.

Serves 6.

Vegetarian Dishes

Vegetarians and non-vegetarians alike will find these recipes offer new food ideas for the family. Provided the right balance is chosen to give essential elements the body needs, vegetarian foods can be nutritious, satisfying and full of variety.

Wholemeal Herbed Quiche

Wholemeal Pastry

½ cup wholemeal self-raising flour	½ teaspoon paprika
½ cup wholemeal plain flour	125 g (4 oz.) vegetable margarine
½ teaspoon vegetable salt	1 egg yolk
	extra paprika

Filling

4 shallots or spring onions	185 g (6 oz.) cheddar cheese
3 tablespoons chopped parsley	3 eggs
¼ teaspoon oregano	vegetable salt
½ teaspoon basil	⅓ cup cream
	⅓ cup milk

Pastry: Sift flours, salt and paprika into bowl; return husks in sifter to flour. Rub in vegetable margarine until mixture resembles coarse breadcrumbs. Add egg yolk; mix with knife until just combined. Turn out on to lightly-floured surface; knead lightly. Carefully roll out pastry on floured surface to line 23 cm (9 in.) flan tin. Trim edges. Refrigerate for 30 minutes. Bake in hot oven 10 to 12 minutes or until pastry is light golden brown. Remove from oven; allow to become cold. When cold, spoon in prepared filling. Dust with extra paprika. Return to moderate oven; cook a further 20 to 25 minutes or until filling is set.

Filling: Place finely-chopped shallots, parsley, oregano, basil, grated cheese, beaten eggs, salt, cream and milk in bowl; mix well.
   Serves 4 to 6.

Wholemeal Herbed Quiche — a crisp pastry shell holds a creamy herb-and-cheese flavoured filling.

Hot Lentil Soup

250 g (8 oz.) brown lentils	1 stick celery
1½ litres (6 cups) water	2 tomatoes
1 tablespoon oil	1 clove garlic
1 potato	470 g (15 oz.) can savoury
2 onions	brown lentils
1 carrot	vegetable salt

Wash lentils; drain. Cover with cold water and leave to stand 2 hours. Drain.

Heat oil in large saucepan; add finely-chopped onions and crushed garlic; saute until onions are golden brown. Add lentils, water, peeled and chopped tomatoes; finely chop remaining vegetables; add to mixture with vegetable salt. Bring to boil; reduce heat; cover and simmer 30 minutes or until lentils are tender.

Add undrained savoury lentils; cook a further 10 minutes.

Serves 4.

Thick Vegetable Soup

¼ cauliflower	2 sticks celery
1 red pepper	2 tablespoons vegetable oil
4 courgettes	1½ litres (6 cups) water
1 potato	3 cups water, extra
2 carrots	vegetable salt
2 onions	

Wash vegetables; roughly chop cauliflower; remove seeds from red pepper and slice thinly; roughly chop courgettes; peel and chop potato; peel and slice carrots; roughly chop celery; peel and roughly chop onions; reserve vegetable peelings.

Heat oil in pan, add vegetable peelings, cook over high heat until golden brown; add water, reduce heat, simmer uncovered 20 minutes. Strain and reserve liquid, discarding peelings. Place reserved liquid in large pan, add prepared vegetables, simmer covered on low heat until vegetables are tender.

Place cooked vegetables and their liquid in blender, blend at high speed 15 seconds or until vegetables are finely chopped but not a puree. (You will need to do this in several lots.) Add extra water; season with salt; mix well; reheat gently.

Serves 4 to 6.

Potato Onion Fritters

750 g (1½ lb.) old potatoes	½ teaspoon vegetable salt
1 large onion	½ teaspoon thyme
2 tablespoons chopped	3 eggs
parsley	2 tablespoons oil

½ cup wholemeal plain	1 teaspoon paprika
flour	¼ cup oil, extra
2 tablespoons wheatgerm	

Peel and grate potatoes, place grated potato in sieve, press well to extract all liquid. Place potato, peeled and very thinly sliced onion, parsley, flour, wheatgerm, salt, thyme, eggs, oil and paprika in bowl; mix well.

Heat extra oil in large frying pan, drop large tablespoonfuls of mixture into pan, spreading out thinly. Cook very gently until golden brown, turn and brown other side. Drain on absorbent paper. Repeat with remaining mixture. Sprinkle a little vegetable salt over each fritter.

Makes approximately 15.

Soy Bean Patties

315 g (10 oz.) can soy	¼ teaspoon mixed herbs
beans	1 tablespoon soy sauce
½ cup wheatgerm	pinch vegetable salt
½ cup finely chopped	2 cups wholemeal
walnuts	breadcrumbs
6 shallots or spring onions	¼ cup sesame seeds
½ teaspoon basil	⅓ cup oil

Place undrained soy beans in electric blender, blend on medium speed 1 minute or until smooth. Place soy bean mixture in bowl, add wheatgerm, walnuts, finely chopped shallots (or spring onions), basil, mixed herbs, soy sauce and salt; mix well.

Divide mixture into 6 equal portions. Drop each portion into combined breadcrumbs and sesame seeds. Press crumbs firmly on to patties, shaping into rounds.

Heat oil in large frying pan, add patties, cook gently until golden brown underneath, approximately 4 minutes; turn and brown other side.

Makes 6 patties.

Herbed Sunflower Seed Loaf

1½ cups sunflower seeds	1 teaspoon mixed herbs
¾ cup sesame seeds	3 tablespoons chopped
1 cup walnuts	parsley
315 g (10 oz.) can soy	2 eggs
beans	2 tablespoons cider
1 large carrot	vinegar
1 large onion	2 tablespoons oil
1 stick celery	1 teaspoon vegetable salt

Place sunflower seeds, sesame seeds and walnuts in electric blender, blend on medium speed 1 minute or until mixture is finely ground.

Transfer mixture to large bowl together with rinsed and well-drained soy beans, peeled and grated carrot, peeled and finely chopped onion, finely chopped celery, mixed herbs, parsley, eggs, vinegar, oil and salt; mix very well with hands.

Press mixture into well-greased 23 cm x 12 cm (9 in. x 5 in.) loaf tin. Cook in moderate oven 60 minutes or until loaf is firm to touch and edges are light golden brown. Allow to cool slightly before turning out of tin. Serve hot or cold.

Serves 6.

Hot Garlic Beans

250 g (8 oz.) green beans	¼ teaspoon marjoram
250 g (8 oz.) courgettes	¼ teaspoon rosemary
90 g (3 oz.) vegetable margarine	½ teaspoon vegetable salt
	½ cup water
3 cloves garlic	4 tablespoons chopped parsley
315 g (10 oz.) can soy beans	6 shallots or spring onions

Wash and string beans, cut into large pieces. Cut courgettes into diagonal slices.

Heat margarine in pan, add crushed garlic and rinsed and drained soy beans; saute gently 3 minutes. Add beans and courgettes, toss gently 2 minutes. Add marjoram, rosemary, salt and water, stir until combined. Bring to boil, reduce heat, simmer covered 3 minutes or until beans are just crisp. Remove lid, increase heat, boil uncovered 2 minutes or until nearly all liquid has evaporated. Add parsley and chopped shallots (or spring onions); mix well.

Serves 4 to 6.

Beetroot and Cashew Nut Salad

4 medium beetroot	½ cup plain yoghurt
2 tablespoons lemon juice	1 teaspoon raw sugar, extra
2 tablespoons oil	
¼ teaspoon caraway seeds	4 shallots or spring onions
1 tablespoon raw sugar	3 tablespoons chopped parsley
¼ teaspoon vegetable salt	60 g (2 oz.) cashew nuts

Place peeled and grated raw beetroot, lemon juice, oil, caraway seeds, sugar and salt in bowl; mix well. Cover and refrigerate 1 hour.

Place yoghurt in bowl, add extra sugar; mix well.

Place cashew nuts on baking tray, cook in moderate oven 5 minutes or until golden brown; cool, chop roughly.

Spoon beetroot mixture into salad bowl, top with yoghurt mixture. Sprinkle over combined chopped shallots (or spring onions) and parsley. Top with cashew nuts.

Serves 4 to 6.

Vegetarian Combination

2 teaspoons wholemeal plain flour	2 cloves garlic
	2 tablespoons chopped parsley
3 carrots	
6 courgettes	1 tablespoon lemon juice
1 aubergine	1 tablespoon water
1 red pepper	90 g (3 oz.) vegetable margarine
125 g (4 oz.) green beans	
4 shallots or spring onions	vegetable salt

Place flour in oven bag. Shake until bag is well coated with flour. Slice carrots thinly. Cut courgettes into 2 cm (¾ in.) slices. Peel aubergine and cut into 2.5 cm (1 in.) cubes. Seed pepper, slice thinly. String beans, cut into 2.5 cm (1 in.) pieces. Chop shallots (or spring onions). Place vegetables in bag.

Combine crushed garlic, chopped parsley, lemon juice, water, margarine and salt. Add to vegetables. Close bag with tie. Place bag in baking dish. Make 4 holes in top. Bake in moderate oven 40 to 50 minutes or until vegetables are cooked. .. Serves 4.

Cauliflower Rolls

½ small cauliflower	½ cup plain yoghurt
6 shallots or spring onions	½ teaspoon vegetable salt
½ green pepper	1 cup wholemeal breadcrumbs
2 tablespoons chopped parsley	oil for deep-frying
250 g (8 oz.) carton cottage cheese	

Batter

2 cups wholemeal self-raising flour	½ teaspoon vegetable salt
	1⅔ cups water

Break cauliflower into small flowerettes, then chop roughly, so that cauliflower is in very small pieces. Place cauliflower, chopped shallots (or spring onions), seeded and finely chopped pepper, parsley, cottage cheese, yoghurt and vegetable salt into bowl; mix well.

Drop tablespoonfuls of mixture into breadcrumbs, roll into balls. Place into prepared batter, then spoon into deep hot oil; fry until golden brown. Drain on absorbent paper.

Batter: Sift flour and salt into bowl, gradually add water, mixing to a smooth batter.

Serves 4.

Hunza Pie

Wholemeal Pastry

2 cups wholemeal plain flour	250 g (8 oz.) vegetable margarine
1 teaspoon vegetable salt	¼ cup water, approx.
1 cup wheatgerm	

Filling

1.25 kg (2½ lb.) old potatoes	vegetable salt
2 tablespoons oil	1 tablespoon kelp granules
	1 small bunch spinach

Pastry: Sift flour and salt into bowl, add husks in sifter to flour. Add wheatgerm, lightly mix into flour. Rub in margarine until mixture resembles fine breadcrumbs. Add water, mix to a firm dough; a tablespoon or two more water may be needed. Turn out on to lightly floured surface, knead lightly. Divide pastry in half. Roll out one half of pastry to fit 23 cm (9 in.) pie plate.

Filling: Peel potatoes, cut into quarters, boil until tender, drain. Place potatoes in bowl; mash very lightly. Add salt, kelp, oil, and washed and shredded spinach; mix well. Let stand until cold.

Spoon spinach filling into pastry case, packing down well. Roll out remaining pastry to cover pie dish. Trim and decorate edges. Brush with water, make a few slits in top of pastry. Bake in hot oven 15 minutes or until pastry is golden brown; reduce heat to moderate, cook further 15 minutes. Serve hot or cold.

Serves 6.

Vegetable Pancakes

Pancakes

1 cup wholemeal plain flour	vegetable margarine
1 teaspoon vegetable salt	1 cup fresh wholemeal breadcrumbs
2 tablespoons oil	30 g (1 oz.) vegetable margarine, extra
1¼ cups skim milk	

Filling

500 g (1 lb.) tomatoes	4 shallots or spring onions
30 g (1 oz.) vegetable margarine	1 tablespoon chopped parsley
2 onions	vegetable salt
2 sticks celery	

Pancakes: Sift flour and salt in bowl; add oil; mix in well. Gradually add skim milk; mix until smooth.

Heat pan; grease lightly with a little vegetable margarine. From small jug pour 2 to 3 tablespoons batter into pan; cook slowly, loosening edges with knife until set and browned underneath. Toss or turn; brown on other side; remove from pan. Repeat with remaining batter.

Divide filling between pancakes, roll up, put pancakes in ovenproof dish. Combine breadcrumbs and melted extra margarine, sprinkle over pancakes, bake in moderate oven 15 to 20 minutes or until crumbs are golden brown.

Filling: Heat margarine in pan, add peeled and sliced onions and chopped celery; saute until onions are tender. Add tomatoes cut into thick wedges, simmer covered 5 minutes. Add chopped shallots (or spring onions) and parsley, season with salt, stir until combined.

Serves 4.

Potato-Mushroom Casserole

60 g (2 oz.) vegetable margarine	2 cups water
3 large onions	1 teaspoon mixed herbs
500 g (1 lb.) small mushrooms	1 teaspoon paprika
1 red pepper	1 teaspoon raw sugar
60 g (2 oz.) vegetable margarine, extra	1 tablespoon soy sauce
4 tablespoons wholemeal plain flour	vegetable salt
	30 g (1 oz.) cheddar cheese

Potato Topping

500 g (1 lb.) old potatoes	3 tablespoons milk
30 g (1 oz.) vegetable margarine	

Heat margarine in large pan, add peeled and roughly chopped onions; saute gently until onions are light golden brown. Add halved mushrooms and seeded and cubed red pepper, saute 5 minutes, stirring occasionally; remove vegetables from pan.

Melt extra margarine in pan; add flour; stir until flour is dark golden brown (do not allow to burn); remove from heat. Add water; stir until combined. Return pan to heat; stir until sauce boils and thickens. Add herbs, paprika, raw sugar, soy sauce and salt; stir until combined. Return vegetables to pan; reduce heat; simmer covered 10 minutes. Spoon mixture into ovenproof dish; cool.

When cold, spoon prepared Potato Topping over top of casserole, bringing to 2.5 cm (1 in.) of edge. Sprinkle grated cheese over. Cook in hot oven 25 minutes or until casserole is heated through and topping is golden brown.

Potato Topping: Peel potatoes, cook until tender; drain. Push potatoes through sieve into bowl, add margarine and milk; mix well. Use Potato Topping while still hot.

Serves 4 to 6.

Potato-Mushroom Casserole makes a substantial vegetarian meal on its own, or would make an unusual vegetable accompaniment.

Date Crumble Slice

Base

½ cup wholemeal plain flour
½ cup wholemeal self-raising flour
2 tablespoons raw sugar
½ teaspoon cinnamon
¼ teaspoon nutmeg
60 g (2 oz.) vegetable margarine
1 egg
2 tablespoons skim milk

Filling

500 g (1 lb.) dates
1 cup water
¾ cup orange juice
1 teaspoon grated orange rind
1 tablespoon honey

Crumble Topping

½ cup wholemeal plain flour
½ cup wholemeal self-raising flour
½ cup rolled oats
½ teaspoon cinnamon
¼ teaspoon mixed spice
2 tablespoons bran
¼ cup raw sugar, lightly packed
125 g (4 oz.) vegetable margarine

Base: Sift all dry ingredients into bowl, return husks in sifter to bowl. Rub in margarine until mixture resembles fine breadcrumbs. Add combined egg and milk; mix lightly. Spread mixture over base of 28 cm x 18 cm (11 in. x 7 in.) shallow cake tin which has been lined with grease-proof paper. Cook in moderate oven 15 minutes or until light golden brown and cooked through. Allow to become cold.

When cold, spread prepared filling evenly over base. Sprinkle prepared Crumble Topping over, pressing down firmly. Cook in moderately hot oven 15 to 20 minutes or until top is golden brown. Allow to become cold before removing from tin.

Filling: Place chopped dates, water, orange juice, orange rind and honey in pan, bring to boil, reduce heat, simmer covered 5 minutes. Remove lid and simmer a further 10 minutes or until date mixture is very soft and thick; cool.

Crumble Topping: Sift flours into bowl, return husks in sifter to bowl. Add remaining dry ingredients; mix lightly. Rub in margarine until mixture resembles coarse breadcrumbs.

Banana Wheatgerm Muffins

⅓ cup oil
⅔ cup honey
3 eggs, separated
3 large bananas
½ cup wheatgerm
1¼ cups wholemeal self-raising flour
1 teaspoon cinnamon

Beat oil, honey and egg yolks until thick and creamy. Add mashed bananas (there should be enough mashed banana to make 1 cup), beat well. Stir in wheatgerm, sifted flour and cinnamon; mix well.

Beat egg whites until soft peaks form. Lightly fold into cake mixture. Spoon tablespoonfuls of mixture into greased muffin tins or deep patty tins. Bake in moderate oven 20 minutes or until golden brown.

Makes approx. 36.

Apricot Buckwheat Pancakes

Pancakes

2 cups wholemeal self-raising flour
1 teaspoon baking powder
1 teaspoon cinnamon
¼ teaspoon nutmeg
1 tablespoon raw sugar
½ cup packaged roasted buckwheat
¼ cup unprocessed bran
2 eggs, separated
2 cups skim milk

Apricot Topping

185 g (6 oz.) dried apricots
2 cups water
½ cup raw sugar
60 g (2 oz.) vegetable margarine
¼ cup sour cream
extra sour cream
cinnamon

Pancakes: Sift flour, baking powder, cinnamon and nutmeg into bowl, return any husks in sifter to bowl. Add buckwheat, sugar and bran to bowl; mix lightly. Make a well in centre of dry ingredients, add egg yolks and milk, mix to a smooth batter. Beat egg whites until soft peaks form, fold into batter mixture.

Heat pancake pan, grease well, pour ¼ cup batter mixture over pan, spreading out evenly; cook slowly until golden brown underneath. Toss or turn pancake, brown on other side; keep warm while making remaining pancakes.

Place pancakes on serving plate, spoon prepared Apricot Topping over each pancake; top with a spoonful of extra sour cream and sprinkle with a little cinnamon.

Apricot Topping: Place finely chopped apricots and water into pan, bring to boil, reduce heat, simmer covered 25 minutes or until apricots are tender.

Place apricots with their liquid, sugar, margarine and sour cream in electric blender, blend on medium speed until mixture is pureed.

Serves 6.

Wheatgerm Wafers

½ cup wholemeal plain flour
2 teaspoons baking powder
½ teaspoon vegetable salt
1 teaspoon raw sugar
¾ cup wheatgerm
60 g (2 oz.) vegetable margarine
2 tablespoons water

Sift flour, baking powder and salt into bowl, return any husks in sifter to bowl. Add sugar and half cup of wheatgerm; mix lightly. Rub in margarine until mixture resembles fine breadcrumbs. Stir in water quickly but gently.

Gather dough into ball and place on floured surface; knead lightly. Roll out to 2.5 cm (1 in.) in thickness, sprinkle over remaining wheatgerm and continue to roll until dough is wafer-thin. Cut into rounds using a 5 cm (2 in.) round cutter. Place on lightly greased oven trays. Cook in moderate oven 10 to 15 minutes or until light golden brown. Allow to cool on trays.

Makes approx. 30.

Ginger Pumpkin Pie

Pastry

1 cup wholemeal plain flour	2 tablespoons sesame seeds
½ cup wholemeal self-raising flour	125 g (4 oz.) vegetable margarine
¼ teaspoon nutmeg	1 egg yolk
¼ teaspoon mixed spice	2 tablespoons water
2 tablespoons raw sugar	extra nutmeg
pinch vegetable salt	

Filling

2 eggs	½ teaspoon cinnamon
¾ cup plain thick yoghurt	¼ teaspoon mixed spice
1 teaspoon ground ginger	¼ cup honey
	750 g (1½ lb.) pumpkin

Pastry: Sift flours, nutmeg, mixed spice and salt into bowl, return any husks in sifter to bowl. Add sesame seeds and sugar; mix lightly. Rub in margarine until mixture resembles fine breadcrumbs. Add egg yolk and water; mix to a firm dough. Turn out on to lightly floured surface; knead lightly.

Roll out pastry to cover base and sides of 23 cm (9 in.) pie plate. Decorate edges. Refrigerate 30 minutes. Cook in moderate oven 12 to 15 minutes or until light golden brown. Remove from oven, allow to become cold.

When cold, spoon in prepared filling. Sprinkle with extra nutmeg. Return to moderate oven, cook further 35 to 40 minutes or until filling has set. Allow pie to cool, then refrigerate until cold.

Filling: Remove seeds from pumpkin, cut pumpkin into pieces, remove skin. Place pumpkin in boiling salted water, cover, reduce heat, simmer 20 minutes or until pumpkin is tender; drain well. Push pumpkin through fine sieve. You will need 1½ cups pumpkin.

Place eggs, ginger, cinnamon, mixed spice, honey and yoghurt in bowl; whisk well. Add pumpkin, mix well.

Honey Fruit Cake

125 g (4 oz.) vegetable margarine	1 cup sultanas
1 cup honey	125 g (4 oz.) dates
2 eggs	2 cups wholemeal self-raising flour
1 cup sunflower seeds	¼ cup ground soya
¼ cup sesame seeds	1 cup water
½ cup wheatgerm	1 teaspoon mixed spice

Beat margarine until soft and creamy, gradually add honey, beating well until very soft and creamy. Add eggs one at a time, beating well after each addition. Place sunflower seeds, sesame seeds, wheatgerm, sultanas and chopped dates in bowl, add margarine mixture; mix well.

Sift flour, ground soya and mixed spice, return any husks in sifter to flour. Fold flour mixture and water alternately into creamed mixture. Spoon into deep 20 cm (8 in.) round cake tin, which has been lined with greased greaseproof paper. Bake in moderately slow oven 1¼ to 1½ hours or until cake is cooked when tested.

Cashew Honey Butter

250 g (8 oz.) roasted unsalted cashew nuts	1 teaspoon honey
¼ cup oil	¼ teaspoon cinnamon

Place nuts in electric blender, blend on medium speed 15 seconds or until finely chopped. Gradually add oil, blend until mixture is smooth and creamy; stop blender occasionally to scrape down sides to incorporate all nuts. Add honey and cinnamon, blend further 10 seconds. Store in refrigerator.

Makes 1 cup.

Honey Orange Fruit

500 g (1 lb.) dried fruits (these can be an assortment of apples, apricots, peaches, prunes and pears)

1 cup orange juice	3 tablespoons honey
1 teaspoon grated orange rind	2.5 cm (1 in.) piece cinnamon stick
2 cups water	4 whole cloves

Place whole fruits, orange juice, orange rind and water in large bowl; cover, and stand overnight. Next day, place fruit with the liquid in large saucepan, add honey, cinnamon stick and cloves. Bring to boil, reduce heat, simmer covered 30 minutes or until fruit is very tender. Pour into large bowl; cover, and refrigerate until cold.

To serve, spoon fruit into serving bowls, with the liquid. Top with plain yoghurt.

Serves 6.

Salads

Colourful salads add variety to any meal, and we've chosen our favourites here. It is becoming increasingly popular to serve a special salad as a light first course for a dinner party; many of the salads given here would be ideal for this purpose.

Paella Salad

2 tablespoons oil	3 chicken stock cubes
60 g (2 oz.) butter	2.5 cm (1 in.) piece
2 onions	cinnamon stick
1 red pepper	salt, pepper
1 green pepper	6 shallots or spring onions
125 g (4 oz.) bacon	125 g (4 oz.) small
2 cloves garlic	mushrooms
500 g (1 lb.) long-grain rice	125 g (4 oz.) stuffed green
2 tomatoes	olives
2 sticks celery	1 tablespoon chopped
1 cup frozen peas	parsley
1 teaspoon saffron	1½ tablespoons french
3 teaspoons curry powder	dressing
4½ cups water	

Heat oil and butter in large pan; saute peeled and chopped onions, thinly-sliced peppers, chopped bacon and crushed garlic 2 minutes. Stir in rice, peeled and roughly-chopped tomatoes, sliced celery, peas, saffron, curry powder, water, crumbled stock cubes and cinnamon stick; season with salt and pepper. Cover pan; simmer very gently 15 to 20 minutes or until almost all liquid has been absorbed. Remove lid; add sliced shallots, sliced mushrooms and sliced olives; stir into rice. Cover; simmer gently 3 minutes. Remove lid; check at this stage if rice is cooked and all liquid has evaporated. If rice needs further cooking, add extra ½ cup boiling water; re-cover; cook a further 2 to 3 minutes. Stir in parsley and french dressing. Serve hot or cold.

Serves 6 to 8.

Paella Salad — saffron-flavoured rice, studded with colourful vegetables, can be served hot or cold. It's a great salad for a buffet or barbecue.

Festive Coleslaw

¾ cup long-grain rice	3 sticks celery
½ cabbage	⅓ cup toasted flaked
2 green peppers	almonds
2 red peppers	3 tablespoons chopped
8 radishes	parsley
1 onion	125 g (4 oz.) black
8 shallots or spring onions	olives
440 g (15 oz.) can corn	
kernels	

Dressing

½ cup mayonnaise	4 tablespoons french
salt, pepper	dressing

Cook rice in large saucepan of boiling, salted water until tender, approx. 12 minutes; drain well; cool. Remove coarse outer leaves of cabbage. Cut into quarters; remove core; shred finely. In large bowl combine shredded cabbage, rice, coarsely-chopped red and green peppers, sliced radishes, peeled and chopped onion, chopped shallots, drained corn, diced celery, almonds, parsley and halved and pitted black olives; refrigerate several hours. Just before serving, add dressing; toss well.

Dressing: Put all ingredients in screw-top jar; shake well.
    Serves 8.

Italian Salad

470 g (15 oz.) can	60 g (2 oz.) black olives
artichoke hearts	1 red pepper
3 small onions	1 green pepper
3 tomatoes	

Dressing

¼ cup vinegar	2 cloves garlic
¼ cup oil	salt, pepper

Drain artichokes and chop roughly; peel onions and cut into quarters; cut tomatoes into wedges; cut red and green peppers into chunks. Combine vegetables in bowl with olives; pour prepared dressing over; combine well.

Dressing: Put all ingredients into screw-top jar. Secure lid; shake well to combine.
    Serves 4.

Vegetable Salad

500 g (1 lb.) brussel	60 g (2 oz.) slivered
sprouts	almonds
4 rashers bacon	salt, pepper
1 red pepper	2 tablespoons chopped
2 sticks celery	parsley
15 g (½ oz.) butter	lettuce

Yoghurt Dressing

½ cup yoghurt (or sour	½ small onion
cream)	salt, pepper
½ cup mayonnaise	1 teaspoon lemon juice

Remove rind from bacon; cut bacon into strips. Remove stalk and seeds from red pepper; cut into thin strips. Slice celery diagonally into 2.5 cm (1 in.) lengths. Cook brussel sprouts in boiling, salted water 5 minutes; drain well. Heat butter; gently saute almonds until light golden colour, about 1 minute. Add bacon, celery and red pepper. Cook until bacon is lightly cooked and vegetables just tender, about 3 minutes. Season well with salt and pepper. Place brussel sprouts on bed of crisp lettuce; spoon the vegetable mixture over. Sprinkle with parsley. Serve the dressing separately.

Yoghurt Dressing: Combine yoghurt or sour cream, mayonnaise, finely-chopped onion and lemon juice. Season with salt and pepper. Refrigerate at least 15 minutes.
    Serves 6.

Garden Vegetable Salad

500 g (1 lb.) fresh broccoli	1 red pepper
(or 375 g pkt frozen	¾ cup french dressing
broccoli)	1 clove garlic
½ small cauliflower	2 tablespoons chopped
250 g (8 oz.) mushrooms	parsley

Slice mushrooms; put in bowl with ½ cup french dressing, crushed garlic and parsley; allow to stand 1 hour. Remove stems and leaves from fresh broccoli; cut into small flowerets. (If using frozen, defrost and cut into small flowerets.) Cut cauliflower into flowerets. Chop pepper into 2.5 cm (1 in.) cubes. Put cauliflower, pepper and broccoli into boiling, salted water; boil 2 minutes; drain; rinse under cold, running water; drain well.

    Toss cauliflower and pepper with mushrooms and dressing. Toss broccoli with remaining dressing. Arrange mushrooms, cauliflower and pepper on plate, broccoli down centre.
    Serves 4.

Artichoke and Orange Salad

400 g (13 oz.) can	6 shallots or spring onions
artichoke halves	90 g (3 oz.) stuffed green
3 oranges	olives
1 green pepper	lettuce
1 cucumber	

Dressing

2 tablespoons french	1 tablespoon red wine
dressing	pinch basil

Drain artichokes; put into bowl with prepared dressing; refrigerate 1 hour. Peel oranges; remove white pith; cut into segments. Add to artichoke mixture with seeded and cubed pepper, peeled, halved and thinly-sliced cucumber, chopped shallots and sliced olives. Serve on crisp lettuce leaves.

Dressing: Combine french dressing, red wine and basil in screw-top jar; shake well.
  Serves 6.

Hot Vegetable Salad

1 large aubergine	2 cloves garlic
3 red peppers	1 teaspoon thyme
3 green peppers	125 g (4 oz.) black olives
4 courgettes	2 tablespoons french
3 small onions	dressing
2 tomatoes	2 tablespoons chopped
125 g (4 oz.) mushrooms	parsley
2 tablespoons oil	salt, pepper

Cut aubergine into 2.5 cm (1 in.) cubes. Place aubergine on absorbent paper; sprinkle with about 1 tablespoon salt; stand 20 minutes; rinse; pat dry. Remove seeds from peppers; cut peppers into 2.5 cm (1 in.) cubes. Slice courgettes diagonally. Peel onions; cut into quarters. Peel and quarter tomatoes. Slice mushrooms.

  Heat oil in large pan; add onions, peppers and crushed garlic; stir over high heat 3 minutes. Add aubergine and courgettes; cook over high heat until vegetables are just tender. Add quartered tomatoes, sliced mushrooms, black olives, thyme, salt and pepper; cook 2 minutes. Stir in dressing and parsley.
  Serves 6.

Mushroom and Spinach Salad

250 g (8 oz.) small	125 g (4 oz.) gruyere or
mushrooms	swiss cheese
4 tablespoons french	4 shallots or spring onions
dressing	60 g (2 oz.) stuffed olives
1 clove garlic	1 tablespoon chopped
¼ teaspoon mixed herbs	parsley
6 spinach leaves	

Slice mushrooms thinly. Combine french dressing, crushed garlic and mixed herbs in bowl; add sliced mushrooms; toss thoroughly; refrigerate 1 hour. Wash spinach; chop leaves roughly. Cook spinach in boiling, salted water 1 minute; drain; rinse under cold water; pat dry. Add to mushroom mixture with thinly-sliced squares of cheese, diagonally-sliced shallots, sliced olives and parsley; mix well.
  Serves 6.

Tomato Cucumber Salad

2 small cucumbers	2 tablespoons chopped
salt	parsley
3 tomatoes	salt, pepper
2 onions	1 tablespoon french
2 tablespoons chopped	dressing
chives	

Peel cucumbers; slice very thinly. Put into bowl; sprinkle lightly with salt; stand 30 minutes. Rinse thoroughly under cold running water until excess salt is removed; drain well. Cut tomatoes into thin wedges. In mixing bowl combine tomatoes, thinly-sliced onions and cucumber. Add chives, parsley, salt, pepper and french dressing.
  Serves 4 to 6.

Almond-Bean Salad

500 g (1 lb.) green beans	salt, pepper
3 rashers bacon	2 tablespoons chopped
125 g (4 oz.) mushrooms	parsley
45 g (1½ oz.) butter	2 tablespoons french
⅓ cup slivered almonds	dressing

Top, tail and string beans; cut in half; cook in boiling, salted water until just tender, approx. 5 minutes; drain. Remove rind from bacon; cut bacon into strips. Slice mushrooms. Melt butter in pan; add almonds; cook until light golden brown. Add bacon strips; cook 2 minutes. Add mushrooms; cook until heated through. Remove from pan; drain well. Combine beans, bacon, mushrooms, almonds, salt, pepper and parsley. Add french dressing; toss lightly.
  Serves 4 to 6.

Courgette and Orange Salad

3 oranges	30 g (1 oz.) butter
4 courgettes	2 tablespoons chopped
4 shallots or spring onions	parsley
60 g (2 oz.) stuffed green	salt, pepper
olives	french dressing
1 onion	crisp lettuce

Peel oranges; cut into slices. Cut courgettes diagonally; chop shallots finely; peel and slice onion; crush garlic. Saute courgettes in butter until just tender, about 5 minutes. Remove from pan. Add onion rings to pan; cook gently until lightly golden. Arrange crisp lettuce leaves on serving plate or bowl; top with orange slices; sprinkle over a little french dressing; top with courgettes and onion, then shallots, sliced olives and parsley. Season with salt and pepper. Sprinkle french dressing over.
  Serves 4.

Curried Potato and Ham Salad

500 g (1 lb.) potatoes	2 thin slices bread
3 hard-boiled eggs	60 g (2 oz.) butter
60 g (2 oz.) ham	2 tablespoons grated
1 stick celery	parmesan cheese
6 shallots or spring onions	lettuce

Dressing

½ cup sour cream	½ cup french dressing
¼ cup mayonnaise	salt, pepper
2 teaspoons curry powder	

Peel potatoes; cut into 2.5 cm (1 in.) cubes; cook in boiling, salted water until just tender; drain; cool. Chop eggs roughly; chop ham; slice celery into 1 cm (½ in.) slices; chop shallots. Combine potatoes, eggs, ham, celery and shallots in bowl; pour prepared dressing over; mix thoroughly. Line salad bowl with lettuce leaves; spoon in salad.

Remove crusts from bread; cut bread into 1 cm (½ in.) cubes. Melt butter in frying pan; add bread; toss until well coated with butter; continue cooking over low heat until golden brown, stirring frequently. Add cheese; toss well; cool. Spoon croutons over top of salad just before serving.

Dressing: Combine all ingredients in a screw-top jar. Secure lid; shake to combine.
Serves 4 to 6.

Spinach and Pepper Salad

1 bunch spinach	3 small onions
1 tablespoon oil	125 g (4 oz.) mushrooms
60 g (2 oz.) bacon	2½ tablespoons french
1 clove garlic	dressing
3 green peppers	salt, pepper
3 red peppers	

Chop spinach into large pieces; remove white stalks. Wash spinach; put in pan with only the water that clings to leaves. Cover; bring to boil; reduce heat; simmer 2 minutes; drain well. Heat oil in large pan; add chopped bacon, crushed garlic, thinly-sliced peppers and peeled and quartered onions. Saute over high heat, stirring continually, until vegetables are just tender. Stir in sliced mushrooms, french dressing, spinach, salt and pepper; cook 1 minute.
Serves 6.

Bean Sprout Salad

560 g (1 lb. 2 oz.) can bean sprouts	6 radishes
230 g (7½ oz.) can water chestnuts	2 onions
	3 shallots or spring onions
300 g (10 oz.) can corn kernels	2 tablespoons chopped parsley
1 cup shredded cabbage	1 small bunch watercress

Dressing

2 tablespoons french dressing	¼ teaspoon sesame oil
2 teaspoons vinegar	1 teaspoon dry sherry
2 teaspoons soy sauce	1 teaspoon ground ginger
	pinch sugar

Drain bean sprouts; rinse thoroughly under cold water; drain well. Drain water chestnuts; cut into slices. Combine in bowl bean sprouts, water chestnuts, drained corn, cabbage, sliced radishes, peeled and quartered onions, diagonally-sliced shallots, parsley and washed watercress leaves; toss well; refrigerate. Just before serving, stir in dressing.

Dressing: Combine all ingredients in screw-top jar; shake well.
Serves 6 to 8.

Brandied Mushroom Salad

60 g (2 oz.) butter	¼ cup french dressing
250 g (8 oz.) mushrooms	½ teaspoon sugar
250 g (8 oz.) brussel sprouts	2 tablespoons brandy
	4 shallots or spring onions
salt, pepper	

Heat butter in large frying pan; add sliced mushrooms and sliced brussel sprouts; fry very quickly 2 minutes, tossing vegetables constantly. Add salt, pepper, french dressing, sugar and brandy. Bring liquid to boil; boil uncovered 3 minutes, still tossing vegetables constantly. Add sliced shallots; mix lightly. Serve immediately.
Serves 2.

Hot Brandied Spinach Salad

1 bunch spinach	½ teaspoon dry mustard
250 g (8 oz.) bacon	2 tablespoons lemon juice
60 g (2 oz.) butter	1 tablespoon sugar
1 teaspoon worcester-shire sauce	2 tablespoons vinegar
	2 tablespoons brandy

Choose very young, fresh green spinach for this recipe. Remove white stalks; cut or tear in half lengthways, then across. Wash well; pat dry. Put into wooden salad bowl.

Remove rind from bacon. Chop bacon and bacon fat separately. Put bacon fat and butter in pan; saute over low heat 5 minutes; remove the bacon fat pieces from pan. Add bacon to pan; saute until it is crisp. Add worcestershire sauce, mustard, lemon juice, sugar and vinegar. Stir well; bring to the boil; reduce heat; simmer 1 minute.

Tilt pan a little and pour brandy on to the dry section of the pan; when warm, set aflame. When flames die down, pour combined dressing over spinach; toss well.
Serves 4 to 6.

Celery Victor Salad

Hot Pasta and Bacon Salad

375 g (12 oz.) shell
  macaroni
1 cup frozen peas
15 g (½ oz.) butter
3 rashers bacon
6 shallots or spring onions
1 tablespoon capers

2 tablespoons chopped
  parsley
2 tablespoons french
  dressing
2 tablespoons mayonnaise
salt, pepper

Cook macaroni, uncovered, in large saucepan of boiling, salted water until just tender, approx. 10 minutes. Add frozen peas; cook 2 minutes; drain well. Heat butter in small pan; saute chopped bacon 2 minutes; drain well. In a bowl combine pasta, peas, bacon, chopped shallots, finely-chopped capers, parsley, french dressing, mayonnaise, salt and pepper.

Serves 6.

Celery Victor Salad

6 sticks celery
2 cups water
2 chicken stock cubes
3 tomatoes
125 g (4 oz.) black olives

45 g (1½ oz.) can anchovy
  fillets
⅓ cup bottled italian
  dressing

Cut celery into 5 cm (2 in.) diagonal pieces. Heat water in saucepan; add crumbled chicken stock cubes; stir until dissolved. Add celery; boil uncovered 5 minutes; drain. Rinse under cold running water to give good green colour; drain again. Put celery, tomatoes cut into wedges, black olives and drained chopped anchovy fillets in salad bowl. Add dressing; toss lightly.

Serves 4 to 6.

Curried Bean Salad

125 g (4 oz.) green beans
310 g (10 oz.) can red kidney beans
310 g (10 oz.) can baby butter beans
300 g (10 oz.) can broad beans
1 tablespoon oil
3 small onions

2 sticks celery
1 red pepper
2 cloves garlic
1 tablespoon french dressing
1 tablespoon chopped parsley
salt, pepper

Curry Mayonnaise

½ cup mayonnaise
2 tablespoons french dressing
2 teaspoons curry powder

1 teaspoon lemon juice
few drops tabasco sauce
salt, pepper

Top and tail beans; slice diagonally; cook in boiling, salted water 2 minutes; drain well. Heat oil in large pan; saute peeled and quartered onions, sliced celery, red pepper cut into thin strips and crushed garlic until vegetables are just tender. Add green beans, drained and rinsed red kidney beans, drained baby butter beans, drained broad beans and french dressing to vegetables in pan. Stir over low heat until hot; stir in parsley; season with salt and pepper. Serve with Curry Mayonnaise.

Curry Mayonnaise: Combine all ingredients in small bowl; mix well.
Serves 6.

Curried Seafood Salad

1½ cups long-grain rice
500 g (1 lb.) cooked prawns
500 g (1 lb.) scallops
60 g (2 oz.) butter
2 sticks celery
2 tablespoons chopped parsley
3 shallots or spring onions

1 small red pepper
½ cup french dressing
2 teaspoons curry powder
1 teaspoon turmeric
2 teaspoons lemon juice
salt, pepper
¼ teaspoon sugar

Gradually add rice to large saucepan of boiling, salted water; boil uncovered 12 minutes or until rice is tender; drain. Spread rice out on flat tray and leave 2 hours or until rice is dry.

Shell prawns; remove back vein. Heat butter in pan; add scallops; cook gently, stirring, 3 minutes or until scallops are tender; drain. Place rice in large bowl; add prawns, scallops, finely-chopped celery, parsley, chopped shallots, seeded and finely-chopped pepper; toss lightly.

Combine french dressing, curry powder, turmeric, lemon juice and sugar in bowl; season with salt and pepper. Add dressing to rice mixture; toss thoroughly. Refrigerate until ready to serve.
Serves 6.

Crabmeat Salad

500 g (1 lb.) large cooked prawns
170 g (6 oz.) can crabmeat
½ cucumber

1 large red pepper
6 shallots or spring onions
lettuce
1 ripe avocado

Dressing

¾ cup mayonnaise
2 tablespoons dry white wine

1 tablespoon tomato sauce
¼ cup cream
few drops tabasco sauce

Shell prawns; remove vein from back portion of prawn. If prawns are too large, cut through centre, the length of the prawn. Put prawns, drained and flaked crabmeat, peeled and thinly-sliced cucumber, seeded and sliced red pepper and diagonally-sliced shallots into bowl; toss lightly. Refrigerate several hours. Arrange salad in lettuce cups; decorate with peeled, stoned and thinly-sliced avocado. Serve dressing separately.

Dressing: Combine all ingredients in small bowl; mix well. Refrigerate before serving.
Serves 4.

Lychee and Orange Salad

1 lettuce
2 x 565 g (1 lb. 14 oz.) cans lychees
2 oranges
6 shallots or spring onions
3 sticks celery
1 red pepper

2 tablespoons flaked almonds
3 tablespoons chopped parsley
2 tablespoons french dressing

Drain lychees. Peel oranges; remove all white pith; cut oranges into segments. Put lychees, orange segments, sliced shallots, sliced celery, seeded and sliced red pepper and parsley in mixing bowl; toss lightly; refrigerate before serving. Wash lettuce; separate lettuce cups on to serving dish or shred finely. Just before serving, add french dressing to salad; toss lightly; arrange over lettuce. Sprinkle with toasted almonds.

To toast almonds: Put almonds in small pan; stir over heat until lightly toasted; remove from pan immediately.
Serves 6.

Hot Cauliflower Salad

½ small cauliflower
4 small onions
250 g (8 oz.) courgettes
15 g (½ oz.) butter
3 rashers bacon
3 small tomatoes

2 tablespoons french dressing
1 tablespoon chopped parsley
salt, pepper

Curry Mayonnaise

1 cup mayonnaise	1 teaspoon lemon juice
3 teaspoons curry powder	salt, pepper
1 clove garlic	

Cut cauliflower into large flowerets. Cook uncovered in boiling, salted water until just tender, approx. 6 to 8 minutes. Add peeled and halved onions and sliced courgettes; cook 2 minutes; drain well. Heat butter in small pan; saute chopped bacon 1 minute; remove from heat; drain well.

In bowl combine cauliflower, onions, courgettes, bacon, peeled and quartered tomatoes, french dressing, parsley, salt and pepper. Serve with Curry Mayonnaise.

Curry Mayonnaise: Combine all ingredients in bowl. Mix well.
Serves 6.

Hot Potato Salad

1 kg (2 lb.) old potatoes	¼ cup sour cream
2 sticks celery	⅓ cup french dressing
1 onion	salt, pepper
½ red pepper	2 rashers bacon
2 tablespoons chopped parsley	2 hard-boiled eggs
	90 g (3 oz.) cheese

Peel and dice potatoes; wash well; cook in boiling, salted water until tender; drain well. Slice celery diagonally; peel and finely chop onion; slice red pepper. Combine hot potatoes, celery, onion, pepper and parsley in bowl.

Mix sour cream and dressing together until smooth; season with salt and pepper; pour over potato mixture; mix lightly; spoon into shallow ovenproof dish. Dice bacon; saute in pan until crisp. Drain; sprinkle over top of potatoes with shelled, chopped eggs. Grate cheese; sprinkle over top of bacon and eggs; heat under hot griller until cheese has melted and is golden brown. This salad is delicious as an accompaniment to steak, chops, etc.
Serves 6.

Pineapple Salad

1 lettuce	4 sticks celery
1 small pineapple	½ cucumber
1 red pepper	125 g (4 oz.) black olives

Dressing

½ cup cream	1 small onion
½ cup mayonnaise	1 teaspoon vinegar
½ cucumber	salt, pepper

Wash lettuce; dry well. Tear lettuce leaves into pieces; place in salad bowl. Remove skin from pineapple; cut pineapple lengthwise into quarters.

Remove centre core from each quarter; cut fruit into large pieces. Add to lettuce with seeded and cubed red pepper, sliced celery, peeled and sliced cucumber and black olives. Toss lightly. Refrigerate until ready to serve. Serve prepared dressing separately.

Dressing: Combine cream and mayonnaise together. Mix well. Add peeled and chopped cucumber, finely-chopped onion, vinegar, salt and pepper.
Serves 4 to 6.

Mango and Orange Salad

1 lettuce	3 sticks celery
500 g (1 lb.) can mango slices	6 shallots or spring onions
3 oranges	1 cucumber

Cream Dressing

⅓ cup mayonnaise	½ teaspoon grated orange rind
⅓ cup cream	
2 tablespoons chopped parsley	1 teaspoon french mustard
	salt, pepper

Wash lettuce; gently separate lettuce cups on to large serving plate. Peel oranges and remove all white pith; cut oranges into segments. To make celery curls, cut celery into 8 cm (3 in.) sticks and slice into very thin strips, leaving intact at one end. Put into iced water until celery curls. Score skin of cucumber with fork; cut cucumber into thin slices. Divide mango slices, oranges, celery curls and cucumber evenly between lettuce cups. Sprinkle chopped shallots over. Refrigerate until ready to serve. Serve dressing separately.

Cream Dressing: Combine all ingredients in bowl; mix well. Let stand 15 minutes before using. NOTE: This salad is particularly good with cold roast pork or chicken.
Serves 6.

Orange and Pear Salad

822 g (1 lb. 13 oz.) can pear halves	1 tablespoon dry sherry
4 oranges	2 teaspoons creme de menthe
1 tablespoon chopped mint	1 tablespoon chopped preserved ginger

Drain pear halves; reserve ½ cup syrup. Cut pears into thin slices; put into bowl. Remove skin and all white pith from oranges; cut into segments. Combine reserved pear syrup with mint, sherry, creme de menthe and chopped ginger; mix well. Pour over oranges and pears; cover; refrigerate before serving. This salad is delicious with pork or lamb.
Serves 4.

Recipes for Slimmers

Here are recipes to help you get slim, and stay slim. If you're used to counting in calories, rather than kilojoules, simply divide the number of kilojoules by four; this will give you the number of calories.

Tomato-Mushroom Salad

125 g (4 oz.) mushrooms	2 tablespoons oil
2 medium tomatoes	1 tablespoon chopped
1 onion	parsley
½ cup white vinegar	

Finely slice mushrooms, tomatoes and onion. Combine oil and vinegar in screw-top jar; shake well. Put mushrooms in small bowl. Put tomato and onion slices in another bowl. Divide the dressing between the two bowls. Marinate 15 minutes. Before serving, drain marinade from vegetables. Arrange tomatoes and onion rings round serving plate; fill centre with mushrooms; sprinkle with chopped parsley.
Serves 3.
Approx. 360 kJ per serve.

Orange Slaw

¼ cabbage	1 tablespoon raisins
1 orange	¾ cup natural yoghurt
3 sticks celery	1 tablespoon lemon juice
½ red or green pepper	1 apple

Peel orange; cut into segments. Combine finely-shredded cabbage, sliced celery, chopped pepper and chopped raisins. Add orange segments and yoghurt; toss lightly. Just before serving, peel and core apple; cut into dice; toss in lemon juice; mix lightly into salad.
Serves 4.
Approx. 500 kJ per serve.

Three fresh-tasting salads — from back, Orange Slaw, Tuna and Bean Sprout Salad, Tomato-Mushroom Salad.

Asparagus Soup

340 g (12 oz.) asparagus	salt, pepper
2 chicken stock cubes	2 tablespoons evaporated
1½ cups water	milk

Blend undrained asparagus in electric blender until smooth (or press asparagus with liquid through sieve). Put asparagus in saucepan; add crumbled stock cubes, water, salt and pepper; simmer until liquid is reduced by half. Stir in evaporated milk just before serving.

Serves 2.

Approx. 200 kJ per serve.

Cream of Courgette Soup

500 g (1 lb.) courgettes	1 large onion
2 cups water	pinch nutmeg
2 chicken stock cubes	½ cup skim milk
2 sticks celery	

Put sliced courgettes, water, crumbled stock cubes, chopped celery, peeled and chopped onion and nutmeg into saucepan; stir over high heat until boiling; reduce heat; simmer covered 10 minutes or until courgettes are tender; cool slightly. Put half of mixture into blender; blend on high speed 1 minute or until ingredients are pureed. Repeat with remaining half of mixture. Return mixture to saucepan; add milk. Stir over medium heat until soup boils.

Serves 4.

Approx. 340 kJ per serve.

French Onion Soup

1 onion	2 beef stock cubes
½ teaspoon butter	1 teaspoon dry mustard
1½ cups hot water	30 g (1 oz.) cheese

Peel onion; chop finely. Fry in butter, covered, on very low heat 20 minutes. Add water, crumbled stock cubes and mustard; simmer a further 30 minutes. Spoon into heatproof dishes; sprinkle grated cheese on top; put under hot griller until cheese melts.

Serves 2.

Approx. 340 kJ per serve.

Ginger Bream

500 g (1 lb.) bream fillets	½ teaspoon dry mustard
1 tablespoon soy sauce	½ teaspoon ground ginger
2 teaspoons worcester-	2.5 cm (1 in.) piece green
shire sauce	ginger
2 tablespoons lemon juice	2 shallots or spring onions

Combine soy sauce, worcestershire sauce, lemon juice, mustard, ground ginger, grated green ginger

and finely-chopped shallots in bowl. Add fish fillets; marinate 1 hour. Grill fish fillets until tender, brushing with marinade several times during cooking. Heat remaining marinade; spoon over fish.

Serves 2.

Approx. 1000 kJ per serve.

Tuna and Bean Sprout Salad

220 g can tuna	2 shallots
250 g (8 oz.) can bean	1 small green pepper
sprouts (or fresh bean	1 small red pepper
sprouts)	1 small cucumber
6 radishes	2 tablespoons chopped
1 stick celery	parsley

Dressing

3 tablespoons lemon juice	½ teaspoon dry mustard
1 tablespoon worcester-	1 tablespoon chopped
shire sauce	onion
1 tablespoon chopped	salt, pepper
capers	

Drain tuna and bean sprouts. Wash bean sprouts; drain. Slice radishes, celery, shallots and cucumber; chop peppers. Combine tuna, bean sprouts and vegetables. Add dressing; toss lightly; refrigerate. Sprinkle parsley over.

Dressing: Put all ingredients in screw top jar; shake well.

Serves 4.

Approx. 460 kJ per serve.

Curried Fish Fillets

500 g (1 lb.) bream fillets	2 tablespoons lemon
2 tablespoons curry	juice
powder	1 cup water
1 tablespoon flour	2 tomatoes
1 tablespoon oil	2 tablespoons chopped
1 onion	parsley
1 clove garlic	salt, pepper
2.5 cm (1 in.) piece green	
ginger	

Skin and bone fish fillets; cut into 8 cm to 10 cm (3 in. to 4 in.) pieces. Lightly toss in combined curry powder and flour. Heat oil in pan; saute sliced onion, crushed garlic and peeled and finely-chopped green ginger until onion is tender. Add fish fillets; brown lightly on both sides. Add water, sliced tomatoes, lemon juice and parsley. Season with salt and pepper. Simmer gently 15 minutes or until fish is tender.

Serves 4.

Approx. 780 kJ per serve.

Stuffed Peppers

½ cup rice	1 small onion
250 g (8 oz.) smoked haddock	2 tablespoons chopped parsley
4 peppers	1 teaspoon worcestershire sauce
1 egg	
1 large tomato	1 cup tomato juice

Cook rice in boiling salted water 12 minutes; drain. Cover haddock with cold water; bring to boil. Reduce heat; simmer 3 to 5 minutes; drain. Bone and flake haddock. Cut peppers in half lengthwise; drop into saucepan of boiling water; boil rapidly 2 minutes; drain. Combine haddock with rice, lightly-beaten egg, peeled and finely-chopped tomato, peeled and grated onion, parsley and worcestershire sauce; mix well. Fill pepper halves evenly; put in greased ovenproof dish; pour tomato juice over. Cover; bake in moderate oven 40 to 45 minutes or until peppers are cooked.
Serves 4.
Approx. 700 kJ per serve.

Tuna Curry

2 onions	1 beef stock cube
15 g (½ oz.) butter	200 g can chunk-style tuna
2 teaspoons curry powder	
¼ cabbage	salt, pepper
½ cup water	

Peel and slice onions. Melt butter; saute onions and curry powder 5 minutes. Add shredded cabbage, water and crumbled stock cube. Cover; cook gently 15 minutes. Mix in drained tuna, salt and pepper; heat gently.
Serves 4.
Approx. 540 kJ per serve.

Chicken Salad

1 chicken breast approx. 250 g (8 oz.)	2 tablespoons french dressing
2 sticks celery	1 tablespoon mayonnaise
60 g (2 oz.) mushrooms	lettuce leaves
½ green pepper	

Steam or boil chicken until tender. Remove meat from bones; cut meat into small pieces. Slice mushrooms thinly. Put in small bowl; add 1 tablespoon of the french dressing; stand 15 minutes. Slice celery; chop green pepper. Combine remaining french dressing and mayonnaise. Combine all ingredients; toss lightly. Serve in crisp lettuce leaves.
Serves 2.
Approx. 1000 kJ per serve.

Italian Beef Casserole

½ cup rice	¼ teaspoon mixed herbs
500 g (1 lb.) lean minced steak	1 tablespoon cornflour
1 clove garlic	1 cup skim milk
2 large onions	60 g (2 oz.) cheddar cheese
salt, pepper	¼ teaspoon nutmeg
470 g (15 oz.) can whole tomatoes	2 egg whites
1 cup water	2 tablespoons grated parmesan cheese

Gradually add rice to large quantity of boiling, salted water; boil uncovered 12 minutes or until rice is tender; drain well. Add meat to frying pan; stand over high heat, mashing meat well. Stir until meat is golden brown. Drain off any fat in pan; add crushed garlic and peeled and finely-chopped onions; saute gently 2 minutes. Add undrained tomatoes, water, mixed herbs, salt and pepper; stir until combined. Bring to boil; reduce heat; simmer covered 30 minutes. Remove lid; increase heat; boil until mixture is thick. Spread half the rice over base of greased ovenproof dish; spoon over half the meat. Repeat rice and meat layer.

Place cornflour, milk and nutmeg in pan; stir until combined. Stir over heat until sauce boils and thickens; season with salt and pepper. Add grated cheese; stir until combined; cool. Beat egg whites until soft peaks form; gently fold into sauce. Pour sauce over meat. Sprinkle with parmesan cheese. Bake uncovered in moderately hot oven 30 minutes or until golden brown.
Serves 6.
Approx. 1600 kJ per serve.

Chinese Beef

375 g (12 oz.) beef topside (or tender steak)	2 sticks celery
	1 onion
1 tablespoon soy sauce	¾ cup water
¼ medium cabbage	1 chicken stock cube
250 g (8 oz.) carrots	salt, pepper

Trim any excess fat from meat; cut meat into thin strips; marinate in soy sauce 20 minutes. Heat pan; add meat; saute until browned and tender. Remove from pan; drain. Combine shredded cabbage, peeled and sliced carrots, peeled and chopped onion, sliced celery, water and crumbled stock cube in pan. Cover; bring to boil; reduce heat; simmer until vegetables are tender but still crisp. Season with salt and pepper; add meat; heat through gently.
Serves 4.
Approx. 1224 kJ per serve.

Chicken with Vegetables

2 whole chicken breasts each weighing 250 g (8 oz.)	1 green or red pepper
	1 onion
	2 sticks celery
1 cup unsweetened pineapple juice	2 medium carrots
	2 teaspoons soy sauce
2 cups water	salt, pepper
2 chicken stock cubes	1 tablespoon cornflour

Cut chicken breasts in half, giving four separate pieces. Combine pineapple juice, water and crumbled stock cubes in saucepan. Add chicken breasts. Cover; bring to boil; reduce heat. Simmer 20 minutes or until chicken is tender. Remove chicken from pan. To pineapple mixture add chopped pepper, peeled and quartered onion, chopped celery, peeled and chopped carrots. Bring to boil; reduce heat; simmer until vegetables are just tender. Remove vegetables from pan. Blend cornflour with a little of the pineapple stock; add to saucepan; stir over heat until sauce boils and thickens. Add chicken, vegetables, soy sauce, salt and pepper; heat thoroughly.
Serves 4.
Approx. 1260 kJ per serve.

Devilled Orange Chicken

1 cup orange juice	1 chicken stock cube
1 tablespoon grated orange rind	salt, pepper
	2 whole chicken breasts approx. 250 g (8 oz.) each
½ teaspoon dry mustard	
½ teaspoon nutmeg	
½ teaspoon curry powder	

Cut chicken breasts in half to give four separate pieces. Combine mustard, curry powder, nutmeg, crumbled stock cube, salt and pepper, orange juice and rind. Add chicken breasts. Marinate 1 to 2 hours. Grill until tender, brushing frequently with marinade; turn chicken frequently to avoid burning. Heat any remaining marinade; spoon over chicken.
Serves 4.
Approx. 1000 kJ per serve.

Pineapple with Chicken

1.25 kg (2½ lb.) chicken or chicken pieces	1 cup water
	2 chicken stock cubes
1 tablespoon oil	salt, pepper
1 clove garlic	1 tablespoon cornflour
2.5 cm (1 in.) piece green ginger	¼ teaspoon chilli powder
	2 teaspoons soy sauce
1 cup unsweetened pineapple juice	1 tablespoon dry sherry
	6 shallots or spring onions

Cut chicken into serving sized pieces. Heat oil in large pan; add chicken; fry gently until golden brown on both sides and cooked through, approx. 20 minutes. Remove chicken from pan. Drain off all fat from pan; add crushed garlic and peeled and grated green ginger; saute gently 1 minute. Add combined pineapple juice, water, crumbled stock cubes, salt, pepper, cornflour, chilli powder, soy sauce and sherry; stir until sauce boils and thickens. Return chicken to pan; stir until combined. Cover pan; simmer gently 15 minutes. Just before serving, add chopped shallots; simmer a further 2 minutes.
Serves 4.
Approx. 1800 kJ per serve.

Chicken with Broccoli

1 kg (2 lb.) chicken	2 teaspoons sate sauce
1 tablespoon oil	1 tablespoon tomato sauce
¼ cup water	salt, pepper
375 g (12 oz.) pkt frozen broccoli	¼ cup water, extra
	1 chicken stock cube
1 large red pepper	1 teaspoon cornflour
3 teaspoons soy sauce	

Cut chicken into small serving sized pieces. Heat oil in large frying pan; add chicken; toss in pan until chicken is well coated with oil; cook gently approx. 5 minutes or until light golden brown. Add water; bring to boil; reduce heat; simmer covered 20 minutes or until chicken is tender. Add broccoli cut into small pieces, seeded and thinly-sliced red pepper, soy sauce, sate sauce, tomato sauce, salt, pepper, crumbled stock cube and water which has been combined with the cornflour. Toss chicken in pan until sauce boils and thickens; reduce heat; simmer uncovered 4 minutes.
Serves 4.
Approx. 1100 kJ per serve.

Golden Crumb Chicken with Asparagus

2 large chicken breasts	2 tablespoons oil
1 egg white	470 g (15 oz.) can green asparagus spears
2 tablespoons skim milk	
10 crispbread biscuits	

Cream Sauce

1½ cups water	salt, pepper
3 chicken stock cubes	1 tablespoon cornflour
2 teaspoons french mustard	1 tablespoon cream

Recipe continued overleaf:

Chicken with Broccoli

Cut each chicken breast in half. Carefully remove meat from bones, giving four individual pieces. Pound each chicken breast out very thinly. Beat egg white and skim milk until combined. Place biscuits in electric blender; blend on medium speed until a fine crumb, or crush finely. Dip chicken breasts into egg white mixture, then coat lightly with crumbs. Heat oil in large frying pan; add chicken breasts; fry quickly on both sides until golden brown and cooked through, approx. 2 minutes on each side. Drain on absorbent paper; keep warm. Place chicken on serving plates; top each chicken breast with drained asparagus spears. Spoon prepared sauce over.

Sauce: Place all ingredients in pan; stir until combined. Place over heat; stir until sauce boils and thickens. Reduce heat; simmer 2 minutes, stirring occasionally.

Serves 4.
Approx. 1600 kJ per serve.

Chinese Cutlets

8 lamb cutlets	2 tablespoons tomato
1 tablespoon hoi sin sauce	paste
or fruit chutney	½ cup water
3 teaspoon worcester-	1 clove garlic
shire sauce	2.5 cm (1 in.) piece green
3 teaspoons soy sauce	ginger
2 teaspoons brown sugar	salt, pepper

Combine hoi sin sauce, worcestershire sauce, soy sauce, brown sugar, tomato paste, water, crushed garlic, grated ginger, salt and pepper. Pour over cutlets; marinate 3 hours. Drain; reserve marinade. Put cutlets on a rack over a tray. Bake in moderate oven 25 to 30 minutes or until cooked, brushing frequently with marinade. Serve with salad.

Serves 4.
Approx. 605 kJ per serve.

Mustard Crumbed Cutlets

8 lamb cutlets	3 teaspoons french
6 crispbreads	mustard
4 shallots or spring onions	2 egg whites
½ teaspoon rosemary	

Crush crispbreads finely; put into bowl; add chopped shallots and rosemary. Mix together mustard and egg whites; add to dry ingredients; mix well. Put cutlets in ovenproof dish; bake in moderate oven 15 minutes. Remove from oven; turn cutlets over; press crumb mixture evenly over each cutlet. Return to oven; bake a further 10 minutes, crumb-side up.

Serves 4.
Approx. 715 kJ per serve.

Cutlets Cacciatore

8 lean lamb cutlets

Cacciatore Sauce

470 g (15 oz.) can whole	30 g (1 oz.) mushrooms
tomatoes	1 bayleaf
1 small onion	½ teaspoon mixed herbs
1 tablespoon chopped	½ cup dry white wine
parsley	salt, pepper
1 clove garlic	

Grill cutlets for approx. 7 minutes on each side, until tender and golden brown. Spoon prepared Cacciatore Sauce over cutlets.

Cacciatore Sauce: Put tomatoes and their liquid into pan; mash tomatoes with potato masher. Add finely-chopped onion and parsley, crushed garlic, sliced mushrooms, bayleaf, mixed herbs, white wine, salt and pepper. Cook over high heat 5 minutes to reduce liquid, stirring occasionally.

Serves 4.
Approx. 780 kJ per serve.

Rich Tomato and Lamb's Fry Casserole

3 tablespoons tomato	½ teaspoon basil
paste	¼ teaspoon worcester-
½ cup water	shire sauce
1 chicken stock cube	250 g (8 oz.) lamb's fry
2 onions	(liver, heart and lungs)
125 g (4 oz.) mushrooms	2 tablespoons chopped
salt, pepper	parsley

Soak fry in salted water 1 hour; remove skin; soak in salted water a further 30 minutes. Pat meat dry and cut into very thin slices. Place tomato paste, water, crumbled stock cube, peeled and sliced onions, salt, pepper, basil, worcestershire sauce and sliced mushrooms in pan; stir until mixture comes to boil; reduce heat; simmer covered 10 minutes. Add meat to tomato mixture; simmer uncovered 5 minutes or until meat is cooked. Add parsley; stir until combined.

Serves 2.
Approx. 1328 kJ per serve.

Veal Provencale

500 g (1 lb.) veal steak	¼ cup water, extra
2 teaspoons butter	1 teaspoon worcester-
1 onion	shire sauce
1 tablespoon water	¼ teaspoon oregano
1 chicken stock cube	125 g (4 oz.) mushrooms
2 teaspoons flour	salt, pepper
1½ teaspoons french	2 tablespoons chopped
mustard	parsley
1 cup tomato juice	

Pound veal steaks until very thin. Heat butter in pan; add veal steaks; cook on both sides until golden brown. Remove veal from pan; add to pan peeled and chopped onion, water and crumbled stock cube; saute until onion is tender. Add flour; cook 1 minute. Remove from heat; add mustard, tomato juice, extra water, worcestershire sauce and oregano. Return to heat; stir until sauce boils and thickens. Return veal steaks to pan; add peeled and sliced mushrooms, salt and pepper; reduce heat; simmer covered a further 5 minutes; stir in parsley.
Serves 4.
Approx. 1110 kJ per serve.

Veal Scallopini

500 g (1 lb.) veal steak	salt, pepper
1 tablespoon oil	½ teaspoon oregano
470 g (15 oz.) can tomato juice	2 tablespoons chopped parsley

Divide veal steaks into four 125 g (4 oz.) servings; pound out thinly. Heat oil in pan; add veal steaks; fry quickly on both sides until lightly golden and cooked through; remove from pan. Add tomato juice and oregano to pan; bring to boil; boil uncovered until sauce thickens slightly. Season with salt and pepper. Return steaks to pan; simmer gently until steaks are heated through. Stir in parsley.
Serves 4.
Approx. 860 kJ per serve.

Ginger Pears

1 cup dry ginger ale	4 medium pears
2 slices green ginger	

Peel skin thinly from pears; cut pears into quarters; remove cores. Put pears, ginger ale and sliced ginger in saucepan; bring mixture to boil. Reduce heat; simmer uncovered until pears are tender. Remove pears and sliced ginger from saucepan; return sauce to heat and continue cooking over high heat until liquid is slightly reduced. Pour sauce over pears.
Serves 4.
Approx. 380 kJ per serve.

Passionfruit Fluff

1 lemon flavoured diabetic jelly	2 passionfruit
1 cup hot water	2 tablespoons evaporated milk

Dissolve jelly in hot water; stir in passionfruit pulp. Refrigerate jelly until partly set, then add

chilled evaporated milk. Beat until mixture is thick and lighter in colour. Pour into serving dish or individual serving dishes; refrigerate until set.
Serves 4.
Approx. 120 kJ per serve.

Strawberry Mousse

1 punnet strawberries	1 tablespoon sugar
1 cup non-fat natural yoghurt	2½ teaspoons gelatine
¼ cup skim milk	1 tablespoon water
	3 egg whites

Wash and hull strawberries (reserve 4 for decoration); put in blender with yoghurt, milk and sugar; blend until smooth. Sprinkle gelatine over water; dissolve over hot water; cool. Add to strawberry mixture; mix well. Fold in softly-beaten egg whites. Pour mixture into large souffle dish or 4 small individual dishes; refrigerate until set. Serve topped with a little yoghurt and a reserved whole strawberry.
Serves 4.
Approx. 400 kJ per serve.

Vanilla Junket

2 plain junket tablets	1 teaspoon sugar
2 cups water	1 teaspoon vanilla
2 teaspoons water, extra	grated nutmeg
1½ cups skim milk powder	

Crush junket tablets with the 2 teaspoons water. Heat the 2 cups water until just warm (if hot, junket will not set); sprinkle milk powder over; whisk well. Add sugar and vanilla. Pour over the crushed tablets; mix well. Pour into serving bowls or glasses; sprinkle with nutmeg. Put aside until set, then refrigerate. Top, if desired, with a whole strawberry.
Serves 4.
Approx. 220 kJ per serve.

Creamy Custard

2 tablespoons custard powder	2 tablespoons skim milk powder
2 teaspoons sugar	1 teaspoon vanilla
1 cup hot water	

Combine custard powder, sugar and skim milk powder with a little of the water; gradually blend in remaining water. Stir in vanilla; stir until custard boils and thickens. Serve with plain stewed fruit.
Serves 2.
Approx. 340 kJ per serve.

Suppers & Snacks

Suppers and snacks can be planned, or impromptu affairs — whipped up when the family is hungry. Or sometimes you want to make just small foods to nibble. Here are recipes for every taste and occasion.

Tacos

12 taco shells	470 g (15 oz.) can whole
2 tablespoons oil	tomatoes
750 g (1½ lb.) minced	1 cup water
steak	2 tomatoes
1 large onion	185 g (6 oz.) cheddar
1 clove garlic	cheese
1 teaspoon chilli powder	2 medium onions, extra
salt, pepper	½ small lettuce

Heat oil in frying pan; add meat and peeled and chopped onion; stir until meat is golden brown, mashing meat well. Pour off any surplus fat. Add crushed garlic, chilli powder, salt and pepper; stir 2 minutes. Add undrained mashed tomatoes; add water; stir well. Bring to boil; reduce heat; simmer covered 30 minutes; remove lid from pan; simmer uncovered 10 minutes or until meat is thick. (If desired, drain 300 g can red kidney beans; rinse under cold running water; add to meat mixture.)

While meat is cooking, cut tomatoes into small pieces; grate cheese; peel and thinly slice extra onions; shred lettuce. Place taco shells on baking tray; bake in moderate oven 5 minutes or until hot.

Guests can assemble their own taco shells. The grated cheese goes in first, then the hot meat mixture (the heat helps melt the cheese); top with tomato, onion and lettuce. If desired, top with a slice of avocado (toss avocado slices in a little lemon juice so they keep their bright colour).

Serves 6.

NOTE: Taco shells can be bought in packets of 12 from most supermarkets and food halls.

Tacos — a great food idea from Mexico — make a light but satisfying supper or snack. Taco shells are available in packets from most large food stores and supermarkets.

Smoked Roe Pate

250 g (8 oz.) smoked roe	2 gherkins
250 g (8 oz.) pkt cream cheese	salt, pepper
1 cup sour cream	1 tablespoon lemon juice
2 tablespoons chopped parsley	1 teaspoon french mustard

Carefully remove thin skin from roe. Put cream cheese into bowl; beat until soft and creamy. Add roughly-chopped roe; beat well until combined. Add sour cream, parsley, finely-chopped gherkins, salt, pepper, lemon juice and mustard; mix well. Spoon into serving bowl; cover; refrigerate overnight.

Sesame Chicken Pieces

2 whole chicken breasts	salt, pepper
3 tablespoons oil	½ cup sesame seeds
2 tablespoons soy sauce	¾ cup plain flour
2 cloves garlic	oil for deep-frying

Remove skin from chicken. Carefully remove chicken meat from bones, giving 4 individual pieces. Pound each chicken breast out lightly; cut into bite-size pieces. Put into bowl with oil, soy sauce, crushed garlic, salt and pepper; mix well. Leave to stand several hours. Coat chicken pieces with combined sesame seeds and flour. Deep-fry in hot oil until golden brown; drain on absorbent paper.

Serves 2 to 4.

Eggs Florentine

2 x 250 g (8 oz.) pkts frozen spinach	1¼ cups milk
30 g (1 oz.) butter	½ cup grated parmesan cheese
1 tablespoon cream	salt, pepper
pinch nutmeg	4 eggs
30 g (1 oz.) butter, extra	1 tablespoon fresh breadcrumbs
2 tablespoons flour	

Heat the spinach with the butter and cream. Remove from heat; add nutmeg. Pour mixture into buttered ovenproof dish; keep warm. Melt extra butter in small saucepan. Add the flour; cook over low heat 2 minutes. Remove from heat; gradually add the milk, stirring until smooth. Return to heat; stir until sauce boils and thickens; reduce heat; simmer uncovered 2 minutes. Add parmesan cheese; stir until melted. Season with salt and pepper. Poach the eggs lightly and arrange over spinach. Pour the sauce over;

sprinkle breadcrumbs over sauce. Brown under a hot griller.

Serves 4.

Smoked Oyster Pate

⅔ cup hot water	salt, pepper
1 chicken stock cube	3 tablespoons mayonnaise, extra
2 teaspoons gelatine	
2 x 105 g (3½ oz.) cans smoked oysters	3 shallots or spring onions, extra
3 shallots or spring onions	2 tablespoons chopped parsley
½ cup sour cream	
⅓ cup mayonnaise	

Put water, crumbled stock cube and gelatine in blender; blend on medium speed 30 seconds or until ingredients are well combined. Add drained, chopped oysters, chopped shallots, sour cream, mayonnaise, salt and pepper; blend on high speed until smooth. Pour mixture into serving dish; refrigerate until set. Put extra mayonnaise, finely-chopped extra shallots and parsley into bowl; mix well; spread evenly over top of pate. Refrigerate until ready to serve.

Herbed Rissoles

500 g (1 lb.) minced steak	60 g (2 oz.) butter
1 egg	3 tablespoons flour
3 tablespoons tomato sauce	2½ cups water
2 teaspoons worcestershire sauce	2 beef stock cubes
salt, pepper	2 tablespoons tomato sauce, extra
pinch mixed herbs	pinch mixed herbs, extra
½ cup dry breadcrumbs	1 teaspoon worcestershire sauce, extra
1 onion	

Place steak, egg, tomato sauce, worcestershire sauce, salt, pepper, mixed herbs, breadcrumbs and peeled and finely-chopped onion in bowl; mix very well with hands. Divide mixture into eight equal portions. Roll each portion in hands to form a round ball, then flatten out slightly. Heat butter in large frying pan; add rissoles; fry gently on both sides until brown; remove from pan. Add flour to pan; stir over heat until dark golden brown; remove pan from heat; add water, crumbled stock cubes, salt, pepper, extra tomato sauce, extra mixed herbs and extra worcestershire sauce; stir until combined. Return pan to heat; stir until sauce boils and thickens; reduce heat; add rissoles; simmer covered 30 minutes, stirring occasionally.

Serves 4.

Stuffed Artichokes

8 large artichokes
1 small lemon
salt

Stuffing

60 g (2 oz.) butter
2 medium onions
1 clove garlic
2 x 470 g (15 oz.) cans whole tomatoes
½ teaspoon basil
¼ teaspoon oregano
1 chicken stock cube
salt, pepper
2 tablespoons chopped parsley
300 ml (½ pint) sour cream
30 g (1 oz.) butter, extra
1 cup fresh white bread-crumbs, firmly packed
2 tablespoons grated parmesan cheese

Wash artichokes, then cut off stem at base, so artichokes stand straight and firm. Remove any old outside leaves, then shorten tips with scissors. Cut the very top of each artichoke across with a sharp knife.

Fill a large pan (or several pans) with hot water; add 1 teaspoon of salt and the sliced lemon; add artichokes; bring to boil; reduce heat; simmer covered 30 minutes. Remove from water; drain off any water from inside artichokes by turning upside down. Allow to cool.

To stuff artichokes, pull out centre leaves from each artichoke. When you pull the leaves you will see the hairy 'choke'; gently remove this choke with spoon and discard.

Stuffing: Heat butter in frying pan; add peeled and chopped onions and crushed garlic; saute gently until onion is transparent; add undrained mashed tomatoes, basil, oregano, crumbled stock cube, salt and pepper. Bring to boil; reduce heat; simmer uncovered 20 minutes or until sauce is thick; remove from heat; add parsley; mix well. Heat extra butter in separate pan; add bread-crumbs and parmesan cheese; remove from heat; mix well. Spoon tomato mixture evenly into centre of each artichoke, then top with sour cream, spreading out evenly. Spoon breadcrumb mixture over. Place artichokes in baking dish; pour 1 cup of water into baking dish. Bake in moderate oven 30 minutes or until breadcrumbs are golden.

Serves 8.

NOTE: Each diner pulls off the leaves, dips them into the creamy filling, then eats that and the thick, fleshy end of the leaf, pulling it between the teeth.

Barbecued Meatballs

500 g (1 lb.) minced steak
250 g (8 oz.) sausage mince
1 egg
½ cup fresh breadcrumbs
1 onion
1 teaspoon curry powder
1 tablespoon chopped parsley
salt, pepper

Sauce

½ cup water
½ cup tomato sauce
2 tablespoons vinegar
¼ cup brown sugar
3 teaspoons worcester-shire sauce
2 tablespoons fruit chutney

Combine minced steak, sausage mince, egg, breadcrumbs, peeled and finely-chopped onion, curry powder, parsley, salt and pepper; mix well. Form tablespoonfuls of mixture into balls; put in baking dish; bake in moderate oven 30 minutes, shaking pan occasionally. Pour off any excess fat; pour sauce over meatballs; return to oven; bake a further 15 to 20 minutes, basting occasionally with sauce.

Sauce: Combine all ingredients in saucepan; stir until sugar has dissolved; bring to boil; remove from heat.

Serves 4 to 6.

Crab and Camembert Quiche

375 g (12 oz.) pkt frozen puff pastry
155 g can crab
150 g can camembert cheese
3 eggs
300 ml (½ pint) double cream
¼ cup milk
1 teaspoon french mustard
salt, pepper
2 tablespoons chopped parsley
3 shallots or spring onions

Let pastry come to room temperature. Roll out pastry to 3 mm (⅛ in.) thickness to line 23 cm (9 in.) flan tin. Press pastry well into sides of tin; trim edges. Drain crab; arrange over base of pastry. Cut cheese into 1 cm (½ in.) slices; place over crab. Put eggs, cream, milk, mustard, salt, pepper, parsley and chopped shallots into bowl; whisk well. Pour custard mixture carefully over cheese. Put a baking tray into a very hot oven until tray is very hot; place flan tin on tray; bake in very hot oven 10 minutes or until custard starts to turn light golden brown; reduce heat to moderate; bake a further 20 minutes or until custard is set. Serve hot.

Serves 6 to 8.

Eggs Benedict

4 English muffins
4 slices ham
4 eggs
butter

Poach eggs; saute ham in butter until hot; split muffins in half and toast. (See recipe for English muffins on page 211 if you are unable to buy them.) Butter the toasted muffins; top with a

Recipe continued overleaf:

slice of ham, then with a poached egg; spoon Hollandaise Sauce over. (See recipe for Blender Hollandaise on page 110.)

Serves 4.

Chicken Salad Sandwich

12 slices bread	salt, pepper
butter	4 shallots or spring onions
2½ cups chopped cooked chicken meat (approx. 1 kg (2 lb.) chicken)	1 teaspoon french mustard
⅓ cup mayonnaise	2 tablespoons chopped parsley

Combine in bowl chicken meat, mayonnaise, salt, pepper, finely-chopped shallots, mustard and parsley; mix well. Butter bread. Place buttered side of bread on base of cooking iron. Put 2 tablespoons of filling on top of bread; top with another slice of bread (buttered side up). Close cooking iron. Cook 5 minutes in an electric sandwich iron or 5 minutes on each side in a jaffle iron.

Makes 6 sandwiches.

NOTE: A small barbecued chicken can be used for these sandwiches.

Curried Steak Sandwich

12 slices bread	1 tablespoon tomato sauce
butter	2 teaspoons worcestershire sauce
250 g (8 oz.) minced steak	¾ cup water
1 onion	2 teaspoons cornflour
30 g (1 oz.) butter	2 tablespoons water, extra
2 teaspoons curry powder	salt, pepper

Saute peeled and chopped onion in butter until transparent; add meat; brown well. Add curry powder, tomato sauce, worcestershire sauce and water; mix well. Bring to boil; reduce heat; simmer covered 10 minutes. Mix cornflour to smooth paste with extra water; add to pan; stir until mixture boils and thickens; reduce heat; simmer 1 minute. Season with salt and pepper. Cool. Butter bread. Put one slice (buttered side down) on base of cooking iron. Top with 2 tablespoons filling and cover with another slice of bread (buttered side up). Close cooking iron.

Cook 5 minutes in an electric sandwich iron or 5 minutes on each side in a jaffle iron.

Makes 6 sandwiches.

Chilli Garlic Peanuts

60 g (2 oz.) butter	½ teaspoon chilli powder
500 g (1 lb.) raw peanuts (with red skins left on)	½ teaspoon paprika
1 large clove garlic	¼ teaspoon salt
	¼ teaspoon caraway seeds

Heat butter in large frying pan; add peanuts; stand over very low heat 5 minutes, stirring occasionally. Add crushed garlic; saute gently 2 minutes. Add chilli, paprika, salt and caraway seeds; saute 3 minutes, stirring constantly. Pour peanuts into bowl; allow to become cold.

Serves 6 to 8.

Avocado Dip

1 kg (2 lb.) large prawns	2 lemons
1 large cucumber	283 g (10 oz.) can green asparagus spears

Dip

1 large ripe avocado	½ cup sour cream
1 cup mayonnaise	salt, pepper
1 teaspoon french mustard	1 tablespoon brandy
2 teaspoons lemon juice	1 teaspoon sugar

Shell and remove back vein from prawns; cut cucumber in half lengthwise, then in half again; remove seeds. Cut strips of cucumber into 8 cm (3 in.) pieces, then cut each piece of cucumber in half again lengthwise. Cut lemons into wedges; drain asparagus. Place small bowls in centre of six individual serving plates; arrange prawns, cucumber, lemon wedges and asparagus spears around each bowl; cover and refrigerate until ready to serve, then spoon prepared dip into each bowl.

Dip: Remove seed and skin from avocado; put all flesh into electric blender. Add mayonnaise, mustard, lemon juice, sour cream, salt, pepper, brandy and sugar; blend on medium speed 1 minute or until very smooth. Cover; refrigerate. (Make only 30 minutes before using or avocado may turn brown.) Serves 6.

Rissoles with Onion Gravy

1 pkt brown onion sauce mix	1 egg
	salt, pepper
1 pkt chicken noodle soup	flour
500 g (1 lb.) minced steak	2 tablespoons oil
1 onion	½ cup water

Combine in bowl minced steak, soup mix, peeled and finely-chopped onion, egg, salt and pepper; mix well. Take tablespoonfuls of meat mixture and roll into balls; coat well with flour. Heat oil in frying pan; add meatballs; brown well. Remove meatballs from pan. Mix brown onion sauce as directed on packet; add to pan with water. Bring to boil, stirring; reduce heat; simmer 1 minute; add meatballs; simmer 1 minute.

Serves 4.

Avocado Dip — delicately-coloured with a creamy texture.

Brandied Mustard Steaks

4 fillet steaks	2 teaspoons french
60 g (2 oz.) butter	mustard
1 clove garlic	2 teaspoons worcester-
1 onion	shire sauce
1½ tablespoons flour	2 tablespoons chopped
2 beef stock cubes	parsley
1 cup water	salt, pepper
1 tablespoon brandy	

Flatten steaks slightly; melt butter in pan; add steaks; cook until done as desired; remove from pan; keep warm. Add crushed garlic and peeled and sliced onion to pan drippings; saute gently 3 minutes. Stir in flour; cook 1 minute. Add water, crumbled stock cubes and remaining ingredients; mix well; season with salt and pepper. Simmer 3 minutes; spoon sauce over steaks.

Serves 4.

Potato Curry Pie

Pastry

1½ cups plain flour	⅓ cup water
½ teaspoon salt	1 egg yolk
90 g (3 oz.) butter	

Filling

500 g (1 lb.) minced steak	1 tablespoon worcester-
2 medium onions	shire sauce
1 medium carrot	salt, pepper
30 g (1 oz.) butter	2 beef stock cubes
3 teaspoons curry	2 teaspoons soy sauce
powder	3 cups water
2 tablespoons tomato	3 tablespoons flour
sauce	¼ cup water, extra

Topping

1 kg (2 lb.) old potatoes	⅓ cup milk
60 g (2 oz.) butter	

Pastry: Sift flour and salt into bowl. Place butter and water in pan; stir over heat until butter has melted and water comes to boil. Add egg yolk to flour mixture with boiling water mixture; stir until combined. Turn dough out on to lightly-floured surface; knead very lightly. Cover pastry with bowl; allow to stand 15 minutes, then knead again lightly. Roll out dough to cover base and sides of greased 23 cm (9 in.) pie plate; trim edges. Spoon prepared filling into pie, spreading out evenly. Spoon potato mixture into large piping bag fitted with star nozzle. Pipe potato in circles around pie, starting at pastry edge and completely covering pie (or spread potato evenly over top of pie). Bake in hot oven 10 minutes; reduce heat to moderate; cook a further 25 minutes or until potato is golden brown.

Filling: Place minced steak, peeled and finely-chopped onions, peeled and grated carrot and butter in frying pan; stir over high heat until meat is light golden brown, mashing meat well. Add curry powder, tomato sauce, worcestershire sauce, salt, pepper, crumbled stock cubes, soy sauce and water; stir until combined. Bring to boil; reduce heat; simmer covered 30 minutes. Remove pan from heat; add combined flour and extra water; stir until combined. Return pan to heat; stir until mixture is boiling. Reduce heat; simmer uncovered 20 minutes or until mixture is thick. Allow to become cold.

Topping: Peel and wash potatoes; cut into quarters. Place in boiling salted water; boil covered 20 minutes or until potatoes are tender; drain. Add butter and milk; mash potatoes well. Use while still hot.

Serves 4 to 6.

Steak and Macaroni Slice

Base

1 cup small macaroni	2 shallots or spring onions
30 g (1 oz.) butter	1 clove garlic
2 tablespoons chopped	1 egg
parsley	

Filling

2 tablespoons oil	¼ cup tomato paste
500 g (1 lb.) minced steak	1 cup water
2 onions	1 beef stock cube
470 g (15 oz.) can whole	60 g (2 oz.) mushrooms
peeled tomatoes	salt, pepper

Topping

60 g (2 oz.) butter	2 teaspoons french
4 shallots or spring onions	mustard
¼ cup flour	2 teaspoons worcester-
¾ cup milk	shire sauce
½ cup dry white wine	½ cup sour cream
¼ cup water	60 g (2 oz.) cheddar cheese

Base: Drop macaroni into large saucepan of boiling, salted water; cook 10 minutes or until tender; drain well; put into bowl. Add chopped butter, parsley, chopped shallots, crushed garlic and lightly-beaten egg; mix well. Spoon mixture evenly over greased 28 cm x 18 cm (11 in. x 7 in.) lamington tin.

Filling: Heat oil in pan; add minced steak and peeled and chopped onions; saute until meat is dark golden brown; pour off any excess fat. Add undrained mashed tomatoes, tomato paste, water, crumbled stock cube, sliced mushrooms, salt and pepper; mix well. Bring to boil; reduce heat; simmer uncovered approx. 50 minutes or until nearly all liquid has evaporated. Spoon meat mixture evenly over macaroni.

Topping: Heat butter in pan; add chopped shallots; cook 1 minute. Add flour; cook until light golden brown. Gradually add milk, wine and water; stir until sauce boils and thickens. Reduce heat; simmer 3 minutes. Add mustard and worcestershire sauce; simmer a further 1 minute. Remove from heat; add combined sour cream and lightly-beaten egg. Spoon mixture evenly over meat layer; sprinkle grated cheese over. Bake in moderate oven 30 minutes or until cheese is golden brown and slice has heated through.

Serves 6.

Greek Triangles

1 large bunch spinach (approx. 20 sticks)	2 tablespoons flour
30 g (1 oz.) butter	pinch nutmeg
salt, pepper	¾ cup milk
4 shallots or spring onions	125 g (4 oz.) feta cheese
30 g (1 oz.) butter, extra	500 g (1 lb.) phylo pastry
	oil

Spinach Filling: Wash spinach; coarsely chop leaves. Put in saucepan with butter, salt, pepper and chopped shallots. Cover; bring to boil; reduce heat; cook until spinach is tender. Drain well; chop spinach finely. Melt extra butter in pan; stir in flour and nutmeg; cook stirring 1 minute. Add milk; stir until sauce boils and thickens. Remove from heat; stir in chopped spinach and chopped feta cheese; cool.

Phylo pastry dries out if it is left uncovered, so deal with one sheet at a time and return remainder to packet. Cut each pastry sheet into 8 cm (3 in.) wide strips. Brush each strip with oil. One strip of pastry makes one complete triangle. Put a teaspoonful of filling on end of each pastry strip. Take corner of pastry and fold over to form triangle, covering filling. Lift first triangle up and over to form second triangle. Continue folding over and over until you reach the end of pastry strip. Trim edges if pastry overhangs.

Lower triangles a few at a time into deep hot oil. Fry until golden; drain well. The recipe makes about 90 triangles. It can of course be halved, or you can make just as many as you need, then freeze remaining pastry and filling separately.

Crunchy Sausage Nibbles

500 g (1 lb.) sausage mince	1 tablespoon worcestershire sauce
1 onion	salt, pepper
1 stick celery	½ cup flour
1 egg	1 egg, extra
2 tablespoons tomato paste	2 tablespoons milk
1 teaspoon prepared mustard	1 teaspoon mixed herbs
	3 cups fresh breadcrumbs
	oil for deep-frying

Combine sausage mince, peeled and finely-chopped onion, finely-chopped celery, egg, tomato paste, mustard, worcestershire sauce, salt and pepper; mix well. Take spoonfuls of mixture and roll into lengths about 5 cm (2 in.) long. Roll in flour, then dip in combined beaten extra egg and milk; roll in combined breadcrumbs and herbs. Deep-fry in hot oil until golden brown and cooked through, approx. 5 minutes.

Makes 35.

Wine and Cheese Slice

5 slices white bread	185 g (6 oz.) cheddar cheese
125 g (4 oz.) butter	1 teaspoon worcestershire sauce
2 cloves garlic	1 teaspoon dry mustard
3 eggs	salt, pepper
½ cup water	1 tablespoon chopped parsley
1 cup dry white wine	
1 chicken stock cube	

Toast bread until lightly browned. Combine softened butter and crushed garlic; beat until smooth. Spread garlic butter evenly over each piece of toast. Put toast, evenly, butter-side down, in 28 cm x 18 cm (11 in. x 7 in.) lamington tin. Combine eggs, water and wine in bowl; beat well. Stir in crumbled stock cube, grated cheese, worcestershire sauce, mustard, salt and pepper. Pour mixture over toast; sprinkle parsley over; bake in moderately slow oven 30 minutes or until mixture is set. Serve with a green salad.

Curried Chicken Savouries

2 whole chicken breasts	1½ tablespoons curry powder
250 g (8 oz.) packaged cream cheese	4 shallots or spring onions
60 g (2 oz.) blanched almonds	salt, pepper
2 tablespoons mayonnaise	1 cup packaged dry breadcrumbs
1 tablespoon fruit or mango chutney	½ cup coconut
	oil for deep-frying

Steam or boil chicken until tender; cool. Remove skin, then remove meat from bones; cut meat into small pieces. Beat cream cheese until soft. Add mayonnaise, chutney and curry powder; beat until all ingredients are well combined. Add chicken, very finely-chopped almonds, chopped shallots, salt and pepper; mix well.

Refrigerate mixture several hours until firm, then roll into balls about the size of a walnut. Roll balls in combined breadcrumbs and coconut. Deep-fry in hot oil; drain on absorbent paper.

Makes approx. 25.

Sauces

Sauces add the finishing taste to a dish, whether it's a rich, succulent sauce to spoon generously over steaks, fish, chicken — or a light, sweet sauce to give extra flavour to hot or cold desserts.

Sauce Chasseur

90 g (3 oz.) butter	¼ teaspoon tarragon
250 g (8 oz.) mushrooms	½ teaspoon sugar
1 clove garlic	1 tablespoon tomato
1 onion	paste
2 tablespoons flour	pepper
1 cup dry white wine	4 shallots or spring onions
¼ cup water	1 tablespoon chopped
¾ cup canned beef consomme	parsley

Heat butter in pan; add sliced mushrooms, crushed garlic and peeled and chopped onion; saute until onion is dark golden brown. Add flour; cook 1 minute. Add white wine, water and beef consomme; stir until sauce boils and thickens; reduce heat; simmer uncovered 5 minutes.

Add tarragon, sugar, tomato paste and pepper; cook a further 3 minutes. Add chopped shallots and parsley; simmer a further 2 minutes. Serve with beef or chicken.

Serves 6.

Cumberland Sauce

⅓ cup orange juice	3 teaspoons vinegar
2 tablespoons lemon juice	½ cup port
½ cup bottled red currant jelly	pepper
	4 shallots or spring onions
1 teaspoon french mustard	

Remove rind from half an orange and half a lemon; cut into thin strips (make sure there is no white pith on rind). Put in boiling water; cook 5 minutes; drain; rinse under cold water. Put orange juice, lemon juice, red currant jelly and mustard in saucepan; stir over medium heat until sauce boils; reduce heat; simmer 3 minutes. Add vinegar, port and pepper; cook a further 2 minutes. Add chopped shallots, orange and lemon strips; cook a further 1 minute. Serve with ham or game.

Serves 6.

Sauce Chasseur — a rich-tasting mushroom and wine sauce to add interest to beef or chicken dishes.

Curry-Cream Sauce

2 onions	2 teaspoons lemon juice
60 g (2 oz.) butter	1 tablespoon chopped
3 teaspoons curry powder	parsley
¾ cup mayonnaise	salt
½ cup cream	

Saute peeled and roughly-chopped onions in butter until onions are transparent; add curry powder. Put into blender; blend until of puree consistency. Return to pan with mayonnaise, cream, lemon juice, chopped parsley; season with salt. Stir over heat until sauce just comes to the boil. Remove from heat immediately. Serve with fish or chicken.
   Serves 4.

Creamy Mushroom Sauce

60 g (2 oz.) butter	½ teaspoon worcester-
2 rashers bacon	shire sauce
1 clove garlic	1 chicken stock cube
125 g (4 oz.) mushrooms	salt, pepper
1½ tablespoons flour	¼ cup cream
1 cup water	1 egg
½ cup dry white wine	4 shallots or spring onions

Heat butter in pan; add chopped bacon, crushed garlic and sliced mushrooms; saute until bacon is crisp. Add flour; stir until golden brown. Gradually add water and wine; stir until sauce boils and thickens. Reduce heat; add worcestershire sauce, crumbled stock cube, salt and pepper; simmer a further 3 minutes. Add combined cream and lightly-beaten egg and chopped shallots; stir over low heat 2 minutes or until sauce is heated through. Serve with steak or chicken.
   Serves 4.

Oyster Sauce

about 10 canned fresh	440 g (14 oz.) can cream of
oysters	oyster soup
60 g (2 oz.) butter	1 cup milk
1 onion	¼ cup cream
2 sticks celery	1 egg yolk
1 clove garlic	pepper
1 tablespoon flour	6 shallots or spring onions

Drain oysters; reserve ¼ cup liquid (or make up to ¼ cup with water, if necessary). Heat butter in pan; add peeled and chopped onion, diced celery and crushed garlic; saute until onion is tender. Add flour; stir until golden brown. Add undiluted oyster soup, milk and reserved oyster liquid; stir until sauce boils and thickens; reduce heat; simmer uncovered 5 minutes. Remove from heat; add cream, lightly-beaten egg yolk, pepper and

chopped shallots. Return to heat; stir over low heat until sauce thickens. Serve with grills or fish.
   Serves 6.

Mustard Sauce

30 g (1 oz.) butter	½ cup cream
3 teaspoons french	salt, pepper
mustard	
1 teaspoon worcester-	
shire sauce	

Heat butter in pan; add mustard; cook 1 minute. Add worcestershire sauce, cream, salt and pepper; stir over low heat until sauce just boils. Serve with beef, lamb or fish.
   Serves 4.

Blender Bearnaise

4 egg yolks	1 bay leaf
¼ cup white vinegar	4 peppercorns
¼ cup tarragon vinegar	250 g (8 oz.) butter
1 shallot or spring onion	salt, pepper

Combine vinegars with chopped shallot, bay leaf and peppercorns in saucepan; bring to boil; reduce heat and simmer until liquid is reduced by half. Strain; reserve liquid; cool.
   Put egg yolks into blender; turn on to low speed. Gradually add hot melted butter, no more than a teaspoonful at a time to begin with. When mixture thickens (this is most important — the vinegar should not be added before the mixture thickens or the sauce will become too thin), add 1 teaspoon vinegar mixture; blend a few seconds, then add another teaspoon of vinegar. Continue adding melted butter gradually until mixture re-thickens, then add another teaspoon vinegar. Continue in this way, blending in butter, then vinegar, until all butter and vinegar have been used. Season with salt and pepper.
   Serves 6.

Blender Hollandaise

4 egg yolks	1 tablespoon strained
salt, pepper	lemon juice
125 g (4 oz.) butter	

Put egg yolks, salt, pepper and lemon juice into blender. Heat butter until bubbling, but not coloured. Turn blender on; gradually pour the hot butter, in a thin stream, on to the egg-yolk mixture; it will thicken and turn golden. Keep over hot water until ready to use.

Rich Chocolate Sauce

125 g (4 oz.) dark chocolate	2 tablespoons custard powder
¼ cup sugar	⅓ cup cream
¼ cup water	

Put chopped chocolate, sugar and water in top of double saucepan; stir over simmering water until chocolate has melted. Mix together custard powder and cream; add to chocolate; stir over heat a further 5 minutes or until slightly thickened. Serve hot over icecream.

Serves 4.

Chocolate Brandy Alexander Sauce

125 g (4 oz.) dark chocolate	1 tablespoon brandy
1 egg yolk	1 tablespoon cornflour
¼ cup water	½ cup milk
2 tablespoons Creme de Cacao	½ cup cream

Put roughly-chopped chocolate, egg yolk and water in top of double saucepan; stir over simmering water until chocolate has melted and mixture thickens. Remove from heat; add Creme de Cacao and brandy; allow to cool. Mix cornflour to smooth paste with milk; add to chocolate mixture; stir until smooth. Stir over medium heat until sauce boils and thickens; reduce heat; simmer 2 minutes. Add cream; reheat without boiling.

Serves 4.

Coffee Liqueur Sauce

1 tablespoon cocoa	¾ cup milk
1 tablespoon cornflour	3 tablespoons coffee liqueur (Kahlua or Tia Maria)
3 teaspoons instant coffee powder	
½ cup sugar	60 g (2 oz.) butter

Put cocoa, cornflour, coffee and sugar in saucepan. Gradually add milk, stirring until combined. Stir over medium heat until sauce boils and thickens. Add coffee liqueur; simmer uncovered 3 minutes. Add butter; stir until melted. Serve hot over icecream.

Serves 4.

Caramel Grand Marnier Sauce

60 g (2 oz.) butter	3 tablespoons Grand Marnier
1 cup brown sugar, firmly packed	1 tablespoon cornflour
½ cup water	½ cup cream

Place butter and sugar in pan; stir over heat until butter has melted; add combined remaining ingredients; stir over low heat until sugar dissolves, then stir until sauce boils. Reduce heat; simmer uncovered 3 minutes; stir constantly. Serve hot over icecream or pancakes or over fresh fruit, such as bananas.

Serves 4 to 6.

Marshmallow Raspberry Sauce

250 g (8 oz.) frozen raspberries	100 g (3½ oz.) pkt white marshmallows
½ cup orange juice	3 teaspoons cornflour
2 tablespoons rum	2 tablespoons water
1 tablespoon sugar	

Thaw out frozen raspberries. Put thawed raspberries and their juice into blender; blend on high speed 1 minute or until smooth; strain through fine sieve; discard seeds (or mash well, push through strainer). Put mixture into top of double saucepan with orange juice, rum and sugar; stir over simmering water until sauce boils. Gradually add chopped marshmallows; stir until melted. Blend together cornflour and water until smooth; add to mixture; stir until sauce boils and thickens. Serve hot over icecream.

Serves 4.

Strawberry Daiquiri Sauce

1 punnet strawberries	¼ cup white rum
2 teaspoons icing sugar	1 tablespoon lemon juice

Put washed and hulled strawberries into blender with icing sugar, rum and lemon juice. Blend on high speed 2 minutes or until smooth. Serve over icecream.

Serves 4.

Caramel Sauce

125 g (4 oz.) butter	2 tablespoons golden syrup
1 cup brown sugar, lightly packed	1½ tablespoons cornflour
1 cup water	¼ cup cream

Combine butter and sugar in saucepan; stir over low heat until butter melts and sugar dissolves and mixture turns to thick syrup; bring to boil; reduce heat; simmer 3 minutes. Combine water, golden syrup and cornflour; mix until smooth; add to brown sugar mixture; stir until smooth. Stir until boiling; reduce heat; simmer 2 minutes. Remove from heat; stir in cream. Serve warm or cold.

Serves 4 to 6.

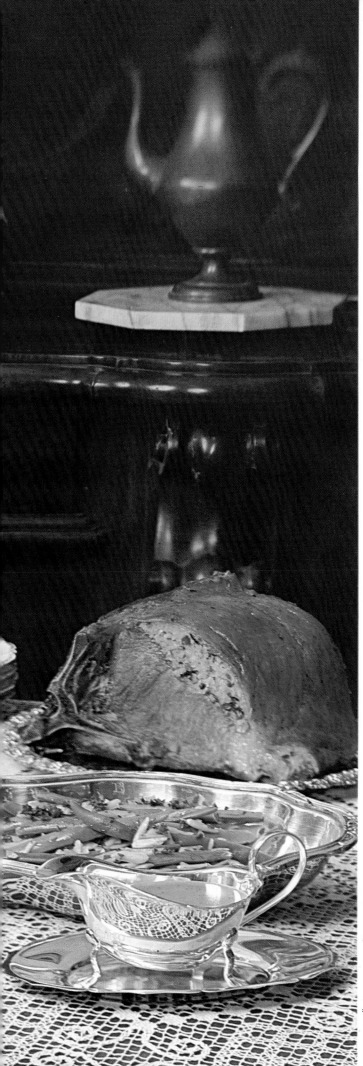

Perfect Dinner Parties

Here's a superb dinner party for six, with lots of do-ahead features. Crumb fish fillets several hours ahead and refrigerate; make up the fish sauce. Stuff beef ready for roasting the day before; cover with plastic food wrap and refrigerate; remove from refrigerator and let come to room temperature before putting in oven. Prepare potato casserole several hours in advance, ready for final reheating. Pears can be prepared completely the day before, but keep pears and liquid separate until serving time.

𝓜enu 1

Almond Crumbed Fish Fillets with Green Ginger Sauce

Sirloin of Beef with Horseradish Stuffing

Potato Casserole
Green Beans

Chocolate Pears* with Liqueur

1 *Almond Crumbed Fish Fillets with Green Ginger Sauce*
2 *Sirloin of Beef with Horseradish Stuffing*
3 *Potato Casserole*
4 *Green Beans*
5 *Chocolate Pears with Liqueur*

*This recipe appears overleaf with full step-by-step instructions.

Almond-Crumbed Fish Fillets

6 fish fillets	¼ cup chopped parsley
2 cups fresh breadcrumbs (about ½ loaf bread)	2 tablespoons lemon juice flour
125 g (4 oz.) slivered almonds	1 egg
30 g (1 oz.) butter	¼ cup milk
salt, pepper	butter for frying

Green Ginger Sauce

1 cup mayonnaise	2 teaspoons grated green ginger
salt, pepper	
2 teaspoons lemon juice	2 tablespoons chopped parsley
⅓ cup sour cream	

Skin fish fillets; pour lemon juice over; let stand 10 minutes. Heat butter in pan; add almonds; stir over low heat until almonds are golden brown. Remove from pan; drain on absorbent paper. Combine breadcrumbs, finely-chopped almonds, salt, pepper and parsley; mix well. Drain fish; roll in flour, then combined beaten egg and milk; coat in breadcrumb mixture; press on firmly.

Heat butter in pan; gently saute fish until golden brown on both sides and cooked through. Serve with lemon wedges and Green Ginger Sauce.

Green Ginger Sauce: Combine all the ingredients and mix well. Refrigerate sauce before serving.

Sirloin of Beef

3 kg (6 lb.) sirloin roast	2 tablespoons port
salt, pepper	1 teaspoon prepared mustard
60 g (2 oz.) butter	
1½ cups water	1 beef stock cube
½ cup cream	1 tablespoon cornflour
1 tablespoon brandy	

Horseradish Stuffing

90 g (3 oz.) butter	salt, pepper
2 rashers bacon	2 tablespoons chopped parsley
125 g (4 oz.) mushrooms	
1 medium onion	1 egg
1½ tablespoons bottled horseradish cream	3 cups fresh breadcrumbs

Run a thin-bladed knife between fat and meat, separating fat from meat but leaving it joined at top and bottom, so that a pocket is formed for stuffing. Spoon in prepared stuffing, pressing in firmly. Put meat, fat side up, in baking dish. Sprinkle salt and pepper over. Put butter on top of fat. Roast in hot oven 20 minutes; reduce heat to moderate for 20 minutes, then increase heat to hot for further 20 minutes.

Remove meat from baking dish; keep warm. Pour off all fat from baking dish. Combine water, cream, brandy, port, mustard and crumbled stock cube; add cornflour; stir until combined. Add to baking dish; stir over low heat until sauce boils and thickens. Reduce heat; simmer 3 minutes. Season with salt and pepper. To carve roast, run knife down and along bone, separating meat from bone; cut meat into slices. Serve sauce separately.

Stuffing: Heat butter in pan; add chopped bacon, sliced mushrooms, peeled and finely-chopped onion; saute gently until onion is soft. Add horseradish cream; stir until combined. Season with salt and pepper. Put breadcrumbs, parsley and egg into bowl; mix well. Add mushroom mixture; mix well.

Potato Casserole

1 kg (2 lb.) potatoes	¼ cup chopped chives (or shallots)
60 g (2 oz.) butter	
¼ cup milk	salt, pepper
250 g (8 oz.) pkt cream cheese	60 g (2 oz.) butter, extra
	1 cup fresh breadcrumbs

Peel the potatoes; boil until tender; drain well. Mash potatoes. Beat butter and cream cheese until soft; add to potatoes; beat well. Season with salt and pepper. Add chives and milk; stir until combined. Spoon into ovenproof dish.

Heat extra butter in frying pan; add breadcrumbs; stir until golden brown. Spoon crumbs over potato. Bake uncovered in moderately hot oven 25 minutes or until heated through.

Green Beans

750 g (1½ lb.) beans	2 teaspoons lemon juice
60 g (2 oz.) butter	2 tablespoons chopped parsley
salt, pepper	

Top, tail and string beans. Put into boiling salted water; cook until just tender; drain. Melt butter in pan; add lemon juice and parsley; stir until combined. Add beans; heat through gently. Season with salt and pepper.

Chocolate Pears with Liqueur Step-by-Step

You will need:

6 pears
1½ cups dry white wine
1½ cups water
¾ cup sugar
4 strips orange rind
8 cm (3 in.) piece cinnamon stick
2 tablespoons Grand Marnier
125 g (4 oz.) milk chocolate
125 g (4 oz.) dark chocolate

1. Peel pears thinly, leaving stems on pears. Trim base of pears so that pears stand upright. Place wine, water, orange rind, sugar and cinnamon stick in pan; stir over low heat until sugar has dissolved. Add pears; cover; simmer gently 20 minutes or until pears are tender. Allow pears to cool in liquid; remove from pan; reserve liquid. Add Grand Marnier to reserved liquid; cover; refrigerate. Refrigerate pears until cold.

2. Gently pat pears dry with absorbent paper to remove any liquid. This is important, so that the chocolate coating will adhere well.

Put chopped milk chocolate and dark chocolate in top of double saucepan over simmering water; stir until chocolate has melted. Allow chocolate to cool until it is just warm. Dip pears into chocolate to coat pears completely. You may need to tilt the pan and use a spoon to help coat pears evenly.

3. Remove pears from chocolate and holding stem gently so that stem does not break, drain off excess chocolate. (Use side of spoon to help drain off excess chocolate at base.) Place on oven tray which has been covered with aluminium foil. Refrigerate until ready to serve. Pour the chilled liquid into individual dishes; put a pear in each dish.

Perfect Dinner Parties

This dinner party for four begins with cold terrine, continues with roast beef fillet and ends with a fabulous dessert. Quantities for recipes, with the exception of the terrine, can be doubled to serve six to eight. The terrine, as given, will serve eight; it is a good big size because any left over makes an excellent luncheon dish. The terrine and chocolate cases for dessert can be prepared the day beforehand.

Menu 2

Ham Terrine*

Roast Fillet of Beef

Avocado Bearnaise
Herbed Potatoes
Baked Tomatoes

Cointreau Strawberries in Chocolate

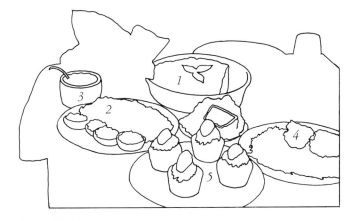

1 Ham Terrine
2 Roast Fillet of Beef
   Baked Tomatoes
3 Avocado Bearnaise
4 Herbed Potatoes
5 Cointreau Strawberries in Chocolate

This recipe appears overleaf with full step-by-step instructions.

Roast Fillet of Beef

2 x 1 kg (2 lb.) pieces of fillet of beef	2 tablespoons flour
90 g (3 oz.) butter	2 cups water
2 tablespoons brandy	2 beef stock cubes
	salt, pepper

Trim all fat and gristle from each piece of fillet. Sprinkle each fillet with black pepper, pressing pepper firmly into meat. Heat butter in large baking dish on top of stove. Add meat; brown quickly on all sides. Remove dish from heat. Pour brandy over. Put dish into moderately hot oven; allow 40 minutes for medium rare, a further 10 minutes for well done.

Remove meat from baking dish; keep warm. Put baking dish on top of stove over heat. When pan drippings are dark golden brown, remove excess fat from pan leaving approx. 4 tablespoons fat. Add flour; stir over heat until flour is dark golden brown; remove pan from heat. Add water; stir until combined. Return pan to heat; stir until sauce boils and thickens. Add crumbled stock cubes, salt and pepper. Simmer gently 10 minutes.

Put sliced meat on to serving plate; spoon over a little of the sauce. Serve remaining sauce and Avocado Bearnaise separately.

Avocado Bearnaise

4 tablespoons white vinegar	salt, pepper
2 shallots or spring onions	4 egg yolks
1 bayleaf	250 g (8 oz.) butter
6 peppercorns	1 tablespoon lemon juice
	1 ripe avocado

Put vinegar, chopped shallots, bayleaf and peppercorns into pan; bring to boil; reduce heat; simmer very gently uncovered until mixture is reduced by half; strain; cool.

Put egg yolks in top of double saucepan; add cooled vinegar; mix well. Melt butter in separate pan; cool. Put top of double saucepan over simmering water; gradually add butter; stir constantly until mixture is thick and creamy; remove from heat immediately. Add lemon juice; season with salt and pepper.

Put sauce in blender; add peeled and chopped avocado; blend on medium speed until smooth. (If you have no blender push avocado through fine nylon or plastic sieve; don't use metal sieve; this darkens avocado. Stir avocado into the sauce.)

Baked Tomatoes

2 medium-sized tomatoes	2 tablespoons chopped parsley
30 g (1 oz.) butter	
salt, pepper	2 shallots or spring onions

Cut tomatoes in half; put into greased ovenproof dish. Dot each tomato half with butter; sprinkle with salt and pepper. Bake uncovered in moderate oven 10 minutes. Place on serving plate; sprinkle combined parsley and chopped shallots over.

Herbed Potatoes

750 g (1½ lb.) old potatoes	1 tablespoon chopped dill or chives (or both)
4 shallots or spring onions	
2 tablespoons chopped parsley	salt, pepper
	90 g (3 oz.) butter

Peel potatoes; slice thinly. Grease 28 cm x 18 cm (11 in. x 7 in.) shallow cake tin; put a layer of potatoes in bottom of pan. Combine finely-chopped shallots, parsley and dill; sprinkle lightly over potatoes; season with salt and pepper. Repeat process with remaining potatoes and herbs, finishing with a layer of potatoes on top.

Melt butter; brush over top of potatoes; cover with aluminium foil; bake in hot oven approx. 1 hour, removing foil during the last 15 minutes of cooking. To serve, cut into squares.

Cointreau Strawberries in Chocolate

125 g (4 oz.) dark chocolate	1 punnet strawberries
¾ cup cream	2 tablespoons Cointreau or Grand Marnier

Chop chocolate roughly; put in top of double saucepan; stir over hot water until melted. Remove from heat; cool a little; put a tablespoon of melted chocolate in 8 cm (3 in.) paper patty case. Spread evenly over base and sides of case with small spatula (see below). Repeat with another three paper cases. Refrigerate until set, then carefully peel off paper; work quickly so that heat of hands does not melt chocolate. Put cases on oven tray; return to refrigerator.

Reserve four strawberries for decoration. Hull remainder; cut in half; pour Cointreau over. Cover until serving time. Whip cream; put a spoonful in base of each chocolate case; spoon strawberries over. Decorate with remaining whipped cream; top with a reserved whole strawberry. Pour liquor from strawberries over the cream.

NOTE: When making the chocolate cases, put three paper patty cases together, one inside the other; this gives firm support when spreading the chocolate. Refrigerate the paper cases for about 30 minutes before filling with chocolate; this will hold the chocolate more firmly.

Ham Terrine Step-by-Step

You will need:

500 g (1 lb.) ham fat
250 g (8 oz.) ham pieces
500 g (1 lb.) chicken livers
250 g (8 oz.) minced pork
250 g (8 oz.) minced veal
3 eggs
½ cup cream
3 tablespoons chopped parsley
90 g (3 oz.) butter
1 medium onion
125 g (4 oz.) mushrooms
2 rashers bacon
¼ teaspoon thyme
salt, pepper
2 tablespoons brandy
2 tablespoons port
2 tablespoons dry sherry
3 bayleaves

1. Ask your delicatessen for good-sized pieces of ham fat, about 15 cm (6 in.) square, if you can get them. Slice ham fat thinly. Line base and sides of oven-proof dish (approx. 5-cup capacity) with fat. There should be enough fat left over to cover top of terrine when it is completed.

2. Heat butter in frying pan; add peeled and very finely-chopped onion, very finely-chopped mushrooms and very finely-chopped bacon. Saute gently until onion is tender.

Put chicken livers into cold salted water; let stand 30 minutes; drain; rinse well. Combine chicken livers, ham, pork mince and veal mince in bowl. Pass this mixture through fine mincer; return to bowl. Place onion mixture, meat mixture, beaten eggs, cream, salt, pepper, brandy, port, dry sherry and thyme in bowl; mix very well. Pour mixture into prepared dish, spreading out evenly.

3. Cover top of meat completely with remaining thin slices of fat. Put bayleaves decoratively on top. Cover dish completely with aluminium foil. Put into baking dish; add enough water to come half-way up sides of dish. Bake in moderate oven 2 hours. Allow to cool, then refrigerate overnight.

Perfect Dinner Parties

Entree and main course in this superb dinner party for six are delightfully easy. Preparation is simple, cooking time is short. You'll like the freshness of the simple salad with its unusual wine dressing. The Strawberry Meringue Gateau takes a little time and trouble, but it can be prepared and assembled several hours beforehand and refrigerated until required. And it's so delicious, you'll want to make it again soon.

Menu 3

Seafood Grand Marnier

Veal with Asparagus
Lemon Sauce

Broccoli, New Potatoes
Tomato and Onion Salad

Strawberry Meringue Gateau*

1 *Seafood Grand Marnier*
2 *Veal with Asparagus*
  Lemon Sauce
3 *Broccoli, New Potatoes*
4 *Tomato and Onion Salad*
5 *Strawberry Meringue Gateau*

This recipe appears overleaf with full step-by-step instructions.

Seafood Grand Marnier

500 g (1 lb.) fresh large prawns	¼ cup cream
250 g (8 oz.) scallops	1 tablespoon Grand Marnier
90 g (3 oz.) butter	1 tablespoon chopped parsley
1 small clove garlic	1 cup rice
salt, pepper	

Gradually add rice to large saucepan of boiling salted water; boil uncovered 12 minutes or until rice is just tender; drain well. Shell prawns; remove back vein. Clean scallops. Divide prawns and scallops evenly between 6 thin bamboo skewers. Heat butter in large frying pan; add seafood skewers; fry quickly on both sides until just golden. Add crushed garlic, salt, pepper and cream; simmer uncovered 3 minutes or until mixture is reduced by half. Add Grand Marnier and parsley; stir until heated through. Spoon a little hot rice on to each serving plate; top with a seafood skewer; spoon sauce over.

Veal with Asparagus

6 veal steaks	90 g (3 oz.) butter
flour	3 tablespoons oil
2 eggs	3 rashers bacon
¼ cup milk	440 g (15½ oz.) can asparagus spears
packaged dry bread-crumbs	

Lemon Sauce

3 egg yolks	salt, pepper
3 tablespoons lemon juice	125 g (4 oz.) butter

Remove rind from bacon; cut each rasher in half; roll up and secure with wooden cocktail stick. Pound veal steaks out thinly. Coat lightly with flour; dip into combined beaten eggs and milk, then into breadcrumbs, pressing crumbs on firmly. Heat butter and oil in large frying pan; add veal steaks; fry gently on both sides until golden brown and cooked through, approx. 3 minutes on each side. Remove from pan.

Add bacon rolls to pan; fry quickly until golden brown; remove from pan; remove wooden sticks. Place veal on serving plate; top each steak with a few drained asparagus spears. Spoon the Lemon Sauce over; top with a bacon roll.

Lemon Sauce: Place egg yolks and lemon juice in top of double saucepan; add roughly-chopped softened butter. Stand pan over simmering water; stir until butter has melted and mixture starts to thicken; remove pan from water; continue stirring until sauce is thick. Season with salt and pepper. Allow to become cold, stirring occasionally. Spoon sauce over meat. (Do not reheat sauce; serve at room temperature.)

Tomato and Onion Salad

1 lettuce	500 g (1 lb.) ripe tomatoes
3 white onions	parsley

Dressing

2 tablespoons oil	salt, pepper
2 tablespoons dry white wine	1 teaspoon sugar
	½ teaspoon basil

Wash lettuce; you will need six small lettuce cups. Dry well; put in plastic bag; refrigerate until crisp. Place lettuce cups on individual serving plates. Slice tomatoes; peel and thinly slice onions. Arrange tomato slices in each lettuce cup; top with onion slices. Garnish with parsley; refrigerate until ready to serve. Before serving, spoon a little of the dressing over the tomatoes and onion.

Dressing: Place all ingredients in screw top jar; shake well. Shake the dressing well again just before serving.

Broccoli

1 kg (2 lb.) broccoli	2 teaspoons butter
salt, pepper	1 teaspoon lemon juice

Wash broccoli; trim off ends of stalks and coarse leaves. Cut deep cross in base of extra thick stalks to facilitate cooking. Place in saucepan with small amount of boiling salted water; boil until tender, approx. 10 to 15 minutes. Drain; add salt, pepper, butter and lemon juice.

If desired, add ½ clove garlic to broccoli while it is cooking; remove garlic before serving.

Strawberry Meringue Gateau

Step-by-step instructions for this dessert are given on the opposite page. The gateau is also shown on the back cover of this book and, in that picture, we've made it even more luscious by giving the meringue layer a coating of chocolate. Here's what you do to make the cake as it appears on the back cover: In top of double saucepan, over simmering water, melt 185 g (6 oz.) dark chocolate and 30 g (1 oz.) butter. Let cool a little, then spread evenly over top and sides of meringue layer. Let stand until set. Top with the strawberries and 3 tablespoons cream, as directed in recipe. Fill remaining cream into piping bag fitted with fluted tube; pipe decorative ring of cream around gateau. Then place cream puffs in position. Pipe any remaining cream into centre of gateau. Complete as the recipe directs.

Strawberry Meringue Gateau Step-by-Step

Meringue Layer
3 egg whites
¾ cup sugar
1½ cups cream
1 tablespoon icing sugar
1 teaspoon vanilla
1 punnet strawberries
2 tablespoons water
4 tablespoons apricot jam

Cream Puffs
½ cup water
30 g (1 oz.) butter
½ cup plain flour
pinch salt
2 eggs
½ cup cream

Almond Praline
60 g (2 oz.) blanched almonds
½ cup sugar
½ cup water

Put almonds on oven tray; put into moderate oven 10 minutes or until golden brown. Put sugar and water into pan; stir over low heat until sugar has dissolved; bring to boil; boil rapidly without stirring until toffee is golden brown. Put almonds on greased oven tray; pour toffee over; allow to set and become cold. Break toffee roughly; put in plastic bag and crush roughly with rolling pin.

1. Beat egg whites until soft peaks form; gradually add sugar; beat until sugar has dissolved. Cover an oven tray with greased greaseproof paper; dust with cornflour; shake off excess; mark 20 cm (8 in.) circle on paper. Spoon meringue mixture into circle; spread out evenly and smoothly. Bake in slow oven 1 hour; remove from oven; allow to cool on tray.

2. Sift flour. Put butter, water and salt into pan. Stir until all butter has melted; bring to rapid boil. Add flour all at once. Stir vigorously with wooden spoon until mixture is thick. When mixture leaves sides of saucepan and forms a smooth ball, remove from heat; cool. Put paste into small bowl of electric mixer; add eggs, one at a time, beating well after each addition. Spoon teaspoonfuls of mixture on to greased oven trays; bake in hot oven 10 minutes; reduce heat to moderate; bake a further 15 to 20 minutes or until golden and crisp. Remove from oven; cut small hole in base of each puff; allow to become cold.
    Whip cream until stiff peaks form; spoon into piping bag fitted with plain nozzle; pipe small amount of cream into each puff through hole in base.

3. Put meringue carefully on serving plate. Put cream, sifted icing sugar and vanilla into bowl; beat until soft peaks form. Wash strawberries (reserve 10 for decoration); hull remaining strawberries; cut in half. Arrange strawberry slices on top of meringue layer; spread 3 tablespoons of cream over strawberries. Arrange filled cream puffs around edge of meringue. Spoon remaining cream into centre, swirling to a peak. Put apricot jam and water into pan; stir over heat until combined and mixture is slightly runny; push through fine sieve. Brush apricot glaze over top of cream puffs and over reserved strawberries; arrange strawberries around cream centre. Sprinkle praline over cream centre and puffs.

Perfect Dinner Parties

This interesting and unusual dinner party menu for four has a delicate balance of food textures and flavours. You'll be particularly delighted with the dessert. The icecream can be made the day beforehand; and see the recipe for the no-trouble-at-all chocolate souffle! Guests take a spoonful of the icecream and a spoonful of the hot souffle.

Menu 4

Prawn and Avocado Cocktail

Chicken and Veal Kiev*

Hot Broccoli Salad
Buttered Wine-Rice

Hot Chocolate Souffle
with Marsala Icecream

1 *Prawn and Avocado Cocktail*
2 *Chicken and Veal Kiev*
3 *Hot Broccoli Salad*
4 *Buttered Wine-Rice*
5 *Hot Chocolate Souffle with Marsala Icecream*

*This recipe appears overleaf with full step-by-step instructions.

Prawn and Avocado Cocktail

750 g (1½ lb.) small prawns	½ lettuce
lemon slices	4 shallots or spring onions
1 avocado	2 tablespoons chopped parsley

Sauce

½ cup cream	¼ cup brandy
¾ cup mayonnaise	few drops tabasco sauce
⅓ cup tomato sauce	pinch curry powder

Shell prawns; remove back vein. Wash prawns and pat dry. Put peeled and chopped avocado, finely-shredded lettuce, chopped shallots and parsley into bowl; toss lightly. Put lettuce mixture in base of 4 individual scallop shells or dishes; top with prawns; cover; refrigerate until ready to serve. On serving, spoon prepared sauce over; decorate with lemon slices.

Sauce: Lightly whip cream. Fold in all other ingredients; mix well.

NOTE: If preparing in advance, peel and chop avocado just before serving; avocados darken on standing.

Hot Broccoli Salad

750 g (1½ lb.) fresh broccoli (or 2 x 250 g (8 oz.) pkts frozen broccoli)	¼ teaspoon grated lemon rind
½ cup canned sliced water chestnuts	½ teaspoon soy sauce
	1 tablespoon dry sherry
1 cm (½ in.) piece green ginger	½ cup water
	1 chicken stock cube
	3 tablespoons oil

Remove stems and leaves from fresh broccoli. If using frozen broccoli, completely defrost broccoli and cut into small flowerets. Put oil, water chestnuts, peeled and grated green ginger and lemon rind into frying pan; simmer until ginger is sizzling. Add broccoli; toss gently in hot oil 1 minute. Add soy sauce, sherry, water and crumbled stock cube. Bring to boil; reduce heat; simmer covered 5 minutes or until broccoli is just crisp. Remove vegetables from pan; put on to serving plate. Increase heat; boil remaining liquid in pan until reduced by half; spoon over broccoli.

Buttered Wine-Rice

90 g (3 oz.) butter	½ cup dry white wine
1 medium onion	4 chicken stock cubes
1 cup rice	salt, pepper
2½ cups hot water	

Heat butter in frying pan; add peeled and finely-chopped onion. Saute gently until onion is tender and lightly golden brown. Add rice; stir 3 minutes.

Dissolve stock cubes in hot water. Add 1 cup of chicken stock to pan; stir until nearly all liquid is absorbed. Add remaining stock and wine; bring to boil; reduce heat; simmer gently, covered, 10 minutes; add salt and pepper.

Chocolate Souffle

2 eggs, separated	½ cup milk
60 g (2 oz.) butter	2 tablespoons sugar
2 tablespoons plain flour	125 g (4 oz.) dark chocolate
½ teaspoon salt	

Melt butter in top of double saucepan over simmering water; remove from heat. Stir in sifted flour and salt; stir until lump free. Stir in milk all at once. Return to heat; stir over simmering water until smooth and thick. Remove from heat. Stir in grated chocolate and sugar while still hot. Stir until dissolved; cool slightly.

Beat egg yolks until pale and fluffy; gradually stir into chocolate mixture with thin-edged metal spoon or spatula. Using clean bowl, beat egg-whites until short moist peaks form. Using thin-edged metal spoon or spatula, fold half the egg-whites into chocolate mixture, then fold in remaining egg whites. Spoon mixture evenly into four greased small individual souffle dishes (approx. ½ cup capacity). Fill mixture to within 1 cm (½ in.) of top. Bake in moderate oven 15 to 20 minutes. Serve with Marsala Icecream.

NOTE: This is an unusual souffle recipe and doesn't need any last-minute preparation. The souffle mixture can be made up on the morning of the party, and put into the individual souffle dishes. Stand the dishes on an oven tray; cover loosely with plastic food wrap; refrigerate. Put them into the oven, on the oven tray, 15 to 20 minutes before serving time.

Marsala Icecream

3 eggs, separated	2 tablespoons marsala
½ cup sugar	2 tablespoons water
1 cup cream	

Put egg yolks, sugar, marsala and water in top of double saucepan or in heatproof bowl. Beat over hot water until mixture is lukewarm. Remove from heat; beat until fluffy and cool, approx. 10 minutes. Whip cream until firm; fold into marsala mixture. Whip egg whites until soft peaks form; fold into marsala mixture. Spoon mixture into deep 20 cm (8 in.) tin. Cover with aluminium foil; freeze until firm, stirring occasionally, so that mixture does not separate. Spoon into individual dishes to serve.

Chicken and Veal Kiev Step-by-Step

You will need:

2 medium-sized whole chicken breasts
4 medium-sized veal steaks
2 eggs
flour
salt, pepper
3 cups fresh white breadcrumbs
    (about ½ loaf bread)
60 g (2 oz.) butter
2 tablespoons oil
375 g (12 oz.) mushrooms

Butter Filling

125 g (4 oz.) butter
salt, pepper
2 tablespoons chopped parsley
4 shallots or spring onions
1 teaspoon french mustard
½ clove garlic
¼ teaspoon oregano
¼ teaspoon thyme

Beat butter until soft and creamy; add salt, pepper, parsley, finely-chopped shallots, mustard, crushed garlic, oregano and thyme; mix well.

1. Remove skin from chicken; cut meat away from bone with sharp knife, giving two chicken fillets from each whole breast. Repeat with other chicken breast.

2. With meat mallet or rolling pin pound chicken fillets and veal out thinly. There should be no holes or the butter will run out during cooking. However, if the flesh does tear, overlap the torn pieces and pound together gently until firm again.

Divide butter filling evenly over chicken breasts. Spread out butter filling to 1 cm (½ in.) from edges of chicken. Brush edges with beaten eggs; put veal on top; press edges together firmly. Trim veal to size of chicken breasts.

3. Coat with flour; dip into beaten eggs, then coat with breadcrumbs. Press breadcrumbs on firmly. Refrigerate until ready to use. Heat butter and oil in pan; add whole mushrooms; saute gently until mushrooms are tender; season with salt and pepper. Remove mushrooms from pan; keep warm until ready to serve. Increase heat so that pan is very hot; add crumbed chicken-and-veal pieces; cook until golden brown on both sides, then reduce heat and cook a further few minutes until cooked through.

International Cookery

In this section we deal with the popular cuisines of China, France, Italy, Greece and America. The foods of each country are given in menu form; choose your favourites for a dinner party.

China

Chinese is probably the most popular of all foreign cuisines — for the lightness of the food, the subtlety of flavour. Here we present a memorable menu of favourite Chinese dishes. The menu given will serve 6 to 8.

Gow Gees

250 g (8 oz.) wonton wrappers
250 g (8 oz.) minced pork
125 g (4 oz.) large fresh prawns
60 g (2 oz.) dried mushrooms
125 g (4 oz.) canned bamboo shoots

6 shallots or spring onions
1 teaspoon grated green ginger
1 clove garlic
2 teaspoons sesame oil
1 tablespoon soy sauce
1 tablespoon dry sherry
oil for deep-frying

Using an 8 cm (3 in.) cutter, cut wonton wrappers into circles; stack a few wrappers on top of each other and cut them all at the same time.

Cover mushrooms with boiling water; stand 30 minutes; drain; chop mushrooms finely. Combine mushrooms with pork, shelled and finely-chopped prawns, finely-chopped bamboo shoots, finely-chopped shallots, ginger, crushed garlic, sesame oil, soy sauce and sherry; mix well. Place small spoonfuls of mixture in centre of each circle. Brush edges of wrappers with water; fold in half; pinch edges together firmly. Drop Gow Gees into deep hot oil; fry until golden brown; remove; drain on absorbent paper. Don't have oil over-hot

Recipe continued overleaf:

Chicken in Ginger Plum Sauce — one of the most delicious chicken dishes in Chinese cuisine! See recipe overleaf.

or Gow Gees will brown before filling is cooked. Serve immediately with Plum Sauce.

NOTE: Wonton wrappers are available from Chinese food stores.

Plum Sauce

½ cup water	1 tablespoon hoi sin sauce
2 teaspoons cornflour	1 teaspoon sesame oil
½ cup bottled plum sauce	1 fresh red chilli or 2 dried
1 tablespoon sugar	chillis
1 tablespoon soy sauce	salt
2 tablespoons sherry	

Blend together water and cornflour; put into saucepan with plum sauce, sugar, soy sauce, sherry, hoi sin sauce, sesame oil, seeded and finely-chopped chilli and salt. Stir until sauce boils and thickens; reduce heat; simmer covered 10 minutes.

NOTE: Chinese plum sauce, hoi sin sauce and sesame oil are available from most large food stores or supermarkets, or from Chinese food stores.

Hors d'Oeuvre Rolls

375 g (12 oz.) pkt puff pastry	1 hard-boiled egg
30 g (1 oz.) butter	½ cup fine noodles, roughly broken
125 g (4 oz.) minced pork	1 tablespoon dry sherry
60 g (2 oz.) mushrooms	salt, pepper
6 shallots or spring onions	1 egg, for glazing
250 g (8 oz.) cooked prawns	oil for deep-frying

Cook noodles in boiling salted water 3 minutes or until tender; rinse under hot water; drain well. Heat butter in pan; add pork mince; saute until well browned. Add finely-chopped mushrooms and shallots; saute a further 2 minutes. Remove from heat; add finely-chopped prawns, finely-chopped egg, finely-chopped noodles, sherry, salt and pepper; mix well.

Have pastry at room temperature. Cut pastry in half; roll each half into rectangle 40 cm x 33 cm (16 in. x 13 in.); with sharp knife trim to 38 cm x 30 cm (15 in. x 12 in.). Cut each rectangle into five 8 cm (3 in.) strips, then cut each strip into four 8 cm (3 in.) squares.

Put a heaped teaspoonful of mixture down the centre of each square, leaving edges free; glaze edges with lightly-beaten egg. Roll up pastry tightly, securing edges together. Deep-fry in hot oil until golden. Drain on absorbent paper. Serve hot with soy sauce.

Short Soup

Soup

2 litres (8 cups) chicken stock	½ teaspoon sesame oil
	1 chicken stock cube
3 shallots or spring onions	

Wontons

25 wonton wrappers (or ¼ pkt)	water
	salt
1 egg	

Wonton Filling

500 g (1 lb.) pork mince	½ teaspoon sesame oil
¼ small cabbage	1 teaspoon grated green ginger
1 tablespoon soy sauce	

Soup: Chop shallots finely; add to saucepan with chicken stock, sesame oil and crumbled stock cube; bring to boil; reduce heat; simmer 3 minutes.

Filling: Combine finely-shredded cabbage with pork mince, soy sauce, sesame oil and grated ginger; mix well. Place a teaspoon of prepared filling slightly below centre of each wonton wrapper. Brush edges of wrapper with lightly-beaten egg. Fold wonton wrapper diagonally in half to form a triangle. Press edges to seal, pressing out any air pockets around filling. Brush a dab of egg on the front right corner of triangles and on the back left corners. With a twisting action, bring the two moistened surfaces together and pinch to seal.

Drop the wontons into vigorously boiling salted water; cook until they float, approx. 15 minutes; drain. Place 3 wontons in the bottom of each soup bowl; pour the hot soup over.

NOTE: Packets of Wonton wrappers are available at Chinese food stores.

Chicken in Ginger Plum Sauce

1.5 kg (3 lb.) chicken	2 tablespoons dry sherry
cornflour	1 clove garlic
½ cup oil	2 medium onions
⅓ cup plum jam	1 red pepper
2 chicken stock cubes	1 stick celery
2 teaspoons cornflour, extra	6 shallots or spring onions
½ cup water	5 cm (2 in.) piece green ginger
3 teaspoons soy sauce	

Steam or boil chicken until tender; cool. Cut chicken into small, serving-sized pieces, leaving meat on bone. Coat chicken pieces lightly in cornflour.

Combine plum jam, crumbled stock cubes, extra cornflour, water, soy sauce, sherry and crushed garlic in bowl. Peel onions; cut into large wedges; seed and slice pepper; slice celery; chop shallots; peel and very thinly slice green ginger.

Heat oil in pan; add chicken; fry until golden brown; remove from pan. Drain off excess oil, leaving 2 tablespoons oil. Add prepared vegetables except shallots; fry quickly 1 minute. Return chicken to pan with plum jam mixture; toss vegetables and chicken until sauce is boiling and thickly coats the chicken. Add shallots; toss well.

Sweet and Sour Fish

1 large whole bream or other whole fish	1 green pepper
	2 sticks celery
1 red pepper	6 shallots or spring onions

Sweet and Sour Sauce

½ cup sugar	1 tablespcon tomato
½ cup white vinegar	sauce
¾ cup water	1 tablespoon cornflour
2 tablespoons tomato paste	¼ cup water, extra

Wash, clean and scale fish; place fish in large baking dish; cover completely with water; place baking dish on top of stove over medium heat; bring to simmering point; simmer very slowly until fish is tender.

Seed red and green peppers; cut into very thin slices; cut celery into 5 cm (2 in.) lengths, then cut into very thin slices. Cut shallots into very thin diagonal slices. Drop peppers and celery into saucepan of boiling salted water; boil 1 minute; drain. Place fish on serving plate; spoon vegetable mixture down centre of fish; spoon over prepared Sweet and Sour Sauce; top with shallots.

Sweet and Sour Sauce: Put sugar, water, vinegar, tomato paste and tomato sauce in saucepan; stir over medium heat until sugar dissolves. Mix cornflour to smooth paste with extra water; add to saucepan. Stir over medium heat until sauce boils and thickens; reduce heat; simmer 1 minute.

Steamed Rice

2 cups long-grain rice water	½ teaspoon salt

Put rice into strainer; wash well under cold running water. Put rice in saucepan; add sufficient cold water to come 2.5 cm (1 in.) above rice. Add salt. Bring to boil; boil rapidly uncovered until water commences to evaporate and steam holes appear in the rice. Then turn heat as low as possible; cover saucepan tightly and allow rice to steam until it is very tender, 15 to 20 minutes. Remove from heat; let stand 5 minutes, then uncover.

Beef in Black Bean Sauce

750 g (1½ lb.) rump steak	⅓ cup sliced bamboo
1 egg white	shoots
1 tablespoon dry sherry	1 teaspoon curry powder
2 tablespoons soy sauce	1 tablespoon black beans
1 teaspoon cornflour	pinch sugar
⅓ cup oil	⅓ cup water
4 shallots or spring onions	2 teaspoons cornflour,
1 red pepper	extra

Cut steak into 5 cm x 5 mm (2 in. x ¼ in.) strips. Combine in bowl with egg white, sherry, soy sauce and cornflour; mix well. Stand 30 minutes.

Put beans in bowl; cover with water; stand 15 minutes; drain and rinse under cold running water; put on to plate; add sugar and 1 teaspoon water; mash well. Chop shallots into 2.5 cm (1 in.) pieces; cut pepper in half; remove seeds; cut each half into thin strips.

Add 2 tablespoons oil to pan; add shallots, red pepper, bamboo shoots and curry powder; saute 2 minutes; remove from pan. Heat remaining oil in pan; add meat and marinade; cook until browned. Return vegetables to pan with bean mixture; combine well. Blend extra cornflour with remaining water; add to pan; stir until mixture boils and thickens.

Lychees with Mandarin Ice

1 cup sugar	¼ cup lemon juice
2 cups water	1 tablespoon Grand
315 g (10 oz.) can mandarin segments	Marnier
	625 g (20 oz.) can lychees

Put sugar and water into pan; stir over low heat until sugar is dissolved. Bring to boil; boil uncovered 3 minutes; cool. Put undrained mandarins in blender; blend 1 minute; push through sieve. Add mandarin juice, lemon juice and Grand Marnier to syrup; stir until combined. Pour into tray; put in freezer until set. Refrigerate lychees until nicely cold. Drain lychees; reserve syrup. Put lychees into serving dishes; spoon some of the reserved syrup over. Flake Mandarin Ice with fork; spoon over lychees.

France

French food is simple, and superb. This elegant three-course menu, to serve four, is one you will be proud to present, yet preparation is so easy.

Grand Marnier Pate

Base

¾ cup hot water	2 tablespoons cold water
2 chicken stock cubes	3 orange slices
1½ teaspoons gelatine	½ cup water, extra

Pate

500 g (1 lb.) chicken livers	1 bayleaf
45 g (1½ oz.) butter	1¼ cups cream
3 rashers bacon	¼ cup Grand Marnier
2 onions	2 teaspoons gelatine
½ teaspoon thyme	2 tablespoons water

Base: Put hot water and crumbled stock cubes into saucepan. Sprinkle gelatine over cold water; add to saucepan; stir until combined. Bring to boil; remove from heat; allow to cool. Pour enough of this chicken stock into oiled 23 cm x 12 cm (9 in. x 5 in.) loaf tin to just cover the base. Refrigerate until set. Place orange slices in pan; cover with extra water; bring to boil; reduce heat; simmer 3 minutes; drain. Arrange orange slices decoratively over set layer; carefully pour over remaining stock; refrigerate until firm.

Pate: Cover chicken livers with water; let stand 30 minutes; drain. Chop chicken livers roughly. Melt 30 g (1 oz.) of butter in pan; add livers; saute until browned on all sides. In separate pan, melt remaining 15 g (½ oz.) butter. Saute peeled and chopped onions and chopped bacon until onion is transparent. Add thyme, bayleaf and the livers; simmer a further 5 minutes. Remove from heat; remove bayleaf.

Put mixture with Grand Marnier into electric blender; blend until smooth. Sprinkle gelatine over water; stir over simmering water until gelatine has dissolved. Stir dissolved gelatine into blended mixture. Whip cream until soft peaks form; fold into gelatine mixture. Spread evenly over set base; refrigerate until firm. Unmould on to plate. Cut into slices to serve.

Serve triangles of toast or Melba Toast (see page 11) with the pate. You might also like to add small individual bowls of green salad, tossed in french dressing.

Beef and Mushroom Casserole

1 kg (2 lb.) round steak	1 beef stock cube
8 small onions	1 tablespoon tomato paste
125 g (4 oz.) mushrooms	¼ teaspoon mixed herbs
2 rashers bacon	1 clove garlic
¾ cup dry red wine	30 g (1 oz.) butter
1¾ cups water	2 tablespoons oil
3 tablespoons flour	30 g (1 oz.) butter, extra

Trim any surplus fat from meat; cut meat into 2.5 cm (1 in.) cubes. Trim rind and surplus fat from bacon; chop roughly. Peel onions; leave them whole; slice or halve mushrooms.

Heat butter and oil in pan. Add about a quarter of the steak at a time to pan; brown well on all sides; remove from pan; repeat with remaining meat; remove from pan. When all meat is browned, add whole onions; cook until light golden brown; add bacon; cook stirring 1 minute; remove from pan.

Heat extra butter in pan; add flour; cook until dark golden brown. Remove pan from heat; gradually add water and wine; stir until well combined. Return to heat; add crumbled stock cube, crushed garlic, tomato paste and mixed herbs. Stir until sauce boils and thickens. Put meat, bacon, onions and mushrooms in ovenproof dish or four individual ovenproof dishes; pour sauce over; mix through lightly. Cook, covered, in moderate oven 1½ hours or until meat is tender.

Creamed Potatoes

750 g (1½ lb.) potatoes	1 cup hot milk
30 g (1 oz.) butter	salt, pepper

Peel potatoes; place in boiling salted water; cover; boil until potatoes are tender, approx. 20 minutes; drain well; mash or push through sieve. Return potato to pan; add butter; mix well. Gradually add hot milk, beating continuously until all the milk is added. Season with salt and pepper.

Green Peas

750 g (1½ lb.) peas	30 g (1 oz.) butter
3 large lettuce leaves	1 chicken stock cube
1 onion	salt, pepper
½ cup hot water	15 g (½ oz.) butter, extra

Shell peas; shred lettuce; peel and finely chop onion. Place prepared vegetables in pan; add butter, water, crumbled stock cube, salt and pepper. Cover; cook over low heat 15 to 20 minutes or until peas are just tender. Add extra butter; mix well.

Mille Feuilles — layers of flaky pastry are layered with jam and cream to make a delectable dessert. See recipe overleaf.

Mille Feuilles

375 g (12 oz.) pkt puff pastry	raspberry (or other) jam 1½ cups cream

Icing

½ cup icing sugar	1½ tablespoons lemon
15 g (½ oz.) butter	juice

Divide pastry in half; roll out each half to 18 cm x 28 cm (7 in. x 11 in.). Place on oven slides; bake in hot oven 12 minutes or until pastry is golden brown; cool. If pastry puffs greatly, press down gently with hands to flatten. Cut each pastry in half lengthways, giving four 9 cm x 28 cm (3½ in. x 11 in.) pieces. Trim edges with sharp knife; crush the odd bits of pastry cut off into crumbs; reserve.

Spread a thin layer of jam on one pastry piece; top with a layer of whipped cream. Place another piece of pastry on top; repeat with two layers of jam, cream and pastry, finishing with plain pastry on top; press down gently. Spread prepared icing over top of final pastry piece. Decorate with crushed crumbs along sides.

Icing: Sift icing sugar into bowl; add softened butter and lemon juice; beat until smooth.

You might like to serve a small selection of French cheeses with the coffee, and there are many interesting varieties to choose from. Brie, Port-Salut and Camembert are probably the most popular, also Fondu aux Raisins, or 'grape cheese'; this has a delightfully mild flavour, enhanced by the grape seeds and skins from the local wine pressings which cover its rind.

Or you might like to serve our version of the famous 'walnut cheese' of France.

Walnut Herb Cheese

250 g (8 oz.) pkt cream cheese	1 tablespoon chopped chives
1 teaspoon french mustard	1 tablespoon chopped parsley
salt, pepper	125 g (4 oz.) walnut halves
1 tablespoon brandy	

Beat cream cheese until just soft; add mustard, salt, pepper, brandy, chives and parsley; stir until just combined. Pat out half the cheese mixture into 8 cm (3 in.) round, making sure that top and sides are even; cover top of cheese with walnut halves. Pat remaining cheese out on top of walnuts, making sure that top and sides are smooth. Arrange remaining walnuts over cheese. Cover; refrigerate — preferably overnight.

Italy

There's the full flavour of Italy in every course of this carefully planned menu to serve six. A variety of crisp seafoods forms the first course, then veal with a delicious sauce, two salads, and a mouth-watering dessert.

Fritto Misto

500 g (1 lb.) fresh prawns	500 g (1 lb.) small squid
about 24 canned fresh oysters	2 onions oil for deep-frying

Batter

1½ cups plain flour	¼ teaspoon turmeric
⅓ cup self-raising flour	1¾ cups water
salt	

Lemon Garlic Sauce

1 cup mayonnaise	4 shallots or spring onions
2 cloves garlic	2 tablespoons chopped
3 teaspoons lemon juice	parsley
1 teaspoon grated lemon rind	salt, pepper

Batter: Sift dry ingredients into bowl. Add water gradually, beating well after each addition; batter should be of thin consistency. Shell prawns, leaving tail intact; remove back vein. Coat prawns, oysters, cleaned squid and peeled and sliced onion rings lightly in flour; dip into batter; drain off excess batter. Deep-fry in hot oil until golden brown. Serve with Lemon Garlic Sauce.

Sauce: Put mayonnaise in bowl with crushed garlic, lemon juice, lemon rind, chopped shallots, parsley, salt and pepper; mix well.

Veal with Basil

6 large veal steaks	⅓ cup dry white wine
flour	½ cup water
salt, pepper	2 teaspoons cornflour
60 g (2 oz.) butter	2 tablespoons brandy
⅓ cup oil	½ teaspoon sugar
60 g (2 oz.) butter, extra	1 teaspoon basil
1 clove garlic	¾ cup thickened cream
2 teaspoons french mustard	3 tablespoons chopped parsley

Pound veal steaks out very thinly. Coat with flour which has been seasoned with salt and pepper; shake off excess flour from steaks. Heat butter and oil in large frying pan; add steaks; fry until golden brown on both sides and cooked through; remove from pan; keep warm.

Drain off all fat from pan; add extra butter, crushed garlic and mustard; stir until butter has melted; add combined wine, water and cornflour; stir until sauce is boiling. Reduce heat; add brandy, sugar, basil and cream; stir until combined; simmer uncovered 3 minutes; add parsley. Place veal steaks on serving plates; spoon sauce over.

Hot Rice Salad

2 cups long-grain rice	3 rashers bacon
310 g can butter beans	2 tablespoons chopped
2 cloves garlic	parsley
45 g can anchovies	salt, pepper
125 g (4 oz.) green olives	½ cup bottled italian
125 g (4 oz.) black olives	dressing
1 red pepper	

Chop bacon; saute with crushed garlic until bacon is crisp; remove from pan. Drain anchovies; chop roughly; cut pepper in half; remove seeds; chop pepper into 1 cm (½ in.) cubes. Cook rice in large saucepan of boiling salted water 12 minutes or until tender; drain; add bacon and garlic, anchovies, pepper, drained and rinsed butter beans, green and black olives, parsley, salt, pepper and italian dressing; toss well.

Mixed Salad

1 small lettuce	2 sticks celery
1 small onion	3 large tomatoes
½ cucumber	2 hard-boiled eggs
1 green pepper	bottled italian dressing

Wash lettuce; drain well; pat dry; tear into large pieces; place in plastic bag in refrigerator to crisp. Peel and thinly slice onion and cucumber. Wash green pepper; remove seeds and slice thinly. Wash celery; cut into diagonal slices. Wash tomatoes; remove core; cut into wedges. Shell eggs; cut into wedges. Put vegetables into bowl; sprinkle with italian dressing; toss lightly. Top with wedges of egg.

Custard Liqueur Puffs

Puffs

1 cup water	pinch salt
75 g (2½ oz.) butter	4 large eggs
1 cup plain flour	

Custard

⅓ cup cornflour	1 teaspoon vanilla
⅓ cup custard powder	30 g (1 oz.) butter
600 ml carton milk	½ cup sugar
300 ml carton cream	

Chocolate Sauce

125 g (4 oz.) dark	½ cup water
chocolate	2 teaspoons cornflour
30 g (1 oz.) butter	¼ cup water, extra
⅓ cup sugar	1 teaspoon vanilla

Puffs: Place water and butter in pan over heat; stir until butter has melted; bring to boil; add sifted flour and salt all at once to the boiling mixture; stir well until mixture forms a ball in saucepan; remove pan from heat; allow dough to cool to warm. Place dough in small bowl of electric mixer; add eggs one at a time; beat mixture well after each addition. Mixture should be smooth, very thick and glossy.

Drop tablespoons of mixture on to greased baking trays; allow room for spreading. Bake in hot oven 10 minutes or until golden brown; reduce heat to moderate; cook a further 20 to 25 minutes. Remove from oven; cut in half; remove any soft centre. Allow to become cold. Before serving, spoon prepared custard into centre of each puff; make sure that puffs are well filled; place tops on puffs. Serve 2 puffs per person. Spoon 1 teaspoon of a favourite liqueur over each puff, then spoon chocolate sauce over each puff.

Custard: Place cornflour, custard powder and sugar in saucepan; stir until combined. Gradually add milk, mixing until smooth and free of lumps. Add cream, vanilla and butter; stir until combined. Place pan over heat; stir until custard boils; reduce heat; simmer uncovered 4 minutes, stirring constantly. Pour custard into bowl; cover with plastic food wrap. When custard has cooled to warm, mix well and fill into puffs immediately.

Chocolate Sauce: Place chopped chocolate, butter, sugar, water and vanilla in small pan; stir over low heat until chocolate has melted. Add combined extra water and cornflour; stir until sauce boils; reduce heat; simmer uncovered 2 minutes, stirring constantly. Sauce can be served hot or cold.

Amaretti

250 g (8 oz.) blanched	2 egg whites
almonds	1 cup castor sugar

Put almonds in blender; blend on high speed 3 minutes or until almonds are finely ground. Beat egg whites until firm peaks form; fold in combined sugar and almonds. Roll heaped teaspoonfuls of mixture into balls; flatten between palms of hands. Put on to greased oven trays that have been lightly dusted with cornflour. Leave to stand 4 hours. Bake in moderately slow oven approx. 20 minutes or until very light golden brown; cool on trays. Makes approx. 35 biscuits to serve with coffee.

Greece

Greek cuisine is centuries old. In Europe, Greece was among the first to establish a particular style of cooking — the mixing and combining of spices and ingredients to produce new, delightful flavours. Honey, lemon, cinnamon are popular flavourings. When they are in season, you might like to add to this menu a bowl of fresh, purple figs. Quantities in this menu will serve six.

Taramasalata

250 g (8 oz.) smoked cod's roe	pepper
2 small potatoes	½ cup olive oil
4 thick slices white bread	2 tablespoons lemon juice

Peel, wash and quarter potatoes. Place in boiling salted water; reduce heat; simmer covered 10 minutes or until potatoes are tender; drain well. Return potatoes to pan; shake over heat until potatoes are dry, approx. 1 minute; cool.

Remove crusts from bread slices; place bread in bowl; cover with warm water; allow to stand 3 minutes. Place bread in large strainer; press with hand to extract as much water as possible. Place cod's roe, potatoes, bread and pepper in electric blender or food processor; blend until smooth. Gradually blend in combined lemon juice and oil; blend until combined and very smooth. Spoon mixture into serving bowls; cover; refrigerate several hours. Serve crusty bread with Taramasalata and the Yoghurt and Cucumber Dip.

Yoghurt and Cucumber Dip

1 cup natural yoghurt	1 large clove garlic
1 small cucumber	3 shallots or spring onions
salt, pepper	

Remove rind from cucumber; grate cucumber on coarse grater; drain off excess liquid; drain very well. Place yoghurt, cucumber, salt, pepper, crushed garlic and finely-chopped shallots in bowl; mix well. Cover bowl; refrigerate several hours.

Stuffed Vine Leaves

250 g (8 oz.) vine leaves	½ teaspoon cinnamon
½ cup long grain rice	3 tablespoons chopped parsley
1 medium onion	
60 g (2 oz.) pine nuts	1 clove garlic
salt, pepper	1 cup water
250 g (8 oz.) minced steak	⅓ cup lemon juice
¼ teaspoon nutmeg	2 tablespoons olive oil

Lemon Sauce

3 egg yolks	salt, pepper
3 tablespoons lemon juice	125 g (4 oz.) butter

Separate leaves; rinse under running warm water; drain well. Spread each leaf out flat. Place rice, peeled and finely-chopped onion, pine nuts, salt, pepper, minced steak, nutmeg, cinnamon, crushed garlic and parsley in bowl; mix well. Place 1 teaspoonful of meat mixture on to each leaf; fold in sides; roll up into small cylinder shape. Place rolls in medium-sized saucepan, stacking them neatly and firmly in layers on top of each other. Add water, lemon juice and oil; place a saucer on top of rolls, then a small weight on top of saucer; cover with lid. Bring to boil; reduce heat; simmer 60 minutes. Drain off liquid from pan. Place rolls on serving plate; serve with bowl of lemon sauce.

Lemon Sauce: Place egg yolks, lemon juice, salt and pepper in top of double saucepan; stir until combined. Add chopped butter. Stand saucepan over simmering water; stir until sauce thickens; remove from heat immediately; stir 1 minute longer.

Greek Lamb

1.5 kg (3 lb.) shoulder of lamb	¼ teaspoon nutmeg
30 g (1 oz.) butter	¼ teaspoon cinnamon
425 g (15 oz.) can whole tomatoes	½ teaspoon rosemary
¼ cup tomato paste	salt, pepper
1 cup dry white wine	1 teaspoon sugar
1 cup water	4 medium potatoes
½ teaspoon grated lemon rind	6 small onions
	4 medium carrots
	3 tablespoons chopped parsley

Stuffing

½ cup long-grain rice	2 tablespoons chopped parsley
1 medium onion	
60 g (2 oz.) butter	1 stick celery
salt, pepper	¼ teaspoon nutmeg
1 egg	

Ask butcher to bone out the shoulder of lamb. Open lamb out, skin-side down, on board. Spoon prepared stuffing over lamb, pressing down firmly. Roll up and secure with string at 5 cm (2 in.) intervals. Place lamb in baking dish;

Recipe continued overleaf:

Greek Lamb is flavoured with lemon and a subtle blend of spices. Vegetables cook with the lamb in a richly-coloured sauce.

spread butter over lamb. Bake in moderately hot oven 30 minutes. Place undrained tomatoes in electric blender; blend 1 minute on medium speed, or mash well. Push tomato mixture through sieve to discard seeds. Place in bowl; add tomato paste, wine, water, lemon rind, nutmeg, cinnamon, rosemary, salt, pepper and sugar; stir until combined. Pour over lamb in baking dish; return to oven for 20 minutes. Add peeled and halved potatoes, peeled onions and peeled carrots cut into 5 cm (2 in.) pieces. Cover baking dish; bake a further 60 minutes or until vegetables are tender. Spoon sauce occasionally over meat and vegetables. Just before serving, add parsley; mix through lightly.

Stuffing: Gradually add rice to large quantity of boiling salted water; boil uncovered 12 minutes or until rice is tender; drain. Heat butter in pan; add peeled and finely-chopped onion and finely-chopped celery; saute 2 minutes or until onion is transparent. Remove pan from heat; add salt, pepper, rice, egg, parsley and nutmeg; mix well. Allow to cool.

Greek Salad

1 small red pepper	2 sticks celery
1 small green pepper	1 cucumber
1 large onion	1 small lettuce
125 g (4 oz.) black olives	125 g (4 oz.) feta cheese
2 ripe tomatoes	¼ cup french dressing

Cut red and green peppers into rings; remove any seeds. Peel onion; cut into wedges; separate into pieces. Cut tomatoes into wedges. Cut celery into slices. Cut cucumber into cubes. Wash and dry lettuce; tear into pieces. Put all prepared vegetables into salad bowl; add olives; cover; refrigerate until ready to serve. Add salad dressing; toss well; top salad with sliced feta cheese.

Greek Custard Slice

500 g (1 lb.) phylo pastry	2 strips lemon rind
185 g (6 oz.) butter	2 tablespoons honey
1½ cups sugar	¼ cup lemon juice
1½ cups water	

Custard

2 litres (8 cups) milk	1½ teaspoons vanilla
1½ cups semolina	4 eggs
1¼ cups sugar	

Custard: Place milk in large pan; bring just to simmering point; reduce heat immediately. Gradually sprinkle semolina over milk, stirring constantly. Stir until mixture boils and thickens. Simmer uncovered 5 minutes, stirring constantly.

Remove pan from heat; allow mixture to cool slightly. Beat eggs until combined; gradually add to milk mixture with sugar and vanilla; mix well. Allow mixture to become cold.

Lay phylo pastry out flat. Place a 25 cm x 27.5 cm (10 in. x 11 in.) baking dish on top of pastry. Using this dish as a guide, cut around baking dish through pastry sheets, cutting pastry sheets 1 cm (½ in.) larger than dish. Lay one sheet of pastry on base of well-greased baking dish; brush well with melted butter. Continue layering pastry and brushing with melted butter until half pastry is used.

Pour cold custard over pastry in baking dish, spreading out evenly. Place another sheet of pastry on top of custard; brush with melted butter; repeat with remaining pastry and butter; brush top of pastry well with butter. Place baking dish in refrigerator until very cold. With very sharp knife cut through pastry to base, cutting into 8 cm (3 in.) diamonds. Bake in hot oven 15 minutes or until light golden brown; reduce heat to moderate; cook a further 40 minutes or until dark golden brown. Remove from oven; mark into diamonds again.

Place sugar, water, lemon rind, honey and lemon juice in pan; stir over heat until sugar has dissolved. Bring to boil; boil uncovered 3 minutes; remove lemon rind. Spoon hot syrup over pastry, allowing to soak in between diamonds. Allow to cool, then refrigerate overnight before serving.

Greek Shortbread

125 g (4 oz.) unsalted butter	2 cups plain flour
½ cup pure icing sugar	¼ teaspoon baking powder
1 egg yolk	1 cup pure icing sugar, extra
1 tablespoon brandy	

Cream butter and sifted icing sugar until very light and fluffy; add egg yolk and brandy; beat well. Add sifted flour and baking powder; mix until combined. Turn mixture out on to lightly-floured surface; knead lightly. Take a tablespoonful of mixture; roll into a 10 cm (4 in.) roll, making sure that roll is thinner at each end. Form into a horseshoe shape. Repeat with remaining mixture.

Place on greased oven trays. Bake in moderate oven 20 minutes. Sift extra icing sugar on to a tray; place hot cooked biscuits in icing sugar, turning to make sure biscuits are well coated with icing sugar. When cold, store biscuits in air-tight container with icing sugar until required.

Makes approx. 24 biscuits to serve with coffee.

America

The style of American cooking varies greatly from North to South. This dinner party menu for four uses simple, interesting recipes from the South.

Guacamole

1 large ripe avocado	1 teaspoon lemon juice
1 clove garlic	2 teaspoons grated onion
¼ teaspoon chilli powder	salt

Sprinkle a bowl with a little salt and rub with half the cut clove of garlic. Remove stone from avocado; spoon the green flesh into the bowl. Mash well; add salt, chilli powder and lemon juice. Stir in onion and finely-chopped remaining half of garlic clove. If desired, sliced olives or cooked, crisp, crumbled bacon can be added. If preparing in advance, cover with a thin layer of mayonnaise or sour cream to prevent darkening.

Just before serving, stir well, stirring in the mayonnaise or sour cream. Serve on crisp lettuce as a salad, or serve as an appetiser with corn chips. (These are available at specialty food shops. If unable to obtain them, use potato crisps.)

Shrimp Creole

1 kg (2 lb.) prawns	½ teaspoon salt
1 onion	185 g (6 oz.) can tomato
45 g (1½ oz.) butter	paste
2 tablespoons flour	470 g (15 oz.) can whole
1 bayleaf	tomatoes
2 sticks celery	2 cups water
½ green pepper	pinch cayenne
½ teaspoon chilli sauce	

Shell and devein prawns. Saute peeled and finely-chopped onion in butter until transparent. Blend in flour, crushed bayleaf, finely-chopped celery, chopped green pepper, chilli sauce, salt, tomato paste, mashed undrained tomatoes, water and cayenne. Cook slowly, stirring occasionally, until thickened, approx. 30 minutes. Stir in prawns; cook a further few minutes or until prawns are heated through. Serve with hot rice.

Tossed Salad

Arrange crisp leaves of lettuce in salad bowl. Top with quartered tomatoes, cucumber slices, onion rings, sliced, canned artichoke hearts and a sprinkle of chopped chives. Just before serving, toss with french dressing.

Cornbread

1 cup self-raising flour	½ teaspoon salt
1 cup cornmeal	60 g (2 oz.) butter
1 teaspoon baking powder	1 cup milk
2 tablespoons sugar	1 egg

Sift flour, baking powder and salt into bowl. Add sugar and cornmeal; combine well. Put butter and milk in saucepan; stir over low heat until butter melts; add to dry ingredients with beaten egg; mix well. Pour mixture into greased 23 cm x 12 cm (9 in. x 5 in.) loaf tin. Bake in moderately hot oven 25 to 30 minutes or until cooked when tested. Turn out and cool on wire rack; cut into slices; serve buttered.

Southern Pecan Pie

Pastry

1 cup plain flour	90 g (3 oz.) butter
½ teaspoon salt	2 tablespoons iced water

Filling

3 eggs	1 cup golden syrup (or corn
⅔ cup sugar	syrup)
pinch salt	125 g (4 oz.) pecan halves
75 g (2½ oz.) butter	

Pastry: Sift flour and salt into bowl; cut in butter coarsely; sprinkle with water. Gather dough into ball. Refrigerate 10 minutes. Roll out to 23 cm (9 in.) circle. Line 20 cm (8 in.) pie plate with dough; trim, but leave 1 cm (½ in.) overhang; fold overhanging pastry back and under; flute edges.

Filling: Beat together eggs, sugar, salt, golden syrup and melted, cooled butter; add pecans. Pour into pastry shell. Bake in moderately hot oven 40 to 50 minutes or until set and golden brown. Serve cool or slightly warm, topped with icecream.

Almond Crisps

250 g (8 oz.) whole	3 tablespoons plain flour
blanched almonds	2 eggs
1 cup castor sugar	

Put almonds on to baking tray; place in moderate oven 5 minutes or until golden brown. Place in blender; blend until finely chopped. Combine nuts, sugar and sifted flour; mix well. Add lightly-beaten eggs; stir until well combined. Roll heaped teaspoonfuls of mixture into balls with damp hands; place on greased oven trays, allowing room for spreading. Bake in moderate oven 15 minutes or until light golden brown.

Makes approx. 30 biscuits to serve with coffee.

Barbecues

Appetites seem to sharpen in the open air; when there's a barbecue, everybody's hungry! And there are recipes here to suit all occasions, whether it's a simple family barbecue or a special party by the pool.

Chinese Plum Sauce

1 large onion	2 teaspoons soy sauce
1 red pepper	2 tablespoons dry sherry
5 cm (2 in.) piece green ginger	salt
	¼ cup water
2 tablespoons oil	2 chicken stock cubes
1 clove garlic	2 teaspoons cornflour
⅓ cup plum jam	2 shallots or spring onions

Peel onion; cut into large pieces. Seed and slice red pepper. Peel green ginger; cut into paper-thin slices. Heat oil in frying pan; add onion, pepper, ginger and crushed garlic; toss quickly over high heat for 1 minute. Add plum jam, soy sauce, sherry and salt; toss quickly for 2 minutes. Add combined water, crumbled stock cubes and cornflour; stir until sauce boils and thickens, tossing vegetables constantly. Simmer 1 minute. Add chopped shallots; stir until just combined. Serve with barbecued steaks, chops etc.

Serves 4 to 6.

Salami Salad

250 g (8 oz.) Danish salami	1 lettuce
250 g (8 oz.) Polish salami	⅓ cup french dressing
250 g (8 oz.) cheddar cheese	3 tablespoons chopped parsley
1 red pepper	salt, pepper
125 g (4 oz.) green olives	
125 g (4 oz.) black olives	

Remove rind from salamis. Cut Danish salami into 2.5 cm (1 in.) cubes. Cut Polish salami into 5 cm x 1 cm (2 in. x ½ in.) strips. Cut cheese into cubes. Seed pepper; cut into cubes. Combine salamis, cheese, pepper, green and black olives; add salt, pepper, parsley and french dressing; toss lightly.

Refrigerate until ready to serve. Cut lettuce into slices; arrange around salad bowl; toss salad; spoon into centre of lettuce.

Serves 6 to 8.

Chinese Plum Sauce, in centre, is a great accompaniment to barbecued steaks. At left, colourful Salami Salad.

Hot Frankfurt Salad

500 g (1 lb.) frankfurts	60 g (2 oz.) butter
500 g (1 lb.) onions	2 teaspoons curry powder
500 g (1 lb.) potatoes	1 tablespoon finely-chopped parsley
500 g (1 lb.) carrots	salt, pepper
500 g (1 lb.) broccoli	

Melt butter in pan; add thickly-sliced frankfurts, sliced onions and peeled and diced potatoes. Saute over low heat, stirring occasionally, for 15 minutes or until potatoes are tender.

Cut broccoli into flowerets; drop broccoli and thinly-sliced carrots into boiling salted water. Return to boil; cook 2 to 3 minutes; drain. Add broccoli, carrots and curry powder to potato mixture; mix lightly; cook a further 5 minutes. Sprinkle with parsley; season with salt and pepper.

Serves 4 to 6.

Glazed Onions

500 g (1 lb.) small onions	1 tablespoon brown vinegar
3 rashers bacon	1 teaspoon soy sauce
1 tablespoon oil	1 tablespoon dry sherry
3 tablespoons tomato sauce	salt, pepper
2 teaspoons brown sugar	2 tablespoons chopped parsley

Peel onions and cut off as little of the root end as possible so that onions will keep their shape during cooking. Place onions in pan; cover with water; bring to boil. Reduce heat; simmer covered 5 minutes; drain.

Place oil in pan; add well-drained onions and chopped bacon; saute until bacon is crisp. Add tomato sauce, brown sugar, vinegar, soy sauce, sherry, salt and pepper; stir until combined. Simmer uncovered until liquid is reduced and sauce coats onions thickly. Just before serving, add parsley; mix lightly.

Serves 4.

Barbecue Beans

2 large onions	440 g (15 oz.) can tomato soup
60 g (2 oz.) butter	1 tablespoon vinegar
4 rashers bacon	1 teaspoon soy sauce
1 clove garlic	1 tablespoon worcestershire sauce
1 stick celery	salt, pepper
300 g (10 oz.) can red kidney beans	1 teaspoon dry mustard
396 g (14 oz.) can borlotti beans	½ cup water
300 g (10 oz.) can soy beans	

Place peeled and roughly-chopped onions, butter, chopped bacon, crushed garlic and chopped celery in large pan; saute until onions are transparent. Add drained and washed kidney beans, drained borlotti beans and drained soy beans; stir until combined. Add undiluted soup, vinegar, soy sauce, worcestershire sauce, salt, pepper, mustard and water; stir until combined. Bring to boil; reduce heat; simmer uncovered 20 minutes, stirring occasionally.

Serves 6 to 8.

Bean and Pepper Salad

300 g (10 oz.) can red kidney beans	1 green pepper
300 g (10 oz.) can soy beans	2 sticks celery
1 red pepper	1 large onion
	470 g (15 oz.) can pineapple pieces

Dressing

¼ cup white vinegar	salt, pepper
⅓ cup oil	¼ teaspoon dry mustard
1 tablespoon pineapple syrup from can	1 clove garlic, crushed

Rinse kidney beans and soy beans in strainer under cold running water; drain. Put drained beans, seeded and cubed peppers, sliced celery, peeled and chopped onion and drained pineapple (reserve 1 tablespoon syrup) into salad bowl. Add prepared salad dressing; toss well. Refrigerate until ready to serve, tossing occasionally. Serve with crisp lettuce.

Dressing: Put all ingredients into screw-top jar; shake well.

Serves 6.

Lemon and Honey Chicken

1.5 kg (3 lb.) chicken (or chicken pieces)	2 tablespoons white vinegar
3 tablespoons lemon juice	1 tablespoon honey
2 tablespoons oil	salt, pepper
	1 clove garlic

Steam or boil chicken 45 minutes; remove from heat; allow to become cold. Break into serving pieces. Place chicken, lemon juice, oil, vinegar, honey, salt, pepper and crushed garlic in bowl; mix well. Cover bowl; marinate for several hours or refrigerate overnight.

Place chicken on barbecue plate. Do not have plate too hot or chicken will brown too quickly. Cook chicken gently until golden brown on all sides, brushing frequently with marinade.

Serves 4.

Curried Crispy Potatoes

1 kg (2 lb.) old potatoes	2 teaspoons curry powder
30 g (1 oz.) butter	salt, pepper
2 tablespoons oil	¼ cup dry white wine
½ cup sour cream	6 shallots or spring onions
1 chicken stock cube	2 tablespoons chopped
½ teaspoon sugar	parsley

Peel and wash potatoes; cut into 2.5 cm (1 in.) cubes. Heat butter and oil in large frying pan; add potatoes; fry gently until golden brown and cooked through, approx. 15 minutes.

Place sour cream, crumbled stock cube, sugar, curry powder, salt, pepper, wine, chopped shallots and parsley in bowl; mix well. Add to potatoes; bring to boil. Reduce heat; simmer uncovered 3 minutes or until sauce thickly coats the potatoes.

Serves 6.

Continental Potato Cakes

500 g (1 lb.) potatoes	½ teaspoon salt
1 egg	oil for frying
1 tablespoon flour	

Peel potatoes; chop roughly; put in blender; blend on high speed until smooth. Add egg, flour and salt. Blend for a further 1 minute. Pour enough oil into frying pan to cover base; drop tablespoonfuls of mixture into hot oil; fry gently 6 minutes or until golden brown, turning once. Drain on absorbent paper. Sprinkle with salt.

Makes approx. 25.

Damper

3 cups self-raising flour	½ cup milk
1½ teaspoons salt	½ cup water
90 g (3 oz.) butter	extra flour

Sift flour and salt into bowl; rub in butter until mixture resembles fine breadcrumbs, fairly even in size. Make a well in centre of dry ingredients; add combined milk and water all at once; mix lightly with sharp knife in cutting motion. Turn out on to lightly floured surface; knead lightly. Knead dough into round; place on greased oven tray. Pat dough out to a 15 cm (6 in.) circle. With sharp knife, cut two slits across dough like a cross, approx. 1 cm (½ in.) deep.

Brush top of dough with milk; sift a little extra flour over dough. Bake in hot oven 10 minutes or until golden brown. Reduce heat to moderate; cook a further 15 minutes.

Shallot Buns

4 individual round	2 tablespoons chopped
buns	parsley
125 g (4 oz.) butter	salt, pepper
4 shallots or spring onions	1 teaspoon french mustard

Make 4 equal cuts in each bun, cutting just to bottom crust, but not right through. Beat butter in bowl until light and creamy. Add finely-chopped shallots, parsley and mustard; mix well. Season with salt and pepper. Spread butter mixture on both sides of bun slices. Wrap each bun in aluminium foil. Heat in moderate oven 10 minutes.

Serves 4.

Hot Camembert Rolls

6 small bread rolls	125 g (4 oz.) butter
250 g (8 oz.) can	1 small clove garlic
camembert cheese	salt, pepper

Cut bread rolls into 4 equal slices, cutting just to bottom crust but not right through. Carefully remove white rind from cheese. Cut cheese into small pieces. Place butter, cheese, crushed garlic, salt and pepper in pan; stir over very low heat until butter has melted and mixture has combined (it will look like a thick white sauce); this will take about 5 minutes. As soon as it is combined, remove pan from heat; allow to cool slightly.

Spread cheese mixture between bread slices. Spread a little cheese mixture over top of bread rolls. Place on oven tray; bake in moderate oven 10 minutes or until tops of bread rolls are golden brown.

Serves 6.

Savoury Rye Bread

1 small loaf unsliced rye	6 shallots or spring onions
bread	2 tablespoons grated
125 g (4 oz.) butter	parmesan cheese
1 teaspoon prepared	salt, pepper
mustard	

Cut bread into 2 cm (¾ in.) slices, cutting just to bottom crust but not right through; then cut down centre of bread, once again cutting just to bottom crust. Combine softened butter, mustard, chopped shallots, cheese, pepper and salt; mix well. Spread both sides of each bread slice with butter mixture; spread any remaining mixture over top of loaf.

Wrap securely in aluminium foil; heat on barbecue or in moderate oven 20 to 25 minutes.

Serves 4 to 6.

Shallot and Bacon Bread

1 cup plain flour	125 g (4 oz.) cheddar
1½ cups self-raising	cheese
flour	8 shallots or spring onions
125 g (4 oz.) butter	2 tablespoons chopped
2 teaspoons salt	parsley
½ teaspoon pepper	3 rashers bacon
1 teaspoon prepared	1 egg
mustard	⅓ cup milk
½ teaspoon paprika	sesame seeds

Sift all dry ingredients into bowl. Rub in butter until mixture resembles fine breadcrumbs. Add grated cheese, finely-chopped shallots and parsley. Remove rind from bacon; chop bacon into very small pieces. Place in pan; fry until bacon is crisp. Add bacon with bacon fat to flour mixture; mix lightly.

Make well in centre of dry ingredients; add well-beaten egg and milk. Turn out on lightly-floured surface; knead lightly. Divide dough in half; roll with hands into cylindrical shape approx. 25 cm (10 in.) long. Repeat with remaining dough.

Place diagonal cuts across top of each roll; brush with milk, then sprinkle with sesame seeds. Place on greased oven tray. Bake in moderate oven 25 minutes or until golden brown and cooked through. Serve hot with butter.

Makes 2 loaves.

Shish Kebab

1.5 kg (3 lb.) boned leg	salt, pepper
of lamb	60 g (2 oz.) butter
¼ cup rice	500 g (1 lb.) mushrooms
2 tablespoons chopped	1 red pepper
mint	1 green pepper
1 tablespoon brown	3 onions
vinegar	bayleaves
1 tablespoon curry powder	¼ cup oil
1 teaspoon worcester-	2 tablespoons dry sherry
shire sauce	1 clove garlic

Cut meat into 5 cm (2 in.) cubes. With a sharp-pointed knife cut 2 cm (¾ in.) pockets into each lamb cube. Gradually add rice to large saucepan of boiling salted water. Cook uncovered 10 minutes or until tender; drain. Combine rice, chopped mint, vinegar, curry powder, worcestershire sauce, salt and pepper in bowl. Add softened butter; mix well. Put ½ teaspoonful of rice stuffing into each lamb pocket.

Cut red and green peppers in half; remove seeds; cut into 2.5 cm (1 in.) pieces. Peel onions; cut into wedges. Thread lamb, peppers, onion wedges, mushrooms and bayleaves on skewers. Crush garlic; combine with oil and sherry. Grill or

barbecue kebabs, brushing with oil mixture while cooking.

Serves 6.

Chicken Sate

2 whole chicken breasts	1 teaspoon turmeric
½ teaspoon grated lemon	¼ teaspoon cinnamon
rind	1½ teaspoons salt
10 shallots or spring	2 teaspoons sugar
onions	2 tablespoons roasted
2 teaspoons ground	peanuts
coriander	1 tablespoon oil
1 teaspoon ground cumin	oil for basting

Sate Sauce

90 g (3 oz.) unsalted	3 tablespoons peanut
peanuts	butter
2.5 cm (1 in.) piece green	1 teaspoon chilli powder
ginger	2 teaspoons curry powder
½ cup mango or fruit	2 teaspoons soy sauce
chutney	1 cup water
¼ cup raisins	salt, pepper
¼ cup sultanas	1 clove garlic

Cut chicken meat from bones; cut into 2.5 cm (1 in.) cubes. Place lemon rind and roughly-chopped shallots in blender; blend on high speed 30 seconds or until shallots are finely-chopped (or chop these ingredients very finely); place mixture in bowl. Stir in coriander, cumin, turmeric, cinnamon, salt, sugar, finely-chopped or blended peanuts and oil; mix well. Add chicken; mix well with spoon.

Thread chicken pieces on thin bamboo skewers; grill, turning occasionally, until cooked through. Baste with oil several times during cooking to keep moist.

Traditional accompaniments are sliced cucumber, sliced onion and hot boiled rice. If desired, saute some slivered almonds and sultanas in hot oil for 3 minutes and stir into rice.

Sate Sauce: Place peanuts, peeled and grated ginger, chutney, raisins, sultanas, peanut butter, chilli powder, curry powder, soy sauce, water, salt, pepper and crushed garlic in electric blender; blend on medium speed 1 minute or until nuts are finely chopped; place in pan. (If you do not have an electric blender, place all ingredients in pan with finely-chopped nuts and chopped raisins.) Bring mixture to boil; reduce heat; simmer uncovered 15 minutes or until mixture is thick.

Serves 6.

Skewered foods cook beautifully on the barbecue. In front, Shish Kebab; on barbecue, Beef and Chicken Sates, served with a rich sate sauce.

Beef Sate

1 kg (2 lb.) rump steak	1 clove garlic
2 tablespoons tomato paste	3 tablespoons white vinegar
3 tablespoons tomato sauce	salt, pepper
3 teaspoons curry powder	2 tablespoons oil
½ teaspoon chilli powder	1 teaspoon soy sauce
1 teaspoon garam masala	1 tablespoon water
2 teaspoons ground cumin	3 tablespoons oil, extra

Sate Sauce

4 tablespoons peanut butter	30 g (1 oz.) butter
½ teaspoon chilli powder	1 medium onion
⅓ cup brown malt vinegar	1 teaspoon soy sauce
3 tablespoons sugar	salt, pepper
	1 cup water

Remove all fat from meat. Cut meat into strips approx. 2.5 cm (1 in.) thick, then cut each strip into 5 mm (¼ in.) pieces. Put tomato paste, tomato sauce, curry powder, chilli powder, garam masala, soy sauce and water into bowl; mix well. Add meat; mix well. Let stand overnight or for several hours.

Drain marinade from meat; reserve marinade for sauce. Thread meat on bamboo skewers. Put under hot grill; grill until golden brown and cooked through. Turn skewers frequently, brushing with extra oil. Serve with Sate Sauce.

Sate Sauce: Heat butter in pan; add peeled and finely-chopped onion; saute gently until onion is golden brown. Add remaining ingredients; mix well. Add reserved marinade; stir until combined. Bring to boil; boil uncovered 5 minutes or until sauce is thick. Serve hot or cold.

Serves 6.

Glazed Pork Rashers

1.25 kg (2½ lb.) pork rashers	2 tablespoons brown vinegar
2 tablespoons soy sauce	2 tablespoons orange marmalade
2.5 cm (1 in.) piece green ginger	2 tablespoons tomato sauce
2 tablespoons honey	1 clove garlic
2 tablespoons sweet sherry	salt, pepper

Place pork rashers in single layer in large baking dish. Bake in moderate oven 40 minutes. Drain off all fat from baking dish. Pour over pork rashers combined soy sauce, peeled and grated green ginger, honey, sherry, vinegar, marmalade, tomato sauce, crushed garlic, salt and pepper. Return baking dish to oven for 40 minutes; spoon glaze frequently over pork.

Serves 4 to 6.

Barbecue Steaks with Beer

4 barbecue steaks (approx. 250 g (8 oz.) each)	2 teaspoons prepared mustard
370 ml (¾ pint) can beer	2 tablespoons tomato sauce
1 tablespoon worcestershire sauce	1 tablespoon cornflour
1 tablespoon soy sauce	

Combine beer, worcestershire, soy and tomato sauces and mustard; pour over steaks; marinate 2 hours. Cook steaks on barbecue until tender, brushing frequently with marinade. Add remaining marinade to cornflour. Stir over heat until sauce boils and thickens; spoon over steaks.

Serves 4.

Hamburgers au Poivre (Pepper Hamburgers)

500 g (1 lb.) minced steak	2 teaspoons worcestershire sauce
3 teaspoons whole black peppercorns	¼ cup lemon juice
1 teaspoon salt	1 tablespoon finely-chopped parsley
60 g (2 oz.) butter	2 shallots or spring onions

Shape minced steak into 8 even-sized hamburgers. Crush peppercorns with a hammer. Sprinkle crushed pepper on both sides of each hamburger, pressing pepper well into meat.

Sprinkle salt evenly over base of frying pan; put pan over high heat. When salt begins to brown (about 3 minutes) add hamburgers. Cook until well browned on each side. Reduce heat; cook a further 2 to 3 minutes depending on thickness of hamburgers, until meat is cooked. Remove from pan; keep warm

Melt butter in frying pan; add parsley and finely-chopped shallots; saute 1 to 2 minutes. Add lemon juice and worcestershire sauce; bring to boil. Reduce heat and simmer 2 to 3 minutes. Pour sauce over hamburgers.

Serves 4.

Minted Pineapple Burgers

750 g (1½ lb.) minced steak	1 egg
1 medium onion	470 g (15 oz.) can sliced pineapple
salt, pepper	packaged dry breadcrumbs
¼ cup tomato sauce	30 g (1 oz.) butter
1 tablespoon soy sauce	¼ cup oil

Minted Butter

125 g (4 oz.) butter	2 shallots or spring onions, finely chopped
2 tablespoons finely-chopped mint	¼ teaspoon dry mustard
salt, pepper	

Put steak, peeled and finely-chopped onion, salt, pepper, tomato sauce, soy sauce and egg into bowl; mix well. Divide meat into 6 equal portions. Drain pineapple rings; cut rings into quarters. Take 2 pieces of pineapple and carefully mould 1 portion of meat around the pineapple; repeat with remaining meat, forming into neat, flat burger shapes. Coat firmly with breadcrumbs.

Heat oil and butter in frying pan; add burgers; fry until golden brown on both sides and cooked through. Put burgers on serving plate; top each with a spoonful of Minted Butter.

Minted Butter: Beat butter until light and creamy. Add remaining ingredients; mix well. Refrigerate until butter is firm.

Serves 6.

NOTE: This mixture also makes excellent bite-sized burgers to serve with drinks. Cut pineapple rings into 2.5 cm (1 in.) pieces (or use 470 g (15 oz.) can pineapple pieces instead); mould meat mixture around 1 piece pineapple at a time; roll in dry breadcrumbs and cook as above.

Minted Wine Chops

6 forequarter lamb chops	2 tablespoons port
1 cup dry red wine	2 tablespoons dry sherry
2 tablespoons brown sugar	1 tablespoon cornflour
1 teaspoon french mustard	2 tablespoons water
3 tablespoons chopped mint	1 chicken stock cube
	salt, pepper

Place wine, brown sugar, mustard, mint, port, sherry, crumbled stock cube, salt and pepper in pan; bring to boil. Reduce heat; simmer uncovered 3 minutes. Remove pan from heat; add combined cornflour and water; stir until combined. Return pan to heat; stir until sauce boils and thickens. Reduce heat; simmer uncovered 3 minutes.

Place chops on hot barbecue plate; brown lightly on both sides; continue cooking chops, brushing each side of chops with sauce, until cooked. Serve with any remaining sauce spooned over.

Serves 4 to 6.

Lychee Prawn Sticks

500 g (1 lb.) large fresh prawns	1 clove garlic
6 small mushrooms	2.5 cm (1 in.) piece green ginger
3 rashers bacon	1 teaspoon honey
565 g (18 oz.) can lychees	1 tablespoon dry sherry
3 tablespoons oil	salt, pepper
½ teaspoon chilli powder	

Shell prawns; remove back vein. Remove rind from bacon rashers; cut each rasher in half; roll up. Drain lychees. Thread ingredients on thin bamboo skewers in this order: lychee, prawn, mushroom, bacon roll, lychee, prawn. There should be enough ingredients for 6 skewers. Place on tray.

Combine oil, chilli powder, crushed garlic, peeled and grated green ginger, honey, sherry, salt and pepper in bowl; mix well. Pour this mixture over skewers. Marinate for 3 hours or overnight, turning skewers occasionally.

Place skewers on hot grill; cook quickly on both sides until prawns are cooked through, approx. 5 minutes; brush marinade over frequently.

Serves 6.

Rosemary Glaze for Meats

½ cup oil	3 teaspoons finely-chopped fresh rosemary (or 1 teaspoon chopped dried rosemary)
½ cup white vinegar	
2 teaspoons salt	
¼ teaspoon pepper	
1 teaspoon sugar	

Place all ingredients in bowl; mix well. This mixture can be brushed over meat while cooking on barbecue, or brushed over spit-roasted meat during cooking time. Each time glaze is used, stir well.

Red Wine Marinade

½ cup dry red wine	1 teaspoon worcester-shire sauce
2 tablespoons port	
1 tablespoon honey	¼ teaspoon chilli powder
1 tablespoon tomato sauce	¼ teaspoon caraway seeds
	½ teaspoon paprika
salt, pepper	

Place all ingredients in saucepan; stir over low heat until combined. Bring to boil; reduce heat; simmer uncovered 3 minutes. Allow to become cold. Brush marinade over meat while grilling.

Pineapple Ginger Marinade

1 cup canned pineapple juice	⅓ cup sweet sherry
	2 tablespoons oil
¼ cup soy sauce	1 teaspoon dry mustard
2 teaspoons grated green ginger	½ teaspoon curry powder
	1 clove garlic, crushed

Combine all ingredients; blend well. Add steaks; stand 1 hour. Remove from marinade; grill over the barbecue until cooked to taste (rare, medium or well done), brushing steaks several times with the marinade as they cook. Marinade is sufficient for 6 steaks.

To Serve with Drinks and Coffee

Here are pates, unusual dips, delightful little nibbles you will be proud to serve to guests with drinks. And, to serve with after-dinner coffee, here are ideas that are just a little different — they make the perfect sweet ending to the meal.

Italian Canapes

1 small french bread stick	2 tablespoons grated parmesan cheese
125 g (4 oz.) salami	1 tablespoon chopped parsley
125 g (4 oz.) mozzarella cheese	paprika

Tomato Sauce

60 g (2 oz.) butter	1 teaspoon oregano
1 onion	1 teaspoon sugar
470 g (15 oz.) can whole peeled tomatoes	salt, pepper
2 cloves garlic	2 tablespoons chopped parsley
1 teaspoon basil	

Cut bread into 1 cm (½ in.) slices; toast one side of each slice of bread. Choose small salami, about the same size as the bread rounds. Put a slice of salami on untoasted side of each slice of bread; top with a spoonful of tomato mixture. Slice mozzarella; cut into about the same size as the bread rounds. Arrange mozzarella slices on top of tomato mixture; sprinkle evenly with parmesan cheese.

Put under griller; grill until cheese has melted and is lightly browned. Sprinkle tops with chopped parsley or paprika.

Tomato Sauce: Melt butter in pan; add peeled and finely-chopped onion and crushed garlic; saute until onion is transparent. Add undrained mashed tomatoes, basil, oregano, sugar, salt and pepper; combine well. Bring to boil; reduce heat; simmer 20 to 25 minutes or until thick. Remove from heat; add parsley; allow to cool.

Makes approx. 20.

Italian Canapes and, at left, Stuffed Mushrooms — they're perfect to serve with drinks, and so easy to make.

Stuffed Mushrooms

375 g (12 oz.) small mushrooms	1 tablespoon milk
1½ cups fresh bread-crumbs	1 teaspoon worcester-shire sauce
1 clove garlic	1½ teaspoons french mustard
6 shallots or spring onions	salt, pepper
1 onion	1 tablespoon lemon juice
2 tablespoons chopped parsley	60 g (2 oz.) butter
¼ teaspoon thyme	125 g (4 oz.) cheddar cheese
1 egg	paprika

Choose mushrooms of even size. Remove stems from mushrooms and chop stems finely. Put breadcrumbs in bowl; add crushed garlic, chopped shallots, peeled and chopped onion, chopped parsley, thyme and chopped mushroom stems; mix well. Combine egg, milk, worcestershire sauce, mustard, salt and pepper; mix well. Add to breadcrumbs; mix until all ingredients are combined. Fill mushroom caps with mixture.

Heat butter in ovenproof dish; add lemon juice. Put mushrooms in dish; sprinkle on grated cheese and paprika. Bake in moderate oven 7 to 10 minutes or until cheese is golden brown.

Makes approx. 15.

Mushrooms Kilpatrick

about 30 canned fresh oysters	500 g (1 lb.) small mushrooms
2 tablespoons lemon juice	125 g (4 oz.) bacon
2 teaspoons worcester-shire sauce	60 g (2 oz.) butter
salt, pepper	2 tablespoons chopped parsley

Drain oysters. Put in bowl; add lemon juice, worcestershire sauce, salt and pepper; marinate 30 minutes. Stem mushrooms. Drain oysters; reserve liquid. Put an oyster in the cap of each mushroom; sprinkle on finely-chopped bacon.

Heat butter in ovenproof dish; add reserved liquid. Put mushrooms in dish; bake in moderate oven 10 minutes or until bacon is crisp. Remove from oven and sprinkle parsley over.

Makes approx. 30.

Camembert Pate

185 g (6 oz.) pkt camembert cheese	6 shallots or spring onions
90 g (3 oz.) butter	salt, pepper
few drops tabasco sauce	2 tablespoons cream

Remove rind from camembert. Beat camembert and softened butter until smooth. Add tabasco, chopped shallots, salt and pepper; mix well. Stir in cream; mix well. Spoon into serving dish; refrigerate until firm.

Cheese Puffs

375 g (12 oz.) pkt puff pastry	2 teaspoons curry powder
125 g (4 oz.) cheddar cheese	6 shallots or spring onions
2 tablespoons chopped parsley	salt, pepper
	1 egg
	2 tablespoons milk

Cut pastry in half; roll each half out thinly on lightly floured board. Cut into rounds using 8 cm (3 in.) cutter. Combine grated cheese, parsley, curry powder, finely-chopped shallots, salt and pepper. Put small teaspoonfuls of filling into centre of each round; brush edges of pastry with combined beaten egg and milk. Fold edges together; pinch well.

Put puffs on greased oven trays; brush well with the egg-glaze. Bake in moderately hot oven 15 to 20 minutes or until golden brown.

Makes approx. 30.

Crunchy Cheese Biscuits

125 g (4 oz.) butter	1 cup self-raising flour
90 g (3 oz.) cheddar cheese	1 cup crushed cornflakes
½ teaspoon salt	1 egg
¼ teaspoon cayenne	1 tablespoon milk

Cream butter until soft. Add grated cheese, salt, cayenne, sifted flour and cornflakes. Combine beaten egg and milk. Reserve two teaspoons for glazing. Add remaining egg and milk to cornflake mixture and mix thoroughly.

Roll teaspoonfuls of mixture into balls; put on lightly-greased oven trays about 5 cm (2 in.) apart Press tops lightly with fork. Glaze with reserved egg and milk mixture. Bake in moderate oven 8 to 10 minutes.

Makes approx. 35.

Savoury Cheese Roll

250 g (8 oz.) packaged cream cheese	2 gherkins
60 g (2 oz.) butter	4 shallots or spring onions
1 tablespoon grated parmesan cheese	salt, pepper
2 tablespoons tomato sauce	¼ cup chopped parsley

Beat cream cheese and butter until smooth. Add parmesan cheese, tomato sauce, finely-chopped gherkins, chopped shallots, salt and pepper. Divide mixture in half; roll each half in chopped parsley, forming two neat rolls. Wrap in grease-proof paper; refrigerate several hours. Slice; serve with savoury biscuits.

English Potted Cheese

250 g (8 oz.) cheddar cheese	few drops tabasco sauce
1 teaspoon french mustard	2 tablespoons dry sherry
salt, pepper	1 teaspoon port
½ teaspoon worcestershire sauce	3 shallots or spring onions
	1 tablespoon chopped parsley

Grate cheese; combine with all ingredients except shallots and parsley; beat well. This can be done in the small bowl of an electric mixer. Chop shallots and parsley finely; mix into the cheese. Serve with hot toast.

Cheese Bites

75 g (2½ oz.) gruyere cheese	⅓ cup plain flour
75 g (2½ oz.) emmenthaler cheese	1 teaspoon baking powder
	salt, pepper
1 egg	14 slices square white bread
2½ tablespoons milk	
1 clove garlic	oil for deep-frying

Grate cheeses; put into small bowl of electric mixer. Add egg, milk, crushed garlic, sifted flour, baking powder, salt and pepper. Beat on medium speed 5 minutes.

With 4 cm (1½ in.) pastry cutter, cut 4 rounds from each slice of bread (or remove crusts from bread, cut each slice into 4 squares). Spread about 2 teaspoonfuls of mixture on each bread piece, right to outer edges. Put in hot oil, cheese-side down; fry until golden brown on both sides, about 2 minutes, turning once. Drain on absorbent paper.

Makes 56.

Anchovy Toasts

2 x 45 g (1½ oz.) cans anchovy fillets	pepper
3 tablespoons mayonnaise	1 small egg white
4 shallots or spring onions	60 g (2 oz.) cheddar cheese
1 small clove garlic	7 to 8 slices thick toasting bread
1 tablespoon chopped parsley	oil for deep-frying

Remove crusts from bread. Cut each slice into 4 squares. Arrange on oven slides; cook until golden brown.

Drain anchovy fillets; reserve oil; mash anchovies well with fork, beating in a little of the reserved oil. Stir in mayonnaise, finely-chopped shallots, crushed garlic, parsley and pepper; mix well. Fold in lightly-beaten egg-white. Drop teaspoonfuls of mixture on to each bread square; top with grated cheese. Bake in moderately hot oven 7 to 10 minutes until puffy and golden brown.

Makes approx. 30.

Creamy Salmon-Wine Dip

250 g (8 oz.) packaged cream cheese	3 tablespoons dry white wine
220 g (7 oz.) can red salmon	2 cloves garlic
	few drops tabasco sauce
1 small onion	salt, pepper

Beat cream cheese until soft and creamy. Drain salmon; remove skin and bones; add salmon to cream cheese; mix well. Add finely-chopped onion, white wine, crushed garlic, tabasco sauce, salt and pepper. Spoon into serving dish. Refriger-ate several hours before serving.

Curried Ham and Egg Balls

60 g (2 oz.) butter	1 tablespoon grated parmesan cheese
⅓ cup flour	
1 tablespoon curry powder	½ teaspoon mixed herbs
1 cup milk	1 tablespoon chopped parsley
1 onion	
60 g (2 oz.) ham	extra flour for coating
2 hard-boiled eggs	1 egg, extra
salt, pepper	2 tablespoons milk, extra
2 cups fresh breadcrumbs	oil for deep-frying

Melt butter; put butter, flour, curry powder, milk, peeled and roughly-chopped onion in blender; blend until smooth. Put in saucepan over medium heat; stir until sauce boils and thickens. Reduce heat; simmer 1 minute. Add finely-chopped ham and shelled, finely-chopped hard-boiled eggs; season with salt and pepper.

Combine breadcrumbs, cheese, mixed herbs and parsley. Roll tablespoonfuls of ham mixture into balls; coat lightly with extra flour; dip in combined beaten extra egg and extra milk. Coat with breadcrumb mixture; dip in egg mixture again; coat with crumb mixture again. Deep-fry in hot oil until golden brown; drain.

Makes approx. 20.

Curried Chicken Balls

60 g (2 oz.) butter	2 cups finely-chopped
3 tablespoons plain flour	chicken meat (approx.
1 cup milk	½ chicken)
salt, pepper	500 g (1 lb.) prawns
1 tablespoon curry	packaged dry breadcrumbs
powder	oil for deep-frying
¼ teaspoon chilli powder	2 tablespoons chopped
½ teaspoon grated lemon	parsley
rind	4 shallots or spring onions
2 teaspoons lemon juice	¼ cup mayonnaise

Batter

1 cup plain flour	½ cup water
¼ teaspoon salt	2 egg whites

Shell and devein prawns; chop prawns roughly. Heat butter in pan; add flour; stir until combined. Remove pan from heat; add milk; stir until combined. Return pan to heat; stir until sauce boils and thickens; add curry powder, chilli powder, lemon rind, lemon juice, salt and pepper; simmer sauce uncovered 3 minutes. Add finely-chopped chicken meat, prawns, parsley and chopped shallots. Allow mixture to become cold; add mayonnaise; mix well. Place bowl in refrigerator until mixture is well chilled.

Take tablespoonfuls of mixture; drop into prepared batter; remove with slotted spoon; drain lightly. Place in breadcrumbs; roll into balls. Place balls in deep hot oil; fry few minutes until golden brown; drain on absorbent paper.

Batter: Sift flour and salt into a bowl. Gradually add water, mixing to a smooth batter. Just before using add unbeaten egg whites; mix well.

Makes approx. 20.

Chinese Pork Balls

500 g (1 lb.) minced	2.5 cm (1 in.) piece green
pork	ginger
230 g (7 oz.) can water	1 tablespoon soy sauce
chestnuts	salt, pepper
60 g (2 oz.) ham	cornflour
6 shallots or spring onions	oil for deep-frying

Sauce

½ cup water	¼ cup brown sugar,
½ cup tomato sauce	lightly packed
2 tablespoons vinegar	1 tablespoon worcester-
2 teaspoons soy sauce	shire sauce

Put pork, finely-chopped water chestnuts, finely-diced ham, chopped shallots, grated ginger, soy sauce, salt and pepper into mixing bowl; mix ingredients together with hands; refrigerate 1 hour. Roll heaped teaspoonfuls of pork mixture into small balls. Put on trays which have been lined with aluminium foil. Refrigerate several hours until firm.

Toss pork balls lightly in cornflour; shake off excess. Lower pork balls, a few at a time, into deep hot oil; fry until golden brown; drain well. Remove pork balls to serving dish; accompany with sauce; serve hot.

Sauce: Combine water, tomato sauce, vinegar, sugar, worcestershire sauce and soy sauce in small saucepan. Stir over low heat until sauce boils; reduce heat; simmer gently 2 minutes.

Makes approx. 30.

Hot Garlic Wine Dip

60 g (2 oz.) butter	3 cloves garlic
2 tablespoons flour	250 g (8 oz.) packaged
1 cup dry white wine	cream cheese
salt, pepper	250 g (8 oz.) cheddar
2 teaspoons french	cheese
mustard	4 shallots or spring onions

Heat butter and crushed garlic in pan; add flour; stir until combined. Remove pan from heat; add white wine; stir until combined. Return pan to heat; stir until sauce boils and thickens. Reduce heat; simmer uncovered 3 minutes. Season with salt and pepper. Add mustard; add finely-chopped cream cheese; stir over very low heat until cheese has melted. Very gradually add grated cheddar cheese, stirring constantly until cheese has melted. Do not boil cheese mixture.

Remove from heat; add finely-chopped shallots; stir until combined. Pour into serving dish; serve hot with toast triangles.

Almond Biscuits

250 g (8 oz.) ground	few drops almond essence
almonds	1 egg-white, extra
¾ cup castor sugar	1 cup icing sugar, approx.
1 egg white	60 g (2 oz.) flaked almonds
½ teaspoon honey	

Beat egg white until firm peaks form; fold in honey and almond essence. Combine ground almonds and sugar; stir in egg white mixture. Cover; let stand 12 hours or overnight.

Beat extra egg white until firm peaks form; add half the egg white to almond mixture. Roll teaspoonfuls of mixture into small balls; roll in sifted icing sugar. Place on greased oven trays; flatten slightly with base of glass. Brush tops of biscuits lightly with remaining egg white. Press a few flaked almonds on top of each biscuit. Bake in moderately slow oven 20 minutes.

Makes approx. 30.

Almond Biscuits — a small biscuit, delicious to serve with coffee.

Honey Walnuts

250 g (8 oz.) walnut halves	1 teaspoon soy sauce
¾ cup honey	castor sugar
1 tablespoon lemon juice	oil for frying

Combine honey, lemon juice and soy sauce; pour over walnuts; allow to stand a few hours, stirring occasionally. Drain walnuts; toss in castor sugar; cook in enough hot oil to cover until golden. Remove from pan; drain well.

French Hazelnut Creams

¼ cup sugar	125 g (4 oz.) butter
¼ cup water	125 g (4 oz.) dark chocolate, extra
2 eggs	
60 g (2 oz.) dark chocolate	30 g (1 oz.) solid white vegetable shortening
2 tablespoons coffee liqueur (Tia Maria or Kahlua)	30 g (1 oz.) whole roasted hazelnuts

Put sugar and water in saucepan; stir over low heat until sugar has dissolved; bring to boil; boil 2 minutes; remove from heat. Beat eggs until pale and frothy; add hot syrup in gradual stream, beating continually until thick. Melt chocolate in top of double saucepan over simmering water; add to egg mixture with coffee liqueur; mix well; cool. Add softened butter; beat until mixture is thick and creamy; refrigerate 30 minutes.

Fill mixture into piping bag fitted with 1 cm (½ in.) plain tube; pipe into swirls on sheet of greased greaseproof paper; pipe swirls approx. 2.5 cm (1 in.) in diameter, bringing centre to a peak. Halve the hazelnuts; press half hazelnut into peak of each swirl; refrigerate several hours until firm.

Melt extra chocolate and vegetable shortening in top of double saucepan over simmering water; cool. Dip swirls into chocolate mixture; coat well. Put on sheet of greased greaseproof paper; refrigerate until set. Keep refrigerated.

Makes approx. 60.

Almond Caramel Chocolate

45 g (1½ oz.) butter	185 g (6 oz.) soft caramels
60 g (2 oz.) blanched almonds	2 tablespoons cream
	125 g (4 oz.) dark chocolate

Melt butter in saucepan; add chopped almonds; saute until lightly golden brown. Add chopped caramels; stir over low heat until soft and melted; pour off any excess butter. Add cream; stir over low heat until well combined. Spread mixture evenly into 18 cm (7 in.) square shallow baking tin which has been lined with greased aluminium foil; bring foil 5 cm (2 in.) above sides of tin. Refrigerate until set.

Put chopped chocolate in top of double saucepan; stir over simmering water until melted. Spread evenly over caramel; refrigerate until set. Cut into squares; keep refrigerated.

Chocolate Hazelnut Creams

185 g (6 oz.) butter	2 teaspoons instant coffee powder
1 cup icing sugar	
1 tablespoon coffee liqueur (Tia Maria or Kahlua)	90 g (3 oz.) ground hazelnuts

Chocolate Coating

185 g (6 oz.) dark chocolate	1 teaspoon instant coffee powder
30 g (1 oz.) solid white vegetable shortening	

Beat butter until light and fluffy. Gradually beat in sifted icing sugar. Add combined coffee liqueur and coffee powder; beat well. Fold in ground hazelnuts. Refrigerate until butter mixture is just firm.

Spoon half of mixture into rough log shape about a quarter of the way down a sheet of greased greaseproof paper. Fold paper over roll, then, with a ruler, push against the butter mixture, so that mixture forms a smooth roll. Roll butter mixture in greaseproof paper; refrigerate until hard. Repeat process with remaining mixture.

Cut into slices 5 mm (¼ in.) thick. Dip into cooled chocolate; coat evenly; shake off excess chocolate. Put on greased greaseproof paper. Refrigerate until set.

Chocolate Coating: Put chopped chocolate, vegetable shortening and coffee powder in top of double saucepan; stir over simmering water until melted; cool.

Makes approx. 50.

Chestnut Chocolates

125 g (4 oz.) dark chocolate	1 tablespoon creme de cacao
125 g (4 oz.) butter	1 tablespoon brandy
¼ cup icing sugar	185 g (6 oz.) dark chocolate, extra
250 g (8 oz.) can sweetened chestnut puree	15 g (½ oz.) solid white vegetable shortening
½ cup cream	

Place chopped chocolate in top of double saucepan; stir over gently simmering water until chocolate has melted; remove from heat; allow to cool. Cream butter until soft and creamy; gradually beat in sifted icing sugar and chestnut puree; beat until mixture is light and fluffy. Gradually stir in cooled chocolate. Whip cream lightly; stir in creme de cacao and brandy; fold gently into chocolate-chestnut mixture; mix well. Cover bowl; refrigerate until mixture is very firm, preferably overnight.

Keeping hands wet, roll heaped teaspoonfuls of mixture into small balls. Put chocolate balls on trays which have been lined with aluminium foil; refrigerate until firm. Put chopped extra chocolate and vegetable shortening in top of double saucepan; stir over simmering water until chocolate has melted; remove from heat immediately. Using fork, dip each chocolate ball into melted chocolate; drain off excess; place on aluminium foil until set.

Makes approx. 50.

Rum and Raisin Chocolate

125 g (4 oz.) dark chocolate	¾ cup raisins
30 g (1 oz.) solid white vegetable shortening	1 tablespoon rum

Topping

125 g (4 oz.) white chocolate	1 tablespoon instant coffee powder
1 tablespoon cream	

Put chopped chocolate and vegetable shortening in top of double saucepan; stir over simmering water until melted. Remove from heat; add chopped raisins. When completely cold, add rum; mix well. Spread mixture evenly into 18 cm (7 in.) square shallow baking tin which has been lined with greased aluminium foil; bring foil 5 cm (2 in.) above sides of tin. Refrigerate until set.

Spread topping evenly over chocolate; refrigerate until set. Cut into squares. Keep refrigerated.

Topping: Put chopped white chocolate in top of double saucepan; stir over simmering water until melted. Add combined coffee and cream; mix well.

Ginger Honey Chocolate

60 g (2 oz.) flaked almonds	1 tablespoon chopped preserved ginger
200 g (6½ oz.) white chocolate	1 tablespoon ginger syrup
1 tablespoon honey	1 tablespoon cream

Put almonds on baking tray; bake in moderate oven 5 minutes or until golden brown; remove from tray immediately; cool. Put chopped white chocolate, honey and 1 tablespoon ginger syrup in top of double saucepan; stir over simmering water until chocolate has melted. Add chopped preserved ginger and cream; mix well.

Spread mixture evenly into 18 cm (7 in.) square shallow baking tin which has been lined with greased aluminium foil; bring foil 5 cm (2 in.) above sides of tin. Sprinkle with toasted flaked almonds. Refrigerate until set. When set, lift out; cut into small squares. Keep refrigerated.

Chocolate Ginger Lychees

625 g (1 lb. 4 oz.) can lychees	185 g (6 oz.) dark chocolate
60 g (2 oz.) preserved ginger	15 g (½ oz.) solid white vegetable shortening

Drain lychees; allow to stand 1 hour on absorbent paper, or until lychees are dry on outside. Cut ginger into thin slivers. Carefully stuff each lychee with ginger.

Put chocolate and vegetable shortening in top of double saucepan. Stir over simmering water until chocolate has melted. Allow to cool slightly. Dip lychees into chocolate; carefully lift out with fork, tapping fork gently on side of saucepan to drain excess chocolate from lychees. Put on oven tray lined with greased, greaseproof paper. Refrigerate until set; keep refrigerated.

Chocolate Hazelnut Meringues

3 egg whites	125 g (4 oz.) roasted hazelnuts
1 cup castor sugar	90 g (3 oz.) dark chocolate, extra
½ teaspoon vinegar	
½ teaspoon vanilla	30 g (1 oz.) solid white vegetable shortening
90 g (3 oz.) dark chocolate	

Beat egg whites until soft peaks form; gradually add sugar; beat until stiff and glossy and sugar has dissolved. Beat in vinegar and vanilla. Fold in very finely-chopped chocolate and very finely-chopped hazelnuts. Spoon mixture into piping bag fitted with plain nozzle; pipe into 5 cm (2 in.) lengths. Bake in slow oven 40 to 45 minutes or until cooked. Loosen and cool on trays.

Chop extra chocolate and vegetable shortening; put into top of double saucepan; stir over simmering water until chocolate melts. Dip half of meringue in chocolate; put on greased aluminium foil to set.

Makes approx. 30.

Sweet Pies

It is not easy to choose a favourite from this selection of popular pies — they're all delicious! There's a delightful variety of fillings; you'll want to try them all.

Creamy Apple Tart

Pastry

1¼ cups plain flour
90 g (3 oz.) butter
1 egg yolk
¼ cup castor sugar

2 teaspoons water
½ cup apricot jam
1 tablespoon water, extra

Creamy Filling

2 tablespoons custard powder
2 tablespoons sugar
½ teaspoon vanilla

1 cup milk
½ cup cream
1 egg yolk

Topping

4 large green apples
½ cup sugar
1 cup water
½ cup dry white wine

2.5 cm (1 in.) cinnamon stick
4 whole cloves

Sift flour on board; make well in centre. Put sugar in centre; make well in sugar. Put softened butter, egg yolk and water in centre of sugar. Work butter, egg yolk, sugar and water with knife until soft and creamy. Work in flour with knife. Knead lightly. Refrigerate 30 minutes or until pastry is firm.

Roll out pastry to cover base and sides of 23 cm (9 in.) flan tin. Prick base well. Bake in moderate oven 15 minutes or until pale golden brown; cool. Fill with prepared Cream Filling. Arrange apples decoratively over custard. Stir apricot jam and extra water in pan over low heat until combined. Push through fine sieve. Brush thickly over apples; cool.

Filling: Put custard powder and sugar into pan; gradually add milk; mix until smooth. Add vanilla and cream. Stir over heat until mixture boils. Reduce heat; simmer uncovered 3 minutes, stirring constantly. Remove pan from heat; allow to cool slightly. Add egg yolk; mix well. Return pan to heat; stir until mixture just comes to boil. Remove from heat; cover; let stand until warm.

Recipe continued overleaf:

Creamy Apple Tart — a creamy filling is topped with wine-flavoured apples, then coated thickly with apricot glaze.

Topping: Peel, quarter and core apples. Cut apples into thick, even slices. Put sugar, water, wine, cinnamon stick and cloves into large pan; add apple slices. Cover; bring to boil. Reduce heat; simmer gently 3 minutes or until apples are just firm and still hold their shape. Drain liquid from apples; separate slices. Cool.

Apple and Blackberry Pie

Pastry

1½ cups plain flour	1 tablespoon sugar
¾ cup self-raising flour	1 egg yolk
⅓ cup custard powder	4 tablespoons water, approx.
⅓ cup cornflour	
pinch salt	1 egg white for glazing
185 g (6 oz.) butter	extra sugar

Filling

4 large green apples	water
1 strip lemon rind	2 tablespoons cornflour
4 whole cloves	2 tablespoons sugar
½ cup water	
380 g (13 oz.) can blackberries	

Pastry: Sift flours, custard powder and salt into bowl. Rub in butter until mixture resembles fine breadcrumbs. Add sugar; mix well. Make a well in centre of dry ingredients; add egg yolk and water. Mix to a firm but pliable dough. Turn out on to lightly floured surface; knead lightly. Roll out just over half the pastry to line 23 cm (9 in.) pie plate. Spoon in prepared filling evenly.

Roll out remaining pastry to cover pie. Brush edges of pie with lightly beaten egg white; cover pie with pastry, pressing edges together. Trim edges and decorate. Brush top with lightly-beaten egg white; sprinkle with extra sugar. Cut a few slits in top to allow steam to escape. Bake in hot oven 10 minutes or until light golden brown. Reduce heat to moderate; cook a further 20 to 25 minutes or until pie is golden brown.

Filling: Peel, core and slice apples. Place apples, lemon rind, cloves and water in pan; bring to boil. Cover; reduce heat; simmer 8 to 10 minutes or until apples are just tender. Place apples in sieve to drain off excess liquid.

Drain blackberries; reserve syrup. You will need 1 cup of this syrup; a little water may be needed to make up to 1 cup. Place syrup in pan; add cornflour and sugar; stir until cornflour is dissolved. Place over heat; stir until sauce boils and thickens. Reduce heat; simmer uncovered 2 minutes. Place apples, blackberries and thickened liquid in bowl; mix well. Allow to become completely cold.

Strawberry Cream Pie

125 g (4 oz.) plain sweet biscuits	3 eggs
60 g (2 oz.) butter	½ cup cream
125 g (4 oz.) pkt cream cheese	½ cup milk
	1 punnet strawberries
½ cup sugar	¼ cup strawberry jam
1 teaspoon vanilla	1 tablespoon water

Put finely-crushed biscuits in bowl; add melted butter; mix well. Put two wide strips of greased greaseproof paper over base and sides of deep 20 cm (8 in.) round cake tin (this makes it easy to remove pie from tin when cooked). Cover the base of the tin with a circle of aluminium foil. Press prepared biscuit crumb over base. Refrigerate while preparing filling.

Beat cream cheese until soft and creamy; add sugar; beat well. Add eggs one at a time, beating well after each addition. Add milk, cream and vanilla; beat until combined. Pour mixture over biscuit base. Cook in moderately slow oven 45 minutes or until custard is set. Allow to cool, then refrigerate until well chilled.

To turn out, place base of cake tin in hot water for a few seconds; lift pie on to serving plate. Arrange hulled, halved strawberries over top. Stir strawberry jam and water over low heat until smooth. Push through sieve. Brush this glaze over strawberries. Decorate with whipped cream.

Hazelnut Cherry Pie

Hazelnut Pastry

½ cup plain flour	1 egg yolk
½ cup ground hazelnuts	60 g (2 oz.) butter
pinch salt	1 tablespoon water
2 tablespoons sugar	

Cream Filling

4 egg yolks	2 teaspoons rum
3 tablespoons sugar	3 x 470 g (15 oz.) cans black cherries
1 teaspoon vanilla	
1¼ cups cream	2 teaspoons gelatine, extra
1 teaspoon gelatine	1 tablespoon rum, extra

Pastry: Sift flour, salt and hazelnuts on board; make large well in centre. Put sugar in centre; make well in sugar. Add softened butter, egg yolk and water. With spatula, work butter, egg yolk, sugar and water together until creamy. Work in flour, using cutting motion with spatula. With hands, work mixture into soft dough; knead lightly. Press pastry out to cover base and sides of 23 cm (9 in.) flan tin. Prick base and sides of pastry well. Refrigerate 15 minutes before baking. Bake in moderate oven 15 minutes or until pastry is golden brown.

Filling: Put egg yolks, sugar and vanilla in top of double saucepan; stir until combined. Gradually beat in cream. Add gelatine; stir until combined. Place saucepan over simmering water; stir constantly until mixture thickens and lightly coats back of wooden spoon. Remove from heat; stir in rum immediately. Allow cream filling to become cold before pouring into prepared pastry case. Refrigerate until filling has set.

Drain cherries; reserve 1 cup cherry syrup. Arrange well-drained cherries over filling; return to refrigerator. Put reserved syrup, extra gelatine and extra rum in saucepan; stir over low heat until gelatine has dissolved. Refrigerate until liquid is the consistency of egg white, then spoon evenly over cherries. Refrigerate until set.

Passionfruit Mallow Slice

Base

125 g (4 oz.) plain sweet biscuits	60 g (2 oz.) butter

Topping

1 pkt lemon jelly crystals	2 x 110 g (3½ oz.) pkts white marshmallows
1 cup boiling water	
½ cup passionfruit pulp (about 4 passionfruit)	⅓ cup milk
	1 cup cream
1 tablespoon grated lemon rind	½ cup cream, extra

Base: Crush biscuits finely; add melted butter; mix well. Press over base of 28 cm x 18 cm (11 in. x 7 in.) shallow cake tin lined with aluminium foil. Refrigerate while preparing topping.

Topping: Dissolve jelly in boiling water; add passionfruit pulp; refrigerate until partially set. Combine chopped marshmallows and milk in pan; stir over low heat until marshmallows melt; cool. Whip cream; fold into cooled marshmallow mixture. Add lemon rind to partially set jelly; stir into marshmallow mixture. Pour on to prepared base; refrigerate until set. Whip extra cream until soft peaks form; spread over top of slice.

Choc-Orange Slice

Base

125 g (4 oz.) plain sweet biscuits	60 g (2 oz.) butter

Filling

2 eggs	⅓ cup orange juice
½ cup sugar	1 tablespoon gelatine
1 cup milk	1 tablespoon Grand Marnier or Cointreau
2 teaspoons grated orange rind	½ cup cream

Topping

90 g (3 oz.) dark chocolate	1 teaspoon gelatine
½ cup cream	2 teaspoons water

Base: Crush biscuits finely; add melted butter; mix well. Press over base of 28 cm x 18 cm (11 in. x 7 in.) shallow cake tin which has been lined with aluminium foil. Refrigerate while preparing filling.

Filling: Place eggs, sugar and milk in top of double saucepan; stir over simmering water until mixture has thickened. Stir in orange rind. Sprinkle gelatine over orange juice; dissolve over hot water. Stir dissolved gelatine into egg mixture; add Grand Marnier; mix well. Beat cream until soft peaks form; fold into egg mixture. Pour on prepared base; refrigerate until mixture has set. When set, spread prepared topping over. Refrigerate until firm.

Topping: Place roughly-chopped chocolate in top of double saucepan; stir over simmering water until chocolate has melted. Remove from heat; stir in cream. Soften gelatine in water; dissolve over hot water; stir into chocolate mixture.

Caramel Banana Pie

Base

250 g (8 oz.) plain sweet biscuits	1 teaspoon cinnamon
	125 g (4 oz.) butter

Filling

250 g (8 oz.) packaged cream cheese	2 tablespoons rum
	2 eggs
60 g (2 oz.) butter	2 bananas
½ cup brown sugar, lightly packed	1 tablespoon lemon juice
	1 tablespoon brown sugar, extra
¼ cup sour cream	
1 teaspoon vanilla	

Crush biscuits finely; combine with cinnamon. Add melted butter; mix well. Press two-thirds of biscuit mixture over base and sides of greased 20 cm (8 in.) pie plate. Slice bananas; sprinkle with lemon juice and the extra sugar; arrange decoratively over crumb crust. Pour filling over; sprinkle remaining crumb mixture evenly over top. Bake in moderately slow oven 50 to 60 minutes or until set. Cool; refrigerate a few hours or overnight.

Filling: Melt butter; add brown sugar; stir until sugar has dissolved. Remove from heat; allow to cool slightly. Beat cream cheese until smooth; add caramel mixture, sour cream, vanilla, rum, eggs; beat well.

Cool Desserts

We have gathered together in this section a collection of mouth-watering recipes. Family or special occasion desserts — they're all here; every page will tempt you.

Ogen Melon Ice

2 small ripe ogen melons
1 cup sugar
½ cup water

1 tablespoon Grand Marnier

Cut ogen melons in half. Remove seeds; scoop out melons to 5 mm (¼ in.) around skin. Place melon flesh in blender; blend on high speed until smooth, or mash well to a puree.

Place sugar and water in saucepan. Stir over low heat until all sugar has dissolved; bring to boil; boil rapidly 2 minutes. Remove syrup from heat immediately; cool slightly.

Stir in ogen melon and Grand Marnier. Place in shallow icecream tray; cool; freeze until firm, stirring occasionally. To serve, run fork across ice to flake; pile into individual serving dishes.

Serves 4.

Mangoes and Ginger Wine Ice

940 g (1 lb. 14 oz.) can mangoes
½ cup green ginger wine

60 g (2 oz.) preserved ginger

Ginger Wine Ice

2 cups hot water
¾ cup sugar

1 cup green ginger wine
2 teaspoons lemon juice

Drain mangoes, reserve syrup; put syrup, ginger wine and chopped ginger in saucepan; bring to boil. Reduce heat; simmer 2 minutes; drain; cool. Put mangoes into serving glasses; pour syrup over; refrigerate until cold. Before serving, top with Ginger Wine Ice.

Ginger Wine Ice: Dissolve sugar in hot water; add ginger wine and lemon juice; cool. Pour into refrigerator trays and freeze. Stir occasionally. Flake lightly with fork before serving.

Serves 4 to 6.

Ogen Melon Ice — light, full of fresh-fruit flavour — makes a perfect summertime dessert.

Grapefruit Sherbet

2 cups grapefruit juice (approx. 4 grapefruit)	2 egg whites
½ cup sugar	¼ cup sugar, extra gin

Put grapefruit juice and sugar in saucepan; stir over medium heat until sugar has dissolved; bring to boil. Remove from heat; allow to become cold. Put grapefruit liquid in freezer tray; freeze until partly frozen.

Beat egg whites until soft peaks form; add extra sugar; beat until dissolved. Using fork, fold egg-white mixture through grapefruit mixture. Return to freezer; freeze until firm, stirring occasionally with fork to blend mixture evenly.

Spoon into individual serving glasses or, if desired, spoon into scooped out grapefruit halves. Before serving, spoon 2 teaspoons gin over each serving.

Serves 4.

Poor Man's Apple Brulee

6 apples	1 tablespoon sugar, extra
2 tablespoons sugar	½ teaspoon vanilla
1 teaspoon grated lemon rind	1½ cups milk
2 tablespoons water	½ cup cream
3 tablespoons custard powder	⅓ cup brown sugar, firmly packed

Peel, quarter and core apples. Cut apples into thick slices. Place apples, sugar, lemon rind and water in pan; cover; bring to boil. Reduce heat; simmer gently 5 minutes or until apples are just tender. Put apples into heatproof dish.

Put custard powder and extra sugar into pan; gradually add milk; stir until combined. Add cream and vanilla. Stir over low heat until mixture boils and thickens; reduce heat; simmer uncovered 2 minutes; cool slightly. Pour custard mixture over apples.

Cover dish; refrigerate until cold. Just before serving, sieve brown sugar on top of custard. Put under griller until sugar melts.

Serves 4.

Lemon Torte

Pastry

1⅓ cups plain flour	3 egg yolks
⅓ cup sugar	½ teaspoon vanilla
90 g (3 oz.) butter	

Filling

2 eggs	1 teaspoon grated lemon rind
⅓ cup sugar	
¼ cup lemon juice	60 g (2 oz.) butter
1 tablespoon water	1 cup cream

Icing

1½ cups icing sugar	90 g (3 oz.) flaked almonds
1 tablespoon lemon juice	

Sift flour on to table; make a well in centre and in it place softened butter, sugar, egg yolk and vanilla. Using the fingertips of one hand, work butter, sugar, egg yolks and vanilla together until well blended. Gradually draw in the flour with a spatula; bring together with hands to form a ball. Knead lightly until smooth. Refrigerate 30 minutes before using.

Divide pastry into three; roll each piece into 20 cm (8 in.) round; place circles of pastry on greased oven trays; bake in moderate oven 10 to 12 minutes, or until pale biscuit colour. Loosen pastry with spatula immediately on removing from oven; leave on trays for few minutes before placing on wire racks to cool.

Whip cream until firm peaks form. Place almonds on oven tray; bake in moderate oven 8 to 10 minutes or until golden brown.

Place a layer of pastry on serving plate; spread approx. 3 tablespoons of prepared filling over pastry; swirl 1 tablespoon cream through filling with small spatula. Place another layer of pastry on top and repeat process with remaining filling and 1 tablespoon cream. Place remaining layer of pastry on top. Spread prepared icing over top of cake; allow to set. Use remaining cream to spread around sides of cake and pipe decorative border on top. Press toasted almonds evenly around edge of cake. Refrigerate several hours or overnight.

Filling: Put beaten eggs and sugar in top of double saucepan; stir until combined. Gradually add strained lemon juice and water; stir until combined. Add lemon rind and roughly-chopped butter. Place pan over simmering water; stir until mixture thickly coats the back of a wooden spoon.

Icing: Sift icing sugar into bowl; add lemon juice; beat well until smooth.

Strawberry Champagne Sorbet

2 punnets strawberries	2 egg whites
1½ cups champagne, dry white wine or sparkling wine	½ cup sugar, extra
	¼ cup water, extra
	¼ teaspoon cream of tartar
¼ cup sugar	¼ cup Grand Marnier or Cointreau
½ cup water	

Put sugar and water in saucepan; stir over low heat until sugar has dissolved. Combine champagne and sugar syrup; pour into freezer tray; freeze until partially set.

Wash and hull 8 of the strawberries; chop

roughly; push through fine sieve; discard seeds. Put extra sugar, extra water and cream of tartar in saucepan; stir over low heat until sugar dissolves; increase heat; boil rapidly 2 minutes. Beat egg whites until soft peaks form; pour the hot syrup into the egg whites in a very thin stream, beating until thick.

Fold champagne mixture into meringue with pureed strawberries; pour back into freezer tray; freeze until set, stirring occasionally with fork to blend mixture evenly.

Wash and hull remaining strawberries; arrange in dishes. Coat strawberries in each dish with 2 teaspoons of Grand Marnier. Use fork to flake the sorbet; spoon on top of strawberries.
Serves 6.

Orange and Rum Dessert Cake

250 g (8 oz.) butter	2 eggs
1 cup sugar	2 cups self-raising flour
2 tablespoons grated orange rind	¾ cup milk
	¾ cup raisins
1 tablespoon grated lemon rind	

Syrup

1 cup orange juice	1 cup sugar
2 tablespoons lemon juice	¼ cup rum

Cream butter, sugar, orange and lemon rinds until light and fluffy. Add eggs one at a time, beating well after each addition. Fold in sifted flour alternately with the milk; fold in chopped raisins.

Grease deep 20 cm (8 in.) round cake tin; line base with greased greaseproof paper. Spread cake mixture evenly in tin; bake in moderate oven 1¼ hours or until cooked when tested. Cool 5 minutes in tin; turn out on to plate or tray; make several holes in cake with skewer so that syrup will be absorbed through cake. Gradually pour prepared syrup over cake. Serve with cream

Syrup: Combine orange juice, lemon juice and sugar in saucepan; stir over low heat until sugar dissolves; bring to boil. Reduce heat; simmer 5 minutes. Stir in rum.

Caramel Praline Pears

825 g (30 oz.) can pear halves	vanilla ice cream

Caramel Sauce

30 g (1 oz.) butter	½ cup hot water
¼ cup brown sugar	2 tablespoons Grand Marnier
¼ cup condensed milk	
1 tablespoon golden syrup	

Praline

30 g (1 oz.) slivered almonds	½ cup sugar
	¼ cup water

Drain pears; spoon into 6 individual serving dishes; top with a scoop of vanilla ice cream. Pour the warm sauce over; sprinkle with praline.

Caramel Sauce: Combine butter, brown sugar, condensed milk and golden syrup in saucepan. Cook over low heat, stirring constantly until mixture leaves sides of saucepan and is a rich golden colour. Remove from heat; gradually stir in hot water. Return to heat; stir a further 1 to 2 minutes. Stir in Grand Marnier.

Praline: Put almonds into lightly greased pan; stir over heat until lightly browned, approx. 5 minutes; remove pan from heat and set aside.

Put sugar and water into saucepan; stir over low heat until sugar has dissolved. Increase heat; boil rapidly uncovered without stirring approx. 5 minutes or until a light golden colour. Remove from heat; pour over almonds; leave to cool and set.

Break into pieces; grind to coarse powder in electric blender, or put through metal mouli grater or chop finely.
Serves 6.

Cream Cheese Strudel

500 g (1 lb.) packaged cream cheese	½ teaspoon vanilla
250 g (8 oz.) cottage cheese	250 g (8 oz.) pkt phylo pastry
½ cup sugar	125 g (4 oz.) butter
½ cup raisins	sugar, extra
	icing sugar

Beat cream cheese until light and fluffy. Add sieved cottage cheese, sugar, chopped raisins and vanilla; mix well. Place one sheet of phylo pastry on board; brush with melted butter. Repeat with second, third and fourth layers, brushing each layer with butter. Place half the filling on one end of pastry; fold edges in 2.5 cm (1 in.) to seal filling. Roll pastry up firmly. Make another roll with remaining pastry and filling. Put rolls on to lightly-greased oven trays; brush tops of rolls with remaining melted butter; sprinkle with extra sugar. Bake in hot oven 10 minutes; reduce heat to moderate; bake a further 10 minutes or until golden brown. Refrigerate strudel several hours before serving. Sprinkle tops with sifted icing sugar.

NOTE: Phylo (or filo or strudel) pastry can be bought from most large food halls or from Continental pastry shops.

Hazelnut Praline Puffs

Hazelnut Praline Puffs

Puffs

1 cup water	pinch salt
60 g (2 oz.) butter	4 eggs
1 cup plain flour	2 cups cream

Praline

90 g (3 oz.) roasted hazelnuts	½ cup sugar
	½ cup water

Caramel Sauce

125 g (4 oz.) butter	100 g (2½ oz.) pkt white marshmallows
¾ cup brown sugar, lightly packed	2 tablespoons milk

Sift flour. Put water, butter and salt into saucepan; stir until all butter has melted; bring to rapid boil. Add flour all at once. Stir vigorously with wooden spoon until mixture is thick. When mixture leaves sides of saucepan and forms a smooth ball, remove from heat. Spread mixture up sides of small bowl of electric mixer; allow to cool. Add eggs one at a time, beating well on medium speed after each addition.

Put tablespoons of mixture on greased oven trays; bake in hot oven 10 minutes. Reduce heat to moderate; bake a further 20 minutes or until golden. Split puffs while still hot; scoop out with small spoon any of the uncooked mixture from inside; allow to cool.

Whip cream; fold in half the prepared praline; fill puffs with this cream; spoon caramel sauce over and sprinkle with remaining praline.

Praline: Put hazelnuts into small greased pan. Put sugar and water into saucepan; stir over low heat until sugar dissolves. Increase heat; bring to boil; boil uncovered without stirring until light golden brown. Remove from heat; pour over hazelnuts; allow to cool. Break into pieces; put in plastic bag; crush with rolling pin.

Caramel Sauce: Combine all ingredients in saucepan. Stir over low heat until marshmallows are dissolved; simmer 3 minutes.

Coffee Liqueur Cheesecake

Coffee Liqueur Cheesecake

Crumb Crust

250 g (8 oz.) plain sweet biscuits	125 g (4 oz.) butter

Filling

375 g (12 oz.) packaged cream cheese	1 tablespoon instant coffee powder
¾ cup castor sugar	1 tablespoon coffee liqueur (Tia Maria or Kahlua)
3 teaspoons plain flour	
3 eggs	
¾ cup sour cream	1 tablespoon water
1 tablespoon lemon juice	1 egg yolk
90 g (3 oz.) dark chocolate	

Cream

3 teaspoons instant coffee powder	1 cup cream
1 teaspoon hot water	1 tablespoon sugar

Crumb Crust: Crush biscuits finely; add melted butter; mix well. Press crumb mixture on base and sides of 20 cm (8 in.) springform pan. Refrigerate while preparing filling.

Filling: Beat cream cheese until softened; combine with sugar and flour; beat well. Beat in eggs, sour cream and lemon juice. Pour half cheesecake mixture into prepared crumb crust.

Put roughly-chopped chocolate, coffee powder, liqueur, water and lightly-beaten egg yolk in top of double saucepan; stir over simmering water until chocolate melts and mixture becomes thick. Remove from heat; cool slightly.

Swirl half chocolate mixture gently through cheesecake mixture in crust with small spatula. Top with remaining cheesecake mixture; swirl remaining chocolate through top half of cheesecake.

Bake in moderately slow oven 1 hour to 1 hour 10 minutes or until set. Remove from oven; allow to become cold; refrigerate overnight. Remove sides from pan; put cheesecake on to serving plate; top with prepared cream.

Cream: Dissolve coffee powder in hot water. Put cream, coffee and sugar in bowl; refrigerate 30 minutes; beat until thick.

Strawberry Cheesecake

Crumb Crust

250 g (8 oz.) plain sweet biscuits	125 g (4 oz.) butter

Filling

250 g (8 oz.) packaged cream cheese	2 tablespoons water
⅓ cup sugar	1 punnet strawberries
2 eggs, separated	2 teaspoons lemon juice
⅓ cup sugar, extra	1½ cups cream
1 tablespoon gelatine	1 teaspoon icing sugar

Crumb Crust: Combine finely-crushed biscuit crumbs with melted butter; mix well. Press over sides and base of greased 20 cm (8 in.) springform pan.

Filling: Sprinkle gelatine over water; dissolve over hot water. Beat cream cheese and sugar until smooth. Beat egg yolks and extra sugar until light and creamy. Put in top of double saucepan over simmering water; stir until sugar dissolves and mixture is thick. Remove from heat; add dissolved gelatine. Gradually add egg yolk mixture to cream cheese mixture; beat until smooth.

Reserve 5 strawberries; mash remainder with fork. Fold mashed strawberries into cream cheese mixture with lemon juice. Whip cream; fold half into strawberry mixture. Lastly fold in softly-beaten egg whites. Spoon into crumb crust; refrigerate until set.

Press reserved strawberries through sieve; combine with sifted icing sugar. Spread remaining whipped cream over top of cheesecake; using small spoon, swirl strawberry puree through cream.

Apricot Ripple Cheesecake

Biscuit Crust

250 g (8 oz.) pkt plain sweet biscuits	125 g (4 oz.) butter

Filling

185 g (6 oz.) dried apricots	2 tablespoons Grand Marnier
2½ cups water	
1 tablespoon sugar	1 cup cream
250 g (8 oz.) pkt cream cheese	1 tablespoon gelatine
	¼ cup water
¾ cup castor sugar	1 egg white

Biscuit Crust: Place finely-crushed biscuits in bowl; add melted butter; mix well. Press biscuit crumbs over base and sides of lightly-greased 20 cm (8 in.) round springform pan. Refrigerate while preparing filling.

Filling: Place apricots and water in pan; bring to boil. Reduce heat; simmer covered 25 to 30 minutes or until apricots are very tender. Place apricots with their liquid in electric blender; add sugar. Blend on medium speed for 30 seconds or until pureed; allow to become cold.

Place cream cheese in small bowl of electric mixer; beat until smooth; add castor sugar and Grand Marnier; beat until sugar has dissolved. Place gelatine and water in bowl; stir until combined. Stand bowl over simmering water until gelatine is dissolved. Gradually add gelatine mixture to cream cheese mixture, beating well.

Place cream in bowl; beat until soft peaks form. Place egg white in bowl; beat until firm peaks form. Fold cream and egg white into cream cheese mixture. Pour into prepared crumb crust. Spoon apricot mixture on top of cream cheese mixture. Swirl apricot mixture into cream cheese mixture with a fork. Place in refrigerator until set. If desired, decorate with whipped cream.

Strawberry Mallow Mousse

1 punnet strawberries	2 tablespoons Grand Marnier
100 g (3½ oz.) pkt white marshmallows	
	2 teaspoons water
1 teaspoon gelatine	1 cup cream
1 tablespoon lemon juice	2 egg whites

Sprinkle gelatine over water; dissolve over hot water. Wash and hull strawberries; chop roughly. Put strawberries and marshmallows into saucepan; stir over low heat until marshmallows have melted. Add gelatine, lemon juice and Grand Marnier; refrigerate until cold and slightly thickened.

Fold in whipped cream and softly-beaten egg whites. Spoon into four individual serving dishes. Refrigerate until set.

Serves 4.

Chocolate Mousse with Rum Cream

100 g (3½ oz.) pkt white marshmallows	30 g (1 oz.) butter
	2 eggs, separated
125 g (4 oz.) dark chocolate	pinch salt

Rum Cream

3 egg yolks	1½ tablespoons rum
¼ cup sugar	1 cup cream
1 tablespoon lemon juice	

Chop chocolate and marshmallows. Put in top of double saucepan with butter; stir over hot water until mixture has melted; remove from heat. Add lightly-beaten egg yolks; return to heat; stir over hot water 3 minutes until mixture is smooth and thick. Allow to cool until slightly set.

Beat egg whites with salt until soft peaks form; fold through chocolate mixture. Spoon into

4 individual serving glasses; refrigerate until set.

Pour Rum Cream over; refrigerate until set. Decorate, if desired, with grated chocolate just before serving.

Rum Cream: Beat egg yolks, sugar and lemon juice until mixture is thick and light lemon in colour. Gradually add rum; mix well. Fold in whipped cream.

Serves 4.

Hazelnut Praline Mousse

3 eggs, separated
⅓ cup sugar
½ cup orange juice

2 teaspoons gelatine
1 cup cream

Praline

1 cup water
1 cup sugar

125 g (4 oz.) roasted
hazelnuts

Beat egg yolks and sugar until thick and creamy. Put in top of double saucepan over simmering water; stir until sugar has dissolved. Sprinkle gelatine over orange juice; dissolve over hot water; combine with egg yolk mixture; cool. Fold in whipped cream, softly-beaten egg whites and crushed hazelnut praline.

Spoon into serving dish or 4 individual serving dishes; refrigerate until set. Before serving, top with extra whipped cream and extra chopped roasted hazelnuts.

Praline: Grease oven tray or swiss roll tin; put hazelnuts on tray. Combine sugar and water in saucepan; stir over low heat until sugar dissolves. Bring to boil; boil until golden toffee colour (approx. 10 minutes); allow bubbles to subside. Pour toffee over hazelnuts in tray and allow to set.

Break toffee roughly; put in blender and blend 2 minutes, stopping blender and stirring occasionally, until praline is fairly fine. Praline can also be crushed by putting it in a plastic bag and crushing with a rolling pin. Serves 4.

Black Forest Icecream

2 litre carton vanilla
icecream
500 g (1 lb.) dark chocolate
30 g (1 oz.) solid white
vegetable shortening
2 x 425 g (15 oz.) cans
black cherries

2 tablespoons Cherry
Heering, maraschino
or brandy
2 tablespoons cornflour
2 tablespoons water

Put an oven tray into freezer, so that it is very cold. Remove icecream container from freezer. Scoop icecream into balls with icecream scoop; place immediately on tray in freezer. Freeze until very hard. Put chocolate and white shortening into top

of double saucepan; stand over hot water; stir until melted; cool. Cover an oven tray with aluminium foil. Dip icecream balls into chocolate; lift out with forks; place on foil-covered tray. Place in freezer until ready to serve. Drain cherries; reserve 1½ cups of syrup. Put reserved cherry syrup and Cherry Heering into pan. Bring to boil; remove from heat; add cornflour mixed with water. Stir until mixture boils and thickens. Add pitted cherries. Pour hot sauce over icecream balls.

Serves 6.

Strawberry Chocolate Mousse

1 punnet strawberries
2 tablespoons Grand
Marnier or Cointreau
1 tablespoon icing sugar
2 eggs, separated
¼ cup sugar
1 tablespoon orange juice

1 teaspoon gelatine
2 teaspoons water
½ cup cream
60 g (2 oz.) dark chocolate
30 g (1 oz.) solid white
vegetable shortening

Reserve 2 strawberries for decoration; wash and hull remainder. Slice half the strawberries; put in bowl with 1 tablespoon of the Grand Marnier and sifted icing sugar. Mash remaining strawberries with fork.

Beat egg yolks and sugar until light and fluffy. Put in top of double saucepan over simmering water; stir until sugar dissolves. Sprinkle gelatine over water; dissolve over hot water; stir into egg-yolk mixture; cool. Add orange juice and remaining Grand Marnier and mashed strawberries to egg mixture. Fold in whipped cream and softly-beaten egg whites. Refrigerate mixture until slightly set.

Spoon sliced strawberries and liquid into 4 individual serving dishes or glasses. Top with the strawberry mousse; refrigerate until set.

Put chocolate and vegetable shortening in top of double saucepan; stand over simmering water until melted; cool. Spoon a thin layer of chocolate over each mousse; refrigerate until set. To serve, decorate each with extra whipped cream and reserved, halved strawberries. Serves 4.

Melon in Champagne

Watermelon, ogen melons or honeydew melons — or a combination of these — can be used. Scoop out balls of melon with melon-baller, or cut melon into dice. Place ½ cup water, ½ cup sugar and ¼ cup green ginger wine in saucepan; stir over heat until sugar is dissolved. Bring to boil; boil 3 minutes; cool; refrigerate. To serve, place melon balls in 6 tall glasses; pour approx. 1½ tablespoons of the ginger syrup into each glass; top up with cold champagne.

Serves 6.

Strawberry Meringue Mousse

1 punnet strawberries	4 tablespoons skim milk powder
3 tablespoons castor sugar	¼ teaspoon vanilla
1 cup water	2 egg whites
3 teaspoons gelatine	½ cup castor sugar, extra

Sprinkle gelatine over water in small bowl; stand bowl over simmering water until gelatine has dissolved; allow to become cold. Put washed, hulled strawberries, sugar, gelatine mixture, skim milk powder and vanilla in blender; blend on medium speed 30 seconds. Pour mixture into 4 individual heatproof dishes. Place in refrigerator until set. Beat egg whites until soft peaks form; gradually add extra sugar to egg whites; beat until dissolved. Spoon mixture into piping bag fitted with fluted nozzle. Pipe meringue decoratively on top of each mousse. Place dishes on baking tray; place in hot oven 3 minutes or until meringue is very light golden colour. Refrigerate again until mousse is firm.

Serves 4.

NOTE: This is an excellent low-kilojoule (or low-calorie) dessert for dieters. Approx. 680 kilojoules (170 calories) per serving.

Chocolate Meringue Torte

4 egg whites	60 g (2 oz.) dark chocolate, extra
1 cup sugar	
15 g (½ oz.) dark chocolate	1 punnet strawberries
1½ cups cream	

Filling

¾ cup cream	2 tablespoons ground hazelnuts
1 tablespoon brandy	

Beat egg whites until soft peaks form; gradually add sugar, beating well after each addition. Fold in the grated 15 g (½ oz.) chocolate. Grease lightly two 18 cm (7 in.) sandwich tins; line base with lightly-greased greaseproof paper. Sprinkle tins lightly with flour; tap out excess flour. Spread meringue mixture evenly into tins; bake in moderately slow oven 40 to 45 minutes. Turn out on to wire rack to cool. (Cakes have a rather untidy appearance at this stage, but don't worry. When assembled as directed, the cake looks beautiful, tastes better!) When meringues are cold, join together with the filling. Whip cream until firm peaks form. Cover sides and top of cake with whipped cream; pipe decorative edge of cream around top of cake. Press extra grated chocolate around sides of cake with spatula. Decorate top with halved strawberries. Refrigerate for several hours.

Filling: Whip cream until soft peaks form; fold in hazelnuts and brandy.

Toffee Almond Pears

6 firm pears	5 cm (2 in.) piece cinnamon stick
1 cup sugar	
1 cup water	4 whole cloves
1½ cups dry white wine	½ cup sugar, extra
5 cm (2 in.) strip orange rind	½ cup water, extra
	60 g (2 oz.) flaked almonds
5 cm (2 in.) strip lemon rind	300 ml (½ pint) double cream

Peel pears thinly with potato peeler, making sure that no skin remains. Place sugar, water, wine, orange and lemon rinds, cinnamon stick and cloves in pan; stir over heat until sugar is dissolved. Add pears; simmer uncovered 20 minutes or until pears are just tender, turning occasionally. Cool. Place pears and liquid in bowl; cover and refrigerate overnight. Place almonds on baking tray; bake in moderate oven 5 minutes or until almonds are golden. Remove pears from syrup; pat dry with absorbent paper. Place pears in individual serving bowls.

Beat cream until soft peaks form; fill into piping bag fitted with star nozzle; pipe cream around base of each pear. Place extra sugar and extra water in pan; stir over low heat until sugar is dissolved. Bring to boil; boil uncovered 4 minutes or until mixture is golden brown. Remove pan from heat; allow toffee to cool slightly. Spoon toffee over top of each pear; sprinkle almonds over toffee. Serve the cold wine liquid separately with pears.

Baked Custard Cream

30 g (1 oz.) butter	1 tablespoon self-raising flour
3 tablespoons castor sugar	
2 eggs, separated	2 cups milk
1 tablespoon plain flour	1 teaspoon vanilla

Cream butter and sugar until light and fluffy. Add egg yolks one at a time, beating well after each addition. Add sifted flours; combine well. Put milk in small saucepan; stir over low heat until milk reaches simmering point; remove from heat; stir in vanilla. Gradually beat milk into creamed mixture, beating all the time; mix well. Beat egg-whites until soft peaks form; gently fold into custard. Put custard into lightly-greased ovenproof dish; put in large baking dish with enough hot water to come half-way up sides of dish. Bake in moderate oven 50 to 60 minutes or until custard is firm. Cool, then refrigerate.

Serves 4 to 6.

How to Make a Perfect Pavlova

It is one of Australia's most popular desserts — this crisp shell of meringue with a favourite filling. Here's how to make it perfectly, with a lemon-cream filling that makes use of the egg yolks left from the pavlova.

You will need:

4 egg whites
1 cup castor sugar
¼ cup granulated sugar
1 tablespoon cornflour
1 teaspoon lemon juice

Custard Cream

4 egg yolks
¼ cup sugar
1 teaspoon vanilla
1 tablespoon cornflour
¾ cup milk
½ cup cream

Beat egg yolks, sugar, vanilla and cornflour until smooth and creamy. Put into saucepan, gradually add cream and milk, stir until smooth. Stir over medium heat until sauce thickens, bring to boil, reduce heat, simmer 2 minutes. Remove from heat, allow to become cold, stirring occasionally.

1. Beat egg whites until soft peaks form, gradually add castor sugar, beating until dissolved (approx. 8 minutes). Fold combined granulated sugar and cornflour into meringue with lemon juice. Picture shows firm, shiny consistency of finished meringue.

2. Place sheet of greaseproof paper, trimmed to size of tray, on greased oven tray, brush paper lightly with melted butter, dust with sifted cornflour. Shake off excess cornflour. Mark 23 cm (9 in.) circle on paper. Spread 3 heaped tablespoons of meringue into circle.

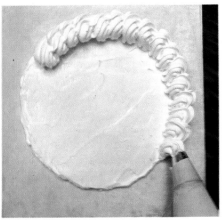

3. Fill remaining meringue into piping bag fitted with star tube. Pipe decoratively around edge of pavlova as shown. Bake in slow oven 40 minutes, remove from oven, allow to become cold. Spoon prepared Custard Cream into pavlova, top with fruit salad or any other fruit; if desired, decorate with whipped cream and strawberries.

Icecream

Here are some of our favourite recipes for icecream — each completely different, each the very best recipe of its type. To prevent ice crystals forming, icecream must freeze fast; set the freezer control at its coldest; return to normal setting when icecream has frozen.

Economical Icecream

470 g (15 oz.) can evaporated milk	1 cup cold water
1½ teaspoons gelatine	1 cup non-fat milk powder
½ cup boiling water	½ cup sugar
	1 teaspoon vanilla

Dissolve gelatine in boiling water. Add cold water; pour into large bowl of electric mixer. Add evaporated milk (it does not need to be chilled), milk powder and sugar. Beat until combined and free from lumps. Freeze until firm.

Remove from refrigerator and allow to stand until softened slightly. Empty into chilled mixing bowl; mash down with potato masher. Beat at high speed until light and fluffy and doubled in bulk. Add vanilla. Spoon into freezer trays; freeze until set.
Serves 6.

Low Calorie Vanilla Icecream

2½ teaspoons gelatine	¼ cup sugar
1 tablespoon water	2 cups water, extra
2 cups skim milk powder	2 teaspoons vanilla

Sprinkle gelatine over 1 tablespoon water; dissolve over hot water; cool. Combine milk powder, sugar, extra water and vanilla in bowl; beat until milk powder has dissolved; add gelatine; beat well.

Pour mixture into freezer trays; freeze until set. When set, put mixture into large bowl of electric mixer; beat until doubled in bulk. Pour mixture into freezer trays; freeze until firm.
Serves 8.

Lemon Sherbet Icecream

½ cup milk	¾ cup lemon juice
2 teaspoons gelatine	1 cup milk, extra
1 cup sugar	300 ml (½ pint) cream
1 cup boiling water	

Put milk and gelatine into small saucepan; stir over low heat until gelatine has dissolved; do not boil. Dissolve sugar in boiling water; add lemon juice and gelatine mixture; cool; then add extra milk and cream. Pour into freezer tray; freeze until partly frozen. Pour mixture into small bowl of electric mixer; beat until slightly thickened. Pour back into freezer tray; freeze until firm, stirring occasionally.
Serves 6.

Coffee Icecream

1½ cups milk	½ cup castor sugar
2 tablespoons instant coffee powder	1 cup cream
	¼ teaspoon cinnamon
4 egg yolks	

Heat milk, but do not allow to boil. Add coffee powder; stir until dissolved. Allow to stand 15 minutes. Beat egg yolks until thick and creamy. Gradually add sugar, beating well until mixture is light and fluffy. Add coffee-milk gradually; beat in cream and cinnamon. Place coffee mixture in top of double saucepan over gently simmering water; beat with rotary beater 10 minutes until mixture has increased in volume and is thick.

Pour into freezer tray; leave until almost frozen. Remove from freezer; beat 10 minutes on electric mixer. Return to freezer; freeze until almost firm; beat again on electric mixer for 10 minutes. Return to freezer to set.

Remove from freezer and place in refrigerator about 5 minutes before serving time for icecream to soften slightly. Top each serving with whipped cream; pour over a little coffee liqueur (Kahlua or Tia Maria).
Serves 6.

Coconut Icecream

875 g (1¾ lb.) coconut	3 litres (12 cups) boiling water
1 cup sugar	
½ teaspoon salt	

Put coconut, sugar and salt into large bowl; pour boiling water over; stir well; let stand 20 minutes. Strain coconut through fine sieve, then, using hands, press out excess liquid from coconut; strain again. Pour coconut liquid into refrigerator trays (the coconut is now discarded); freeze until solid. (Mixture will separate into layers, but reconstitutes perfectly on beating, as below.)

Turn into large bowl of electric mixer; beat on low speed until mixture is mushy and evenly combined. Return to refrigerator trays; freeze again until firm.

Serve plain, or as a topping for fresh fruit salad.

Super Rich Icecream

4 eggs, separated   1 cup cream
1 cup icing sugar   1 teaspoon vanilla

Beat egg yolks lightly. Beat egg whites until firm peaks form; gradually beat in sifted icing sugar. Fold in egg yolks, then whipped cream; stir in vanilla. Pour into freezer trays; freeze until set.
    Serves 6.

Passionfruit Icecream Slice

2 tablespoons cornflour   1¼ cups sugar
2 tablespoons flour   90 g (3 oz.) butter
3 teaspoons grated lemon   4 passionfruit
    rind   2 egg yolks
1 cup lemon juice   1 litre (1¾ pints) vanilla
1½ cups water   icecream

Put sifted cornflour and flour into saucepan with lemon rind. Gradually add lemon juice and water; blend until smooth; add sugar; mix well. Stir over medium heat until mixture boils and thickens; reduce heat; simmer 5 minutes. Add butter; stir until melted. Add passionfruit pulp; mix well. Remove from heat; stir in lightly-beaten egg yolks. Return to heat; stir over low heat 2 minutes; cool completely. When cold, spoon half the lemon mixture over base of 28 cm x 18 cm (11 in. x 7 in.) shallow cake tin which has been lined with greased aluminium foil; bring foil 5 cm (2 in.) above sides; this makes it easy to remove slide from tin. Return to freezer; freeze until firm.
    Soften icecream; spread evenly over lemon mixture; freeze until firm. Spoon rest of lemon mixture over icecream; freeze until firm. To serve, cut in slices.
    Serves 6 to 8.

Liqueur Icecream

5 eggs   2 tablespoons Cointreau
¾ cup sugar   ¼ cup sugar, extra
1¼ cups cream

Place eggs and the ¾ cup sugar in top of double saucepan. Beat over hot water until the sugar dissolves and mixture is lukewarm. Remove from heat; beat until thick and creamy. Whip cream and extra sugar until firm. Fold egg mixture and Cointreau into cream; combine well.
    Spoon mixture into freezer tray. Freeze until firm, stirring occasionally.
    Serves 6.
NOTE: Other liqueurs can be used in place of the Cointreau; Creme de Menthe is delicious, too.

Irish Coffee Icecream

4 egg yolks   2 tablespoons Irish whisky
½ cup castor sugar   (or other whisky)
1 tablespoon instant   300 ml (½ pint) cream
    coffee powder

Beat egg yolks, sugar and coffee powder in top of double boiler over hot water until thick and creamy. Remove from heat. When cold, fold in whisky and whipped cream. Spoon into refrigerator tray; freeze until set.
    This is a beautifully soft-textured icecream. Top each serving, if desired, with whipped cream.
    Serves 4.

French Custard Icecream

½ cup sugar   1 teaspoon gelatine
3 egg yolks   2 teaspoons hot water
½ cup milk   1½ cups cream
2 teaspoons vanilla

Sprinkle gelatine over water; dissolve over hot water. Beat egg yolks and sugar until light and fluffy; add milk and vanilla; combine well. Put custard mixture in top of double saucepan over simmering water; stir until custard becomes thick and coats back of wooden spoon. Remove from heat; add gelatine; beat with rotary beater until custard becomes lukewarm. Add cream; mix well.
    Pour mixture into freezer tray; freeze until firm. Spoon icecream mixture into small bowl of electric mixer; beat on high speed until light and fluffy. Pour back into freezer tray; freeze until firm.
    Serves 4 to 6.

Italian Gelato

1¼ cups pure icing sugar   2 egg whites
½ cup lemon juice   ¼ cup pure icing sugar,
3 cups water   extra

Put icing sugar, lemon juice and water into saucepan. Stir over low heat until sugar has dissolved. Bring to boil; boil uncovered 15 minutes; allow to cool. Pour into refrigerator trays and leave to freeze overnight. Beat egg-whites until firm peaks form; gradually beat in extra sifted icing sugar. Spoon in lemon mixture; beat 5 minutes until mixture is smooth and white. Return to freezer trays; freeze overnight until the mixture is firm.
    Serves 4 to 6.

Hot Desserts

These are desserts the family will hurry home to in the cold winter weather. Or, at other times of the year, these desserts provide the perfect balance to a light meal.

German Plum Tart

2¼ cups self-raising flour	⅓ cup milk
pinch salt	2 x 825 g (1 lb. 13 oz.) cans
60 g (2 oz.) butter	dark plums
¼ cup castor sugar	castor sugar, extra
1 egg	

Sift flour and salt into large mixing bowl; rub in butter until mixture resembles fine breadcrumbs; stir in sugar; mix well. Mix with lightly-beaten egg and enough milk to make a soft dough. Knead lightly. Roll pastry out on lightly-floured surface to line base and sides of 20 cm (8 in.) or 23 cm (9 in.) flan tin.

Drain plums; remove stones and cut in half. Arrange plums decoratively over pastry, cut side up. Bake in hot oven 20 to 30 minutes. Remove from oven; sprinkle tart generously with extra castor sugar. Serve hot with cream.

Serves 6.

NOTE: When in season, fresh plums can be substituted for the canned plums; or other canned fruit, such as apricots or peaches, can be substituted.

Caramel Baked Apples

6 green apples	2 tablespoons plain flour
1½ teaspoons cinnamon	1½ cups water
1 cup brown sugar, lightly packed	30 g (1 oz.) butter

Core apples; do not peel. Make a slit around centre of apples, so that apples do not burst during cooking. Place apples in ovenproof dish. Sprinkle over combined cinnamon, sugar and flour. Add water to pan; place a piece of butter on top of each apple. Bake uncovered in moderate oven 1 hour or until apples are tender. Stir sauce occasionally during cooking time.

Serves 6.

German Plum Tart — sugar-topped plums top a delicious cake pastry. Serve it warm, with cream.

Upside-Down Caramel Banana Cake

185 g (6 oz.) butter	⅓ cup coconut
¾ cup castor sugar	2 cups self-raising flour
2 eggs	pinch salt
1 teaspoon vanilla	½ cup milk

Upside-Down Topping

60 g (2 oz.) butter	2 large bananas
½ cup brown sugar	

Beat butter and sugar until light and creamy. Add eggs one at a time, beating well after each addition; mix in vanilla. Stir in coconut. Fold in sifted dry ingredients alternately with milk.

Upside-Down Topping: Blend softened butter with brown sugar; do not overmix. Spread over base of greased deep 20 cm (8 in.) round cake tin. Arrange sliced bananas decoratively over brown sugar mixture. Spread cake mixture over. Bake in moderate oven 55 to 60 minutes or until cooked when tested. Stand in tin 5 minutes before turning out on serving plate. Serve hot with custard.

Serves 6.

Hot Apricots with Sour Cream

470 g (15 oz.) can apricot halves	1 cup sour cream
½ cup sugar	1 egg
2 tablespoons self-raising flour	1 teaspoon vanilla

Topping

2 tablespoons sugar	2 teaspoons butter
1 teaspoon cinnamon	

Combine sugar and flour; add sour cream, egg and vanilla; beat until smooth. Drain apricots. Put apricots in base of 20 cm (8 in.) pie plate. Spoon the sour cream mixture over. Bake in moderate oven 35 minutes. Remove from oven; sprinkle with topping. Return to oven for 10 minutes.

Topping: Combine sugar and cinnamon. Rub in the butter.

Serves 4.

Rum Plums with Cinnamon Cream

2 x 825 g (1 lb. 13 oz.) cans dark plums	2 tablespoons rum
2.5 cm (1 in.) piece cinnamon stick	1 cup cream
4 whole cloves	2 teaspoons sugar cinnamon

Drain plums; reserve syrup. Cut plums in half; place in bowl. Place syrup in pan with cinnamon stick and cloves; bring to boil. Reduce heat; simmer uncovered 5 minutes; remove from heat. Add rum; stir until combined; strain syrup over plums.

Spoon plums with syrup into serving bowls. Place cream and sugar in bowl; beat until soft peaks form. Spoon on top of plums; sprinkle with a little cinnamon.

Serves 4.

Coconut Peach Pudding

2 x 425 g (14 oz.) cans unsweetened pie peaches	1 teaspoon vanilla
	2 eggs
¼ cup sugar	½ cup self-raising flour
90 g (3 oz.) butter	½ cup coconut
¼ cup sugar, extra	1 tablespoon castor sugar

In small saucepan combine pie peaches with sugar; stir over low heat until sugar has dissolved. Transfer to greased ovenproof dish. Cream butter, extra sugar and vanilla until light and creamy. Add eggs one at a time, beating well after each addition. Stir in sifted flour; mix thoroughly. Spoon mixture evenly over pie peaches.

Combine coconut with castor sugar; sprinkle evenly on top. Bake in moderate oven 50 to 55 minutes or until cooked. Serve with custard or cream.

Serves 4 to 6.

Boiled Date Pudding

1.5 kg (3 lb.) dates	2 teaspoons grated lemon rind
185 g (6 oz.) butter	
1 cup brown sugar, firmly packed	2 cups fresh white bread-crumbs
2 cups water	1 small apple
¼ teaspoon salt	1 small carrot
½ teaspoon bicarbonate of soda	1 cup plain flour
	1 teaspoon cinnamon
3 eggs	½ teaspoon nutmeg
2 teaspoons grated orange rind	½ teaspoon mixed spice
	¼ cup rum

Put 750 g (1½ lb.) roughly-chopped dates, butter, sugar, water and salt into large saucepan. Stir over low heat until butter has melted; bring to boil. Reduce heat; simmer uncovered 8 minutes stirring continually. Remove from heat; stir in soda. Allow to stand until mixture is completely cold.

Stir in lightly-beaten eggs, orange rind, lemon rind, grated carrot, peeled and grated apple and rum. Add sifted dry ingredients and remaining chopped dates; mix until well combined. Put mixture into centre of floured pudding cloth; tie corners and sides of cloth securely.

Put into large boiler of boiling water; boil rapidly covered 4 to 4½ hours. Replenish with more boiling water approx. every 20 minutes as water evaporates; water must never go off the boil. Allow pudding to dry completely before removing cloth. Serve hot or cold with custard or cream.

Serves 6 to 8.

NOTE: See section on Christmas Cookery for correct way to boil a pudding.

Baked Rice Custard

2 tablespoons short-grain rice	⅓ cup sugar
2 cups water	1 teaspoon vanilla
pinch salt	2½ cups milk
3 eggs	¼ cup sultanas
	cinnamon or nutmeg

Bring water and salt to the boil. Gradually add rice. Boil rapidly uncovered 10 minutes; drain well. Beat eggs, sugar and vanilla together; add rice and sultanas. Add milk gradually; stir to combine.

Pour into ovenproof dish. Sprinkle with cinnamon or nutmeg. Stand in baking dish with enough water to come halfway up sides of dish. Bake in moderate oven 35 minutes. After this time, slip a long fork under the skin that has formed on top; stir gently to distribute rice evenly through custard. Reduce heat to moderately slow; bake a further 15 minutes and stir with fork again. Cook a further 15 to 20 minutes, or until custard is set.

Serves 4.

French Apple Pudding

1 cup apricot jam	1 cup castor sugar
2 tablespoons brandy	2 eggs
1 tablespoon lemon juice	1 cup milk
2 tablespoons grated lemon rind	3 cups self-raising flour
125 g (4 oz.) butter	3 green apples

Combine jam, lemon juice and brandy in saucepan. Bring to boil, stirring; reduce heat; simmer 2 minutes. Cool. Pour into greased 2 litre (approx. 4 pint) pudding basin. Cream butter and sugar until light and creamy. Stir in lemon rind. Add eggs; beat well. Gradually beat in milk. Sift flour and fold through creamed mixture.

Peel, core and roughly chop apples. Add to pudding mixture. Spoon over apricot mixture. Cover with foil and steam 3½–4 hours. Serve warm with cream or custard.

Serves 8–10.

Flambe Strawberries

1 lemon	2 punnets strawberries
2 oranges	½ cup brandy
½ cup sugar	

Remove rind from the oranges and lemon in large strips, taking care not to include any of the white pith; squeeze lemon and oranges. Put sugar, lemon and orange rinds and juice in saucepan; cook slowly 5 minutes, pressing rinds with spoon to extract all flavour possible. Remove rinds.

Add the hulled strawberries to pan; spoon syrup gently over strawberries until they are coated with it. Warm brandy; pour over strawberries; set aflame. Serve with cream, or spoon over vanilla icecream.

Serves 6.

Peaches in Port

825 g (1 lb. 10 oz.) can peach halves	½ cup sugar
½ cup port	1 tablespoon lemon juice
½ cup bottled red currant jelly	¼ teaspoon cinnamon
	¼ cup brandy

Combine port, red currant jelly, sugar, lemon juice and cinnamon in frying pan. Stir over medium heat until sugar has dissolved. Bring to boil; add drained peach halves. Reduce heat; simmer 5 minutes. Add brandy; set aflame. Serve with cream or icecream.

Serves 4.

Apple Fritters

3 apples	flour
½ cup dry white wine	oil for deep-frying
1 tablespoon brown sugar	½ cup sugar
1 teaspoon grated lemon rind	1 teaspoon cinnamon

Peel and core apples; cut into 1 cm (½ in.) slices. Put apple slices into bowl; add wine, brown sugar and lemon rind; stir well. Cover; refrigerate overnight.

Drain apple slices; dust lightly with flour; dip in batter; allow excess batter to drain off; deep-fry in hot oil until golden brown and cooked. Drain; toss in combined sugar and cinnamon.

Batter: Sift 1 cup plain flour, 1 tablespoon sugar and 1 teaspoon cinnamon into bowl; gradually add ¾ cup water; beat until smooth. Beat one egg white until firm peaks form; lightly fold into batter; mix until smooth.

Serves 4.

Hot Rum-Cherry Pancakes

Pancakes

½ cup plain flour	1 egg
pinch salt	¾ cup milk

Batter

1 cup plain flour	pinch salt
1 tablespoon oil	2 egg whites
¾ cup water	

Filling

250 g (8 oz.) packaged cream cheese	½ cup cream
1 teaspoon grated lemon rind	2 teaspoons rum
2 tablespoons sugar	470 g (15 oz.) can black cherries
	oil for deep-frying

Cherry Rum Sauce

30 g (1 oz.) butter	1 teaspoon lemon juice
2 tablespoons sugar	1 tablespoon water
2 tablespoons rum	1 teaspoon cornflour

Pancakes: Sift flour and salt into bowl; make well in centre. Add whole egg; work in flour from sides; add milk a little at a time. Beat well until bubbles rise to surface; stand 1 hour. Heat pan; grease lightly. From small jug pour 2 to 3 tablespoons of batter into pan; cook slowly, loosening edges with knife, until set and lightly browned underneath. Toss or turn; brown on other side.

Makes 6.

Batter: Sift flour and salt into bowl; add oil and water; mix to a smooth batter. Just before using, fold in softly-beaten egg whites.

Filling: Place cream cheese, lemon rind and sugar in bowl; beat until soft and creamy. Put cream into bowl; beat until soft peaks form. Fold cream and rum into cream cheese mixture. Drain cherries; reserve syrup. Fold well-drained cherries into cheese mixture. Divide filling evenly between pancakes; fold into envelope shape, brushing last fold with some of the prepared batter to hold it firm. Dip pancakes into prepared batter; place in deep hot oil; fry until golden brown; drain on absorbent paper. Serve immediately with prepared Cherry Rum Sauce.

Cherry Rum Sauce: Heat butter in frying pan; add sugar; stir until sugar is bubbling. Add rum and set aflame. When flames die down, add lemon juice and 1 cup of the reserved cherry syrup; stir until combined. Combine water and cornflour; add to sauce; stir until sauce boils and thickens. Simmer, uncovered, 5 minutes.

Serves 6.

NOTE: The amount of syrup in a can of cherries varies, according to the individual brands. If can does not contain 1 cup syrup, make up to 1 cup with extra water.

Hot Strawberry Souffle

2 punnets strawberries	1 cup milk
2 tablespoons castor sugar	½ cup castor sugar, extra
1 teaspoon cinnamon	1 teaspoon grated orange rind
125 g (4 oz.) butter	1 tablespoon brandy
4 tablespoons plain flour	4 eggs, separated

Strawberry Ripple Cream

300 ml (½ pint) double cream	1 tablespoon castor sugar
	¼ teaspoon vanilla

Wash, hull and dry strawberries. Reserve 6 strawberries for Strawberry Ripple Cream. Halve remaining strawberries; divide between 6 individual souffle dishes. Sprinkle half the combined cinnamon and castor sugar over strawberries.

Melt butter in top of double saucepan over simmering water; remove pan from heat. Add flour; stir until combined. Add milk, extra castor sugar, orange rind and brandy; stir until combined. Return pan over simmering water; stir until mixture is thick; remove from heat. Allow to cool slightly.

Beat egg yolks until thick and creamy; gently fold into souffle mixture. Beat egg whites until soft peaks form; fold in gently. Place souffle dishes on oven tray. Slowly pour souffle mixture over strawberries in each souffle dish.

Bake in moderate oven 15 minutes or until golden brown. Remove from oven; sprinkle with remaining cinnamon mixture. Serve immediately. Serve Strawberry Ripple Cream separately.

Strawberry Ripple Cream: Mash reserved strawberries well. Place cream, sugar and vanilla in bowl; beat until soft peaks form. Gently fold mashed strawberries through cream.

Serves 6.

Delicious Fruit Pudding

1 cup mixed fruit	1 teaspoon bicarbonate of soda
½ cup sugar	
60 g (2 oz.) butter	1 cup self-raising flour
1 cup water	

Place fruit, sugar, butter and water in pan. Stir over low heat until butter has melted; simmer mixture 5 minutes, stirring occasionally. Remove from heat; stir in sifted soda and sifted flour; mix well. Put into well-greased 1 litre (4 cup) pudding basin. Cover; steam 2 hours; replenish saucepan with boiling water every 20 minutes.

Serves 4.

Hot Rum-Cherry Pancakes

Apple Brown Betty

4 apples	1 tablespoon grated lemon
6 slices white bread	rind
½ cup sultanas	1 egg
½ cup brown sugar, firmly	125 g (4 oz.) butter
packed	

Peel apples; grate into bowl. Remove crusts from bread; cut bread into 1 cm (½ in.) cubes; mix with grated apple. Add sultanas, brown sugar, grated lemon rind, lightly-beaten egg and melted butter; mix well. Spoon mixture into four lightly-greased individual ovenproof dishes. Bake in moderate oven 10 minutes. Serve with cream or custard.

Serves 4.

Apple Roll

375 g (12 oz.) pkt puff	470 g (15 oz.) can pie apple
pastry	¾ cup sultanas
60 g (2 oz.) butter	1 egg
⅓ cup brown sugar, firmly	sugar
packed	

Roll pastry out on lightly-floured board to 30 cm x 38 cm (12 in. x 15 in.) rectangle. Spread softened butter evenly over pastry; sprinkle with brown sugar; spread pie apple evenly over sugar; sprinkle with sultanas. Fold edges over; roll up as for swiss roll; tuck ends under.

Put on greased oven tray; brush pastry with lightly-beaten egg; sprinkle with sugar. Bake in hot oven 10 minutes; reduce heat to moderate; bake a further 25 to 30 minutes or until golden brown and pastry is cooked through. Serve with cream.

Serves 6.

Apple Pudding

30 g (1 oz.) butter	411 g (14½ oz.) can
1 tablespoon sugar	sweetened pie apple
1 egg	¼ cup coconut
1 tablespoon self-raising	1 tablespoon sugar, extra
flour	

Beat butter and sugar until light and creamy. Add lightly-beaten egg; beat well. Stir in sifted flour. Spread apple over base of small, greased ovenproof dish. Spread butter mixture evenly over apple. Combine coconut and extra sugar; sprinkle on top. Bake in moderate oven 35 minutes or until golden.

Serves 2.

Brandied Caramel Apples

60 g (2 oz.) butter	2 tablespoons brandy
½ cup brown sugar, firmly	½ teaspoon cinnamon
packed	pinch nutmeg
4 large green apples	pinch mixed spice

Peel apples; cut into quarters; remove cores; cut into slices. Melt butter in frying pan; add sugar; stir until combined. Add apples; stir until apples are coated with caramel. Add remaining ingredients; bring to boil; boil 3 minutes. Serve with cream.

Serves 4.

Baked Banana Slice

Pastry

60 g (2 oz.) butter	pinch salt
2 tablespoons sugar	½ cup milk
2 cups self-raising flour	1 egg, separated
⅓ cup cornflour	castor sugar, extra

Filling

60 g (2 oz.) butter	1 teaspoon vanilla
⅔ cup castor sugar	2 cups coconut
2 eggs	6 bananas

Cream butter and sugar until light and fluffy. Gradually add lightly-beaten egg yolk, beating well after each addition. Stir in sifted dry ingredients alternately with milk. Mix until pastry forms a soft, pliable dough; form into a round; refrigerate 30 minutes.

Roll out half the pastry on lightly-floured surface to line greased 28 cm x 18 cm (11 in. x 7 in.) lamington tin. Spoon filling evenly into pastry shell; roll remaining pastry to cover filling. Brush with lightly-beaten egg white; sprinkle lightly with extra sugar. Bake in moderate oven 35 to 40 minutes or until golden. Serve warm with cream or custard.

Filling: Cream butter and sugar until light and fluffy. Gradually add lightly-beaten eggs, beating well after each addition. Stir in vanilla, coconut, peeled and thinly-sliced bananas.

Serves 6.

Banana Fritters

8 bananas	¼ teaspoon salt
3 tablespoons plain flour	½ cup milk
⅓ cup cornflour	1 egg white
1½ teaspoons baking	½ cup castor sugar
powder	oil for deep-frying

Peel bananas; cut in half across. Sift flour, cornflour, baking powder and salt into bowl. Mix to smooth batter with the milk. Beat egg white until soft peaks form; fold lightly into batter.

Drop banana pieces into batter, then deep fry in hot oil until golden brown. Remove and drain on absorbent paper. Toss in sugar; serve hot with icecream or cream.

Serves 4.

Rum Cream Bananas

250 g (8 oz.) packaged cream cheese	2 tablespoons cream
	1 tablespoon rum
1/3 cup brown sugar, lightly packed	30 g (1 oz.) butter
	8 bananas
1/4 teaspoon cinnamon	1/3 cup cream, extra
1 egg, separated	cinnamon, extra

Have cream cheese at room temperature. Beat cream cheese until soft and fluffy. Gradually add brown sugar and cinnamon; beat well. Add lightly-beaten egg yolk; beat until combined. Stir in rum and cream; mix well. Beat egg white until soft peaks form; fold gently into cream cheese mixture.

Peel bananas; halve lengthwise. Melt butter in pan; gently saute bananas over low heat until golden and just tender. Place alternate layers of bananas and cream cheese mixture in small oven-proof dish, finishing with a layer of cream cheese mixture. Spoon extra cream over; sprinkle with a little extra cinnamon; bake in moderate oven 15 to 20 minutes until heated through and bubbly on top.

Serves 4.

Apricot Crumble Slice

Base

125 g (4 oz.) butter	1 cup plain flour
1/2 cup sugar	1/2 cup self-raising flour
1 egg	

Filling

125 g (4 oz.) dried apricots	3/4 cup sugar
2 cups hot water	

Topping

1 1/2 cups coconut	90 g (3 oz.) butter
1 cup rolled oats	1/4 cup honey

Cream butter and sugar until light and fluffy; add egg; beat well. Fold in sifted flours. Grease 18 cm x 28 cm (7 in. x 11 in.) shallow cake tin; line base with greased greaseproof paper. Spread mixture evenly over base of tin; spoon apricot filling evenly over base; sprinkle evenly with prepared topping.

Bake in moderately hot oven 10 minutes; reduce heat to moderate; cook a further 20 to 25 minutes or until golden brown. Cool in tin 5 minutes; turn out; serve hot or cold with cream.

Filling: Put apricots and water in bowl; stand 30 minutes. Put apricots and liquid into saucepan; bring to boil. Reduce heat; simmer covered 10 minutes. Add sugar; stir until dissolved; simmer a further 10 minutes uncovered. Put apricots and syrup in blender; blend to pulp, or push apricots and syrup through sieve; cool.

Topping: Combine coconut and rolled oats in bowl; add combined melted butter and honey; mix well.

Fig and Apricot Slice

Pastry

1 cup plain flour	125 g (4 oz.) butter
1/2 cup self-raising flour	1 egg, separated
2 1/2 tablespoons cornflour	1/3 cup milk
2 1/2 tablespoons custard powder	1 tablespoon sugar

Filling

500 g (1 lb.) dried figs	1 cup brown sugar, lightly packed
250 g (8 oz.) dried apricots	
3 cups boiling water	1/4 teaspoon nutmeg
1 teaspoon grated lemon rind	1 teaspoon mixed spice
	1 teaspoon cinnamon
2 tablespoons orange juice	2 tablespoons cornflour
	1/4 cup water, extra

Sift dry ingredients into bowl; rub in butter until mixture resembles fine breadcrumbs. Add combined egg yolk and milk; mix to a firm dough. Turn out on lightly-floured surface; knead lightly. Roll out half the pastry to line base of greased and greased-paper lined 28 cm x 18 cm (11 in. x 7 in.) shallow cake tin or 20 cm (8 in.) square slab tin. Prick pastry well; bake in hot oven 10 minutes or until light golden brown; allow to become cold.

Spread prepared cold filling over pastry base. Roll out remaining pastry to cover filling. Brush with lightly-beaten egg white and sprinkle with sugar. Bake in moderately hot oven 20 to 25 minutes or until golden brown. Serve warm with cream or custard.

Filling: Chop apricots and figs roughly; place in bowl; add water; allow to stand 2 hours. Place figs and apricots with water in saucepan; add lemon rind, orange juice, nutmeg, mixed spice and cinnamon; stir over heat until mixture boils. Reduce heat; simmer covered 30 minutes or until figs and apricots are tender. Add sugar; stir until dissolved; simmer 3 minutes, stirring constantly. Gradually add combined cornflour and extra water; stir until mixture boils and thickens. Simmer 2 minutes. Allow to become cold.

NOTE: Fresh figs in season can be used instead of the dried figs in this recipe. You will need about 12 large figs. Peel and chop figs; cook as above. (There is no need to soak them with the apricots.)

Cakes

Sometimes the occasion calls for a simple cake, sometimes for one that is scrumptious — a really gorgeous gateau! Recipes for all types of cake are given in this section — you can make a different choice every day.

Almond Cream Rings

Choux Pastry

1 cup water	1 cup plain flour
75 g (2½ oz.) butter	4 large eggs
pinch salt	60 g (2 oz.) flaked almonds

Vanilla Cream

2 eggs, separated	1½ cups milk
6 tablespoons castor sugar	½ teaspoon vanilla
1 tablespoon plain flour	icing sugar
1 tablespoon cornflour	

Choux Pastry: Put water, butter and salt into pan; bring to boil. Add sifted flour all at once; stir vigorously over heat until mixture is very thick and leaves sides of pan. Put into small bowl of electric mixer; allow to cool until warm. Add eggs one at a time, beating well after each addition. Mixture should be smooth and glossy.

Fill mixture into piping bag fitted with 1 cm (½ in.) plain tube. Grease baking trays; mark 6 cm (2½ in.) circles on tray. Pipe choux pastry round edges of circles. With wet finger, smooth joins together. Arrange flaked almonds lightly on top. Bake in hot oven 3 minutes; reduce heat to moderate; cook a further 20 minutes. Make a small slit in sides of pastry to allow steam to escape.

Vanilla Cream: Put egg yolks, 4 tablespoons sugar, ½ cup milk and sifted flour and cornflour into bowl; beat lightly until combined. Put remaining milk in pan; bring to boil. Remove from heat immediately; pour over egg yolk mixture, beating well. Return mixture to pan; stir until mixture comes to boil. Reduce heat; stir 1 minute. Remove from heat; add vanilla; stir until combined.

Recipe continued overleaf:

Almond Cream Rings — delightfully light pastries filled with vanilla cream.

When cold, beat egg whites until soft peaks form; add remaining sugar; beat until firm peaks form. Gently fold into cold cream. Fill mixture into piping bag fitted with plain tube. Cut choux pastries in half; remove any uncooked pastry. Fill with cream. Place tops in place. Dust each with sifted icing sugar.

Makes approx. 12.

Hazelnut Loaf Cake

125 g (4 oz.) butter	1 teaspoon grated lemon
½ cup castor sugar	rind
3 eggs	1¼ cups plain flour
90 g (3 oz.) ground	½ teaspoon bicarbonate of
hazelnuts	soda
2 tablespoons lemon juice	

Beat butter and sugar until light and creamy. Gradually add lightly-beaten eggs, beating well after each addition. Stir in ground hazelnuts, lemon juice and lemon rind; mix well. Fold in sifted dry ingredients. Spoon mixture into greased and paper-lined 23 cm x 12 cm (9 in. x 5 in.) loaf tin. Bake in moderate oven 45 to 50 minutes.

Date and Walnut Cake

125 g (4 oz.) butter	½ cup self-raising flour
1 cup castor sugar	½ teaspoon nutmeg
1 cup cooked mashed	2 teaspoons grated lemon
potato	rind
2 eggs	125 g (4 oz.) chopped
125 g (4 oz.) dates	walnuts
½ cup plain flour	¼ cup milk

Chop dates; put in saucepan with milk; bring to boil. Remove from heat; leave to cool. Cream butter, sugar and lemon rind until light and fluffy. Add eggs one at a time, beating well after each addition. Add mashed potato gradually; beat well. Fold in sifted flours and nutmeg. Fold in chopped walnuts, date-and-milk mixture.

Place mixture in greased 23 cm x 12 cm (9 in. x 5 in.) loaf tin, with base lined with greased greaseproof paper. Bake in moderate oven 55 to 60 minutes. Cool in tin before turning out.

Banana Walnut Loaf

90 g (3 oz.) butter	1¼ cups self-raising flour
⅓ cup sugar	pinch salt
1 egg	⅓ cup plain yoghurt
1 large banana	2 tablespoons finely-
1 teaspoon lemon juice	chopped walnuts

Beat butter and sugar until light and creamy. Add lightly-beaten egg; beat well. Stir in combined peeled, mashed banana and lemon juice. Fold in sifted dry ingredients alternately with yoghurt. Stir in half the chopped walnuts; mix until smooth. Spoon mixture into greased and greased-paper lined 18 cm (7 in.) square shallow baking tin; sprinkle with remaining walnuts.

Bake in moderate oven 40 minutes or until cooked when tested. Allow cake to cool 5 minutes in tin; turn out and cool on wire rack. When cold, cut into slices; serve with butter.

Sultana Coconut Cake

125 g (4 oz.) butter	2 cups self-raising flour
¾ cup sugar	½ cup coconut
1 teaspoon grated orange	⅔ cup orange juice
rind	1 cup sultanas
2 eggs, separated	

Cream butter, sugar and orange rind until light and fluffy. Add egg yolks one at a time, beating well after each addition. Fold in sifted flour and coconut alternately with orange juice. Stir sultanas into mixture.

Beat egg whites until soft peaks form; fold into mixture. Spread mixture evenly into greased 23 cm x 12 cm (9 in. x 5 in.) loaf tin which has been lined with greased greaseproof paper. Bake in moderate oven 60 to 65 minutes or until cake is cooked. Turn on to wire rack to cool.

Coconut Cake

125 g (4 oz.) butter	1¼ cups coconut
1 cup castor sugar	½ cup self-raising flour
1 teaspoon vanilla	¾ cup semolina
4 eggs, separated	pinch salt

Lemon Icing

1 cup icing sugar	1 tablespoon lemon juice
15 g (½ oz.) butter	

Beat butter until creamy. Gradually add sugar, beating until mixture is light and fluffy. Add egg-yolks one at a time, beating well after each addition; beat in vanilla. Stir in coconut; mix well. Fold in sifted dry ingredients. Beat egg-whites until firm; fold gently into mixture. Spoon into greased and greased-paper lined 23 cm x 12 cm (9 in. x 5 in.) loaf tin. Bake in moderate oven 55 to 60 minutes. When cold, dust with sifted icing sugar or top with Lemon Icing; sprinkle with extra coconut.

Lemon Icing: Sift icing sugar into top of double saucepan. Stir in softened butter and lemon juice;

combine well. Stir over gently simmering water until mixture is of good spreading consistency. Remove from heat; spread over top of cake.

Coconut Teacake

60 g (2 oz.) butter
½ cup castor sugar
½ teaspoon vanilla
1 egg

1½ cups self-raising flour
½ cup milk
⅓ cup raspberry (or other) jam

Topping

30 g (1 oz.) butter
2 tablespoons sugar
½ teaspoon vanilla
1 egg

1½ cups coconut
2 tablespoons self-raising flour

Beat butter and sugar until light and fluffy. Add vanilla and egg; beat well. Sift flour; add to creamed mixture alternately with milk; mix until smooth. Grease 20 cm (8 in.) round sandwich tin; line base with greased greaseproof paper. Spoon half of cake mixture into base of tin; spread evenly.

Mix jam until smooth; spread over cake mixture; spoon remaining cake mixture to cover. Cover top of cake with topping mixture; bake in moderate oven 35 to 40 minutes, or until cooked when tested.

Topping: Cream butter, sugar and vanilla until creamy. Add egg; beat well. Fold in coconut and sifted flour; mix well.

Pineapple Coconut Cake

½ cup honey
½ cup coconut
½ cup chopped mixed nuts
60 g (2 oz.) butter
2½ cups self-raising flour
1 teaspoon cinnamon
¼ teaspoon nutmeg

1 cup castor sugar
½ teaspooon bicarbonate of soda
1 cup sour cream
2 eggs
470 g (15 oz.) can crushed pineapple

Grease deep 20 cm (8 in.) round cake tin; line base with greased greaseproof paper. Pour honey over base, spreading out evenly. Sprinkle combined coconut and nuts over honey, pressing down firmly. Heat butter in pan; when melted, evenly spoon butter over coconut mixture.

Sift flour, sugar, cinnamon, nutmeg and soda into large bowl. Put sour cream and eggs into separate bowl; beat until combined. Drain pineapple. Add drained pineapple and sour cream mixture to flour mixture; beat with wooden spoon until smooth, approx. 4 minutes. Pour mixture evenly into cake tin.

Bake in moderate oven 1 hour 15 minutes or until skewer inserted comes out clean. (If cake becomes too brown during cooking, put a sheet of brown paper lightly over cake.) Allow to cool slightly before turning out of tin.

Chocolate Coconut Cake

125 g (4 oz.) butter
1 cup brown sugar, lightly packed
1 egg
1 cup self-raising flour

1 tablespoon cocoa
1 cup coconut
1 tablespoon icing sugar
½ cup milk

Cream butter and sugar until light and fluffy. Add egg; beat well. Stir in sifted flour and cocoa; beat lightly until smooth. Spread half mixture evenly into a greased 20 cm (8 in.) square shallow baking tin. Combine coconut, icing sugar and milk; mix until smooth; spread evenly over cake mixture. Spoon remaining cake mixture on top of evenly filling.

Bake in moderate oven 30 minutes or until cooked when tested. If desired, top with chocolate icing.

Moist Chocolate Cake

125 g (4 oz.) butter
¾ cup castor sugar
⅔ cup mashed cooked potato, loosely packed
60 g (2 oz.) dark chocolate

⅓ cup cocoa
2 eggs
1½ cups self-raising flour
½ teaspoon salt
⅓ cup milk

Icing

45 g (1½ oz.) dark chocolate
½ teaspoon oil

2 tablespoons water
1 cup icing sugar, approx.

Put chocolate over hot water to melt; remove from heat; cool. Cream butter; add sugar and cold potato; beat well. Add melted chocolate and sifted cocoa; add eggs one at a time, beating well after each addition. Fold in sifted flour and salt alternately with milk.

Spoon mixture into 2 greased 20 cm (8 in.) round sandwich tins. Bake in moderate oven 25 to 30 minutes. Cool on wire rack. When cold, sandwich layers together with whipped cream; top with Chocolate Icing.

Icing: Combine roughly-chopped chocolate, oil and water in top of double saucepan or in small heatproof basin. Stir over hot water until chocolate has melted. Gradually beat in sifted icing sugar; beat until smooth and of good spreading consistency. Quickly pour over cold cake; spread evenly.

NOTE: This mixture can also be baked as a plain loaf cake. Fill cake mixture into 23 cm x 12 cm (9 in. x 5 in.) loaf tin which has been greased and had the base lined with greased greaseproof paper. Bake in moderate oven 45 to 50 minutes.

Dark Chocolate Cake

1¾ cups self-raising flour	1¼ cups sugar
½ teaspoon bicarbonate of soda	125 g (4 oz.) butter
	1 cup milk
¼ teaspoon salt	1 teaspoon vanilla
½ cup cocoa	2 eggs

Chocolate Icing

1½ cups icing sugar	2 teaspoons butter
2 teaspoons cocoa	2 tablespoons water

Sift dry ingredients into large bowl; add sugar. Add melted butter gradually; mix well. Add milk and vanilla; beat well. Add lightly-beaten eggs gradually, beating well after each addition.

Put mixture into greased and greased-paper lined deep 20 cm (8 in.) round cake tin. Bake in moderate oven 65 minutes or until cooked when tested. Top with Chocolate Icing when cold.

Chocolate Icing: Sift together icing sugar and cocoa; mix in melted butter and water; beat until smooth.

Orange Cake

90 g (3 oz.) butter	½ cup water
1 teaspoon grated orange rind	3 eggs
	¾ cup sugar
3 tablespoons orange juice	1¼ cups self-raising flour

Put butter, orange rind, orange juice and water in saucepan; stir until butter has melted. Beat eggs and sugar until thick and creamy. Fold sifted flour into egg mixture. Add hot liquid; fold in lightly. Pour into greased deep 20 cm (8 in.) round cake tin, which has the base lined with greased grease-proof paper. Bake in moderate oven 35 to 40 minutes. Turn on to wire rack to cool.

Lumberjack Cake

2 medium apples	1½ cups plain flour
185 g (6 oz.) dates	½ teaspoon salt
1 teaspoon bicarbonate of soda	60 g (2 oz.) butter, extra
1 cup boiling water	½ cup brown sugar, firmly packed
125 g (4 oz.) butter	⅓ cup milk
1 cup sugar	60 g (2 oz.) shredded coconut
1 egg	
1 teaspoon vanilla	

Combine peeled, cored and finely-chopped apples, chopped dates, bicarbonate of soda and boiling water; allow to cool until lukewarm. Cream butter and sugar until light and fluffy; add egg and vanilla; beat well. Sift flour and salt; beat into creamed mixture alternately with cooled fruit mixture. Pour mixture into deep greased and greased-paper lined 20 cm (8 in.) square cake tin. Bake in moderate oven 1 hour 10 minutes, or until cooked when tested.

Combine extra butter, brown sugar, milk and coconut in pan; stir over low heat until butter and sugar have melted. Spread coconut mixture over hot cake; bake a further 20 minutes or until topping is golden brown.

Cinnamon Apricot Cake

60 g (2 oz.) butter	pinch salt
½ cup castor sugar	1 teaspoon baking powder
250 g (8 oz.) butter, extra	¼ cup unprocessed bran
1 cup brown sugar, firmly packed	¼ cup wheatgerm
1 teaspoon grated orange rind	2 teaspoons cinnamon
	¾ cup milk
3 eggs	910 g (1 lb. 13 oz.) can apricot halves
2½ cups wholemeal self-raising flour	

Grease deep 20 cm (8 in.) square cake tin. Line base with greased greaseproof paper. Melt butter in pan; pour butter over base of tin. Sprinkle castor sugar evenly over butter.

Beat extra butter, orange rind and brown sugar until very light and creamy; add eggs one at a time, beating well after each addition. Sift flour, salt, baking powder and cinnamon into bowl; return any husks in sifter to flour. Add wheatgerm and bran; stir until combined. Fold flour mixture alternately into butter mixture with milk; mix well.

Drain apricots; place over base of prepared tin, cut side down. Spoon cake mixture evenly over apricots. Bake in moderate oven 65 to 70 minutes or until cake is cooked when tested. Cool on wire rack.

Apricot Loaf

1 cup milk	125 g (4 oz.) dried apricots
1 cup packaged All Bran	1 tablespoon honey
1 cup brown sugar, firmly packed	1 cup self-raising flour

Combine milk, All Bran, brown sugar, chopped apricots and honey in bowl. Cover; stand overnight. Next day, add sifted flour; mix well.

Grease 20 cm x 10 cm (8 in. x 4 in.) loaf tin; line base with greased greaseproof paper. Spoon cake mixture evenly into tin; bake in moderate oven 1 hour or until cooked when tested. Turn out and cool on wire rack. Serve sliced and buttered.

Apricot Loaf

Cherry Madeira Cake

185 g (6 oz.) butter	3 eggs
⅔ cup castor sugar	1 cup plain flour
1 teaspoon grated lemon rind	1 cup self-raising flour
	185 g (6 oz.) glace cherries

Cream butter until light and fluffy; gradually beat in sugar. Add grated lemon rind; mix well. Beat eggs lightly; add gradually to mixture; beat well. Sift flours; lightly fold into creamed mixture. Halve cherries; fold into mixture.

Turn mixture into greased deep 18 cm (7 in.) cake tin which has been lined with greased grease-proof paper. Bake in moderate oven 75 minutes or until cake is cooked. Turn on to wire rack to cool.

Black Forest Cherry Cake

8 eggs, separated	½ cup cocoa
1 whole egg	2 x 440 g (14 oz.) jars
1 cup sugar	morello cherries
1 tablespoon warm water	(or 2 x 470 g (15 oz.) cans
1 cup sponge cake crumbs	cherries)
90 g (3 oz.) ground almonds	2 tablespoons Kirsch
	¼ cup cornflour
½ cup self-raising flour	4 cups cream

Grease deep 23 cm (9 in.) square or round cake tin; dust lightly with flour. Beat egg-yolks with whole egg, sugar and water until pale and fluffy. Fold in the crumbs and ground almonds; fold in softly-beaten egg-whites and finally the sifted flour and cocoa. Pour mixture into prepared tin; bake in moderate oven 35 to 40 minutes or until cooked when tested. Turn out on to wire rack covered with teatowel; allow to become cold.

Remove stones from cherries; dissolve cornflour in a little of the cherry syrup; put into saucepan with cherries and remaining cherry syrup. Stir over medium heat until sauce boils and thickens; reduce heat; simmer 2 minutes; allow to become cold.

Put cream and Kirsch into bowl; beat until thick. Cut cake horizontally into 4 even layers. Put one layer of cake on large serving plate. Spread one-third of the cherry filling over cake layer; spread approx. ½ cup of the cream over the cherry filling; continue layering in this way, ending with the final cake layer. Spread remaining cream over top and sides of cake and, if desired, pipe decoratively around top edge of cake and sprinkle with chocolate shavings. Refrigerate several hours before serving.

Boiled Fruit Cake

125 g (4 oz.) butter	¼ teaspoon ground ginger
1 cup sugar	2 eggs
½ cup brown sugar, lightly packed	1 cup plain flour
	1 cup self-raising flour
1 cup milk	1 cup dry sherry
500 g (1 lb.) mixed fruit	1 teaspoon bicarbonate of
1 teaspoon cinnamon	soda
½ teaspoon nutmeg	1 tablespoon milk, extra

Place in saucepan butter, sugars, milk, fruit and spices. Stir until boiling; reduce heat; simmer 5 minutes. Let cool; add sherry and soda. Beat eggs; add to fruit mixture; add sifted flours and extra milk. Place mixture in deep 20 cm (8 in.) round cake tin which has been lined with two thicknesses of brown paper and one of greaseproof paper. Decorate top of cake, if desired, with blanched almonds. Bake in moderate oven 1¾ hours or until cooked with tested.

Golden Fruit Loaf

2 cups self-raising flour	1 cup warm milk
½ cup sugar	60 g (2 oz.) butter
½ cup sultanas	2 tablespoons golden
½ teaspoon salt	syrup

Sift dry ingredients into bowl; add sultanas. Put milk, butter and golden syrup in pan; put over low heat until butter has melted. Pour over dry ingredients; mix thoroughly.

Pour mixture into greased and greased-paper lined 23 cm x 12 cm (9 in. x 5 in.) loaf tin. Bake in moderate oven 40 minutes or until cooked when tested. Turn out and cool on wire rack.

Light Fruit Cake

½ cup sugar	1 cup sugar, extra
½ cup water	1 cup self-raising flour
250 g (8 oz.) butter	1 teaspoon vanilla
2 teaspoons glycerine	500 g (1 lb.) sultanas
2½ cups plain flour	60 g (2 oz.) mixed peel
4 eggs	185 g (6 oz.) glace cherries

Combine sugar and water in saucepan; stir over low heat until sugar is dissolved. Remove from heat; cool.

Cream butter and glycerine until butter is just softened; do not overcream. Add sifted plain flour; beat until just combined. Beat eggs until foamy; gradually add extra sugar; beat until dissolved. Gradually add egg mixture to creamed mixture; beat only until combined. Stir in sifted self-raising flour, cold syrup, vanilla, sultanas, peel and halved cherries.

Spoon into lined deep 20 cm (8 in.) square or 23 cm (9 in.) round cake tin. Bake in moderately slow oven 2 to 2¼ hours.

Wholemeal Boiled Fruit Cake

375 g (12 oz.) pkt mixed fruit	1 egg
60 g (2 oz.) dates	1 cup wholemeal plain flour
125 g (4 oz.) vegetable margarine	1 cup wholemeal self-raising flour
1 cup raw sugar	pinch salt
1 tablespoon golden syrup	⅓ cup chopped walnuts
1 cup water	

Line a deep 20 cm (8 in.) round cake tin with two thicknesses of greaseproof paper, bringing paper 5 cm (2 in.) above edges of tin. Put mixed fruit, chopped dates, margarine, sugar, golden syrup and water in saucepan; stir over low heat until margarine has melted; bring to boil; boil uncovered 2 minutes. Remove from heat; allow to become completely cold. Add lightly-beaten egg; mix well. Add sifted dry ingredients and walnuts; mix well. Spread evenly into prepared tin; bake in moderately slow oven 1¾ hours or until cooked when tested. Cover with aluminium foil until cold; when cold, remove from tin; re-wrap in aluminium foil; store in the foil until required.

Banana Sour Cream Cake

125 g (4 oz.) butter	⅓ cup sour cream
1 teaspoon vanilla	2 cups self-raising flour
1 cup sugar	¼ teaspoon bicarbonate of soda
2 eggs	
1 cup mashed bananas (approx. 3 bananas)	

Beat butter with vanilla until soft and creamy; gradually beat in the sugar. Add eggs one at a time, beating well after each addition. Add combined mashed bananas and sour cream alternately to the mixture with the sifted dry ingredients. Spoon into greased deep 20 cm (8 in.) cake tin; bake in moderate oven 1¼ hours or until cooked when tested. Let stand in tin 10 minutes before turning out to cool on wire rack.

Halva Cake

125 g (4 oz.) butter	¾ cup semolina
½ cup sugar	1 cup self-raising flour
2 teaspoons grated orange rind	90 g (3 oz.) ground almonds
2 eggs	1½ tablespoons sugar, extra
3 tablespoons brandy	

Syrup

1¼ cups orange juice	2 tablespoons Grand Marnier
½ cup sugar	

Cream butter, sugar and orange rind until light and fluffy. Add eggs one at a time, beating well after each addition. Gradually beat in brandy. Add sifted dry ingredients; stir until mixture is combined. Spoon mixture into greased deep 20 cm (8 in.) cake tin which has base lined with greased greaseproof paper.

Bake in hot oven 10 minutes; reduce heat to moderate; bake a further 30 minutes. Remove cake from tin and put on ovenproof dish. Spoon over the Orange Syrup; sprinkle top with extra sugar; return to oven and cook a further 15 minutes.

Orange Syrup: Combine orange juice and sugar in saucepan; stir over low heat until sugar dissolves; bring to boil. Remove from heat; add Grand Marnier.

Apple Patty Cakes

2 cups self-raising flour	3 eggs
¾ cup sugar	¼ cup milk
1 teaspoon cinnamon	½ teaspoon vanilla
125 g (4 oz.) softened butter	1 tablespoon lemon juice
	1 apple

Sift dry ingredients into small basin of electric mixer; add softened butter, eggs, milk, vanilla and lemon juice. Beat on medium speed 2 minutes. Add peeled, grated apple; beat a further 1 minute. Drop tablespoonfuls of mixture into deep, greased patty tins; bake in moderately hot oven 12 to 15 minutes or until golden brown.

Makes approx. 24.

Quick Apple Cake

Mock Yeast Cake

2 eggs	2 teaspoons vinegar
1 cup castor sugar	2½ cups self-raising flour
1 cup milk	1 cup sultanas

Topping

½ cup plain flour	½ cup castor sugar
60 g (2 oz.) butter	2 teaspoons cinnamon

Beat eggs and sugar until light and fluffy. Heat milk in saucepan until warm; add vinegar; stir until combined. Gradually add milk to egg mixture, beating well after each addition. Fold in sifted flour; add sultanas; mix well. Put mixture into deep 20 cm (8 in.) square cake tin which has the base lined with greased greaseproof paper. Sprinkle topping over evenly. Bake in moderate oven approx. 1 hour or until cooked when tested.

Topping: Sift flour into bowl; rub in butter until mixture resembles fine breadcrumbs. Add sugar and cinnamon; mix well.

Quick Apple Cake

2 teaspoons instant coffee powder	½ cup canned pie apple
2 cups hot water	250 g (8 oz.) butter
1½ cups brown sugar	1 egg
375 g (12 oz.) raisins	3¼ cups plain flour
2 teaspoons cinnamon	2 teaspoons bicarbonate of soda
1 teaspoon ground cloves	

Dissolve coffee in hot water. Combine brown sugar, chopped raisins, cinnamon, cloves, pie apple, butter and dissolved coffee in pan. Stir over low heat until butter melts; cool. Add lightly-beaten egg; mix well. Add sifted flour and soda; mix well. Pour mixture into greased and greased-paper lined 28 cm x 23 cm (11 in. x 9 in.) baking dish. Bake in moderate oven 40 to 45 minutes or until cooked when tested.

This makes a delicious family dessert cake, served hot from the oven with cream or custard. If serving as cake, it will cut better if left to stand overnight.

How to Make a Perfect Sponge

Here's how to make a light-as-a-feather, melt-in-the-mouth sponge cake, filled with cream and passionfruit. The top can be dusted with sifted icing sugar or spread with passionfruit icing.

You will need:

4 eggs
¾ cup castor sugar
⅔ cup plain flour
⅓ cup cornflour
1 teaspoon baking powder
1 cup cream
2 tablespoons passionfruit pulp
  (approx. 2 passionfruit)

Passionfruit Icing

1 cup icing sugar
1 teaspoon butter
2 tablespoons passionfruit pulp
  (approx. 2 passionfruit)

Sift icing sugar into bowl, add butter and enough passionfruit pulp to mix to a stiff paste. Put bowl over simmering water, stir 1 minute or until icing is of a thin consistency; remove from heat, spread over top of cake, allow to set.

1.   Put eggs into small bowl of electric mixer, beat on medium to high speed until mixture is thick and creamy. Mixture will rise almost to the top of the bowl; beating time is 5 to 8 minutes. Gradually beat in sugar, beat until sugar has dissolved.

2.   Sift dry ingredients several times so that all ingredients are thoroughly combined; with spatula or metal spoon, gently fold dry ingredients into egg-yolk mixture. Do this lightly and quickly, so that the airy sponge mixture is not broken down, but make sure that all flour is mixed in. Pour mixture into two well-greased deep 20 cm (8 in.) round cake tins. (Some champion sponge makers weigh the tins after pouring in the mixture, to make sure both tins have an equal amount of mixture.)

3.   Bake in moderate oven 20 to 25 minutes; cake is cooked when it shrinks slightly from side of tin, as shown in picture, or when top, pressed with fingertips, springs back lightly and fingertips leave no impression. Cover a wire rack with a clean teatowel, turn cakes out of tins immediately they are cooked. Carefully invert so that tops of cakes are uppermost. When cakes are completely cold, spread one cake with whipped cream, top with passionfruit pulp. Put the second cake on top, ice with passionfruit icing.

Apple Cinnamon Coffee Cake

60 g (2 oz.) butter	½ teaspoon cinnamon
½ cup castor sugar	½ cup milk
½ teaspoon vanilla	½ cup sultanas
1 egg	1 green apple
1½ cups self-raising flour	1 teaspoon cinnamon, extra
1 teaspoon instant coffee powder	1 teaspoon sugar, extra

Cream butter, sugar and vanilla until light and fluffy. Add egg; beat well. Fold in sifted flour, coffee powder and cinnamon alternately with milk. Add sultanas; mix well.

Grease 20 cm (8 in.) round sandwich tin; line base with greased greaseproof paper. Spread cake mixture evenly into tin. Peel apple; cut into quarters; remove core. Cut each quarter crosswise into thin slices. Arrange apple slices evenly around edge of cake and in the centre of cake. Sprinkle top of cake with combined extra cinnamon and sugar.

Bake in moderate oven 30 to 35 minutes or until cooked when tested. Turn out of tin; cool on wire rack; serve buttered.

Raisin Gingerbread

45 g (1½ oz.) butter	¼ teaspoon bicarbonate of soda
⅓ cup treacle	
⅓ cup brown sugar, lightly packed	1 egg
	⅓ cup warm milk
1 cup self-raising flour	1½ tablespoons preserved ginger
pinch salt	
1½ teaspoons ground ginger	½ cup raisins

Put butter, treacle and brown sugar into saucepan; stir over low heat until sugar dissolves; cool. Sift flour, salt, ground ginger and soda into bowl; add cooled sugar mixture, lightly-beaten egg and warmed milk; mix well. Stir in chopped ginger and finely-chopped raisins.

Pour mixture into 18 cm (7 in.) square shallow baking tin which has been greased and greased-paper lined. Bake in moderate oven 35 to 40 minutes or until cake is cooked.

Baking Dish Ginger Cake

185 g (6 oz.) butter	½ cup milk
½ cup water	1 teaspoon vanilla
½ cup golden syrup	2 eggs
3 cups self-raising flour	2 tablespoons ground ginger
1 cup castor sugar	

Lemon Icing

2½ cups icing sugar	2 tablespoons lemon juice
2 teaspoons butter	

Put butter, water and golden syrup into pan; stir over low heat until butter has melted and mixture combined; allow to become cold. Sift flour, sugar and ginger into large bowl; make well in centre of dry ingredients; add butter mixture, well-beaten eggs, vanilla and milk. Gradually mix in flour mixture, then beat very well.

Grease 23 cm x 32.5 cm (9 in. x 13 in.) baking dish; line base with greased greaseproof paper. Pour cake mixture in; spread evenly. Bake in moderate oven 35 to 40 minutes or until cooked when tested. When cold, top with Lemon Icing.

Lemon Icing: Sift icing sugar into bowl; add softened butter and lemon juice; stir until conbined. Stand bowl over simmering water; stir until icing is shiny and of good spreading consistency. A teaspoon or two of milk may be needed if icing is too thick.

Italian Ricotta Cake

250 g (8 oz.) ricotta cheese	2 teaspoons baking powder
1 cup sugar	
3 eggs	⅓ cup sultanas
1 teaspoon vanilla	⅓ cup chopped mixed peel
2 cups self-raising flour	glace cherries

Cream together ricotta cheese and sugar until light and fluffy. Add eggs one at a time, beating well after each addition. Add vanilla. Fold in sifted dry ingredients, fruit and peel. Spoon mixture into greased and greased-paper lined 23 cm x 12 cm (9 in. x 5 in.) loaf tin. Press glace cherries lightly and decoratively along top (you'll need about 10 cherries). Bake in moderate oven 1 hour 10 minutes or until cooked when tested.

Chocolate Lamington Bar

90 g (3 oz.) butter	¼ cup milk
⅓ cup sugar	raspberry jam
1 egg	½ cup cream
½ teaspoon vanilla	coconut
1¼ cups self-raising flour	

Icing

1⅓ cups icing sugar	15 g (½ oz.) butter
2 tablespoons cocoa	¼ cup milk

Beat butter until creamy; add sugar; beat until light and fluffy. Add lightly-beaten egg and vanilla; beat well. Fold in sifted dry ingredients alternately with the milk. When all ingredients are added, beat mixture lightly until smooth. Spoon mixture into greased and paper-lined

25 cm x 8 cm (10 in. x 3 in.) bar tin. Bake in moderate oven 35 to 40 minutes; allow to become completely cold before icing. Thinly trim brown top, base and sides from cake; cut cake in halves lengthwise. Spread raspberry jam over one side of cut surface; spread with lightly-whipped cream; join halves together. Spread chocolate icing evenly over top and sides of cake, making sure all cake is covered. Sprinkle with coconut; let stand until icing has set.

Icing: Sift icing sugar and cocoa into heatproof basin or top of double saucepan. Add softened butter and milk; stir with wooden spoon to mix thoroughly. Stand over hot water; stir constantly until icing is of good coating consistency. Keep icing over hot water while icing cake.

Tea Loaf

¾ cup sultanas	¾ cup brown sugar, firmly
¾ cup currants	packed
1 cup strong black tea	1 egg
1¾ cups self-raising flour	2 tablespoons marmalade
¼ teaspoon salt	

Put sultanas and currants in bowl; add strong black tea; leave to stand overnight. Next day, add sifted flour and salt to fruit; mix well. Stir in brown sugar. Beat egg and marmalade together; add to fruit mixture; mix well. Pour mixture into greased 23 cm x 12 cm (9 in. x 5 in.) loaf tin which has the base lined with greased, greaseproof paper. Bake in moderate oven approx. 1 hour or until loaf is cooked with tested. Turn out on to wire rack; cool. Serve sliced with butter.

Caramel Hazelnut Gateau

Cake

8 large eggs	⅔ cup cornflour
1½ cups castor sugar	60 g (2 oz.) ground
1⅓ cups plain flour	hazelnuts
2 teaspoons baking	3 x 300 ml cartons
powder	thickened cream

Filling

90 g (3 oz.) butter	¼ cup milk, extra
1 cup brown sugar, lightly	2 tablespoons Grand
packed	Marnier or Cointreau
1½ cups milk	300 ml (½ pint) double
1 tablespoon cornflour	cream

Cake: Put eggs into large bowl of electric mixer; beat on highest speed until thick and creamy; gradually beat in sugar; beat until all sugar is dissolved. Sift dry ingredients several times; sift over egg mixture, then sift the hazelnuts over; fold in quickly but lightly. Do not over-mix; this is a sponge mixture. Pour into greased deep 28 cm (11 in.) round cake tin. Bake in moderately hot oven 40 minutes or until cake is firm to touch and shrinks slightly from sides of tin. Turn out on to wire rack to cool.

When cold, cut cake into four even layers. Place first layer of cake on serving plate; spread with half the prepared caramel filling; place second layer of cake on caramel. Whip one carton of cream; spread over cake layer. Place third layer of cake on cream; spread over remaining caramel; top with remaining cake layer. Beat remaining 2 cartons of cream until soft peaks form; spread two-thirds of cream over top and sides of cake; fill remaining cream into large piping bag fitted with star nozzle; pipe decoratively around cake; place hazelnuts on top of cake. If desire, drizzle decoratively with melted chocolate. You'll need about 30 g (1 oz.). Refrigerate.

Filling: Melt butter in pan; add sugar; stir until sugar is bubbling; remove pan from heat; add milk. Return pan to heat; stir until sugar dissolves; add combined extra milk and cornflour; stir until filling boils and thickens; add Grand Marnier; stir over low heat 2 minutes. Remove from heat; pour into bowl; allow to cool; cover with plastic food wrap; put into refrigerator until cold. Beat cream until soft peaks form; fold into caramel mixture.

NOTE: This is a superb, special-occasion cake.

Lamington Wedges

1 pkt vanilla cake mix	coconut

Chocolate Icing

2 cups icing sugar	2 tablespoons strawberry
3 tablespoons cocoa	jam
1½ cups water	

Make up cake mix as directed on packet. Pour mixture into two greased 20 cm (8 in.) sandwich tins. Bake in moderate oven 30 to 35 minutes or until cooked when tested. Cut each cake into four quarters, then cut each quarter into three, giving 12 triangles from each cake. Dip each triangle into prepared icing, then toss in coconut.

Makes 24.

Chocolate Icing: Sift icing sugar and cocoa into basin; add warmed sieved jam and water; beat well.

NOTE: This is a very thin, liquid icing which coats the cakes beautifully.

Cool Desserts

We have gathered together in this section a collection of mouth-watering recipes. Family or special occasion desserts — they're all here; every page will tempt you.

Ogen Melon Ice

2 small ripe ogen melons   1 tablespoon Grand
1 cup sugar   Marnier
½ cup water

Cut ogen melons in half. Remove seeds; scoop out melons to 5 mm (¼ in.) around skin. Place melon flesh in blender; blend on high speed until smooth, or mash well to a puree.

Place sugar and water in saucepan. Stir over low heat until all sugar has dissolved; bring to boil; boil rapidly 2 minutes. Remove syrup from heat immediately; cool slightly.

Stir in ogen melon and Grand Marnier. Place in shallow icecream tray; cool; freeze until firm, stirring occasionally. To serve, run fork across ice to flake; pile into individual serving dishes.

Serves 4.

Mangoes and Ginger Wine Ice

940 g (1 lb. 14 oz.) can   60 g (2 oz.) preserved
   mangoes   ginger
½ cup green ginger wine

Ginger Wine Ice

2 cups hot water   1 cup green ginger wine
¾ cup sugar   2 teaspoons lemon juice

Drain mangoes, reserve syrup; put syrup, ginger wine and chopped ginger in saucepan; bring to boil. Reduce heat; simmer 2 minutes; drain; cool. Put mangoes into serving glasses; pour syrup over; refrigerate until cold. Before serving, top with Ginger Wine Ice.

Ginger Wine Ice: Dissolve sugar in hot water; add ginger wine and lemon juice; cool. Pour into refrigerator trays and freeze. Stir occasionally. Flake lightly with fork before serving.

Serves 4 to 6.

Ogen Melon Ice — light, full of fresh-fruit flavour — makes a perfect summertime dessert.

Grapefruit Sherbet

2 cups grapefruit juice (approx. 4 grapefruit)	2 egg whites
½ cup sugar	¼ cup sugar, extra
	gin

Put grapefruit juice and sugar in saucepan; stir over medium heat until sugar has dissolved; bring to boil. Remove from heat; allow to become cold. Put grapefruit liquid in freezer tray; freeze until partly frozen.

Beat egg whites until soft peaks form; add extra sugar; beat until dissolved. Using fork, fold egg-white mixture through grapefruit mixture. Return to freezer; freeze until firm, stirring occasionally with fork to blend mixture evenly.

Spoon into individual serving glasses or, if desired, spoon into scooped out grapefruit halves. Before serving, spoon 2 teaspoons gin over each serving.

Serves 4.

Poor Man's Apple Brulee

6 apples	1 tablespoon sugar, extra
2 tablespoons sugar	½ teaspoon vanilla
1 teaspoon grated lemon rind	1½ cups milk
2 tablespoons water	½ cup cream
3 tablespoons custard powder	⅓ cup brown sugar, firmly packed

Peel, quarter and core apples. Cut apples into thick slices. Place apples, sugar, lemon rind and water in pan; cover; bring to boil. Reduce heat; simmer gently 5 minutes or until apples are just tender. Put apples into heatproof dish.

Put custard powder and extra sugar into pan; gradually add milk; stir until combined. Add cream and vanilla. Stir over low heat until mixture boils and thickens; reduce heat; simmer uncovered 2 minutes; cool slightly. Pour custard mixture over apples.

Cover dish; refrigerate until cold. Just before serving, sieve brown sugar on top of custard. Put under griller until sugar melts.

Serves 4.

Lemon Torte

Pastry

1⅓ cups plain flour	3 egg yolks
⅓ cup sugar	½ teaspoon vanilla
90 g (3 oz.) butter	

Filling

2 eggs	1 teaspoon grated lemon rind
⅓ cup sugar	60 g (2 oz.) butter
¼ cup lemon juice	1 cup cream
1 tablespoon water	

Icing

1½ cups icing sugar	90 g (3 oz.) flaked almonds
1 tablespoon lemon juice	

Sift flour on to table; make a well in centre and in it place softened butter, sugar, egg yolk and vanilla. Using the fingertips of one hand, work butter, sugar, egg yolks and vanilla together until well blended. Gradually draw in the flour with a spatula; bring together with hands to form a ball. Knead lightly until smooth. Refrigerate 30 minutes before using.

Divide pastry into three; roll each piece into 20 cm (8 in.) round; place circles of pastry on greased oven trays; bake in moderate oven 10 to 12 minutes, or until pale biscuit colour. Loosen pastry with spatula immediately on removing from oven; leave on trays for few minutes before placing on wire racks to cool.

Whip cream until firm peaks form. Place almonds on oven tray; bake in moderate oven 8 to 10 minutes or until golden brown.

Place a layer of pastry on serving plate; spread approx. 3 tablespoons of prepared filling over pastry; swirl 1 tablespoon cream through filling with small spatula. Place another layer of pastry on top and repeat process with remaining filling and 1 tablespoon cream. Place remaining layer of pastry on top. Spread prepared icing over top of cake; allow to set. Use remaining cream to spread around sides of cake and pipe decorative border on top. Press toasted almonds evenly around edge of cake. Refrigerate several hours or overnight.

Filling: Put beaten eggs and sugar in top of double saucepan; stir until combined. Gradually add strained lemon juice and water; stir until combined. Add lemon rind and roughly-chopped butter. Place pan over simmering water; stir until mixture thickly coats the back of a wooden spoon.

Icing: Sift icing sugar into bowl; add lemon juice; beat well until smooth.

Strawberry Champagne Sorbet

2 punnets strawberries	2 egg whites
1½ cups champagne, dry white wine or sparkling wine	½ cup sugar, extra
	¼ cup water, extra
	¼ teaspoon cream of tartar
¼ cup sugar	¼ cup Grand Marnier or Cointreau
½ cup water	

Put sugar and water in saucepan; stir over low heat until sugar has dissolved. Combine champagne and sugar syrup; pour into freezer tray; freeze until partially set.

Wash and hull 8 of the strawberries; chop

roughly; push through fine sieve; discard seeds. Put extra sugar, extra water and cream of tartar in saucepan; stir over low heat until sugar dissolves; increase heat; boil rapidly 2 minutes. Beat egg whites until soft peaks form; pour the hot syrup into the egg whites in a very thin stream, beating until thick.

Fold champagne mixture into meringue with pureed strawberries; pour back into freezer tray; freeze until set, stirring occasionally with fork to blend mixture evenly.

Wash and hull remaining strawberries; arrange in dishes. Coat strawberries in each dish with 2 teaspoons of Grand Marnier. Use fork to flake the sorbet; spoon on top of strawberries.

Serves 6.

Orange and Rum Dessert Cake

250 g (8 oz.) butter	2 eggs
1 cup sugar	2 cups self-raising flour
2 tablespoons grated orange rind	¾ cup milk
	¾ cup raisins
1 tablespoon grated lemon rind	

Syrup

1 cup orange juice	1 cup sugar
2 tablespoons lemon juice	¼ cup rum

Cream butter, sugar, orange and lemon rinds until light and fluffy. Add eggs one at a time, beating well after each addition. Fold in sifted flour alternately with the milk; fold in chopped raisins.

Grease deep 20 cm (8 in.) round cake tin; line base with greased greaseproof paper. Spread cake mixture evenly in tin; bake in moderate oven 1¼ hours or until cooked when tested. Cool 5 minutes in tin; turn out on to plate or tray; make several holes in cake with skewer so that syrup will be absorbed through cake. Gradually pour prepared syrup over cake. Serve with cream

Syrup: Combine orange juice, lemon juice and sugar in saucepan; stir over low heat until sugar dissolves; bring to boil. Reduce heat; simmer 5 minutes. Stir in rum.

Caramel Praline Pears

825 g (30 oz.) can pear halves	vanilla ice cream

Caramel Sauce

30 g (1 oz.) butter	½ cup hot water
¼ cup brown sugar	2 tablespoons Grand Marnier
¼ cup condensed milk	
1 tablespoon golden syrup	

Praline

30 g (1 oz.) slivered almonds	½ cup sugar
	¼ cup water

Drain pears; spoon into 6 individual serving dishes; top with a scoop of vanilla ice cream. Pour the warm sauce over; sprinkle with praline.

Caramel Sauce: Combine butter, brown sugar, condensed milk and golden syrup in saucepan. Cook over low heat, stirring constantly until mixture leaves sides of saucepan and is a rich golden colour. Remove from heat; gradually stir in hot water. Return to heat; stir a further 1 to 2 minutes. Stir in Grand Marnier.

Praline: Put almonds into lightly greased pan; stir over heat until lightly browned, approx. 5 minutes; remove pan from heat and set aside.

Put sugar and water into saucepan; stir over low heat until sugar has dissolved. Increase heat; boil rapidly uncovered without stirring approx. 5 minutes or until a light golden colour. Remove from heat; pour over almonds; leave to cool and set.

Break into pieces; grind to coarse powder in electric blender, or put through metal mouli grater or chop finely.

Serves 6.

Cream Cheese Strudel

500 g (1 lb.) packaged cream cheese	½ teaspoon vanilla
250 g (8 oz.) cottage cheese	250 g (8 oz.) pkt phylo pastry
½ cup sugar	125 g (4 oz.) butter
½ cup raisins	sugar, extra
	icing sugar

Beat cream cheese until light and fluffy. Add sieved cottage cheese, sugar, chopped raisins and vanilla; mix well. Place one sheet of phylo pastry on board; brush with melted butter. Repeat with second, third and fourth layers, brushing each layer with butter. Place half the filling on one end of pastry; fold edges in 2.5 cm (1 in.) to seal filling. Roll pastry up firmly. Make another roll with remaining pastry and filling. Put rolls on to lightly-greased oven trays; brush tops of rolls with remaining melted butter; sprinkle with extra sugar. Bake in hot oven 10 minutes; reduce heat to moderate; bake a further 10 minutes or until golden brown. Refrigerate strudel several hours before serving. Sprinkle tops with sifted icing sugar.

NOTE: Phylo (or filo or strudel) pastry can be bought from most large food halls or from Continental pastry shops.

Hazelnut Praline Puffs

Hazelnut Praline Puffs

Puffs

1 cup water	pinch salt
60 g (2 oz.) butter	4 eggs
1 cup plain flour	2 cups cream

Praline

90 g (3 oz.) roasted hazelnuts	½ cup sugar
	½ cup water

Caramel Sauce

125 g (4 oz.) butter	100 g (2½ oz.) pkt white marshmallows
¾ cup brown sugar, lightly packed	2 tablespoons milk

Sift flour. Put water, butter and salt into saucepan; stir until all butter has melted; bring to rapid boil. Add flour all at once. Stir vigorously with wooden spoon until mixture is thick. When mixture leaves sides of saucepan and forms a smooth ball, remove from heat. Spread mixture up sides of small bowl of electric mixer; allow to cool. Add eggs one at a time, beating well on medium speed after each addition.

Put tablespoons of mixture on greased oven trays; bake in hot oven 10 minutes. Reduce heat to moderate; bake a further 20 minutes or until golden. Split puffs while still hot; scoop out with small spoon any of the uncooked mixture from inside; allow to cool.

Whip cream; fold in half the prepared praline; fill puffs with this cream; spoon caramel sauce over and sprinkle with remaining praline.

Praline: Put hazelnuts into small greased pan. Put sugar and water into saucepan; stir over low heat until sugar dissolves. Increase heat; bring to boil; boil uncovered without stirring until light golden brown. Remove from heat; pour over hazelnuts; allow to cool. Break into pieces; put in plastic bag; crush with rolling pin.

Caramel Sauce: Combine all ingredients in saucepan. Stir over low heat until marshmallows are dissolved; simmer 3 minutes.

Coffee Liqueur Cheesecake

Coffee Liqueur Cheesecake

Crumb Crust

250 g (8 oz.) plain sweet biscuits	125 g (4 oz.) butter

Filling

375 g (12 oz.) packaged cream cheese	1 tablespoon instant coffee powder
¾ cup castor sugar	1 tablespoon coffee liqueur (Tia Maria or Kahlua)
3 teaspoons plain flour	
3 eggs	
¾ cup sour cream	1 tablespoon water
1 tablespoon lemon juice	1 egg yolk
90 g (3 oz.) dark chocolate	

Cream

3 teaspoons instant coffee powder	1 cup cream
1 teaspoon hot water	1 tablespoon sugar

Crumb Crust: Crush biscuits finely; add melted butter; mix well. Press crumb mixture on base and sides of 20 cm (8 in.) springform pan. Refrigerate while preparing filling.

Filling: Beat cream cheese until softened; combine with sugar and flour; beat well. Beat in eggs, sour cream and lemon juice. Pour half cheesecake mixture into prepared crumb crust.

Put roughly-chopped chocolate, coffee powder, liqueur, water and lightly-beaten egg yolk in top of double saucepan; stir over simmering water until chocolate melts and mixture becomes thick. Remove from heat; cool slightly.

Swirl half chocolate mixture gently through cheesecake mixture in crust with small spatula. Top with remaining cheesecake mixture; swirl remaining chocolate through top half of cheesecake.

Bake in moderately slow oven 1 hour to 1 hour 10 minutes or until set. Remove from oven; allow to become cold; refrigerate overnight. Remove sides from pan; put cheesecake on to serving plate; top with prepared cream.

Cream: Dissolve coffee powder in hot water. Put cream, coffee and sugar in bowl; refrigerate 30 minutes; beat until thick.

Strawberry Cheesecake

Crumb Crust

250 g (8 oz.) plain sweet biscuits	125 g (4 oz.) butter

Filling

250 g (8 oz.) packaged cream cheese	2 tablespoons water
⅓ cup sugar	1 punnet strawberries
2 eggs, separated	2 teaspoons lemon juice
⅓ cup sugar, extra	1½ cups cream
1 tablespoon gelatine	1 teaspoon icing sugar

Crumb Crust: Combine finely-crushed biscuit crumbs with melted butter; mix well. Press over sides and base of greased 20 cm (8 in.) springform pan.

Filling: Sprinkle gelatine over water; dissolve over hot water. Beat cream cheese and sugar until smooth. Beat egg yolks and extra sugar until light and creamy. Put in top of double saucepan over simmering water; stir until sugar dissolves and mixture is thick. Remove from heat; add dissolved gelatine. Gradually add egg yolk mixture to cream cheese mixture; beat until smooth.

Reserve 5 strawberries; mash remainder with fork. Fold mashed strawberries into cream cheese mixture with lemon juice. Whip cream; fold half into strawberry mixture. Lastly fold in softly-beaten egg whites. Spoon into crumb crust; refrigerate until set.

Press reserved strawberries through sieve; combine with sifted icing sugar. Spread remaining whipped cream over top of cheesecake; using small spoon, swirl strawberry puree through cream.

Apricot Ripple Cheesecake

Biscuit Crust

250 g (8 oz.) pkt plain sweet biscuits	125 g (4 oz.) butter

Filling

185 g (6 oz.) dried apricots	2 tablespoons Grand Marnier
2½ cups water	1 cup cream
1 tablespoon sugar	1 tablespoon gelatine
250 g (8 oz.) pkt cream cheese	¼ cup water
¾ cup castor sugar	1 egg white

Biscuit Crust: Place finely-crushed biscuits in bowl; add melted butter; mix well. Press biscuit crumbs over base and sides of lightly-greased 20 cm (8 in.) round springform pan. Refrigerate while preparing filling.

Filling: Place apricots and water in pan; bring to boil. Reduce heat; simmer covered 25 to 30 minutes or until apricots are very tender. Place apricots with their liquid in electric blender; add sugar. Blend on medium speed for 30 seconds or until pureed; allow to become cold.

Place cream cheese in small bowl of electric mixer; beat until smooth; add castor sugar and Grand Marnier; beat until sugar has dissolved. Place gelatine and water in bowl; stir until combined. Stand bowl over simmering water until gelatine is dissolved. Gradually add gelatine mixture to cream cheese mixture, beating well.

Place cream in bowl; beat until soft peaks form. Place egg white in bowl; beat until firm peaks form. Fold cream and egg white into cream cheese mixture. Pour into prepared crumb crust. Spoon apricot mixture on top of cream cheese mixture. Swirl apricot mixture into cream cheese mixture with a fork. Place in refrigerator until set. If desired, decorate with whipped cream.

Strawberry Mallow Mousse

1 punnet strawberries	2 tablespoons Grand Marnier
100 g (3½ oz.) pkt white marshmallows	2 teaspoons water
1 teaspoon gelatine	1 cup cream
1 tablespoon lemon juice	2 egg whites

Sprinkle gelatine over water; dissolve over hot water. Wash and hull strawberries; chop roughly. Put strawberries and marshmallows into saucepan; stir over low heat until marshmallows have melted. Add gelatine, lemon juice and Grand Marnier; refrigerate until cold and slightly thickened.

Fold in whipped cream and softly-beaten egg whites. Spoon into four individual serving dishes. Refrigerate until set.

Serves 4.

Chocolate Mousse with Rum Cream

100 g (3½ oz.) pkt white marshmallows	30 g (1 oz.) butter
125 g (4 oz.) dark chocolate	2 eggs, separated
	pinch salt

Rum Cream

3 egg yolks	1½ tablespoons rum
¼ cup sugar	1 cup cream
1 tablespoon lemon juice	

Chop chocolate and marshmallows. Put in top of double saucepan with butter; stir over hot water until mixture has melted; remove from heat. Add lightly-beaten egg yolks; return to heat; stir over hot water 3 minutes until mixture is smooth and thick. Allow to cool until slightly set.

Beat egg whites with salt until soft peaks form; fold through chocolate mixture. Spoon into

4 individual serving glasses; refrigerate until set.

Pour Rum Cream over; refrigerate until set. Decorate, if desired, with grated chocolate just before serving.

Rum Cream: Beat egg yolks, sugar and lemon juice until mixture is thick and light lemon in colour. Gradually add rum; mix well. Fold in whipped cream.

Serves 4.

Hazelnut Praline Mousse

3 eggs, separated
1/3 cup sugar
1/2 cup orange juice

2 teaspoons gelatine
1 cup cream

Praline

1 cup water
1 cup sugar

125 g (4 oz.) roasted
hazelnuts

Beat egg yolks and sugar until thick and creamy. Put in top of double saucepan over simmering water; stir until sugar has dissolved. Sprinkle gelatine over orange juice; dissolve over hot water; combine with egg yolk mixture; cool. Fold in whipped cream, softly-beaten egg whites and crushed hazelnut praline.

Spoon into serving dish or 4 individual serving dishes; refrigerate until set. Before serving, top with extra whipped cream and extra chopped roasted hazelnuts.

Praline: Grease oven tray or swiss roll tin; put hazelnuts on tray. Combine sugar and water in saucepan; stir over low heat until sugar dissolves. Bring to boil; boil until golden toffee colour (approx. 10 minutes); allow bubbles to subside. Pour toffee over hazelnuts in tray and allow to set.

Break toffee roughly; put in blender and blend 2 minutes, stopping blender and stirring occasionally, until praline is fairly fine. Praline can also be crushed by putting it in a plastic bag and crushing with a rolling pin. Serves 4.

Black Forest Icecream

2 litre carton vanilla
icecream
500 g (1 lb.) dark chocolate
30 g (1 oz.) solid white
vegetable shortening
2 x 425 g (15 oz.) cans
black cherries

2 tablespoons Cherry
Heering, maraschino
or brandy
2 tablespoons cornflour
2 tablespoons water

Put an oven tray into freezer, so that it is very cold. Remove icecream container from freezer. Scoop icecream into balls with icecream scoop; place immediately on tray in freezer. Freeze until very hard. Put chocolate and white shortening into top

of double saucepan; stand over hot water; stir until melted; cool. Cover an oven tray with aluminium foil. Dip icecream balls into chocolate; lift out with forks; place on foil-covered tray. Place in freezer until ready to serve. Drain cherries; reserve 1½ cups of syrup. Put reserved cherry syrup and Cherry Heering into pan. Bring to boil; remove from heat; add cornflour mixed with water. Stir until mixture boils and thickens. Add pitted cherries. Pour hot sauce over icecream balls.

Serves 6.

Strawberry Chocolate Mousse

1 punnet strawberries
2 tablespoons Grand
Marnier or Cointreau
1 tablespoon icing sugar
2 eggs, separated
1/4 cup sugar
1 tablespoon orange juice

1 teaspoon gelatine
2 teaspoons water
1/2 cup cream
60 g (2 oz.) dark chocolate
30 g (1 oz.) solid white
vegetable shortening

Reserve 2 strawberries for decoration; wash and hull remainder. Slice half the strawberries; put in bowl with 1 tablespoon of the Grand Marnier and sifted icing sugar. Mash remaining strawberries with fork.

Beat egg yolks and sugar until light and fluffy. Put in top of double saucepan over simmering water; stir until sugar dissolves. Sprinkle gelatine over water; dissolve over hot water; stir into egg-yolk mixture; cool. Add orange juice and remaining Grand Marnier and mashed strawberries to egg mixture. Fold in whipped cream and softly-beaten egg whites. Refrigerate mixture until slightly set.

Spoon sliced strawberries and liquid into 4 individual serving dishes or glasses. Top with the strawberry mousse; refrigerate until set.

Put chocolate and vegetable shortening in top of double saucepan; stand over simmering water until melted; cool. Spoon a thin layer of chocolate over each mousse; refrigerate until set. To serve, decorate each with extra whipped cream and reserved, halved strawberries. Serves 4.

Melon in Champagne

Watermelon, ogen melons or honeydew melons — or a combination of these — can be used. Scoop out balls of melon with melon-baller, or cut melon into dice. Place ½ cup water, ½ cup sugar and ¼ cup green ginger wine in saucepan; stir over heat until sugar is dissolved. Bring to boil; boil 3 minutes; cool; refrigerate. To serve, place melon balls in 6 tall glasses; pour approx. 1½ tablespoons of the ginger syrup into each glass; top up with cold champagne.

Serves 6.

Strawberry Meringue Mousse

1 punnet strawberries	4 tablespoons skim milk
3 tablespoons castor	powder
sugar	¼ teaspoon vanilla
1 cup water	2 egg whites
3 teaspoons gelatine	½ cup castor sugar, extra

Sprinkle gelatine over water in small bowl; stand bowl over simmering water until gelatine has dissolved; allow to become cold. Put washed, hulled strawberries, sugar, gelatine mixture, skim milk powder and vanilla in blender; blend on medium speed 30 seconds. Pour mixture into 4 individual heatproof dishes. Place in refrigerator until set. Beat egg whites until soft peaks form; gradually add extra sugar to egg whites; beat until dissolved. Spoon mixture into piping bag fitted with fluted nozzle. Pipe meringue decoratively on top of each mousse. Place dishes on baking tray; place in hot oven 3 minutes or until meringue is very light golden colour. Refrigerate again until mousse is firm.

Serves 4.

NOTE: This is an excellent low-kilojoule (or low-calorie) dessert for dieters. Approx. 680 kilojoules (170 calories) per serving.

Chocolate Meringue Torte

4 egg whites	60 g (2 oz.) dark chocolate,
1 cup sugar	extra
15 g (½ oz.) dark chocolate	1 punnet strawberries
1½ cups cream	

Filling

¾ cup cream	2 tablespoons ground
1 tablespoon brandy	hazelnuts

Beat egg whites until soft peaks form; gradually add sugar, beating well after each addition. Fold in the grated 15 g (½ oz.) chocolate. Grease lightly two 18 cm (7 in.) sandwich tins; line base with lightly-greased greaseproof paper. Sprinkle tins lightly with flour; tap out excess flour. Spread meringue mixture evenly into tins; bake in moderately slow oven 40 to 45 minutes. Turn out on to wire rack to cool. (Cakes have a rather untidy appearance at this stage, but don't worry. When assembled as directed, the cake looks beautiful, tastes better!) When meringues are cold, join together with the filling. Whip cream until firm peaks form. Cover sides and top of cake with whipped cream; pipe decorative edge of cream around top of cake. Press extra grated chocolate around sides of cake with spatula. Decorate top with halved strawberries. Refrigerate for several hours.

Filling: Whip cream until soft peaks form; fold in hazelnuts and brandy.

Toffee Almond Pears

6 firm pears	5 cm (2 in.) piece cinnamon
1 cup sugar	stick
1 cup water	4 whole cloves
1½ cups dry white wine	½ cup sugar, extra
5 cm (2 in.) strip orange	½ cup water, extra
rind	60 g (2 oz.) flaked almonds
5 cm (2 in.) strip lemon	300 ml (½ pint) double
rind	cream

Peel pears thinly with potato peeler, making sure that no skin remains. Place sugar, water, wine, orange and lemon rinds, cinnamon stick and cloves in pan; stir over heat until sugar is dissolved. Add pears; simmer uncovered 20 minutes or until pears are just tender, turning occasionally. Cool. Place pears and liquid in bowl; cover and refrigerate overnight. Place almonds on baking tray; bake in moderate oven 5 minutes or until almonds are golden. Remove pears from syrup; pat dry with absorbent paper. Place pears in individual serving bowls.

Beat cream until soft peaks form; fill into piping bag fitted with star nozzle; pipe cream around base of each pear. Place extra sugar and extra water in pan; stir over low heat until sugar is dissolved. Bring to boil; boil uncovered 4 minutes or until mixture is golden brown. Remove pan from heat; allow toffee to cool slightly. Spoon toffee over top of each pear; sprinkle almonds over toffee. Serve the cold wine liquid separately with pears.

Baked Custard Cream

30 g (1 oz.) butter	1 tablespoon self-raising
3 tablespoons castor	flour
sugar	2 cups milk
2 eggs, separated	1 teaspoon vanilla
1 tablespoon plain flour	

Cream butter and sugar until light and fluffy. Add egg yolks one at a time, beating well after each addition. Add sifted flours; combine well. Put milk in small saucepan; stir over low heat until milk reaches simmering point; remove from heat; stir in vanilla. Gradually beat milk into creamed mixture, beating all the time; mix well. Beat egg-whites until soft peaks form; gently fold into custard. Put custard into lightly-greased ovenproof dish; put in large baking dish with enough hot water to come half-way up sides of dish. Bake in moderate oven 50 to 60 minutes or until custard is firm. Cool, then refrigerate.

Serves 4 to 6.

How to Make a Perfect Pavlova

It is one of Australia's most popular desserts — this crisp shell of meringue with a favourite filling. Here's how to make it perfectly, with a lemon-cream filling that makes use of the egg yolks left from the pavlova.

You will need:

4 egg whites
1 cup castor sugar
¼ cup granulated sugar
1 tablespoon cornflour
1 teaspoon lemon juice

Custard Cream

4 egg yolks
¼ cup sugar
1 teaspoon vanilla
1 tablespoon cornflour
¾ cup milk
½ cup cream

Beat egg yolks, sugar, vanilla and cornflour until smooth and creamy. Put into saucepan, gradually add cream and milk, stir until smooth. Stir over medium heat until sauce thickens, bring to boil, reduce heat, simmer 2 minutes. Remove from heat, allow to become cold, stirring occasionally.

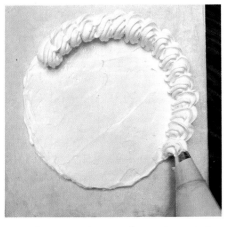

1. Beat egg whites until soft peaks form, gradually add castor sugar, beating until dissolved (approx. 8 minutes). Fold combined granulated sugar and cornflour into meringue with lemon juice. Picture shows firm, shiny consistency of finished meringue.

2. Place sheet of greaseproof paper, trimmed to size of tray, on greased oven tray, brush paper lightly with melted butter, dust with sifted cornflour. Shake off excess cornflour. Mark 23 cm (9 in.) circle on paper. Spread 3 heaped tablespoons of meringue into circle.

3. Fill remaining meringue into piping bag fitted with star tube. Pipe decoratively around edge of pavlova as shown. Bake in slow oven 40 minutes, remove from oven, allow to become cold. Spoon prepared Custard Cream into pavlova, top with fruit salad or any other fruit; if desired, decorate with whipped cream and strawberries.

Icecream

Here are some of our favourite recipes for icecream — each completely different, each the very best recipe of its type. To prevent ice crystals forming, icecream must freeze fast; set the freezer control at its coldest; return to normal setting when icecream has frozen.

Economical Icecream

470 g (15 oz.) can evaporated milk	1 cup cold water
1½ teaspoons gelatine	1 cup non-fat milk powder
½ cup boiling water	½ cup sugar
	1 teaspoon vanilla

Dissolve gelatine in boiling water. Add cold water; pour into large bowl of electric mixer. Add evaporated milk (it does not need to be chilled), milk powder and sugar. Beat until combined and free from lumps. Freeze until firm.

Remove from refrigerator and allow to stand until softened slightly. Empty into chilled mixing bowl; mash down with potato masher. Beat at high speed until light and fluffy and doubled in bulk. Add vanilla. Spoon into freezer trays; freeze until set.

Serves 6.

Low Calorie Vanilla Icecream

2½ teaspoons gelatine	¼ cup sugar
1 tablespoon water	2 cups water, extra
2 cups skim milk powder	2 teaspoons vanilla

Sprinkle gelatine over 1 tablespoon water; dissolve over hot water; cool. Combine milk powder, sugar, extra water and vanilla in bowl; beat until milk powder has dissolved; add gelatine; beat well.

Pour mixture into freezer trays; freeze until set. When set, put mixture into large bowl of electric mixer; beat until doubled in bulk. Pour mixture into freezer trays; freeze until firm.

Serves 8.

Lemon Sherbet Icecream

½ cup milk	¾ cup lemon juice
2 teaspoons gelatine	1 cup milk, extra
1 cup sugar	300 ml (½ pint) cream
1 cup boiling water	

Put milk and gelatine into small saucepan; stir over low heat until gelatine has dissolved; do not boil. Dissolve sugar in boiling water; add lemon juice and gelatine mixture; cool; then add extra milk and cream. Pour into freezer tray; freeze until partly frozen. Pour mixture into small bowl of electric mixer; beat until slightly thickened. Pour back into freezer tray; freeze until firm, stirring occasionally.

Serves 6.

Coffee Icecream

1½ cups milk	½ cup castor sugar
2 tablespoons instant coffee powder	1 cup cream
4 egg yolks	¼ teaspoon cinnamon

Heat milk, but do not allow to boil. Add coffee powder; stir until dissolved. Allow to stand 15 minutes. Beat egg yolks until thick and creamy. Gradually add sugar, beating well until mixture is light and fluffy. Add coffee-milk gradually; beat in cream and cinnamon. Place coffee mixture in top of double saucepan over gently simmering water; beat with rotary beater 10 minutes until mixture has increased in volume and is thick.

Pour into freezer tray; leave until almost frozen. Remove from freezer; beat 10 minutes on electric mixer. Return to freezer; freeze until almost firm; beat again on electric mixer for 10 minutes. Return to freezer to set.

Remove from freezer and place in refrigerator about 5 minutes before serving time for icecream to soften slightly. Top each serving with whipped cream; pour over a little coffee liqueur (Kahlua or Tia Maria).

Serves 6.

Coconut Icecream

875 g (1¾ lb.) coconut	3 litres (12 cups) boiling water
1 cup sugar	
½ teaspoon salt	

Put coconut, sugar and salt into large bowl; pour boiling water over; stir well; let stand 20 minutes. Strain coconut through fine sieve, then, using hands, press out excess liquid from coconut; strain again. Pour coconut liquid into refrigerator trays (the coconut is now discarded); freeze until solid. (Mixture will separate into layers, but reconstitutes perfectly on beating, as below.)

Turn into large bowl of electric mixer; beat on low speed until mixture is mushy and evenly combined. Return to refrigerator trays; freeze again until firm.

Serve plain, or as a topping for fresh fruit salad.

Super Rich Icecream

4 eggs, separated
1 cup icing sugar

1 cup cream
1 teaspoon vanilla

Beat egg yolks lightly. Beat egg whites until firm peaks form; gradually beat in sifted icing sugar. Fold in egg yolks, then whipped cream; stir in vanilla. Pour into freezer trays; freeze until set.
Serves 6.

Passionfruit Icecream Slice

2 tablespoons cornflour
2 tablespoons flour
3 teaspoons grated lemon rind
1 cup lemon juice
1½ cups water

1¼ cups sugar
90 g (3 oz.) butter
4 passionfruit
2 egg yolks
1 litre (1¾ pints) vanilla icecream

Put sifted cornflour and flour into saucepan with lemon rind. Gradually add lemon juice and water; blend until smooth; add sugar; mix well. Stir over medium heat until mixture boils and thickens; reduce heat; simmer 5 minutes. Add butter; stir until melted. Add passionfruit pulp; mix well. Remove from heat; stir in lightly-beaten egg yolks. Return to heat; stir over low heat 2 minutes; cool completely. When cold, spoon half the lemon mixture over base of 28 cm x 18 cm (11 in. x 7 in.) shallow cake tin which has been lined with greased aluminium foil; bring foil 5 cm (2 in.) above sides; this makes it easy to remove slide from tin. Return to freezer; freeze until firm.
Soften icecream; spread evenly over lemon mixture; freeze until firm. Spoon rest of lemon mixture over icecream; freeze until firm. To serve, cut in slices.
Serves 6 to 8.

Liqueur Icecream

5 eggs
¾ cup sugar
1¼ cups cream

2 tablespoons Cointreau
¼ cup sugar, extra

Place eggs and the ¾ cup sugar in top of double saucepan. Beat over hot water until the sugar dissolves and mixture is lukewarm. Remove from heat; beat until thick and creamy. Whip cream and extra sugar until firm. Fold egg mixture and Cointreau into cream; combine well.
Spoon mixture into freezer tray. Freeze until firm, stirring occasionally.
Serves 6.
NOTE: Other liqueurs can be used in place of the Cointreau; Creme de Menthe is delicious, too.

Irish Coffee Icecream

4 egg yolks
½ cup castor sugar
1 tablespoon instant coffee powder

2 tablespoons Irish whisky (or other whisky)
300 ml (½ pint) cream

Beat egg yolks, sugar and coffee powder in top of double boiler over hot water until thick and creamy. Remove from heat. When cold, fold in whisky and whipped cream. Spoon into refrigerator tray; freeze until set.
This is a beautifully soft-textured icecream. Top each serving, if desired, with whipped cream.
Serves 4.

French Custard Icecream

½ cup sugar
3 egg yolks
½ cup milk
2 teaspoons vanilla

1 teaspoon gelatine
2 teaspoons hot water
1½ cups cream

Sprinkle gelatine over water; dissolve over hot water. Beat egg yolks and sugar until light and fluffy; add milk and vanilla; combine well. Put custard mixture in top of double saucepan over simmering water; stir until custard becomes thick and coats back of wooden spoon. Remove from heat; add gelatine; beat with rotary beater until custard becomes lukewarm. Add cream; mix well.
Pour mixture into freezer tray; freeze until firm. Spoon icecream mixture into small bowl of electric mixer; beat on high speed until light and fluffy. Pour back into freezer tray; freeze until firm.
Serves 4 to 6.

Italian Gelato

1¼ cups pure icing sugar
½ cup lemon juice
3 cups water

2 egg whites
¼ cup pure icing sugar, extra

Put icing sugar, lemon juice and water into saucepan. Stir over low heat until sugar has dissolved. Bring to boil; boil uncovered 15 minutes; allow to cool. Pour into refrigerator trays and leave to freeze overnight. Beat egg-whites until firm peaks form; gradually beat in extra sifted icing sugar. Spoon in lemon mixture; beat 5 minutes until mixture is smooth and white. Return to freezer trays; freeze overnight until the mixture is firm.
Serves 4 to 6.

Hot Desserts

These are desserts the family will hurry home to in the cold winter weather. Or, at other times of the year, these desserts provide the perfect balance to a light meal.

German Plum Tart

2¼ cups self-raising flour
pinch salt
60 g (2 oz.) butter
¼ cup castor sugar
1 egg

⅓ cup milk
2 x 825 g (1 lb. 13 oz.) cans
 dark plums
castor sugar, extra

Sift flour and salt into large mixing bowl; rub in butter until mixture resembles fine breadcrumbs; stir in sugar; mix well. Mix with lightly-beaten egg and enough milk to make a soft dough. Knead lightly. Roll pastry out on lightly-floured surface to line base and sides of 20 cm (8 in.) or 23 cm (9 in.) flan tin.

Drain plums; remove stones and cut in half. Arrange plums decoratively over pastry, cut side up. Bake in hot oven 20 to 30 minutes. Remove from oven; sprinkle tart generously with extra castor sugar. Serve hot with cream.

Serves 6.

NOTE: When in season, fresh plums can be substituted for the canned plums; or other canned fruit, such as apricots or peaches, can be substituted.

Caramel Baked Apples

6 green apples
1½ teaspoons cinnamon
1 cup brown sugar, lightly
 packed

2 tablespoons plain flour
1½ cups water
30 g (1 oz.) butter

Core apples; do not peel. Make a slit around centre of apples, so that apples do not burst during cooking. Place apples in ovenproof dish. Sprinkle over combined cinnamon, sugar and flour. Add water to pan; place a piece of butter on top of each apple. Bake uncovered in moderate oven 1 hour or until apples are tender. Stir sauce occasionally during cooking time.

Serves 6.

German Plum Tart — sugar-topped plums top a delicious cake pastry. Serve it warm, with cream.

Upside-Down Caramel Banana Cake

185 g (6 oz.) butter
¾ cup castor sugar
2 eggs
1 teaspoon vanilla

⅓ cup coconut
2 cups self-raising flour
pinch salt
½ cup milk

Upside-Down Topping

60 g (2 oz.) butter
½ cup brown sugar

2 large bananas

Beat butter and sugar until light and creamy. Add eggs one at a time, beating well after each addition; mix in vanilla. Stir in coconut. Fold in sifted dry ingredients alternately with milk.

Upside-Down Topping: Blend softened butter with brown sugar; do not overmix. Spread over base of greased deep 20 cm (8 in.) round cake tin. Arrange sliced bananas decoratively over brown sugar mixture. Spread cake mixture over. Bake in moderate oven 55 to 60 minutes or until cooked when tested. Stand in tin 5 minutes before turning out on serving plate. Serve hot with custard.

Serves 6.

Hot Apricots with Sour Cream

470 g (15 oz.) can apricot
halves
½ cup sugar
2 tablespoons self-raising
flour

1 cup sour cream
1 egg
1 teaspoon vanilla

Topping

2 tablespoons sugar
1 teaspoon cinnamon

2 teaspoons butter

Combine sugar and flour; add sour cream, egg and vanilla; beat until smooth. Drain apricots. Put apricots in base of 20 cm (8 in.) pie plate. Spoon the sour cream mixture over. Bake in moderate oven 35 minutes. Remove from oven; sprinkle with topping. Return to oven for 10 minutes.

Topping: Combine sugar and cinnamon. Rub in the butter.

Serves 4.

Rum Plums with Cinnamon Cream

2 x 825 g (1 lb. 13 oz.) cans
dark plums
2.5 cm (1 in.) piece
cinnamon stick
4 whole cloves

2 tablespoons rum
1 cup cream
2 teaspoons sugar
cinnamon

Drain plums; reserve syrup. Cut plums in half; place in bowl. Place syrup in pan with cinnamon stick and cloves; bring to boil. Reduce heat; simmer uncovered 5 minutes; remove from heat. Add rum; stir until combined; strain syrup over plums.

Spoon plums with syrup into serving bowls. Place cream and sugar in bowl; beat until soft peaks form. Spoon on top of plums; sprinkle with a little cinnamon.

Serves 4.

Coconut Peach Pudding

2 x 425 g (14 oz.) cans
unsweetened pie
peaches
¼ cup sugar
90 g (3 oz.) butter
¼ cup sugar, extra

1 teaspoon vanilla
2 eggs
½ cup self-raising flour
½ cup coconut
1 tablespoon castor sugar

In small saucepan combine pie peaches with sugar; stir over low heat until sugar has dissolved. Transfer to greased ovenproof dish. Cream butter, extra sugar and vanilla until light and creamy. Add eggs one at a time, beating well after each addition. Stir in sifted flour; mix thoroughly. Spoon mixture evenly over pie peaches.

Combine coconut with castor sugar; sprinkle evenly on top. Bake in moderate oven 50 to 55 minutes or until cooked. Serve with custard or cream.

Serves 4 to 6.

Boiled Date Pudding

1.5 kg (3 lb.) dates
185 g (6 oz.) butter
1 cup brown sugar, firmly
packed
2 cups water
¼ teaspoon salt
½ teaspoon bicarbonate of
soda
3 eggs
2 teaspoons grated orange
rind

2 teaspoons grated lemon
rind
2 cups fresh white bread-
crumbs
1 small apple
1 small carrot
1 cup plain flour
1 teaspoon cinnamon
½ teaspoon nutmeg
½ teaspoon mixed spice
¼ cup rum

Put 750 g (1½ lb.) roughly-chopped dates, butter, sugar, water and salt into large saucepan. Stir over low heat until butter has melted; bring to boil. Reduce heat; simmer uncovered 8 minutes stirring continually. Remove from heat; stir in soda. Allow to stand until mixture is completely cold.

Stir in lightly-beaten eggs, orange rind, lemon rind, grated carrot, peeled and grated apple and rum. Add sifted dry ingredients and remaining chopped dates; mix until well combined. Put mixture into centre of floured pudding cloth; tie corners and sides of cloth securely.

Put into large boiler of boiling water; boil rapidly covered 4 to 4½ hours. Replenish with more boiling water approx. every 20 minutes as water evaporates; water must never go off the boil. Allow pudding to dry completely before removing cloth. Serve hot or cold with custard or cream.

Serves 6 to 8.

NOTE: See section on Christmas Cookery for correct way to boil a pudding.

Baked Rice Custard

2 tablespoons short-grain rice	⅓ cup sugar
	1 teaspoon vanilla
2 cups water	2½ cups milk
pinch salt	¼ cup sultanas
3 eggs	cinnamon or nutmeg

Bring water and salt to the boil. Gradually add rice. Boil rapidly uncovered 10 minutes; drain well. Beat eggs, sugar and vanilla together; add rice and sultanas. Add milk gradually; stir to combine.

Pour into ovenproof dish. Sprinkle with cinnamon or nutmeg. Stand in baking dish with enough water to come halfway up sides of dish. Bake in moderate oven 35 minutes. After this time, slip a long fork under the skin that has formed on top; stir gently to distribute rice evenly through custard. Reduce heat to moderately slow; bake a further 15 minutes and stir with fork again. Cook a further 15 to 20 minutes, or until custard is set.

Serves 4.

French Apple Pudding

1 cup apricot jam	1 cup castor sugar
2 tablespoons brandy	2 eggs
1 tablespoon lemon juice	1 cup milk
2 tablespoons grated lemon rind	3 cups self-raising flour
	3 green apples
125 g (4 oz.) butter	

Combine jam, lemon juice and brandy in saucepan. Bring to boil, stirring; reduce heat; simmer 2 minutes. Cool. Pour into greased 2 litre (approx. 4 pint) pudding basin. Cream butter and sugar until light and creamy. Stir in lemon rind. Add eggs; beat well. Gradually beat in milk. Sift flour and fold through creamed mixture.

Peel, core and roughly chop apples. Add to pudding mixture. Spoon over apricot mixture. Cover with foil and steam 3½–4 hours. Serve warm with cream or custard.

Serves 8–10.

Flambe Strawberries

1 lemon	2 punnets strawberries
2 oranges	½ cup brandy
½ cup sugar	

Remove rind from the oranges and lemon in large strips, taking care not to include any of the white pith; squeeze lemon and oranges. Put sugar, lemon and orange rinds and juice in saucepan; cook slowly 5 minutes, pressing rinds with spoon to extract all flavour possible. Remove rinds.

Add the hulled strawberries to pan; spoon syrup gently over strawberries until they are coated with it. Warm brandy; pour over strawberries; set aflame. Serve with cream, or spoon over vanilla icecream.

Serves 6.

Peaches in Port

825 g (1 lb. 10 oz.) can peach halves	½ cup sugar
	1 tablespoon lemon juice
½ cup port	¼ teaspoon cinnamon
½ cup bottled red currant jelly	¼ cup brandy

Combine port, red currant jelly, sugar, lemon juice and cinnamon in frying pan. Stir over medium heat until sugar has dissolved. Bring to boil; add drained peach halves. Reduce heat; simmer 5 minutes. Add brandy; set aflame. Serve with cream or icecream.

Serves 4.

Apple Fritters

3 apples	flour
½ cup dry white wine	oil for deep-frying
1 tablespoon brown sugar	½ cup sugar
1 teaspoon grated lemon rind	1 teaspoon cinnamon

Peel and core apples; cut into 1 cm (½ in.) slices. Put apple slices into bowl; add wine, brown sugar and lemon rind; stir well. Cover; refrigerate overnight.

Drain apple slices; dust lightly with flour; dip in batter; allow excess batter to drain off; deep-fry in hot oil until golden brown and cooked. Drain; toss in combined sugar and cinnamon.

Batter: Sift 1 cup plain flour, 1 tablespoon sugar and 1 teaspoon cinnamon into bowl; gradually add ¾ cup water; beat until smooth. Beat one egg white until firm peaks form; lightly fold into batter; mix until smooth.

Serves 4.

Hot Rum-Cherry Pancakes

Pancakes

½ cup plain flour	1 egg
pinch salt	¾ cup milk

Batter

1 cup plain flour	pinch salt
1 tablespoon oil	2 egg whites
¾ cup water	

Filling

250 g (8 oz.) packaged cream cheese	½ cup cream
	2 teaspoons rum
1 teaspoon grated lemon rind	470 g (15 oz.) can black cherries
2 tablespoons sugar	oil for deep-frying

Cherry Rum Sauce

30 g (1 oz.) butter	1 teaspoon lemon juice
2 tablespoons sugar	1 tablespoon water
2 tablespoons rum	1 teaspoon cornflour

Pancakes: Sift flour and salt into bowl; make well in centre. Add whole egg; work in flour from sides; add milk a little at a time. Beat well until bubbles rise to surface; stand 1 hour. Heat pan; grease lightly. From small jug pour 2 to 3 tablespoons of batter into pan; cook slowly, loosening edges with knife, until set and lightly browned underneath. Toss or turn; brown on other side.
  Makes 6.

Batter: Sift flour and salt into bowl; add oil and water; mix to a smooth batter. Just before using, fold in softly-beaten egg whites.

Filling: Place cream cheese, lemon rind and sugar in bowl; beat until soft and creamy. Put cream into bowl; beat until soft peaks form. Fold cream and rum into cream cheese mixture. Drain cherries; reserve syrup. Fold well-drained cherries into cheese mixture. Divide filling evenly between pancakes; fold into envelope shape, brushing last fold with some of the prepared batter to hold it firm. Dip pancakes into prepared batter; place in deep hot oil; fry until golden brown; drain on absorbent paper. Serve immediately with prepared Cherry Rum Sauce.

Cherry Rum Sauce: Heat butter in frying pan; add sugar; stir until sugar is bubbling. Add rum and set aflame. When flames die down, add lemon juice and 1 cup of the reserved cherry syrup; stir until combined. Combine water and cornflour; add to sauce; stir until sauce boils and thickens. Simmer, uncovered, 5 minutes.
  Serves 6.

NOTE: The amount of syrup in a can of cherries varies, according to the individual brands. If can does not contain 1 cup syrup, make up to 1 cup with extra water.

Hot Strawberry Souffle

2 punnets strawberries	1 cup milk
2 tablespoons castor sugar	½ cup castor sugar, extra
1 teaspoon cinnamon	1 teaspoon grated orange rind
125 g (4 oz.) butter	1 tablespoon brandy
4 tablespoons plain flour	4 eggs, separated

Strawberry Ripple Cream

300 ml (½ pint) double cream	1 tablespoon castor sugar
	¼ teaspoon vanilla

Wash, hull and dry strawberries. Reserve 6 strawberries for Strawberry Ripple Cream. Halve remaining strawberries; divide between 6 individual souffle dishes. Sprinkle half the combined cinnamon and castor sugar over strawberries.

Melt butter in top of double saucepan over simmering water; remove pan from heat. Add flour; stir until combined. Add milk, extra castor sugar, orange rind and brandy; stir until combined. Return pan over simmering water; stir until mixture is thick; remove from heat. Allow to cool slightly.

Beat egg yolks until thick and creamy; gently fold into souffle mixture. Beat egg whites until soft peaks form; fold in gently. Place souffle dishes on oven tray. Slowly pour souffle mixture over strawberries in each souffle dish.

Bake in moderate oven 15 minutes or until golden brown. Remove from oven; sprinkle with remaining cinnamon mixture. Serve immediately. Serve Strawberry Ripple Cream separately.

Strawberry Ripple Cream: Mash reserved strawberries well. Place cream, sugar and vanilla in bowl; beat until soft peaks form. Gently fold mashed strawberries through cream.
  Serves 6.

Delicious Fruit Pudding

1 cup mixed fruit	1 teaspoon bicarbonate of soda
½ cup sugar	
60 g (2 oz.) butter	1 cup self-raising flour
1 cup water	

Place fruit, sugar, butter and water in pan. Stir over low heat until butter has melted; simmer mixture 5 minutes, stirring occasionally. Remove from heat; stir in sifted soda and sifted flour; mix well. Put into well-greased 1 litre (4 cup) pudding basin. Cover; steam 2 hours; replenish saucepan with boiling water every 20 minutes.
  Serves 4.

Hot Rum-Cherry Pancakes

Breads, Buns & Scones

Many people these days are finding it easy and economical to bake their own bread. In this section we give some of our best recipes, plus favourite ways with scones.

Swedish Rye Bread

2 cups rye flour	1 teaspoon brown sugar,
2 cups white plain flour	extra
2 teaspoons salt	1 cup milk
1 tablespoon brown sugar	½ cup water
½ cup bran	2 tablespoons treacle
½ cup wheatgerm	½ cup rye flour, extra
30 g (1 oz.) fresh	
yeast	

Sift flours and salt into large bowl. Add brown sugar, bran and wheatgerm; mix well. Cream yeast with extra sugar; add ½ cup lukewarm milk; mix well. Stand covered in warm place approx. 15 minutes or until frothy. Combine remaining milk, water and treacle in saucepan; stir over low heat until lukewarm. Add to dry ingredients with yeast mixture; mix to a firm dough. Put extra rye flour on board; put dough on this; knead well, kneading in extra flour. Put into lightly-oiled bowl; stand covered in warm place until dough has doubled in bulk, approx. 40 minutes.

Punch dough down; turn out of bowl on to board lightly dusted with rye flour; knead 5 minutes. Divide dough in half; knead into two round shapes; put on to two greased oven trays; stand covered in warm place 15 minutes. Brush top of bread with cold water; sprinkle with sifted rye flour; make several slits on top of bread. Bake in hot oven 15 minutes; reduce heat to moderately hot; bake a further 15 minutes or until bread sounds hollow when tapped on base.

Swedish Rye Bread — a good, firm-textured loaf with excellent flavour.

Wholemeal Bread

30 g (1 oz.) fresh yeast	½ cup full cream milk powder
2 cups warm water	30 g (1 oz.) butter
½ teaspoon salt	1½ cups white plain flour
2 tablespoons honey or treacle	3 cups wholemeal plain flour

Crumble yeast into bowl; gradually add water, mixing until yeast is dissolved; add salt, honey, melted butter and milk powder; whisk until smooth. Sprinkle 1 teaspoon plain flour over yeast mixture; cover bowl; stand in warm place 15 minutes or until yeast starts to bubble. Gradually beat in sifted white flour, beating well. Sift wholemeal flour; return any husks in sifter to flour. Gradually add wholemeal flour to batter mixture, beating well. Mixture should form a soft ball. Turn dough out on to well-floured surface; knead 5 minutes. Place in lightly-oiled bowl; cover; stand in warm place 35 to 40 minutes.

Punch dough down and knead again 5 minutes. Cut bread dough in half; knead one half into oblong shape; place in greased 23 cm x 12 cm (9 in. x 5 in.) loaf tin. Remaining dough can be made into another loaf or cut into eight equal portions and formed into bread rolls. Place bread in warm place until dough rises almost to top of tin, or until bread rolls are almost double in size. Brush tops with water; sprinkle, if desired, with poppy seeds or sesame seeds. To bake bread, bake in hot oven 20 minutes; reduce heat to moderate; bake a further 25 minutes or until cooked. To cook rolls, bake in hot oven 15 to 20 minutes.

Four Flour Bread

30 g (1 oz.) fresh yeast	⅓ cup gluten flour
⅓ cup brown sugar	½ cup soy flour
3¾ cups lukewarm water	¾ cup rye flour
1 kg (2 lb.) wholemeal plain flour	3 teaspoons salt
	⅔ cup rolled oats
	½ cup safflower oil

Cream yeast with 1 teaspoon of the brown sugar; add ¾ cup of the lukewarm water. Let stand in a warm place 10 to 15 minutes, until frothy. Sift flours and salt into large bowl; return husks in sifter to bowl. Mix in remaining brown sugar and oats. Make well in centre of dry ingredients; gradually stir in yeast mixture, oil and remaining water; beat well. Cover; set aside in warm place until dough has about half-doubled in bulk, approx. 30 minutes. (If allowed to fully double in bulk, as is usual with most breads, this bread loses a lot of its good texture.)

Knead dough; cut in half; knead each half well 5 minutes. Cut each of these halves in half again; knead into smooth round shapes. Put two rounds side by side into greased 23 cm x 12 cm (9 in. x 5 in.) loaf tins. Stand in warm place about 15 minutes or until dough rises to within 1 cm (½ in.) of edge of tins. Brush top of bread with water.

Bake in hot oven 20 minutes; reduce heat to moderately hot; bake a further 20 to 25 minutes or until cooked. Turn on to wire racks to cool.

Health Bread

2 cups wholemeal self-raising flour	pinch salt
1 cup stoneground wholemeal flour	1 egg
	1 tablespoon honey
	1½ cups milk

Put egg and honey into bowl; gradually add milk, beating well. Sift self-raising flour. Add egg mixture to combined dry ingredients; mix well. Spoon mixture into greased and greased-paper-lined 23 cm x 12 cm (9 in. x 5 in.) loaf tin. Cover with aluminium foil with a 2.5 cm (1 in.) pleat down centre to allow expansion; press foil firmly around rim of tin to seal completely. Pierce top of foil once with skewer. Bake in moderately hot oven 1½ hours. Remove foil; bake a further 15 minutes or until firm on top.

Boston Brown Bread

1¼ cups cornmeal	1 teaspoon salt
1 cup wholemeal plain flour	½ cup treacle
1 cup rye flour	1 tablespoon castor sugar
1 teaspoon bicarbonate of soda	1½ cups milk
	1 teaspoon vinegar
	¾ cup raisins

Sift flours, soda and salt into large mixing bowl; stir in cornmeal. Add treacle, sugar, combined milk and vinegar and chopped raisins to flour mixture; mix well to combine all ingredients. Grease 3 x 500 g (1-lb.) coffee tins; line bases with greased greaseproof paper. Spoon mixture evenly into tins. Place two thicknesses of greased greaseproof paper over top of tins. Place rounds of aluminium foil over this; tie securely with string. Place tins upright in large saucepan; add enough cold water to come half-way up sides of tins. Cover pan; bring to boil; boil rapidly 2 hours, replenishing water when needed. Remove breads from saucepan; cool slightly in tins; turn on to wire rack to cool completely.

Banana Bread

¼ cup milk	1 cup sugar
1 teaspoon lemon juice	2 cups self-raising flour
250 g (8 oz.) bananas	2 eggs
(approx. 2 bananas)	60 g (2 oz.) butter

Combine milk and lemon juice. Peel and mash bananas; put into bowl of electric mixer. Add sugar, sifted flour, lightly-beaten eggs, softened butter and combined milk and lemon juice. Beat on low speed until combined, then beat on medium speed 2 minutes. Turn mixture into greased 23 cm x 12 cm (9 in. x 5 in.) loaf tin which has the base lined with greased greaseproof paper. Bake in slow oven approx. 1¾ hours or until cooked when tested. Cool in tin 10 minutes before turning out on wire rack to complete cooling.

Blender Bread

1 potato	2 cups wholemeal plain
½ cup water	flour
2 teaspoons sugar	½ cup wheatgerm
30 g (1 oz.) fresh	2 teaspoons salt
yeast	¼ cup sugar, extra
1¼ cups water, extra	1 cup skim milk powder
2 cups plain flour	90 g (3 oz.) butter
¼ cup soy flour	

Peel potato; chop roughly. Put in saucepan with water; cook covered 10 minutes or until potato is tender. Put potato and liquid in blender with sugar, yeast and extra water; blend until smooth. Sift flours, wheatgerm, salt, extra sugar and skim milk powder into large bowl; return husks in sifter to bowl. Rub in butter until mixture resembles fine breadcrumbs. Make well in centre of dry ingredients; add blended liquid; mix well. Turn dough out on to lightly-floured board; knead until smooth. Put dough into lightly-oiled bowl; stand covered in warm place 20 minutes.

Turn dough out on to lightly-floured board; knead again; divide dough in two; shape into two loaves and put in two greased 20 cm x 10 cm (8 in. x 4 in.) loaf tins. Stand covered in warm place until dough reaches edge of tins (approx. 20 minutes). Bake bread in moderately hot oven 35 to 40 minutes or until bread sounds hollow when tapped on base. Turn bread out of tins and cool on wire rack.

Wholemeal Raisin Bread

30 g (1 oz.) fresh	4 cups wholemeal plain
yeast	flour
½ cup brown sugar, lightly	1 teaspoon salt
packed	½ cup wheatgerm
2 cups milk	¾ cup raisins

Cream yeast and one teaspoon of the sugar; add ½ cup lukewarm milk; stand in warm place until frothy, approx. 10 minutes. Sift flour and salt into large bowl; return husks in sifter to bowl; fold in wheatgerm, remaining sugar and chopped raisins. Make well in centre of dry ingredients; add yeast mixture and remaining lukewarm milk. Beat with wooden spoon from centre and out towards sides of bowl; beat well until all flour has been incorporated. Turn out on to floured surface; knead well until smooth. Return to lightly-oiled bowl; cover with cloth; let stand in warm place until doubled in bulk, approx. 30 to 40 minutes. Turn out on to floured surface; knead until smooth; shape into loaf; put into lightly-oiled 23 cm x 12 cm (9 in. x 5 in.) loaf tin. Cover; let rise until dough reaches edge of tin. Brush top with water; bake in hot oven 10 minutes; reduce heat to moderately hot; bake a further 25 to 30 minutes or until cooked.

English Muffins

2 cups wholemeal plain	1¼ cups milk
flour	30 g (1 oz.) fresh
2 cups white plain flour	yeast
2 teaspoons sugar	⅓ cup lukewarm water
1½ teaspoons salt	½ cup cornmeal
1 tablespoon oil	

Sift flours, sugar and salt into bowl; return husks in sifter to bowl. Cream yeast with water; combine with lukewarm milk and oil. Make well in centre of dry ingredients; add yeast and milk mixture; mix to firm dough. Turn dough out on to lightly-floured board; knead until smooth and elastic. Place dough in lightly-oiled bowl; stand covered in warm place until dough doubles in bulk, approx. 40 minutes. Punch dough down and turn out on to board dusted with cornmeal. Roll dough out until 1 cm (½ in.) thick.

Using 10 cm (4 in.) cutter, cut into rounds. Put muffins, cornmeal-side up, about 5 cm (2 in.) apart on ungreased oven trays which have been lightly dusted with cornmeal. Cover trays lightly and stand in warm place until muffins are puffy, approx. 30 to 35 minutes. Lightly grease frying pan; arrange muffins a few at a time in frying pan; cook over low heat until muffins are golden brown on both sides; allow approx. 10 minutes each side. Cool on wire rack.

Before serving, split in half; toast each muffin half; spread with butter.

NOTE: If cooking muffins in an electric frypan, have heat set to 260°F (135°C).

Makes approx. 12.

Herbed Potato Bread

2½ cups plain flour	1 teaspoon sugar
1½ teaspoons salt	1¼ cups milk
1 teaspoon mixed herbs	2 tablespoons chopped
1 cup mashed potato	chives
30 g (1 oz.) fresh	2 tablespoons grated
yeast	parmesan cheese

Sift flour and salt into bowl; add cold mashed potato, herbs, chives and parmesan cheese; mix well. Cream yeast and sugar; add ½ cup lukewarm milk; stand in warm place 10 minutes or until frothy. Add to flour mixture with remaining lukewarm milk; mix well. Turn dough out on to well-floured board; knead 5 minutes. Put dough into lightly-oiled bowl; stand covered in warm place until dough doubles in bulk (approx. 30 minutes).

Turn dough out on to lightly-floured board; knead another 5 minutes. Shape dough into loaf shape; put into greased 23 cm x 12 cm (9 in. x 5 in.) loaf tin; stand covered in warm place until dough reaches edge of tin (approx. 20 to 30 minutes). Brush top of bread with a little milk; bake in hot oven 10 minutes; reduce heat to moderately hot; bake a further 30 to 35 minutes or until bread sounds hollow when tapped on base.

Poppy Seed Plait

Poppy Seed Plait

30 g (1 oz.) fresh	1 egg
yeast	4 cups plain flour
¼ cup sugar	125 g (4 oz.) butter
1 cup milk	1 egg, extra
2 teaspoons salt	poppy seeds

Cream yeast with sugar; add lukewarm milk and salt; let stand 10 to 15 minutes. Add well-beaten egg; mix well. Gradually add sifted flour alternately with melted, cooled butter. Turn out on to board; knead well until smooth. Put dough into lightly-oiled bowl; cover; let stand in warm place until doubled in bulk, approx. 1 hour.

Punch down; turn out on lightly-floured surface; knead until smooth. Divide dough into 3 equal portions. Roll each portion into roll 50 cm (20 in.) long and form into plait, securing at each end. Put on to large greased oven tray. Brush plait well with extra lightly-beaten egg; sprinkle with poppy seeds. Bake in hot oven 10 to 15 minutes or until golden brown; reduce heat to moderate; bake a further 15 to 20 minutes or until bread sounds hollow when tapped on base.

Herbed Potato Bread

Curried Onion Scones

60 g (2 oz.) butter	3 teaspoons curry powder
1 onion	1 egg
3 cups self-raising flour	1 cup milk
salt, pepper	milk, extra

Heat butter in pan; add peeled and chopped onion; saute until onion is tender. Sift flour, salt, pepper and curry powder into bowl. Make well in centre; add combined butter, onion, lightly-beaten egg and milk; mix to a soft dough. Turn out on lightly-floured board; knead lightly. Pat dough to 2 cm (¾ in.) thickness; cut into rounds with 5 cm (2 in.) cutter. Put on greased oven tray. Glaze tops with extra milk. Bake in hot oven 10 to 15 minutes or until cooked.

Makes approx. 16.

Herb Scones

3 cups self-raising flour	2 tablespoons chopped
salt, pepper	chives
60 g (2 oz.) butter	1 egg
2 teaspoons mixed herbs	1 cup milk
4 shallots or spring onions	milk, extra
2 tablespoons chopped parsley	

Sift flour, salt and pepper into bowl; rub in butter until mixture resembles fine breadcrumbs. Add mixed herbs, chopped shallots, parsley and chives; mix well. Make a well in centre; add combined lightly-beaten egg and milk; mix to a soft dough. Turn out on lightly-floured board; knead lightly. Pat out dough to 2 cm (¾ in.) thickness; cut into rounds with 5 cm (2 in.) cutter. Put on to greased oven tray. Glaze tops with extra milk. Bake in hot oven 10 to 15 minutes or until cooked.

Makes approx. 16.

Ham and Cheese Scones

3 cups self-raising flour	4 shallots or spring onions
salt, pepper	1 egg
60 g (2 oz.) butter	1¼ cups milk
90 g (3 oz.) cheddar cheese	milk, extra
60 g (2 oz.) ham	

Sift flour, salt and pepper into bowl; rub in butter until mixture resembles fine breadcrumbs. Add grated cheese, finely-chopped ham and chopped shallots; mix well. Make well in centre; add combined lightly-beaten egg and milk; mix to a soft dough. Turn out on floured surface; knead lightly. Pat out dough to 2 cm (¾ in.) thickness;

cut into rounds with 5 cm (2 in.) cutter. Put on to greased oven tray. Glaze tops with extra milk. Bake in hot oven 10 to 15 minutes or until cooked.

Makes approx. 16.

Orange Raisin Scones

2 cups self-raising flour	30 g (1 oz.) butter
1 tablespoon icing sugar	1 teaspoon grated orange
pinch salt	rind
1 tablespoon full cream milk powder	1 cup raisins
	¾ cup water

Sift flour, icing sugar, salt and milk powder into bowl. Rub in butter until mixture resembles fine breadcrumbs. Add orange rind and chopped raisins. Make well in centre of dry ingredients; add water; mix to a soft dough. Turn out on to a lightly-floured board; knead lightly. Roll or pat dough out to approx. 1 cm (½ in.) thick. Cut into rounds with 5 cm (2 in.) floured cutter. Place on lightly-greased oven tray; brush top of scones with a little milk. Bake in hot oven 10 to 15 minutes or until golden.

Makes approx. 12.

Lemon Crumb Scones

2 cups self-raising flour	1 teaspoon grated lemon
½ teaspoon salt	rind
60 g (2 oz.) butter	1 teaspoon lemon juice
¾ cup milk	4 tablespoons sugar

Sift flour and salt into bowl; rub in butter until mixture resembles fine breadcrumbs. Add milk; mix to a soft dough. Turn dough out on to a lightly-floured board; knead lightly. Roll or pat dough out to approx. 1 cm (½ in.) thickness. Cut into rounds with 5 cm (2 in.) floured scone cutter. Put scones on to lightly-greased oven tray; brush with milk. Combine lemon rind, lemon juice and sugar; sprinkle over scones. Bake in hot oven 12 to 15 minutes or until golden.

Makes approx. 12.

Wheatgerm Scones

3 cups self-raising flour	¾ cup milk
½ teaspoon salt	½ cup water
1 cup wheatgerm	60 g (2 oz.) butter

Sift flour and salt into bowl; add wheatgerm; mix well. Rub in butter until mixture resembles fine breadcrumbs. Combine milk and water; make well in centre of dry ingredients; add liquid; mix to a soft dough. Turn on to lightly-floured board; knead lightly; roll or pat out evenly to about

2.5 cm (1 in.) thickness; cut into rounds with floured 5 cm (2 in.) cutter. Place scones on lightly-greased oven tray; bake in hot oven 15 minutes or until golden. Remove from oven and brush with a little melted butter.

Makes approx. 15.

Cracked Wheat Bread

1¼ cups lukewarm water	4 cups plain flour, extra
30 g (1 oz.) fresh yeast	1 cup cracked wheat
1 teaspoon sugar	1 teaspoon salt
1 teaspoon plain flour	1 tablespoon sugar, extra
	60 g (2 oz.) butter

Place lukewarm water and yeast in bowl; stir until yeast is dissolved; sprinkle sugar and flour over. Cover bowl; stand in warm place 10 minutes or until mixture is frothy. Sift extra flour, salt and extra sugar into bowl; add cracked wheat; mix lightly. Add yeast mixture and melted butter; mix well. Turn out on to floured surface; knead 10 minutes. Place dough in lightly-oiled bowl; cover; stand in warm place 30 minutes or until doubled in bulk. Punch down and knead again 4 minutes. Divide dough in half. Knead each into a loaf shape. Place in two well-greased 23 cm x 12 cm (9 in. x 5 in.) loaf tins. Cover tins; leave in warm place until dough is almost to top of tins. Brush top of each loaf with a little melted butter; sprinkle extra cracked wheat over. Bake in hot oven 30 to 35 minutes or until cooked.

Wholemeal Cheese Bread

1½ cups wholemeal self-raising flour	½ cup cracked wheat
1½ cups white self-raising flour	1 egg
1 teaspoon salt	1¼ cups milk
2 teaspoons dry mustard	2 tablespoons cracked wheat, extra
90 g (3 oz.) butter	1 tablespoon sesame or poppy seeds
2 tablespoons grated parmesan cheese	30 g (1 oz.) butter, extra
2 tablespoons chopped parsley	

Sift flours, salt and mustard into large bowl; return husks in sifter to bowl. Rub in butter until mixture resembles fine breadcrumbs. Add cheese, parsley and cracked wheat to dry ingredients; mix well. Combine beaten egg and milk; make well in centre of dry ingredients; add milk mixture; mix to a soft dough.

Turn dough out on to well-floured surface; knead lightly until dough forms a soft ball. Press dough evenly into well-greased 23 cm x 12 cm (9 in. x 5 in.) loaf tin. Brush top of bread with a little extra milk; sprinkle with extra cracked wheat

and sesame seeds. Bake in moderately hot oven 10 minutes; reduce heat to moderate; bake a further 35 to 40 minutes or until cooked when tested with skewer. Brush bread with extra melted butter 10 minutes before end of cooking time.
NOTE: Cracked wheat is available from health food stores.

Irish Soda Bread

2 cups plain flour	pinch sugar
1 cup self-raising flour	30 g (1 oz.) butter
1 cup boiled sieved potato	1¼ cups buttermilk or sour milk
1 teaspoon bicarbonate of soda	1 egg
1 teaspoon salt	

Sift flours, salt and soda. Rub in butter until mixture resembles fine breadcrumbs. Add potato; mix well. Beat egg with half the buttermilk or sour milk; add to flour mixture; mix in. Add enough of the remaining milk to mix to a soft dough. Put dough into lightly-greased 20 cm (8 in.) sandwich tin. Cut a cross on top with sharp knife. Bake in moderately hot oven 30 to 40 minutes. Cool on wire rack. If soft crust is desired, brush lightly, while hot, with melted butter.

Sticky Buns

155 g (5 oz.) butter	2 large bananas
½ cup brown sugar	½ cup milk
½ cup chopped walnuts	30 g (1 oz.) butter, extra
2 cups self-raising flour	¼ cup brown sugar, extra
½ teaspoon salt	

Cream 125 g (4 oz.) of the butter and the brown sugar until light and fluffy. Spread over base of greased 20 cm (8 in.) sandwich tin. Sprinkle walnuts over butter mixture. Sift flour and salt into bowl. Rub in remaining 30 g (1 oz.) of butter; add mashed bananas; mix to soft dough with milk.

Turn on to lightly-floured board; knead well. Roll to an oblong shape; brush with extra melted butter; sprinkle with extra brown sugar; roll up. Cut into 1 cm (½ in.) slices. Place around tin, cut-side up, covering walnuts. Bake in hot oven 20 minutes or until cooked. If desired, brush top with melted butter to glaze.
NOTE: Instead of using sandwich tin, the mixture can be used to make individual buns. Spread butter-brown sugar mixture into greased deep patty tins; sprinkle with the walnuts; cut dough into just 5 mm (¼ in.) slices; fit one of the slices of dough into each patty tin. Bake in hot oven 15 to 20 minutes.

Makes 12.

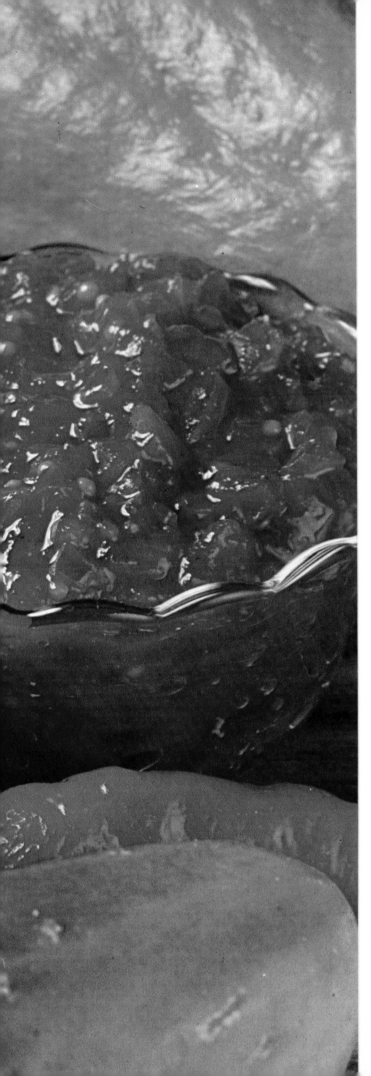

Pickles, Chutneys, Relishes & Jams

Meals gain extra interest when they're accompanied by a colourful pickle or a good flavoured chutney or relish. You'll like the special jam recipes, too.

Chilli Relish

500 g (1 lb.) tomatoes
2 cucumbers
2 red peppers
4 onions
3 red chillies
3 tablespoons salt
2 cups white vinegar
¾ cup white sugar

¾ cup brown sugar, lightly packed
1 tablespoon mustard seeds
2 teaspoons paprika
½ teaspoon chilli powder
2 tablespoons flour
½ cup water

Peel and seed tomatoes; chop finely. Peel cucumbers; cut in half lengthways; remove seeds; chop finely. Peel onions; chop finely. Seed and finely chop peppers and chillies. Put vegetables in bowl; sprinkle with the salt; stand 3 hours; drain and rinse well under cold running water.

Put vinegar, sugars and mustard seeds in saucepan; stir over low heat until sugar dissolves; increase heat; bring to boil. Add vegetables; bring back to boil. Reduce heat; simmer uncovered 5 minutes. Mix paprika, chilli powder and flour to smooth paste with the water; add to vegetable mixture; stir constantly until mixture boils and thickens. Reduce heat; simmer uncovered 20 to 25 minutes or until thick. Pour mixture into hot sterilised jars; seal.

Makes approx. 1 litre (4 cups).
NOTE: Use rubber gloves when handling and chopping the chillies; they can burn the fingers.

In front, Curried Cucumber and Pepper Pickles (see recipe overleaf); at back, Chilli Relish.

Curried Cucumber and Pepper Pickles

2 large cucumbers	3¼ cups white vinegar
1 small marrow	2 cups sugar
2 large onions	2 teaspoons curry powder
2 red peppers	1 teaspoon celery seeds
½ cup salt	1 teaspoon mustard seeds

Wash cucumbers; cut in half lengthways; remove seeds; cut into quarters, then cut into 2.5 cm (1 in.) cubes. Peel marrow; cut in half; remove core; cut into 2.5 cm (1 in.) cubes. Peel onions; cut into 2.5 cm (1 in.) cubes. Cut peppers in half; remove seeds; cut into 2.5 cm (1 in.) cubes. Put vegetables in earthenware or plastic bowl; sprinkle with the salt; stand overnight.

Next day, drain and rinse well. Combine vinegar, sugar, curry powder, celery seeds and mustard seeds. Stir over heat until sugar dissolves; bring to boil. Add drained vegetables; bring back to boil. Reduce heat; simmer 5 minutes. Pour into sterilised jars; seal immediately.

Makes approx. 2 litres (8 cups).

Marrow and Tomato Pickle

1 kg (2 lb.) ripe tomatoes	¼ teaspoon allspice
1 kg (2 lb.) marrow	¼ teaspoon ground ginger
2 onions	1 teaspoon mustard seeds
3 teaspoons salt	1¼ cups sugar
¼ teaspoon paprika	1 cup white vinegar
¼ teaspoon cinnamon	

Remove skins from tomatoes; chop roughly. Peel, core and chop marrow. Peel and finely chop onions. Combine vegetables in large saucepan with salt, paprika, cinnamon, allspice, ginger and mustard seeds. Stir over low heat; bring to boil. Reduce heat; simmer covered 30 minutes or until marrow is tender.

Place sugar and vinegar in small saucepan; stir over low heat until sugar has dissolved. Add sugar and vinegar to pan; simmer gently uncovered approx. 25 to 30 minutes or until mixture is thick. Bottle while hot.

Makes approx. 1½ litres (6 cups).

Curried Cucumber Pickles

6 medium cucumbers	2 cups sugar
3 onions	2 teaspoons curry powder
3 green or red peppers	1 teaspoon celery seeds
½ cup salt	1 teaspoon mustard
water	seeds
3¼ cups white vinegar	

Wash cucumbers; cut into 5 mm (¼ in.) slices. Peel and slice onions. Cut peppers into 1 cm (½ in.) pieces. Put vegetables in earthenware or plastic bowl; sprinkle with the salt; pour water over to cover vegetables; stand 5 hours; drain well.

Combine vinegar, sugar, curry powder, celery seeds and mustard seeds in saucepan. Stir over low heat until sugar dissolves; bring to boil. Add drained vegetables; bring back to boil. Pour into sterilised jars; seal immediately.

Makes approx. 2.5 litres (10 cups).

Sweet and Sour Pickles

2 medium cucumbers	2 cups white vinegar
2 red peppers	2 cups sugar
1 green pepper	¼ teaspoon turmeric
2 small carrots	2 teaspoons celery seeds
6 small onions	1 tablespoon mustard
¼ cauliflower	seeds
¼ cup salt	

Chop unpeeled cucumbers into 1 cm (½ in.) cubes. Seed peppers; cut into 1 cm (½ in.) cubes. Peel carrots; cut into strips. Peel onions; chop into 1 cm (½ in.) cubes. Break cauliflower into flowerets. Combine vegetables in bowl; sprinkle the salt over; let stand a few hours or overnight. Drain vegetables; rinse under cold water.

Combine in saucepan vinegar, sugar, turmeric, celery seeds and mustard seeds; stir over low heat until sugar dissolves. Bring to boil; add vegetables; bring back to boil; remove from heat immediately. Pack vegetables into hot sterilised bottles; pour over enough vinegar liquid to cover; seal.

Makes approx. 1½ litres (6 cups).

Tomato Chutney

1.5 kg (3 lb.) ripe tomatoes	2 teaspoons dry mustard
500 g (1 lb.) onions	¼ cup cornflour
¼ cup salt	¼ cup brown vinegar, extra
water	½ teaspoon nutmeg
2 cups brown malt vinegar	½ teaspoon pepper
2 cups brown sugar	½ teaspoon cinnamon
1 tablespoon curry powder	½ teaspoon ground ginger

Cut tomatoes into thick slices. Peel onions; cut in half; cut into slices. Place tomatoes and onions in large bowl; cover with water; sprinkle salt over; mix through lightly. Cover bowl; stand overnight.

Next day, drain liquid from tomatoes and onions. Place tomatoes and onions in large saucepan; add vinegar; bring to boil uncovered. Add brown sugar; stir over low heat until sugar dissolves. Combine curry powder, mustard and cornflour. Gradually add extra vinegar; mix until smooth and free of lumps. Remove pan from heat; gradually add cornflour mixture; stir until combined. Return pan to heat; stir until mixture boils. Boil uncovered 35 to 40 minutes or until chutney is of good thick consistency.

Five minutes before end of cooking time, add remaining ingredients; mix well. Stir frequently during cooking. Pour mixture into hot sterilised jars; seal.

Makes approx. 1½ litres (6 cups).

Mango Chutney

1 kg (2 lb.) tomatoes	2 cups white vinegar
2 medium onions	1 cup water
1 large cooking apple	450 g (15 oz.) can papaw
1½ cups sugar	pieces
1 tablespoon salt	560 g (1 lb. 2 oz.) can
1 teaspoon ground cloves	mango slices
¼ teaspoon cayenne	¾ cup sultanas
¼ teaspoon chilli powder	60 g (2 oz.) preserved
2 teaspoons mustard	ginger
seeds	

Skin tomatoes; chop roughly. Put in large saucepan; bring to boil. Reduce heat; simmer covered 10 to 15 minutes until soft and pulpy. Remove from heat; push mixture through fine sieve.

Return tomato puree to saucepan. Add peeled and chopped onions, peeled, cored and chopped apple, sugar and salt. Stir over low heat until sugar dissolves. Mix ground cloves, chilli powder and cayenne to a paste with a little of the vinegar. Add this to the tomato mixture with the remaining vinegar, water, mustard seeds, drained and roughly-chopped papaw and mango. Bring to the boil; reduce heat; simmer uncovered 30 minutes. Add sultanas and chopped ginger; simmer a further 30 to 40 minutes or until mixture becomes thick. Pour into hot sterilised jars; seal.

Makes approx. 1½ litres (6 cups).
NOTE: When fresh mangoes and papaw are in season, substitute 2 mangoes, peeled and roughly-chopped, and half a medium papaw, seeded and roughly-chopped, for the canned mango and papaw.

Red Pepper and Tomato Chutney

4 large red peppers	1 tablespoon mustard
500 g (1 lb.) tomatoes	seeds
4 medium onions	2 tablespoons flour
2 tablespoons salt	¼ teaspoon paprika
2 cups white vinegar	¼ teaspoon turmeric
1½ cups sugar	½ cup water

Chop seeded peppers finely; chop peeled tomatoes finely; peel onions and chop finely. Combine vegetables in bowl; sprinkle the salt over; let stand a few hours; drain.

Combine in large saucepan vinegar, sugar and mustard seeds; stir over low heat until sugar dissolves; bring to boil. Add vegetables; bring back to boil; boil 10 minutes. Combine flour, paprika and turmeric; mix to a smooth paste with the water; add to pickle mixture; stir until boiling. Reduce heat; simmer a further 10 minutes or until thick. Pour into hot sterilised jars; seal.

Makes approx. 1 litre (4 cups).
NOTE: This also makes a delicious sandwich spread.

Indian Date and Ginger Chutney

375 g (12 oz.) dates	½ cup brown sugar, firmly
60 g (2 oz.) preserved	packed
ginger	1 teaspoon chilli powder
1 cup white vinegar	1 teaspoon cinnamon
1 cup water	

Chop dates and ginger finely. Combine in saucepan vinegar, water and brown sugar; stir over low heat until sugar has dissolved. Increase heat; bring to boil; add dates, ginger, chilli powder and cinnamon. Bring back to boil; reduce heat; simmer uncovered 10 minutes or until mixture is thick. Pour mixture into hot sterilised jars; seal. Keep refrigerated.

Makes approx. 3½ cups.

Sweet Date Chutney

1 cup sugar	½ teaspoon ground cloves
1½ cups brown vinegar	½ teaspoon cinnamon
250 g (8 oz.) dates	1 clove garlic
1 teaspoon chilli powder	1 teaspoon salt
1 teaspoon ground ginger	60 g (2 oz.) sultanas
1 teaspoon dry mustard	60 g (2 oz.) unsalted
½ teaspoon ground	cashews
cardamom	

Put sugar and vinegar into pan; stir over low heat until sugar has dissolved. Stone dates; chop finely. Add to sugar and vinegar mixture with chilli powder, ginger, mustard, cardamom, cloves, cinnamon and crushed garlic. Bring to boil uncovered; reduce heat; simmer gently 30 minutes or until mixture is thick. Stir in sultanas, finely-chopped cashews and salt. Pour into hot sterilised jars; seal.

Makes approx. 1 litre (4 cups).

Curried Tomato Chutney

750 g (1½ lb.) firm tomatoes	2 cups sugar
500 g (1 lb.) onions	2 tablespoons curry powder
3 large green apples	2 tablespoons flour
¼ cup salt	2 teaspoons turmeric
3 cups white vinegar	½ cup water

Chop peeled tomatoes into 1 cm (½ in.) cubes; cut peeled onions into 1 cm (½ in.) cubes; cut peeled and cored apples into 1 cm (½ in.) cubes. Combine tomatoes, onions and apples in large bowl; sprinkle the salt over. Cover and stand a few hours or overnight.

Combine vinegar and sugar in large pan; stir over low heat until sugar dissolves. Bring to boil; add drained vegetables; bring back to boil. Reduce heat; simmer 10 minutes. Mix flour, curry powder and turmeric to smooth paste with the water; add to pan; stir until mixture boils and thickens. Reduce heat; simmer 10 minutes. Remove from heat; pour into hot sterilised jars; seal when cold.

Makes approx. 2 litres (8 cups).

Indian Aubergine Relish

2 aubergines	1 cup white vinegar
3 tablespoons salt	½ cup water
3 red peppers	⅓ cup sugar
500 g (1 lb.) onions	1 teaspoon turmeric
2 red chillies	1 teaspoon garam masala
2 cloves garlic	1 tablespoon mustard seeds
3 tablespoons oil	salt, pepper
2 tablespoons flour	

Cut aubergines into 2.5 cm (1 in.) slices; sprinkle the 3 tablespoons salt over aubergine slices; stand 30 minutes. Rinse aubergines; pat dry; cut each round into quarters. Seed peppers; cut into 2.5 cm (1 in.) cubes. Peel onions; cut into quarters. Put peppers into large saucepan of boiling water; boil uncovered 3 minutes; remove from water; rinse under cold running water. Put onions and aubergines into same saucepan of boiling water; boil uncovered 3 minutes; remove from water; drain.

Heat oil in large pan; saute crushed garlic and finely-chopped chillies 3 minutes; add prepared vegetables; saute 1 minute. Mix flour to smooth paste with vinegar; put in separate saucepan with water, sugar, turmeric, garam masala and mustard seeds. Stir over medium heat until sauce boils and thickens. Reduce heat; simmer 2 minutes; add salt and pepper. Add sauce to vegetables; stir until mixture comes to boil. Reduce heat; simmer 1 minute. Spoon into hot sterilised jars; seal.

Makes approx. 1¼ litres (5 cups).

NOTE: Garam masala (Indian mixed spice) is obtainable at most large supermarkets or food stores.

Beetroot and Apple Relish

2 bunches beetroot (approx. 10 beetroot)	5 cm (2 in.) piece cinnamon stick
2 large cooking apples	2 teaspoons ground ginger
2 onions	¼ cup flour
2 cups white vinegar	½ cup water, extra
1 cup water	
1 cup sugar	

Peel beetroot; cut off stems; chop beetroot into 1 cm (½ in.) cubes. Peel and core apples; chop into 1 cm (½ in.) cubes. Peel onions; chop roughly. Put vinegar, water and sugar into large saucepan; stir over medium heat until sugar dissolves; bring to boil. Add beetroot, apples, onions and cinnamon stick; bring back to boil. Reduce heat; simmer covered 40 minutes; remove cinnamon stick.

Mix flour and ginger to a smooth paste with the extra water; gradually add to beetroot mixture, stirring all the time; stir until boiling. Reduce heat; simmer uncovered 40 to 50 minutes or until thick. Pour into hot sterilised jars; seal.

Makes approx. 1½ litres (6 cups).

Spiced Pears

4 cups white vinegar	5 cm (2 in.) piece cinnamon stick
2 cups water	8 whole allspice
5 cm (2 in.) strip lemon rind	5 cm (2 in.) piece green ginger
5 cm (2 in.) strip orange rind	2 cups sugar
12 peppercorns	8 firm pears
6 whole cloves	

Place vinegar, water, lemon rind, orange rind, peppercorns, cloves, cinnamon stick, allspice, sugar and peeled and very thinly-sliced ginger in large pan. Stir over low heat until sugar dissolves. Bring to boil; reduce heat; simmer uncovered 5 minutes. Add pears which have been peeled, quartered and had seeds removed. Simmer uncovered 5 minutes. Place pears in hot sterilised jars; pour liquid over; seal.

Delicious as an accompaniment to pork or chicken.

Fig Jam — recipe overleaf

Fig Jam

500 g (1 lb.) dried figs	1/3 cup lemon juice
1 litre (4 cups) water	2 teaspoons grated lemon
3 cups sugar	rind

Chop figs roughly. Put figs and water into bowl; allow to stand overnight. Next day, put figs with water into large pan; bring to boil. Reduce heat; simmer covered 30 to 35 minutes or until figs are tender.

Put sugar in large baking dish; place in moderate oven 7 minutes or until sugar is warm. Add sugar to fig mixture with lemon juice and lemon rind; stir over low heat until sugar dissolves. Bring to boil; boil uncovered 15 to 20 minutes or until jam jells when tested on a cold saucer; stir jam occasionally during cooking time to prevent sticking. Pour into hot sterilised jars; seal.

Makes approx. 3 cups.

Orange Pineapple Jam

3 oranges	3 passionfruit
1½ litres (6 cups) water	1.5 kg (3 lb.) sugar
1 small pineapple	

Slice unpeeled oranges thinly. Put orange slices and water into bowl; allow to stand overnight. Next day, put oranges and water into large pan; bring to boil. Reduce heat; simmer uncovered approx. 10 minutes or until orange rind is tender. Peel pineapple; remove hard core; cut pineapple into pieces. Add pineapple to pan; simmer covered a further 20 minutes.

Put sugar into baking dish; put in moderate oven 7 minutes or until sugar is warm. Add sugar to orange and pineapple mixture with passionfruit pulp; stir over low heat until sugar dissolves. Bring to boil; boil uncovered approx. 35 minutes or until jam jells when tested on cold saucer; stir jam occasionally during cooking time. Pour into hot, sterilised jars; seal.

Makes approx. 1¼ litres (5 cups).

Raspberry Jam

750 g (1½ lb.) frozen	1 tablespoon grated lemon
raspberries	rind
2 cups sugar	1 tablespoon rum or sherry

Put thawed raspberries and their liquid in pan; add sugar and lemon rind. Stir over low heat until sugar dissolves; bring to boil. Boil rapidly uncovered approx. 25 minutes or until jam jells when tested on a cold saucer. Stir in rum; pour into hot, sterilised jars; seal.

Makes approx. 2 cups.

Peach and Passionfruit Jam

2 kg (4 lb.) firm peaches	½ cup lemon juice
(approx. 12 large	3 cups water
peaches)	2 kg (4 lb.) sugar
½ cup passionfruit pulp	
(approx. 4 passionfruit)	

Remove skin and stones from peaches. Chop peaches roughly. Place peaches, passionfruit pulp, lemon juice and water in large pan; bring to boil. Reduce heat; simmer covered 30 minutes or until peaches are very tender. Using a potato masher, mash peaches roughly.

Place sugar in baking dish; place in moderate oven 7 minutes or until sugar is warm. Add sugar to peach mixture; stir over low heat until sugar dissolves; increase heat; bring to boil. Boil uncovered 25 to 30 minutes or until jam jells when tested. Pour into hot sterilised jars; seal.

Makes approx. 2¼ litres (9 cups).

Tomato Jam

1.5 kg (3 lb.) tomatoes	1 tablespoon grated lemon
500 g (1 lb.) apples	rind
(approx. 3 medium	1/3 cup lemon juice
apples)	1.25 kg (2½ lb.) sugar

Skin tomatoes and cut into thin slices. Put tomatoes, peeled, cored and thinly-sliced apples and grated lemon rind into large saucepan; cover; bring to boil. Reduce heat; simmer 30 minutes.

Put sugar into baking dish; place in moderate oven 7 minutes. Add sugar and lemon juice to tomato mixture; stir until sugar is dissolved. Bring to boil. Boil uncovered approx. 40 to 45 minutes or until jam jells when tested on a cold saucer. Stir jam occasionally during cooking time. Pour into hot sterilised jars; seal.

Makes approx. 1.5 litres (6 cups).

Lemon Butter

4 eggs	2 teaspoons grated lemon
¾ cup sugar	rind
½ cup lemon juice	125 g (4 oz.) butter
¼ cup water	

Put beaten eggs and sugar into top of double saucepan; stir until combined. Gradually add lemon juice and water; stir until combined. Add lemon rind and roughly-chopped butter; place pan over simmering water; stir until mixture thickly coats wooden spoon. Pour into hot sterilised jars; seal. Store in refrigerator.

Makes approx. 3 cups.

Apricot and Orange Jam

250 g (8 oz.) dried apricots	1¾ litres (7 cups) water
4 oranges	1.25 kg (2½ lb.) sugar
	2 tablespoons lemon juice

Cut unpeeled oranges in half lengthways; slice each half thinly. Roughly chop apricots. Put oranges and apricots in large saucepan; add the water. Bring to boil; reduce heat; simmer covered 30 to 40 minutes or until oranges and apricots are tender.

Place sugar in large baking dish; put in moderate oven 7 minutes, or until sugar is warm. Add warmed sugar to pan; stir until dissolved; add lemon juice. Bring to boil; boil rapidly uncovered 45 to 55 minutes or until jam jells when tested. Pour into sterilised jars; seal.

Makes approx. 1¾ litres (7 cups).

Pineapple and Lemon Jam

470 g (15 oz.) can pineapple pieces	4 lemons
	1½ cups sugar

Peel lemons; remove white pith. Cut lemons in half; remove seeds. Put lemons in blender with undrained pineapple pieces. Blend on high speed 30 seconds.

Put mixture in pan; add sugar; stir over low heat until sugar dissolves. Bring to boil; boil uncovered approx. 20 minutes or until jam is thick, stirring occasionally to prevent sticking. Pour into sterilised jars; seal. Jam will thicken on standing.

Makes approx. 2 cups.

Brandied Peaches

1.5 kg (3 lb.) peaches	2 cups brandy
water	

Light Sugar Syrup

2 cups sugar	1¼ litres (5 cups) water

Spiced Sugar Syrup

4 cups sugar	6 whole cloves
1 litre (4 cups) water	8 whole allspice
15 cm (6 in.) cinnamon stick	

First blanch peaches by placing them a few at a time in a pan and covering with cold water. Slowly heat the water, and when peaches rise to the surface, remove with a perforated spoon. Repeat with the rest of the peaches. When cool, skin carefully.

Soak skinned peaches for an hour in cold water, drain, then put in the prepared Light Sugar Syrup. Leave, covered, in a cool place for 4 days.

After peaches have been 'candied', drain carefully. Prepare Spiced Sugar Syrup; add brandy, stirring well, as soon as syrup is removed from the heat. Place drained peaches into hot sterilised jars and divide the syrup between them. Seal. Allow to stand for 2 weeks before using.

Light Sugar Syrup: Place sugar and water in large pan; stir over low heat until sugar is dissolved; remove pan from heat.

Spiced Sugar Syrup: Place sugar, water, cinnamon stick, cloves and allspice in large pan; stir over heat until sugar is dissolved; bring to boil. Reduce heat; simmer 3 minutes; remove pan from heat.

NOTE: If bottling peaches in several jars, break cinnamon stick into pieces so that you can add a piece to each jar.

Marmalade

6 oranges	1.5 litres (6 cups) water
2 lemons	1.25 kg (2½ lb.) sugar

Cut fruit into quarters. Cut each quarter into thin slices. Put fruit into large bowl; add water; cover bowl; allow to stand overnight. Next day, put fruit with water into large pan; bring to boil; reduce heat; simmer covered 20 minutes or until rind is very tender. Put sugar into baking dish; place in moderate oven 7 minutes. Add sugar to fruit mixture; stir until dissolved. Bring to boil; boil uncovered 25 to 30 minutes or until jam jells when tested on cold saucer. Pour into hot, sterilised jars; seal.

Makes approx. 2 litres (8 cups).

NOTE: If desired, ¼ cup whisky or brandy can be stirred into the hot jam just before bottling.

Grapefruit and Ginger Jam

2 large grapefruit	60 g (2 oz.) preserved ginger
5 cups sugar	
470 g (15 oz.) can crushed pineapple	1½ litres (6 cups) water

Cut unpeeled grapefruit in half; slice each half thinly. Put grapefruit in saucepan with the water. Bring to boil; reduce heat; simmer covered 20 minutes.

Place sugar in large baking dish; put in moderate oven 7 minutes, or until sugar is warm. Add to grapefruit the warmed sugar, undrained pineapple and chopped ginger. Stir over medium heat until sugar dissolves. Increase heat; bring to boil; boil uncovered 50 to 60 minutes or until jam jells when tested. Pour into hot sterilised jars; seal.

Makes approx. 1½ litres (6 cups).

Christmas Cookery

Christmas dinner — it's probably the year's most important meal! Here is how to cook every important item, food you'll be proud to present. And there's lots of extras to offer to guests who drop in during the holiday period.

Mince Pies

Pastry

2 cups plain flour	1 egg yolk
½ teaspoon baking powder	1 to 2 teaspoons water
155 g (5 oz.) butter	1 teaspoon lemon juice
pinch salt	

Filling

411 g (14½ oz.) mincemeat	1 tablespoon milk
1 egg, separated	castor sugar

Sift dry ingredients; rub in butter until mixture resembles dry breadcrumbs. Mix in lightly-beaten egg yolk, lemon juice and water to form a firm dough. Turn on to lightly-floured surface; knead lightly. Roll out pastry to 5 mm (¼ in.) thickness; cut out 6 cm (2½ in.) rounds with floured plain or fluted cutter. Fit pastry rounds into lightly-greased patty tins.

Place about a teaspoonful of mincemeat in each pastry case. Brush pastry edges with lightly-beaten egg white; place second round of pastry on top; press edges together gently. Brush tops of pies with combined lightly-beaten egg yolk and milk; sprinkle with sugar. Cut two slits in top of each pie to allow steam to escape. Bake in moderate oven 25 to 30 minutes or until pies are golden brown.
Makes approx. 12.

Chocolate Rum Fruits

250 g (8 oz.) mixed glace fruits	¼ cup rum
	125 g (4 oz.) dark chocolate

Chop fruit into bite-size pieces; place in bowl. Add rum; mix well; cover; leave 1 hour or overnight. Drain fruit; place on absorbent paper;

Recipe continued overleaf:

Mince Pies — make them for the family or when guests drop in; they also make an ideal small gift from your kitchen.

pat dry. Put chopped chocolate in top of double saucepan. Stir over simmering water until chocolate has melted. (The hot water should not touch the bottom of the saucepan or the chocolate could overheat.) Remove pan from heat. Place a piece of well-dried fruit on end of skewer; dip into chocolate; gently tap skewer against edge of saucepan to drain off excess chocolate. Use another skewer to push chocolate-fruit gently on to foil; leave to set. Refrigerate until chocolate is firm. Pipe on decorative patterns with the remaining melted chocolate.

Roast Turkey

6 kg (12 lb.) turkey	2 chicken stock cubes
125 g (4 oz.) butter	90 g (3 oz.) butter, extra
2 cups water	

Forcemeat

60 g (2 oz.) butter	1 teaspoon grated lemon
1 large onion	rind
3 rashers bacon	2 tablespoons chopped
6 cups fresh breadcrumbs	parsley
(approx. 1 large	½ teaspoon mixed herbs
sandwich loaf)	salt, pepper
500 g (1 lb.) minced veal	2 eggs
or sausage mince	milk

Herb Stuffing

3 cups fresh breadcrumbs	¼ teaspoon thyme
(approx. ½ loaf)	¼ teaspoon oregano
2 tablespoons chopped	salt, pepper
parsley	60 g (2 oz.) butter
4 shallots or spring onions	1 egg

Herb Stuffing: Put breadcrumbs in bowl with parsley, chopped shallots, thyme, oregano, salt and pepper; mix well. Add melted butter and lightly-beaten egg; mix well.

Forcemeat: Heat butter in pan; add peeled and chopped onion and chopped bacon; saute until onion is tender. Add breadcrumbs, meat, lemon rind, parsley, mixed herbs, salt and pepper; mix well; bind with lightly-beaten eggs; add a little milk if mixture seems too dry.

Fill the herb stuffing into cavity of turkey at neck end; fill loosely; stuffing will swell during cooking. Fill forcemeat stuffing into cavity at other end. Secure openings of turkey by weaving skewer through skin to hold firmly together. Tie legs with string to keep in good shape during cooking. Spread softened butter all over turkey, rubbing butter in well cover breast and legs.

Put water, crumbled stock cubes and extra butter in large baking dish; add turkey. Roast in moderate oven 30 minutes. Baste turkey well, then cover loosely with well-greased sheet of aluminium foil; tuck foil loosely in at sides of turkey. Continue cooking in moderate oven; allow approx. 20 minutes per 500 g (1 lb.); a 6 kg (12 lb.) turkey will take approx. 4 hours to cook. Move foil to baste turkey frequently during cooking time. Remove foil for the last half hour of cooking time to complete browning; baste again.

Roast Pork

1 leg pork	1 cup water
2 tablespoons oil	2 chicken stock cubes
1 teaspoon salt	

Sauce

425 ml (15 fl. oz.) can apple	1 tablespoon soy sauce
juice	3 tablespoons Grand
2 tablespoons flour	Marnier
pepper	

Put pork into large baking dish; rub well with oil, then salt. Bake in hot oven 25 to 30 minutes or until crackling is crisp and golden brown. Add water and crumbled stock cubes to baking dish; reduce heat to moderate; continue cooking, uncovered, until pork is tender; allow 25 to 30 minutes per 500 g (1 lb.), depending on thickness of joint.

Remove pork from baking dish; keep warm. Put baking dish on top of stove over medium heat; cook until pan drippings are reduced by half, leaving approx. 2 tablespoons drippings in pan. Add flour; stir until well browned. Gradually add combined apple juice, soy sauce and Grand Marnier; stir until smooth; stir until sauce boils and thickens. Reduce heat; simmer 1 minute; add pepper.

Brandied Apricot Duck

2 kg (4 lb.) duck	8 shallots or spring onions
4 cups fresh breadcrumbs	1 egg
60 g (2 oz.) butter	2 tablespoons brandy
60 g (2 oz.) bacon	melted butter

Sauce

125 g (4 oz.) dried apricots	¼ cup lemon juice
3 cups water	1 teaspoon soy sauce
¼ cup brown sugar, lightly	1 teaspoon worcester-
packed	shire sauce
¼ cup brandy	

Melt butter in pan; add chopped bacon and chopped shallots; saute until bacon is crisp. Put breadcrumbs in bowl; add bacon and shallot mixture, lightly-beaten egg and brandy; mix well. Fill duck with prepared stuffing; put in baking dish; brush well with melted butter. Roast in hot oven 10 minutes; reduce heat to moderate; roast a further 45 minutes, brushing occasionally with pan juices. Pour off fat; add sauce to pan; roast a further 30 minutes or until duck is tender, brushing occasionally with sauce.

Sauce: Cover apricots with 1½ cups of the water; allow to stand 1 hour. Put apricots and liquid in saucepan; bring to boil; reduce heat; simmer covered 15 minutes or until tender. Put apricots and liquid in blender; blend until smooth. Add brown sugar, brandy, lemon juice, soy sauce, worcestershire sauce and remaining water. Put in saucepan; stir over medium heat until sauce boils; remove from heat. Serves 4.

Creamy Chicken Loaf

1.5 kg (3 lb.) chicken	salt, pepper
½ cup mayonnaise	½ teaspoon prepared
½ cup sour cream	mustard
1 tablespoon chopped	1 teaspoon grated lemon
parsley	rind
2 gherkins	1 tablespoon lemon juice
3 shallots or spring onions	4 hard-boiled eggs
1 tablespoon gelatine	

Steam or boil chicken in usual way until tender; reserve 1 cup of chicken stock. When chicken is cold, remove skin and bones; chop meat very finely. Put mayonnaise, sour cream, parsley, finely-chopped gherkins, finely-chopped shallots, mustard, lemon rind and lemon juice into bowl; stir until combined. Season with salt and pepper.

Put gelatine and reserved chicken stock in pan; stir over low heat until gelatine is dissolved; cool. Add gelatine mixture to mayonnaise mixture; stir until combined. Lightly oil a 23 cm x 12 cm (9 in. x 5 in.) loaf tin; cover base with finely-chopped hard-boiled eggs; spoon chicken mixture over evenly. Cover tin; refrigerate overnight. Turn out of tin; cut into slices.

Serves 4 to 6.

Quick-Mix Christmas Pudding

1.5 kg (3 lb.) can plum	125 g (4 oz.) mixed peel
pudding	1 egg
125 g (4 oz.) prunes	¼ cup dry sherry
125 g (4 oz.) dates	¼ cup orange juice
125 g (4 oz.) sultanas	½ cup rum or brandy
125 g (4 oz.) glace cherries	

Open can; crumble pudding with fingers into large bowl. Remove stones from prunes; chop prunes and dates. Add sultanas, chopped cherries and mixed peel. Combine in bowl with lightly-beaten egg, sherry, rum or brandy and orange juice; mix well. Mix fruit into pudding; combine well. Place mixture in well-greased 2.5 litre (approx. 4½ pint) pudding steamer; steam approx. 2 hours.

Economical Christmas Pudding

125 g (4 oz.) butter	125 g (4 oz.) prunes
1½ cups plain flour	60 g (2 oz.) mixed peel
2 cups fresh breadcrumbs	2 tablespoons sweet
1 cup brown sugar, firmly	sherry
packed	1 apple
1 cup sultanas	2 teaspoons bicarbonate
1 cup raisins	of soda
¾ cup currants	1½ cups milk

Combine sultanas, chopped raisins, currants, chopped prunes and chopped peel in bowl. Add sherry and peeled, grated apple; set aside. Sift flour; rub in butter until mixture resembles coarse breadcrumbs; add breadcrumbs, brown sugar, prepared fruit and the combined milk and soda. Place mixture in greased 2.5 litre (approx. 4½ pint) pudding basin; cover with greased grease-proof paper before securing lid.

Put basin in saucepan filled with enough boiling water to come halfway up sides of pudding basin. Cover; steam rapidly 3½ hours or until cooked. Check every 20 to 30 minutes to see if water in saucepan needs to be replenished. Re-steam 2 hours on day of serving.

Family-Size Pudding

250 g (8 oz.) butter	1 small apple
1 cup brown sugar, firmly	1 small carrot
packed	125 g (4 oz.) mixed peel
1 tablespoon grated	2 cups fresh breadcrumbs
orange rind	1½ cups plain flour
1 tablespoon grated	pinch salt
lemon rind	½ teaspoon nutmeg
4 eggs	1 teaspoon mixed spice
250 g (8 oz.) dates	½ teaspoon bicarbonate of
250 g (8 oz.) raisins	soda
250 g (8 oz.) sultanas	3 tablespoons brandy

Cream butter and sugar until light and fluffy. Add orange and lemon rinds. Add eggs one at a time, beating well after each addition. Chop dates, raisins and peel; peel and grate apple and carrot. Stir fruit, peel, carrot and breadcrumbs into creamed mixture. Sift dry ingredients; fold in; add brandy.

To steam: Place in well-greased 2.5 litre (approx. 4½ pint) pudding basin; steam 4 hours. Re-steam 2 hours on day of serving.

To boil: Follow the step-by-step instructions on page 229. Boil rapidly 4 hours; replenish with boiling water every 20 minutes (water must not go off the boil). Re-boil 2 hours on day of serving.

Glazed Ham Step~by~Step

The Christmas ham takes pride of place on the festive table. Here we make it even more decorative with a cherry-studded surface and a rich sherry glaze.

You will need:

1 leg of ham
250 g (8 oz.) glace cherries
whole cloves
½ cup honey
3 teaspoons french mustard
2 tablespoons dry sherry
2 teaspoons soy sauce
¼ cup brown sugar

1.   Remove rind from ham, run thumb around edge of rind just under skin. Start pulling rind from widest edge of ham, using fingers to loosen it from the fat. When you have pulled it to within 15 cm (6 in.) of shank end, take a very sharp pointed knife and cut through rind around shank end in a decorative pattern. Continue to pull the rind off the fat up to the pattern.

2.   With sharp knife, cut across fat at 5 cm (2 in.) intervals. Make sure that you cut just through the fat and not into the meat. Cut in opposite direction at 5 cm (2 in.) intervals, to make diamonds.

3.   Decorate the ham with whole cloves and halved glace cherries (put halved toothpicks into the ham and press the cherries on to the toothpicks).

4.   Put ham into large baking dish; brush well with combined honey, mustard, sherry, soy sauce and sugar. Put on lowest shelf of moderately hot oven for 60 minutes or until glaze is golden brown. Brush glaze frequently over ham. Glaze ham on the day it is to be served. If glazed the day before, glaze can become thin and the gloss not so rich.

Boiled Christmas Pudding Step-by-Step

There's no more popular pudding at Christmas than the boiled pudding — rich, moist, spicily fragrant. Whichever recipe you use, here is how to boil the pudding so that it will turn out perfectly on Christmas Day.

1. Chop fruit so that all pieces are of even size, about the size of a sultana; scissors are best for this. Dip them in water occasionally if fruit is sticky. When fruit is ready, make up pudding mixture as recipe directs, then prepare the pudding cloth. Use a 75 cm (30 in.) square of unbleached calico. Drop it into a large pan of boiling water; boil 30 minutes. Remove from water; wring out well (protect hands from hot cloth with rubber gloves). Spread out cloth and cover with plain flour (about half a cup). Bring flour to within 10 cm (4 in.) of edges of cloth. The cloth can be left unfloured but flouring gives the pudding a better skin. Put mixture into centre of cloth; it should be round in shape, moulded into a slight peak at the top.

2. Gather corners and sides of cloth round pudding mixture as evenly as possible. Pull corners tightly and firmly to give pudding a good round shape. Make sure that all edges of the pudding cloth are pulled up in hands as shown, so that no water can get into the pudding during boiling.

3. Tie firmly with string about 2.5 cm (1 in.) above top of pudding; this allows room for expansion during cooking. Twist string around cloth about 10 times to give good, firm seal. Make handle from string ends to lift out pudding easily when cooked. Put pudding into large boiler three-quarters full of boiling water; there must be enough rapidly-boiling water to float pudding. Put lid on immediately; boil rapidly for time stated in recipe. Replenish with more boiling water, if necessary, about every 20 minutes. Water must never go off the boil.

4. At end of cooking time, lift pudding from water; suspend from handle of cupboard door or legs of an upturned stool; pudding must be able to swing freely, without touching anything. Tie ends of wet cloth together so they do not touch the pudding. Let hang overnight or until cloth around pudding dries completely. Untie ends of cloth so they will also dry. In hot Christmas weather it is better to store the pudding in the refrigerator. On day of serving, re-boil as recipe directs.

After pudding is cooked, remove it from the water; let stand about 5 minutes or until cloth is dry. Cut string with knife or scissors; carefully and gently pull cloth from pudding. It may be necessary to ease pudding from cloth at top with a knife, then gently pull off remainder of cloth. If you want to flame the pudding when serving, warm ¼ cup brandy, pour it over pudding at the table, set aflame.

Festive Fruit Slice

Pastry

1½ cups self-raising flour	¼ cup castor sugar
⅓ cup custard powder	1 egg
2½ teaspoons cornflour	castor sugar, extra
125 g (4 oz.) butter	

Filling

470 g (15 oz.) can crushed pineapple	1 cup dates
	1 cup prunes
470 g (15 oz.) can apricot halves	60 g (2 oz.) glace cherries
	¾ cup sugar
1 cup sultanas	½ cup brandy
1 cup raisins	1 tablespoon orange juice
1 cup currants	1 tablespoon lemon juice

Pastry: Sift flour, custard powder and cornflour into basin; rub in butter until mixture resembles fine breadcrumbs. Stir in sugar and lightly-beaten egg. Knead lightly on floured board. Refrigerate 1 hour.

Roll out half the pastry to fit greased and greased-paper-lined 28 cm x 18 cm (11 in. x 7 in.) shallow cake tin. Cover evenly with approx. 3½ cups of prepared filling. Roll out the remaining pastry; place on top of filling. Glaze top with a little cold water; sprinkle with extra sugar. Bake in hot oven 20 to 25 minutes. Cool; cut into slices. Serve with icecream or custard.

Filling: Place undrained pineapple and undrained apricot halves in saucepan; add sultanas, chopped raisins, currants, finely-chopped dates, pitted and chopped prunes, chopped cherries and sugar. Stir over low heat until mixture becomes thick and sugar has dissolved; bring to boil; reduce heat; simmer uncovered 5 minutes. Remove from heat; cool slightly; add brandy, orange and lemon juices.

Pour into airtight container; cover and allow to stand overnight or several days before using. NOTE: This recipe makes enough filling for two of the Festive slices, or the remaining fruit mixture can be used as filling for small fruit mince tarts.

Celebration Cake

500 g (1 lb.) sultanas	5 eggs
250 g (8 oz.) raisins	½ cup rum, brandy or sweet sherry
250 g (8 oz.) dates	
125 g (4 oz.) currants	1¾ cups plain flour
125 g (4 oz.) mixed peel	⅓ cup self-raising flour
125 g (4 oz.) glace cherries	1 teaspoon mixed spice
60 g (2 oz.) glace pineapple	½ teaspoon cinnamon
60 g (2 oz.) glace apricots	¼ teaspoon nutmeg
250 g (8 oz.) butter	¼ teaspoon salt
1 cup brown sugar, firmly packed	2 tablespoons rum, brandy or sweet sherry, extra

Chop raisins, dates, peel, cherries, pineapple and apricots; combine in large basin with sultanas, currants and rum; mix well. Cover; stand overnight.

Line a deep 20 cm (8 in.) square or deep 23 cm (9 in.) round cake tin with three thicknesses of greaseproof paper, bringing paper 8 cm (3 in.) above edges of tin.

Beat butter until soft; add sugar; beat only until combined. Add eggs one at a time, beating well after each addition. Add creamed mixture to fruit mixture; mix well. Stir in sifted dry ingredients; mix thoroughly. Spread evenly into prepared tin; bake in slow oven 3 to 3½ hours. When cooked, remove from oven; brush evenly with extra rum. Cover with aluminium foil; leave until cold. Remove from tin; re-wrap in aluminium foil to keep airtight until required.

Fruit and Nut Cake

250 g (8 oz.) dessert dates	250 g (8 oz.) brazil nuts
125 g (4 oz.) glace pineapple	2 eggs
	½ cup brown sugar, lightly packed
125 g (4 oz.) glace apricots	1 teaspoon vanilla
125 g (4 oz.) red glace cherries	1 tablespoon rum
125 g (4 oz.) green glace cherries	90 g (3 oz.) softened butter
	½ cup plain flour
125 g (4 oz.) whole blanched almonds	½ teaspoon baking powder
	pinch salt

Stone dates; chop pineapple and apricots into fairly large pieces; leave remaining fruit and nuts whole. Mix all these well together; reserve ½ cup combined nuts and glace fruits for garnishing. Beat eggs until light and fluffy; add sugar, vanilla, rum and softened butter. Continue beating until well blended. Sift flour with baking powder and salt; add to creamed mixture with fruit and nuts; mix well.

Grease 20 cm (8 in.) ring tin; line base of tin with greased greaseproof paper; spoon mixture evenly into tin. Place reserved fruit on top, pressing gently down into mixture. Bake in slow oven approx. 1½ hours or until cake is firm to touch. Allow cake to cool in tin 10 minutes before turning out on to wire rack to cool. When completely cold, wrap in aluminium foil to keep airtight until required. About an hour or two before serving, brush top of cake with prepared glaze.

Glaze: Combine in small saucepan 1 tablespoon gelatine, 1 tablespoon sugar and ½ cup water; stir over medium heat until sugar and gelatine have dissolved.

Sherry-Sultana Cake

500 g (1 lb.) sultanas	185 g (6 oz.) butter
90 g (3 oz.) glace cherries	1 cup sugar
60 g (2 oz.) glace pineapple	3 eggs
60 g (2 oz.) glace apricots	2 teaspoons cornflour
¾ cup water	½ cup water, extra
¼ cup sherry (sweet or dry)	1¼ cups plain flour
1 tablespoon orange juice	1¼ cups self-raising flour
1 tablespoon lemon juice	

Put sultanas, halved cherries, chopped glace pineapple and apricots, water, sherry, orange and lemon juices together in saucepan. Bring slowly to the boil; reduce heat; simmer gently uncovered 10 minutes or until most of the liquid has been absorbed. Remove from heat; cool.

Cream butter and sugar until light and fluffy; add eggs one at a time, beating well after each addition. Blend cornflour in extra water; add to creamed mixture alternately with sifted dry ingredients; fold in fruit mixture.

Grease deep 23 cm (9 in.) round cake tin; line with greased greaseproof paper. Spread mixture evenly into tin. Bake in moderately slow oven 2½ hours to 3 hours or until cooked when tested.

Irish Fruit Cake

375 g (12 oz.) raisins	⅓ cup whisky
375 g (12 oz.) sultanas	½ small green apple
90 g (3 oz.) glace cherries	30 g (1 oz.) walnuts
90 g (3 oz.) dates	60 g (2 oz.) ground almonds
60 g (2 oz.) prunes	185 g (6 oz.) butter
30 g (1 oz.) glace pineapple	¾ cup castor sugar
60 g (2 oz.) mixed peel	3 eggs
1 teaspoon grated lemon rind	1½ cups plain flour
	¼ teaspoon nutmeg
1 teaspoon grated orange rind	½ teaspoon cinnamon
	¼ teaspoon salt
2 tablespoons lemon juice	1 tablespoon whisky, extra
¼ cup orange juice	

Stone prunes; chop all fruit and mixed peel; combine in large screwtop jar with rinds, juices, whisky and peeled and grated apple. Shake jar well to mix ingredients evenly; store in cool, dry place 3 weeks. Reverse jar each day. (Use jar with plastic, not metal, lid.)

Line 23 cm x 12 cm (9 in. x 5 in.) loaf tin or deep 20 cm (8 in.) round cake tin with two thicknesses of greaseproof paper, bringing paper 5 cm (2 in.) above edge of tin.

Chop walnuts. Beat butter until soft; add sugar; beat only until combined. Add eggs one at a time, beating well after each addition. Put fruit mixture into large basin; add walnuts, almonds and creamed mixture; stir in sifted dry ingredients.

Spread mixture evenly into prepared tin; bake in slow oven approx. 3 hours. Remove from oven; brush evenly with extra whisky; cover with aluminium foil; leave until cold. Remove from tin; re-wrap in foil to keep airtight until required.

Madeira Fruit Cake

250 g (8 oz.) glace cherries	⅓ cup sweet sherry
500 g (1 lb.) sultanas	375 g (12 oz.) butter
125 g (4 oz.) mixed peel	1⅓ cups castor sugar
1 teaspoon grated orange rind	6 eggs
	4 cups plain flour
1 teaspoon grated lemon rind	2 teaspoons baking powder
⅓ cup brandy	

Put halved cherries, sultanas, chopped mixed peel, orange and lemon rinds, brandy and sweet sherry into bowl; mix well. Cover and stand overnight.

Beat butter until soft and creamy; gradually add sugar, beating well. Add eggs one at a time, beating well after each addition. Fold in sifted flour and baking powder alternately with fruit; mix well. Spoon cake mixture into deep 23 cm (9 in.) round cake tin lined with three thicknesses of white paper. Bake in slow oven 3 hours or until cooked when tested. When completely cold, turn out of tin.

Currant-Cherry Cake

1 kg (2 lb.) currants	5 eggs
250 g (8 oz.) glace cherries	2 cups plain flour
250 g (8 oz.) butter	½ teaspoon salt
½ cup rum, brandy or sweet sherry	1 teaspoon mixed spice
	2 tablespoons rum, brandy or sweet sherry, extra
1 cup brown sugar, firmly packed	

Line a deep 20 cm (8 in.) square or deep 23 cm (9 in.) round cake tin with three thicknesses of greaseproof paper, bringing paper 8 cm (3 in.) above edges of tin.

Halve cherries; combine in large basin with currants and rum. Beat butter until soft; add sugar; beat until combined. Add eggs one at a time, beating well after each addition. Add creamed mixture to fruit mixture; mix well. Stir in sifted dry ingredients; mix thoroughly. Spread evenly into prepared tin; bake in slow oven 2½ to 3 hours. When cooked, remove from oven; brush top evenly with extra rum; cover tightly with aluminium foil; leave until cold. Remove from tin; re-wrap in aluminium foil to keep airtight until required.

How to Carve the Christmas Ham

1. Run a thumb under the edge of the ham rind to loosen it, then gently peel off the rind. Turn the ham over and cut around the pelvic bone as shown. Remove the bone for easier carving and tidier slices.

2. Choose a long, thin-bladed knife. Cut across at top of ham, near bone end, as shown, to give flat surface; mainly only fat is cut away.

3. Take long sweeps with the knife to get a good straight — not curved — edge to the ham. Do not press on the knife. Use the whole length of the blade to carve, moving it in a slicing fashion. As you carve, the slices will increase in size but they will still remain perfectly flat and even.

4. When the ham has been carved to the extent shown, turn it over and start carving the other side.

5. Cut across at top, near the bone, as shown; these slices on the reverse side will be much leaner. As you keep carving you will come to the leg bone; carve thin slices from side of bone.

6. Eventually all that remains will be the thick portion at the end of the leg. Remove this and cut in half for easier carving. Place it on a board, fat side up, and cut downward in thin slices.

How to Carve the Christmas Turkey

1. Remove the leg as shown, cutting between the bones at the joint.

2. Place the leg on carving board, cut in half at the joint. Carve the drumstick down into slices, as shown. Cut other piece — the thigh — into slices.

3. Take the knife across the top of the wing into the turkey carcass. But do not remove the wing.

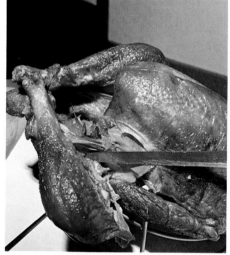

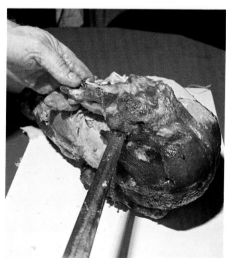

4. Slice the breast down, as shown, to the cut made at the top of the wing; this makes it easy to remove the slices.

5. As you carve you will come against the bone of the carcass; cut small slices from near the breastbone. Toward the end you will be able to cut through the stuffing so that it is incorporated in each slice. You can serve the remaining stuffing separately.

6. Make a cut beneath the wing. Remove wing, it can be carved as the drumstick. Proceed carving in similar way on the other side of the turkey.

Christmas Pudding

1 kg (2 lb.) mixed fruit	2 teaspoons bicarbonate
250 g (8 oz.) dates	of soda
250 g (8 oz.) raisins	3 eggs
2 cups water	2 cups plain flour
1 cup white sugar	2 cups self-raising flour
1 cup brown sugar, lightly	2 teaspoons mixed spice
packed	1 teaspoon cinnamon
1 teaspoon salt	¼ cup rum
250 g (8 oz.) butter	

Put in pan the fruit, chopped dates, chopped raisins, water, sugars, salt and butter. Stir over low heat until butter has melted; bring to boil; reduce heat; simmer uncovered 8 minutes, stirring occasionally; remove from heat; add soda; mix well. Allow mixture to become completely cold.

Beat eggs and rum until combined. Add egg mixture, sifted flours, mixed spice and cinnamon to fruit mixture; mix well.

To boil: See page 229 for how to prepare the cloth and boil the pudding. Boil pudding rapidly 6 hours. On day of serving, re-boil 1½ hours.

To steam: Fill pudding into well-greased 4 litre (8 pint) pudding basin. Cover with greased aluminium foil; place lid on firmly. Steam 6 hours; make sure water comes halfway up sides of basin. Replenish with more boiling water when necessary. Steam a further 1½ hours on day of serving.

Christmas Trifle

1 jam-filled swiss roll	470 g (15 oz.) can
⅔ cup orange juice	pineapple pieces
¼ cup lemon juice	¾ cup passionfruit pulp
2 tablespoons sherry	(approx. 6 passionfruit)
or brandy	250 g (8 oz.) strawberries
470 g (15 oz.) can sliced	2 tablespoons sherry
peaches	or brandy, extra
1 pkt port wine jelly	1½ cups cream
crystals	

Custard

2 cups milk	2 tablespoons sugar
2 tablespoons custard	1 teaspoon vanilla
powder	

Make jelly according to directions on packet; refrigerate until set. Wash and hull strawberries; soak in extra sherry. Cut swiss roll into 1 cm (½ in.) rounds; arrange evenly over base of large bowl. Combine orange juice, lemon juice and sherry; mix well. Spoon over swiss roll slices.

Arrange drained peaches on top or in centre of swiss roll; pour over half the cold custard. Spoon chopped jelly on top of custard, then drained pineapple and passionfruit pulp over jelly. Pour over remaining custard; decorate with whipped cream and strawberries.

Custard: Blend custard powder with a little of the milk; add remainder; mix well. Stir in sugar. Stir over low heat until mixture boils and thickens. Remove from heat; stir in vanilla. Allow to cool.
Serves 8.

Creole Fruit Cake

2 tablespoons instant	6 eggs
coffee powder	3 teaspoons baking
½ cup water	powder
250 g (8 oz.) prunes	¼ teaspoon bicarbonate
500 g (1 lb.) currants	of soda
500 g (1 lb.) sultanas	¼ teaspoon salt
250 g (8 oz.) glace cherries	1 teaspoon nutmeg
250 g (8 oz.) dates	2 teaspoons cinnamon
250 g (8 oz.) mixed peel	1 teaspoon allspice
250 g (8 oz.) walnut pieces	1½ tablespoons cocoa
½ cup dry sherry	½ cup plum jam
½ cup brandy	1 tablespoon grated lemon
250 g (8 oz.) butter	rind
1½ cups brown sugar,	1 tablespoon lemon juice
lightly packed	3½ cups plain flour

Stone prunes, cut in half; place sultanas, currants and halved prunes in bowl; pour sherry and brandy over; mix well; cover; leave overnight or for several days. Cream butter and sugar until light and fluffy; add eggs one at a time, beating well after each addition.

Place fruit in bowl; add whole glace cherries, halved dates, chopped mixed peel, walnut pieces and 1 cup sifted flour; mix well. Dissolve coffee in water. Sift remaining dry ingredients; stir into egg mixture; add fruit, grated lemon rind, lemon juice, jam and dissolved coffee. Mix well. Place mixture in deep 23 cm (9 in.) square cake tin which has been lined with two thicknesses of brown paper and one thickness of greaseproof paper. Bake in slow oven approx. 3½ hours or until cooked when tested.

White Christmas

250 g (8 oz.) solid white	30 g (1 oz.) mixed peel
vegetable shortening	30 g (1 oz.) preserved
3 cups Rice Krispies	ginger
1 cup coconut	30 g (1 oz.) glace apricots
¾ cup icing sugar	30 g (1 oz.) glace pineapple
1 cup milk powder	¼ cup sultanas
	30 g (1 oz.) glace cherries

Melt chopped white vegetable shortening over gentle heat. Combine Rice Krispies, coconut, sifted icing sugar, milk powder and chopped fruits; mix well. Add melted shortening and mix thoroughly.

Press mixture into lightly-greased and grease-proof paper lined 28 cm x 18 cm (11 in. x 7 in.) shallow cake tin. Refrigerate until firm. Cut into bars for serving.

NOTE: For a more economical version, glace fruit and ginger can be omitted; increase amount of sultanas used to ½ cup.

Almond Fruit Slice

3 egg whites	125 g (4 oz.) glace cherries
½ cup castor sugar	
1 cup plain flour	60 g (2 oz.) glace pineapple
125 g (4 oz.) unblanched almonds	60 g (2 oz.) glace apricots

Beat egg whites until soft peaks form; gradually beat in castor sugar, beating well after each addition until all sugar is dissolved. Fold in sifted flour, whole, unpeeled almonds and glace fruits cut into small pieces. Spread into greased 25 cm x 8 cm (10 in. x 3 in.) bar tin. Bake in moderate oven 30 to 35 minutes or until just firm to touch. Turn out of tin to cool.

When cold, wrap in aluminium foil; put aside for one or two days. Using very sharp knife (an electric knife is good for this), cut bread into wafer-thin slices. Put slices on to baking tray; bake in slow oven 45 minutes or until dry and crisp.

Makes approx. 40 slices.

Icecream Cake

2⅓ cups milk	60 g (2 oz.) red glace cherries
1 cup condensed milk	
1 vanilla junket tablet	60 g (2 oz.) green glace cherries
1 tablespoon milk, extra	
1 teaspoon vanilla	125 g (4 oz.) sultanas
1½ tablespoons gelatine	¼ cup orange juice
4 tablespoons water	⅓ cup brandy
60 g (2 oz.) glace apricots	60 g (2 oz.) slivered almonds
60 g (2 oz.) glace pineapple	300 ml (½ pint) double cream

Put milk and condensed milk into saucepan; stir over low heat until just lukewarm; remove from heat. Crush junket tablet; dissolve in the 1 tablespoon extra milk; stir into warm milk with vanilla. Soften gelatine in the water; dissolve over hot water; allow to cool. Stir cooled gelatine mixture into milk mixture; mix well. Pour into shallow tray; freeze for about 30 minutes until set and very cold.

Spoon mixture into large bowl of electric mixer; beat on highest speed 10 minutes. The mixture will double in bulk and have a marshmallow consistency. It is important that mixture be beaten on highest speed of mixer; if beaten slowly, mixture will become warm and will not increase in volume.

Combine chopped glace apricots, chopped glace pineapple, halved cherries, sultanas, orange juice and brandy. Put almonds on oven tray; bake in moderate oven 10 minutes or until golden brown; remove from tray; chop roughly. Fold fruit mixture and almonds into icecream mixture; mix well.

Pour mixture into deep 23 cm (9 in.) round cake tin, which has been greased and lined with greased greaseproof paper. Put into freezer; freeze overnight. To serve, unmould cake on to serving plate; decorate with extra whipped cream, if desired.

Sherry Custard

1½ cups milk	2 tablespoons custard powder
2 tablespoons sugar	
1 teaspoon vanilla	¼ cup sweet sherry

Mix custard powder to a smooth paste with a little of the milk; add remaining milk, sugar, vanilla and sherry. Stir over medium heat until custard boils and thickens; reduce heat; simmer 2 minutes. Serve with the Christmas pudding.

Makes 1½ cups.

Brandy Butter

125 g (4 oz.) butter	1 tablespoon brandy
2 cups icing sugar	

Cream butter; gradually blend in sifted icing sugar and brandy. Refrigerate until firm. If desired, when firm, the butter can be put into a piping bag fitted with fluted tube and decorative rosettes piped on a scone tray. Refrigerate again.

Brandy Custard

¼ cup sugar	pinch salt
½ cup water	2 tablespoons brandy
2 egg yolks	¼ cup cream

Put sugar and water into saucepan; stir over low heat until sugar dissolves; bring to boil; reduce heat; simmer 10 minutes. Beat egg yolks and salt; pour hot syrup in slowly, beating until thick and creamy. Fold in brandy and whipped cream.

Cooking for a Crowd

When you're called upon to cater for a large number of people — perhaps for a family wedding, birthday or anniversary, or for a charity function — quantities needed for a recipe can sometimes be a little bewildering. This section will be of great help. Recipes serve up to 25 or 50. We have also given, with most recipes, quantities to serve just six people, so that you can try out several.

Mango Mousse Trifle

4 x 425 g (15 oz.) cans mangoes in syrup	600 ml (1 pint) double cream
2 teaspoons grated lemon rind	4 egg whites
2 teaspoons grated orange rind	3 x 20 cm (8 in.) sponge cake layers
1 cup castor sugar	2 tablespoons rum
3½ tablespoons gelatine	1 cup milk
1 cup water	600 ml (1 pint) double cream, extra

Reserve 4 slices of mango for decoration. Place mangoes with their syrup in electric blender; blend on medium speed 1 minute or until pureed. You will need to do this in 2 batches. Or mash until smooth. Place mango puree in large bowl; add orange rind, lemon rind and sugar; stir until sugar has dissolved.

Sprinkle gelatine over water in small bowl; stir until combined. Stand bowl over simmering water; stir until gelatine has dissolved; allow to cool slightly. Gradually add gelatine mixture to mango mixture; mix well. Refrigerate until mixture is the consistency of unbeaten egg white.

Beat egg whites in bowl until firm peaks form. Beat cream until soft peaks form. Fold egg whites and cream into mango mixture. Cut sponge cakes into 5 cm (2 in.) cubes. Divide cake over base of three medium-sized serving bowls. Sprinkle combined milk and rum over cake. Pour the mango mousse over. Cover bowls; refrigerate several hours or until set. Beat extra cream until

Recipe continued overleaf:

Mango Mousse Trifle — rum-soaked sponge cake is covered with a creamy mango-flavoured mousse.

firm peaks form; spoon into piping bag with nozzle attached. Pipe edge around each mango mousse. Chop reserved mangoes; pile into centre of mousse.

NOTE: If canned mangoes are difficult to obtain, substitute canned apricots.

Serves 25.

Quantities for Six

425 g (15 oz.) can mangoes in syrup, ½ teaspoon grated lemon rind, ½ teaspoon grated orange rind, ¼ cup castor sugar, 1 tablespoon gelatine, ⅓ cup water, ¾ cup cream, 1 egg white, 20 cm (8 in.) sponge cake, 2 teaspoons rum, ¼ cup milk, ½ cup cream, extra.

Pate with Port

1 kg (2 lb.) chicken livers	375 g (12 oz.) bacon
125 g (4 oz.) butter	1⅓ cups cream
4 small onions	⅓ cup port
250 g (8 oz.) mushrooms	⅓ cup dry sherry
1 teaspoon thyme	1 tablespoon brandy
1 bayleaf	salt, pepper

Clean and dry chicken livers. Heat butter in pan. Saute livers, peeled and finely-chopped onions, thyme, bayleaf, chopped mushrooms and chopped bacon 7 to 10 minutes. Remove from heat; discard bayleaf. Put half mixture into blender with half the cream; blend until smooth; repeat with remaining mixture and cream; push through sieve. Stir in port, sherry and brandy. Season with salt and pepper. Pour into serving dishes; cover with plastic food wrap. This pate can be made two days before serving. Serve with toast triangles.

Serves 25.

Quantities for Six

250 g (8 oz.) chicken livers, 30 g (1 oz.) butter, 1 small onion, 60 g (2 oz.) mushrooms, ¼ teaspoon thyme, 1 small bayleaf, 3 rashers bacon, ⅓ cup cream, 1 tablespoon port, 1 tablespoon dry sherry, 1 teaspoon brandy, salt, pepper.

Chicken in Red Wine

30 chicken legs	700 ml bottle dry red wine
250 g (8 oz.) butter	4½ cups water
185 g (6 oz.) bacon pieces	3 chicken stock cubes
30 tiny onions	1 bayleaf
750 g (1½ lb.) mushrooms	½ teaspoon mixed herbs
2 cloves garlic	1 cup flour
½ cup brandy	salt, pepper

Heat 125 g (4 oz.) of the butter in large frying pan; add chicken legs; brown well; remove from pan. You will need to brown chicken in several batches. Remove all chicken from pan.

Add finely-chopped bacon pieces to pan; saute until crisp; remove from pan. Add peeled, whole onions to pan; saute until golden brown; remove from pan. Add sliced mushrooms and crushed garlic to pan; saute until mushrooms are just tender; remove from pan. Melt remaining butter in pan; add flour; stir until flour is combined and golden brown. Remove from heat. Gradually add all combined liquids. Stir until combined, then add crumbled stock cubes, bayleaf and herbs. Return to heat; stir until sauce boils and thickens; season with salt and pepper.

Pour sauce into large boiler; add bacon, onions and mushrooms. Cover and simmer 1 hour. Add chicken legs to sauce; heat gently until sauce comes to the boil; cover; reduce heat; simmer gently 30 minutes.

To Prepare Ahead: Chicken legs can be cooked and sauce made well in advance, then frozen until required. If freezing, do not cook onions, garlic or mushrooms until sauce is being reheated for serving, then melt some extra butter, saute onions until golden brown and saute mushrooms and garlic as recipe directs. Add them to the sauce when reheating. The sauce may need to simmer longer to cook the onions through.

Serves 25.

Quantities for Six

12 chicken legs, 60 g (2 oz.) butter, 125 g (4 oz.) bacon pieces, 12 tiny onions, 250 g (8 oz.) mushrooms, 1 clove garlic, ¼ cup brandy, 2 cups dry red wine, 1 cup water, 1 chicken stock cube, piece of bayleaf, pinch mixed herbs, 3 tablespoons flour, salt, pepper.

Chicken and Asparagus Mornay

6 x 1.25 kg (2½ lb.) chickens	1 large jar mayonnaise about 682 ml (24 fl. oz.)
2 x 470 g (15 oz.) cans cream of chicken soup	4 x 470 g (15 oz.) cans asparagus cuts
1 litre (4 cups) milk	1 cup chopped parsley
250 g (8 oz.) butter	salt, pepper
1 tablespoon prepared mustard	350 g pkt dry breadcrumbs
1¼ cups flour	125 g (4 oz.) cheese
	125 g (4 oz.) butter, extra

Steam or boil chickens in usual way (reserve 1¾ litres (7 cups) of the chicken stock). Combine reserved chicken stock, milk and undiluted chicken soup in saucepan; stir over heat until hot.

Melt butter in another saucepan; add mustard and flour; stir until smooth; cook 1 minute; add to hot liquid; stir until smooth, then stir until sauce boils and thickens; reduce heat; simmer 2 minutes.

Remove skin and bones from chicken; cut chicken into large pieces; add to sauce with mayonnaise, drained asparagus cuts, parsley, salt and pepper. Pour mixture into 4 large casserole dishes.

Combine breadcrumbs and cheese with extra melted butter; sprinkle over top of casseroles; bake uncovered in moderate oven 30 to 35 minutes or until golden brown.

Serves 50.

To Prepare Ahead: Make as above, one or two days before; put into casserole dishes, but do not put topping on; cover; refrigerate. On day of serving, sprinkle topping over casseroles; bake as above.

Quantities for Six
1.25 kg (2½ lb.) chicken, 1 cup milk, 1½ cups chicken stock, 60 g (2 oz.) butter, 1 teaspoon prepared mustard, ⅓ cup flour, ½ cup mayonnaise, 470 g (15 oz.) can asparagus cuts, 2 tablespoons chopped parsley, salt, pepper, 1 cup packaged dry breadcrumbs, 30 g (1 oz.) cheese, 30 g (1 oz.) butter, extra.

Beef Curry

6 kg (12 lb.) chuck steak	3½ litres (14 cups) hot water
250 g (8 oz.) butter	3 large apples
½ cup oil	3 large bananas
250 g (8 oz.) butter, extra	salt, pepper
6 large onions	2 tablespoons soy sauce
1½ cups plain flour	2 tablespoons brown sugar
6 tablespoons curry powder	5 beef stock cubes

Ask butcher to chop meat into approx. 2.5 cm (1 in.) cubes. Heat a small amount of butter and oil in frying pan; add approx. 500 g (1 lb.) meat; fry very quickly until golden brown; remove from pan. Repeat butter, oil and meat frying until all meat is browned; remove meat from pan.

Add 3 cups of water to pan in which meat was cooked; stir well to take up all brown pan drippings. Heat extra butter in large boiler; add peeled and finely-chopped onions and curry powder; saute until onions are golden brown; add flour; stir until golden brown and free of lumps. Remove pan from heat; add water from pan and remaining 11 cups of water all at once; stir until combined. Return pan to heat; stir until sauce boils and thickens. Add salt, pepper, peeled and grated apples and peeled and chopped bananas, soy sauce, brown sugar and crumbled stock cubes; stir until combined.

Add meat to pan; stir until combined. Bring to boil; reduce heat; simmer covered 2 hours or until meat is very tender. Stir meat frequently during cooking time. If sauce is too thin, remove lid from pan during last 30 minutes of cooking time.

Serves 50.

To Prepare Ahead: Make up recipe as directed 2 days before. Cook meat 1½ hours only, then cook a further 30 minutes on day of serving, or until meat is tender. This casserole is not suitable for freezing.

Quantities for Six
1 kg (2 lb.) chuck steak, 60 g (2 oz.) butter, 2 tablespoons oil, 60 g (2 oz.) butter, extra, 1 onion, 4 tablespoons plain flour, 2 tablespoons curry powder, 3 cups hot water, 1 green apple, 1 banana, salt, pepper, 1 teaspoon soy sauce, 1 tablespoon brown sugar, 2 beef stock cubes.

Herbed Veal with Noodles

6 kg (12 lb.) stewing veal	1½ litres (6 cups) water
125 g (4 oz.) butter	2 x 150 g (5 oz.) cans tomato paste
¾ cup oil	
125 g (4 oz.) butter, extra	4 chicken stock cubes
8 onions	250 g (8 oz.) bacon pieces
4 cloves garlic	2 tablespoons soy sauce
1½ cups flour	4 teaspoons basil
4 x 396 g (14 oz.) cans whole tomatoes	2 teaspoons mixed herbs
	salt, pepper
3 cups dry red wine	½ cup chopped parsley

Trim excess fat and gristle from meat; cut meat into cubes. Heat butter and oil in pan; brown meat well; do this in batches, about 500 g to 750 g (1 lb. to 1½ lb.) of meat at a time, so meat browns well; remove meat from pan. Melt extra butter in pan. Peel and finely chop onions; crush garlic; add to pan; saute gently until onions are transparent.

Add flour; mix well; stir 1 minute over low heat. Stir in undrained mashed tomatoes, wine, water, tomato paste, crumbled stock cubes, chopped bacon pieces and soy sauce. Add basil, mixed herbs, salt and pepper. Stir until sauce boils and thickens.

Return meat to pan; cover; reduce heat; simmer 1 hour or until meat is tender. Just before serving, stir in chopped parsley. Serve with hot buttered noodles. You will need 1 kg (2 lb.) noodles.

Serves 25.

Quantities for Six
1.5 kg (3 lb.) stewing veal, 60 g (2 oz.) butter, 1 tablespoon oil, 30 g (1 oz.) butter, extra, 1 large onion, 1 clove garlic, 3 tablespoons flour, 396 g can tomatoes, ¾ cup red wine, 2 cups water, 2 tablespoons tomato paste, 1 chicken stock cube, 60 g (2 oz.) bacon pieces, 2 teaspoons soy sauce, 1 teaspoon basil, 1 teaspoon mixed herbs, salt, pepper, 2 tablespoons chopped parsley.

Herb Bread

5 long french loaves	3 cloves garlic
750 g (1½ lb.) butter	1 teaspoon mixed herbs
½ cup chopped parsley	

Cut bread at approx. 2.5 cm (1 in.) intervals, making sure you do not cut right through to the bottom crust. Mix softened butter with parsley, crushed garlic and mixed herbs; mix well. Spread butter on each side of each slice of bread; wrap each loaf in aluminium foil. Bake in moderate

Recipe continued overleaf:

oven 15 to 20 minutes.
Serves 50.

Quantities for Six
1 loaf bread, 125 g (4 oz.) butter, 1 tablespoon chopped parsley, 1 clove garlic, ¼ teaspoon mixed herbs.

Green Salad

For this, you will need about 6 lettuces and 1 bottle of french dressing. Tomatoes (cut each tomato into 8 wedges) can be added to salad, with sliced cucumber, black or green olives, sliced white onions, chopped parsley, chopped mint etc.
Serves 50.

Buttered Parsley Rice

2.75 kg (5½ lb.) rice	1 cup chopped parsley
250 g (8 oz.) butter	

Using several boilers, cook rice in boiling salted water until tender, approx. 12 minutes; drain. Melt butter in large boiler; add rice and parsley; toss until well combined.
To Prepare Ahead: Cook rice the day before serving; refrigerate. On day of serving, put rice into large baking dishes; pour the melted butter and parsley over. Heat in moderate oven 15 to 20 minutes, stirring occasionally.
Serves 50.

Quantities for Six
2 cups rice, 60 g (2 oz.) butter, 1 tablespoon parsley.

Cheese Straws

1 cup plain flour	¼ teaspoon salt
60 g (2 oz.) butter	1 egg yolk
90 g (3 oz.) cheddar cheese	1 tablespoon lemon juice
pinch cayenne	

Rub butter into sifted flour until mixture resembles fine breadcrumbs. Add grated cheese, cayenne and salt; mix lightly. Combine egg yolk and lemon juice. Make well in centre of dry ingredients; add egg yolk mixture; mix to a firm dough. Roll pastry out thinly; cut into strips 1 cm x 8 cm (½ in. x 3 in.). Bake on greased oven trays in moderate oven for 12 minutes.
Makes approx. 100 straws.

Creamy Potato Balls

2 kg (4 lb.) potatoes	10 shallots or spring onions
125 g (4 oz.) butter	
½ cup milk	4 eggs, extra
500 g (1 lb.) packaged cream cheese	2 cups milk, extra
	flour
2 eggs	packaged dry breadcrumbs
250 g (8 oz.) bacon	oil for deep-frying

Peel potatoes; chop roughly; cook in boiling salted water until tender; drain; mash with potato masher until smooth and free of lumps. Beat cream cheese and softened butter until smooth; add milk and eggs; beat until combined. Add mashed potato to cream cheese mixture; beat until smooth. Chop bacon; saute in frying pan 2 minutes; add to potato mixture with chopped shallots; cool mixture.
Form tablespoons of mixture into balls; coat lightly with flour; dip in combined beaten extra eggs and milk; coat with breadcrumbs. Coat again with egg-and-milk mixture and breadcrumbs. Deep-fry in hot oil until golden.
Makes approx. 100.
To Prepare Ahead: Prepare as above one or two days before; deep-fry as above; cool; arrange on oven trays; cover with plastic food wrap; refrigerate. On serving day, reheat in moderate oven 15 to 20 minutes or until crisp. These are not suitable for freezing.

Quantities for Six
500 g (1 lb.) potatoes, 30 g (1 oz.) butter, 1 tablespoon milk, 125 g (4 oz.) cream cheese, 1 egg, 2 rashers bacon, 4 shallots, 1 egg, extra, ¼ cup milk, extra.

Do-It-Yourself Pizzas

5 loaves long french bread	1 kg (2 lb.) cheddar cheese
1.5 kg (3 lb.) salami	500 g (1 lb.) stuffed olives

Tomato Sauce

125 g (4 oz.) butter	salt, pepper
3 large onions	1 tablespoon basil
3 x 910 g (1 lb. 13 oz.) cans whole tomatoes	2 teaspoons oregano
4 cloves garlic	1 tablespoon sugar

Cut bread into 1 cm (½ in.) slices. Slice olives. Cut cheese into thin slices. Place prepared Tomato Sauce in serving bowls; arrange bread, salami, cheese and olives on platters around Tomato Sauce. Guests make their own miniature pizzas — topping a bread slice with a slice of salami, cheese, then Tomato Sauce and olives.

Tomato Sauce: Heat butter in large pan; add peeled and chopped onions and crushed garlic; saute gently until onion is tender. Add undrained tomatoes, salt, pepper, basil, oregano and sugar; stir until combined. Mash tomatoes well with potato masher until they are broken into small pieces. Bring to boil; reduce heat; simmer uncovered 60 minutes or until mixture is very thick. Serve hot or cold.
Serves 50.

Do-it-yourself Pizzas — a great idea for a party!

Marshmallow Fruit Pavlova

12 egg whites	1 punnet strawberries
3½ cups castor sugar	¾ cup passionfruit pulp
2 teaspoons white vinegar	4 cups (1½ pints) double
1 teaspoon vanilla	cream
4 large bananas	¼ cup strawberry jam
3 tablespoons lemon juice	2 tablespoons water

Place egg yolks, sugar and vanilla in a large bowl; beat until soft and creamy. Place milk and cream in pan; stand over heat until hot add remainder of sugar, beating well after each addition, until almost all sugar is dissolved. Add vanilla and vinegar; beat until just combined. Pour mixture into 37 cm x 27 cm (15 in. x 11 in.) baking dish, which has been lined with greased greaseproof paper, lightly dusted with cornflour. Spread meringue out evenly. Place in moderate oven 1 minute, then immediately reduce heat to slow; bake 1¼ hours or until meringue has formed a hard crust.

Take out of oven; carefully turn meringue out of tin on to wire rack, leaving top side down. The base of the pavlova now becomes the top. (As the pavlova cools, this top will fall slightly, leaving room for the topping.)

When cold, carefully run large sharp knife under meringue to loosen from cake cooler. Now take four spatulas (you'll need help with this), place spatulas under meringue and lift on to large serving plate or board. Beat cream until firm peaks form; spread cream over meringue, then pipe a border of cream around edge. Peel and slice bananas; dip in lemon juice; wash and hull strawberries; cut in half. Arrange bananas and strawberries over cream; spoon passionfruit pulp over. Place strawberry jam and water in pan; stir over low heat until mixture is combined. Push through fine sieve. Brush this strawberry glaze over strawberries.

Serves 25.

To Prepare Ahead: Make pavlovas up to 3 days ahead. Store in cool, dry place, lightly covered; do not refrigerate. Place fruit and cream on pavlovas 2 hours before serving; store in refrigerator after decorating. This is not suitable for freezing.

Quantities for Six
4 egg whites, 1 cup castor sugar, 1 teaspoon white vinegar, 1 teaspoon vanilla, 2 bananas, 1 punnet strawberries, ¼ cup passionfruit pulp, 1 cup cream, 2 tablespoons strawberry jam, 1 tablespoon water. Make up as directed in recipe, but use small bowl of electric mixer. Use 28 cm x 18 cm (11 in. x 7 in.) shallow cake tin. Bake in slow oven 45 minutes.

NOTE: The Creme Brulee recipe makes use of the egg yolks remaining from this recipe.

Creme Brulee

12 egg yolks	2 teaspoons vanilla
6 cups milk	½ cup castor sugar
1 cup cream	½ cup brown sugar
½ cup sugar	

Place egg yolks, sugar and vanilla in a large bowl; beat until soft and creamy. Place milk and cream in pan; stand over heat until hot. Gradually add hot milk mixture to egg yolks beating well. Pour mixture into large shallow heatproof dish. Place dish in large baking tin; pour in hot water so that water comes half-way up sides of dish. Place in moderately slow oven 1 hour, or until set. Place in refrigerator when cold. On day of serving, sieve combined castor sugar and brown sugar over Brulee. Place under a hot griller until sugars have melted. Return to refrigerator until serving time.

Serves 12. Make two of these to serve 25.

To Prepare Ahead: Make up recipe as directed one or two days before serving; put sugar topping on top of Brulee on day of serving. This is not suitable for freezing.

Quantities for Six
6 egg yolks, 600 ml (1 pint) milk, ½ cup cream, ¼ cup milk powder, ¼ cup sugar, 1 teaspoon vanilla, ¼ cup castor sugar, ¼ cup brown sugar.

NOTE: The Marshmallow Fruit Pavlova makes use of the egg whites remaining from this recipe.

Creme Caramel Grand Marnier

1 cup sugar	½ cup sugar, extra
1 cup water	2 tablespoons Grand
3 cups milk	Marnier
6 eggs	

Combine sugar and water in saucepan. Stir over low heat until sugar dissolves, then cook over heat until syrup boils; reduce heat and simmer until syrup turns light caramel colour. Pour into deep 20 cm (8 in.) round cake tin; allow caramel to cool and set. Beat together milk, eggs, extra sugar and Grand Marnier; pour over caramel. Put tin in baking dish with enough water to come 4 cm (1½ in.) up sides of tin. Bake in moderate oven 1 hour 15 minutes or until custard is set. Cool; refrigerate overnight. Turn out carefully on to deep serving dish.

Each of these creme caramels cuts neatly into 8 wedges; make 4, using the above quantities, to serve 25 generously. They are best made the day before serving; refrigerate in the tins in which they were cooked; turn out on to serving plates the following day.

Brandy Sauce

1·75 litres (7 cups) milk
⅔ cup custard powder
¾ cup sugar
1 cup cream
¼ to ½ cup brandy

Place custard powder and sugar in bowl; gradually add the milk, stirring until combined; pour into large saucepan. Place over low heat; stir until sauce boils and thickens; reduce heat; simmer uncovered 4 minutes. Gradually add brandy to taste. Remove saucepan from heat; allow to cool slightly.

Place cream in bowl; beat until soft peaks form; fold into custard. This custard can be served warm or cold. If served cold, a little extra milk may be needed as it thickens on standing. Serve with canned or stewed fruit or hot steamed puddings.

Gives 25 servings, allowing ⅓ cup per serving.

Pears with Ginger

8 x 910 g (1 lb. 13 oz.) cans pear halves
2 x 250 g (8 oz.) jars preserved ginger in syrup

Place undrained pears in large bowls; add finely-chopped undrained ginger; mix well. Cover bowls; refrigerate overnight. To serve, spoon a pear into each serving dish with some of the ginger and syrup. Serve with cream or icecream.

Quantities for Six
910 g (1 lb. 13 oz.) can pear halves, ½ cup ginger in syrup.

Coffee Liqueur Mousse

1 cup sugar
1 cup water
375 g (12 oz.) dark chocolate
4 eggs
4 tablespoons brandy
4 tablespoons coffee liqueur (Tia Maria or Kahlua)
2 cups cream
1 cup cream, extra strawberries

Combine sugar and water in saucepan; stir over heat until sugar is dissolved; bring to boil; remove from heat.

Chop chocolate; put into blender with lightly-beaten eggs; add boiling syrup gradually in a thin stream; start to blend immediately a portion of the hot syrup is added; blend on low speed. Continue blending and adding hot syrup until chocolate is melted and mixture has thickened slightly. Cool. Add liqueur and brandy; refrigerate at least 1 hour.

Whip cream; fold into chocolate mixture. Put into individual serving dishes or two large serving dishes and refrigerate 2 hours or overnight. Decorate with extra whipped cream and halved strawberries.

To Prepare Ahead: This delicious mousse can be made two days before, covered firmly with plastic food wrap and refrigerated. Decorate before serving.

Serves 25.

Quantities for Six
¼ cup sugar, ¼ cup water, 90 g (3 oz.) dark chocolate, 1 egg, 1 tablespoon brandy, 1 tablespoon coffee liqueur, ½ cup cream, ½ cup cream, extra, strawberries.

Apple Strudel

2 x 375 g (12 oz.) pkts puff pastry
2 x 910 g (1 lb. 13 oz.) cans pie apple
½ cup sultanas
½ cup sugar
2 tablespoons grated lemon rind
2 teaspoons cinnamon
2 tablespoons sugar, extra
1 egg for glazing

Combine apples, sugar, sultanas, lemon rind and cinnamon; do not heat. Roll puff pastry on lightly-floured surface to 2 rectangles approx. 45 cm x 23 cm (18 in. x 9 in.). Cut each pastry rectangle into 2 even pieces giving four 23 cm (9 in.) pastry squares. Put an equal amount of filling over one half of each piece of pastry to within 2.5 cm (1 in.) of edges. Glaze these edges with beaten egg; fold pastry over filling; press edges firmly together. Trim edges with sharp knife. Glaze top of pastry with beaten egg; sprinkle with extra sugar; make several slits in top of pastry to allow steam to escape during cooking. Put on greased baking trays; bake in hot oven 20 to 25 minutes or until pastry is golden brown. Serve with cream or icecream.

Serves 25.

To Prepare Ahead: The strudels can be prepared completely the day beforehand, arranged on baking trays, covered and refrigerated. On the serving day, remove from refrigerator; brush with egg-glaze; bake as directed. If you wish to serve them hot, reheat 15 minutes in moderate oven.

Quantities for Six
375 g (12 oz.) pkt puff pastry (use only half this quantity), 470 g (15 oz.) can pie apple, 1 tablespoon sultanas, 1 tablespoon sugar, 1 teaspoon lemon rind, ½ teaspoon cinnamon, 2 teaspoons sugar, extra, 1 egg for glazing.

Drinks & Punches

Here are cool, cool drinks for all occasions — some in large quantities, suitable for parties and celebrations; some in small quantities for dinner party aperitifs or just pleasant drinking with friends.

Singapore Sling Punch

½ cup gin
¼ cup Cherry Heering
¼ cup grenadine
¼ cup lemon juice
4 x 241 ml bottles soda water

Combine gin, Cherry Heering, grenadine, lemon juice; refrigerate. Just before serving, add chilled soda water. Pour into glasses; add ice cubes. Garnish each glass with an orange slice and a maraschino cherry. Serve with straws.
Makes 1½ litres (6 cups).

Liqueur Punch

¾ cup gin
1½ cups Curacao
1½ x 500 ml bottles dry ginger ale
1½ cups lemonade
2 lemons
125 g (4 oz.) bottle maraschino cherries

Combine gin, Curacao, thinly-sliced lemons and drained maraschino cherries in large bowl. Refrigerate until ready to serve. To serve, add chilled dry ginger ale, lemonade and ice cubes; mix lightly.
Makes 1½ litres (6 cups).

Red Wine Punch

2 cups water
1½ cups sugar
2.5 cm (1 in.) piece cinnamon stick
1 cup orange juice (approx. 3 oranges)
½ cup lemon juice (approx. 2 lemons)
750 ml bottle dry red wine
750 ml bottle soda water
1 punnet strawberries

Put sugar, water and cinnamon stick in saucepan; stir over medium heat until sugar dissolves and syrup comes to boil. Reduce heat; simmer 5 minutes. Remove cinnamon stick; allow syrup to become cold. Add orange and lemon juices and wine. Wash and hull strawberries; cut in half. Add to punch. Refrigerate until ready to serve, then add chilled soda water.
Makes approx. 2 litres (8 cups).

Sparkling Claret Punch

540 g (1 lb. 3 oz.) can pineapple pieces
1 orange
1 lemon
2 strips cucumber rind
½ cup brandy
¼ cup maraschino liqueur
750 ml bottle claret
2 x 285 ml bottles soda water

Place undrained pineapple pieces, sliced orange and lemon, cucumber strips, brandy, maraschino and claret in bowl; mix well; refrigerate. Just before serving, add chilled soda water.
Makes approx. 2 litres (8 cups).

Citrus Wine Punch

½ cup lime juice cordial
¾ cup orange juice
750 ml bottle dry white wine
1 orange
1 lemon
2 x 241 ml bottles dry ginger ale
2 x 241 ml bottles soda water
241 ml bottle lemonade
2 tablespoons chopped mint

Combine lime juice, orange juice, white wine, finely-sliced orange and lemon; mix well; refrigerate. Just before serving, add chilled ginger ale, soda water, lemonade and chopped mint.
Makes approx. 2½ litres (10 cups).

Sparkling Fruit Punch

850 ml can pineapple juice
2 x 241 ml bottles dry ginger ale
750 ml bottle sparkling white wine
¼ cup orange juice
⅓ cup passionfruit pulp
2 oranges
1 lemon
1 punnet strawberries

Put chilled pineapple juice, dry ginger ale, sparkling wine and orange juice in large bowl; stir until combined. Add passionfruit pulp, sliced oranges, sliced lemon and washed and hulled strawberries; mix well. Add ice cubes.
Makes approx. 2 litres (8 cups).

Bubbly Orange Cocktail

1 cup orange juice
¼ cup Cointreau
¼ cup brandy
1 tablespoon icing sugar
12 ice cubes

Combine all ingredients in blender; blend on high speed 2 minutes or until ice cubes are crushed; pour into glasses to serve.
Serves 6.

Punches are popular at parties. You will like all the interesting recipes in this section.

Lemon Daiquiri Punch

1 cup white rum
⅓ cup lime juice cordial
½ cup lemon juice
½ cup sugar

1 cup water
750 ml bottle soda water
2 x 241 ml bottles
  lemonade

Put sugar and water in saucepan; stir over low heat until sugar dissolves; remove from heat; cool. Combine sugar syrup with rum, lime juice and lemon juice; refrigerate until cold. Just before serving, add chilled soda and lemonade. If desired, add a few mint sprigs, lemon slices and slices of cucumber rind.
  Makes approx. 2¼ litres (9 cups).

Minted Punch

1 cup gin
¼ cup creme de menthe
4 x 241 ml bottles
  lemonade

2 x 241 ml bottles soda
  water
mint leaves
ice cubes

Combine refrigerated gin, creme de menthe, lemonade and soda water in a punch bowl; add a few chopped mint leaves. Add ice cubes when serving.
  Makes approx. 1¾ litres (7 cups).

Summer Punch

375 ml bottle Pimm's Cup
3 x 241 ml bottles
  lemonade
2 x 241 ml bottles dry
  ginger ale

1 cucumber
1 orange
1 lemon
ice

Put refrigerated Pimm's Cup, lemonade and dry ginger ale into punch bowl. Add thinly-peeled strips of cucumber rind and thinly-peeled rind of orange and lemon cut into 5 cm (2 in.) strips, then add ice cubes.
  Makes approx. 1½ litres (6 cups).

Fruit Cup Punch

1 medium pineapple
1 cup orange juice
⅓ cup lemon juice
1½ cups sugar

½ cup passionfruit pulp
3 x 241 ml bottles dry
  ginger ale
750 ml bottle lemonade

Peel and dice pineapple. Put in saucepan with orange and lemon juices and sugar; stir over low heat until sugar dissolves. Bring to boil; reduce heat; simmer slowly 15 minutes. Cool; add passionfruit pulp; refrigerate until serving time; then add chilled dry ginger ale and lemonade.
  Makes approx. 2 litres (8 cups).

Caramel Cream Shake

2 eggs
2 tablespoons bottled
  caramel topping

2 cups milk
1 tablespoon icecream
nutmeg

Combine eggs and caramel topping; beat until light and fluffy. Gradually beat in milk and icecream until all ingredients are combined. Pour into serving glasses; top with a sprinkle of nutmeg.
  Serves 2.

Light Grape Drink

1 part dry vermouth
2 parts grape juice

ice cubes

Combine vermouth and chilled grape juice; pour over crushed ice or ice cubes.

Apple-Vermouth

1 part dry vermouth
3 parts apple juice

ice cubes
lemon slice

Combine dry vermouth and chilled apple juice in glass; add a few ice cubes. Decorate with half a lemon slice.
NOTE: This modern combination of vermouth with fruit juices has become a world-wide favourite. If making in quantity to serve at a barbecue, or in small glasses to serve as an unusual pre-dinner drink, one 750 ml bottle of dry vermouth and 1¾ litres (7 cups) apple juice make 2½ litres (10 cups).

Brandied Iced Coffee

1 tablespoon instant
  coffee powder
3 cups hot water
⅓ cup sugar
1 cup milk
2 teaspoons vanilla

⅓ cup brandy
vanilla icecream
300 ml (½ pint) double
  cream
cinnamon

Dissolve instant coffee powder and sugar in hot water; cool. Add milk, vanilla and brandy. Refrigerate until ready to serve. To serve, put a scoop of vanilla icecream in glass; pour on coffee; top with whipped cream; sprinkle with cinnamon.
  Serves 4 to 6.

Measures & Temperatures

Oven Temperatures

The table below gives recommended equivalents.

	°C	°F	Gas Mark
Very slow	120	250	½
Slow	140	275	1
	150	300	2
Moderately slow	160	325	3
Moderate	180	350	4
Moderately hot	190	375	5
Hot	200	400	6
	220	425	7
	230	450	8
Very hot	240	475	9

Cup Measures

	Metric	Imperial
1 cup flour	140 g	4½ oz
1 cup sugar (granulated or castor)	250 g	8 oz
1 cup brown sugar, firmly packed	185 g	6 oz
1 cup icing sugar, sifted	185 g	6 oz
1 cup shortening (butter, margarine, etc.)	250 g	8 oz
1 cup honey, golden syrup, treacle	375 g	12 oz
1 cup fresh breadcrumbs	60 g	2 oz
1 cup packaged dry breadcrumbs	155 g	5 oz
1 cup crushed biscuit crumbs	125 g	4 oz
1 cup rice, uncooked	220 g	7 oz
1 cup mixed fruit or individual fruit such as sultanas, etc.	185 g	6 oz
1 cup nuts, chopped	125 g	4 oz
1 cup coconut, desiccated	90 g	3 oz

Cup and Spoon Measures

Recipes in this book use this standard metric equipment approved by the Australian Standards Association:

(a) 250–ml (8–fl oz) cup for measuring liquids. A litre jug (capacity 4 cups) also is available.

(b) a graduated set of four cups – measuring 1 cup, half, third and quarter cup – for measuring items such as flour, sugar, etc. When measuring in these fractional cups, level off at the brim.

(c) a graduated set of four spoons; tablespoon (20–ml liquid capacity); teaspoon (5–ml); and half and quarter teaspoons.

Note: All spoon measurements are level.

It is important to remember that the Australian 20–ml tablespoon, which has been used throughout this book, differs from both the British and American tablespoons. The table below gives a comparison. The British standard tablespoon holds 17.7 ml and the American 14.2 ml. A teaspoon holds approximately 5 ml in all three countries.

Australian	British	American
1 teaspoon	1 teaspoon	1 teaspoon
1 tablespoon	1 tablespoon	1 tablespoon
2 tablespoons	2 tablespoons	3 tablespoons
3 tablespoons	3½ tablespoons	4 tablespoons
3½ tablespoons	4 tablespoons	5 tablespoons

Liquid Measures

Cups have been used in this book and the following table gives a few examples.

	Metric	Imperial
½ cup	125 ml	4 fl oz
1 cup	250 ml	8 fl oz
1½ cups	375 ml	12 fl oz
2 cups	500 ml	16 fl oz

Index